CONFLICTING AGENTS
Conflict Management in Multi-Agent Systems

MULTIAGENT SYSTEMS, ARTIFICIAL SOCIETIES, AND SIMULATED ORGANIZATIONS
International Book Series

Series Editor: Gerhard Weiss
Technische Universität München

CONFLICTING AGENTS
Conflict Management in Multi-Agent Systems

Edited by

Catherine Tessier
Onera-Cert, Toulouse, France

Laurent Chaudron
Onera-Cert, Toulouse, France

Heinz-Jürgen Müller
Deutsche Telekom, Darmstadt, Germany

SPRINGER SCIENCE+BUSINESS MEDIA, LLC

Library of Congress Cataloging-in-Publication Data

Conflicting agents : conflict management in multi-agent systems / edited by Catherine Tessier, Laurent Chaudron, Heinz-Jürgen Müller.
p. cm. -- (Multiagent systems, artificial societies, and simulated organizations)
Includes bibliographical references and index.
ISBN 978-1-4757-8380-3 ISBN 978-0-306-46985-5 (eBook)
DOI 10.1007/978-0-306-46985-5
1. Intelligent agents (Computer software) 2. Electronic data processing--Distributed processing. I. Tessier, Catherine. II. Chaudron, Laurent. III. Müller, Heinz Jürgen. IV. Series.

QA 76.76I58 C66 2000
006.3'3—dc21 00-064622

Originally published by Kluwer Academic Publishers in 2001
Softcover reprint of the hardcover 1st edition 2001

Printed on acid-free paper.

To Jean-Marc Fouet

Contents

Preface

Conflicts between agents acting in a multi-agent environment arise for different reasons, involve different concepts, and are dealt with in different ways, depending on the kind of agents and on the domain where they are considered. For example, agents may have conflicting beliefs, conflicting goals, or may have to share limited resources. Conflicts may be expressed as mere differences, or as contradictions, or even as social conflicts. They may be avoided, solved, kept, or even created deliberately.

Since more and more concern is attached to agents' teamwork and agents' dialogue, conflicts naturally arise as a key issue to be dealt with, not only with application dedicated techniques, but also with more formal and generic tools.

The aim of this book is to focus on the management of conflicts in multi-agent environments. It is the fruit of thoughts that have been discussed since 1993 in the occasion of several workshops held at IJCAI, AAAI and ECAI.

We deeply thank all the authors for their high-quality contributions and for their cooperation during the editing process. We are most grateful to Jörg Denzinger who gave us judicious advice that helped us putting together the different chapters of the book, and to Jean-Pierre Chrétien who helped us solve some tricky LaTeXproblems.

CATHERINE TESSIER, LAURENT CHAUDRON AND HEINZ-JÜRGEN MÜLLER

Contributing Authors

C.P. Abubucker
Paine College
1235 15th Street
Augusta, GA 30901-3182, USA

Esma Aïmeur
Université de Montréal
Département d'Informatique et de Recherche Opérationnelle
2920 Chemin de la Tour
Montréal, H3C 3J7, Québec, Canada

T. Castelão
Grand Valley State University
One Campus Drive
Allendale, MI 49401-9403, USA

Cristiano Castelfranchi
National Research Council - Institute of Psychology
Division of "Artificial Intelligence, Cognitive and Interaction Modelling"
Viale Marx, 15
00137 Roma, Italy

Laurent Chaudron
Département Commande des systèmes et dynamique du vol
Office national d'études et de recherches aérospatiales
Centre de Toulouse (Cert)
BP 4025
31055 Toulouse Cedex, France

Fabrice Chantemargue
Sente
Rue du Petit-Chêne 18 ter
CH-1003 Lausanne, Suisse
(current address)

Jörg Denzinger
University of Calgary
Computer Science Department
2500 University Drive N.W.
Alberta, Canada T2N 1N4

Rino Falcone
National Research Council - Institute of Psychology
Division of "Artificial Intelligence, Cognitive and Interaction Modelling"
Viale Marx, 15
00137 Roma, Italy

Humbert Fiorino
Imag/Leibniz/Magma
46, avenue Félix-Viallet
38031 Grenoble Cedex, France

Markus Hannebauer
German National Research Center for Information Technology (GMD)
Research Institute for Computer Architecture and Software Technology (FIRST)
Kekuléstraße 7
12489 Berlin, Germany

Hyuckchul Jung
Information Sciences Institute
University of Southern California
4676 Admiralty Way
Marina del Rey, CA 90292, USA

William A. Lawless
Paine College
1235 15th Street
Augusta, GA 30901-3182, USA

Thomas Malsch
Arbeitsbereich Technikbewertung und Technikgestaltung
Technische Universität Hamburg-Harburg
21071 Hamburg, Germany

Heinz-Jürgen Müller
T-Nova Deutsche Telekom Innovationsgesellschaft mbH
Technologiezentrum Darmstadt
64307 Darmstadt, Germany

Jacques Penders
KPN Research
P.O. Box 421
2260 AK Leidschendam, the Netherlands

Milind Tambe
Information Sciences Institute
University of Southern California
4676 Admiralty Way
Marina del Rey, CA 90292, USA

Catherine Tessier
Département Commande des systèmes et dynamique du vol
Office national d'études et de recherches aérospatiales
Centre de Toulouse (Cert)
BP 4025
31055 Toulouse Cedex, France

CONFLICTING AGENTS

Gerhard Weiß
Institut für Informatik
Technische Universität München
80290 München, Germany

Chapter 1

AGENTS' CONFLICTS: NEW ISSUES

Catherine Tessier
Onera-Cert, Toulouse, France
Catherine.Tessier@cert.fr

Heinz-Jürgen Müller
Deutsche Telekom, Darmstadt, Germany
Heinz-Juergen.Mueller@telekom.de

Humbert Fiorino
Imag, Grenoble, France
Humbert.Fiorino@imag.fr

Laurent Chaudron
Onera-Cert, Toulouse, France
Laurent.Chaudron@cert.fr

Abstract The aim of this first chapter is to set the theme of agents' conflicts into scene, to clarify the basic terms and views which will then be deeper discussed in the following chapters, and to give the reader a guideline through the book. Several different points of view on (artificial and human) agents' conflicts will be taken and put into context to the current literature on multi-agent systems and the subsequent chapters. Eventually an agents' conflict handling action model will glue together these views into a general process for designing the conflict behaviour of agents.

1. INTRODUCTION

The term "agent" has been used in Computer Science and more specifically in Artificial Intelligence in various ways. The most typical ones are the "Electronic Assistant" metaphor, which interprets an agent as a system acting on behalf of its user, and the "Artificial Society" metaphor, which interprets agents as members of a Multi-Agent System, designed to solve a problem through collaboration. In both cases there is a need to describe the interactions of the agents, either with its human user or its agent fellow in the artificial society. Though the *action*-part of the inter-actions are most important from a system user's point of view, the interesting question for a system designer is the modelling of the trigger situations and events that enable the interaction to be performed (see (Müller, 1997) for an overview on design techniques for multi-agent systems). This is exactly the point where conflicts enter the stage. As the above mentioned metaphors have their grounding in sociology it is straightforward enough to look for human analogies of trigger situations within teams, groups, and other forms of societies.

The aim of this book is to study conflicts in the context of Multi-Agent Systems (MAS), i.e. artificial societies modelled on the basis of autonomous, interacting agents. Of interest are questions about types of conflict in general and the use of conflicts as trigger functions for activities in MAS in particular. The latter is also dedicated to questions of conflict management, resolution, and avoidance, i.e. the question of how agents cope with conflicts and conflicting situations.

For the introduction chapter we will briefly make an excursion into the definition of agents in order to generate a common understanding of the term. Then we will investigate in general, epistemological considerations in order to get an abstract methodological guideline. Eventually the chapter will close with a preview and classification of the following chapters.

1.1 AN EXCURSION ON AGENT DEFINITIONS

The question about what an agent is has been discussed in the Distributed AI community for over twenty-five years without a generally accepted result. So it should be clear that the following "definition" also reflects a subjective view, though it may be matched to the majority of agent approaches as discussed below.

Definition 1 (Agent) *An* agent *is a system with the following properties:*

1. *It lives in an artificial world W together with other agents*

2. *It has facilities to sense W and to manipulate W*
3. *It has a (at least partial) representation of W*
4. *It is goal-directed, and as a consequence it has the ability to plan its activities*
5. *It can communicate with other agents*

The first property says that an agent needs other agents plus a common world to be an agent. The fourth property implies that it has knowledge about its abilities, i.e. its operations in the world. Properties two, three, and four imply as well that there must be a reasoner or inference mechanism which enables the agent to work with its sensor inputs, world knowledge and plans. Note that *a priori* there is no need for the representation of the other agents and their skills. However, those partner models enhance the behaviour of the society as shown in (Müller and Siekmann, 1991).

The definition coincides with the definition of Franklin and Graesser (Franklin and Graesser, 1996) which is the essence of agency synthesized from a dozen recent definitions:

> An autonomous agent is a system situated within and a part of an environment that senses that environment and acts on it, over time, in pursuit of its own agenda and so as to effect what it senses in the future.

The definition of Jennings and Wooldridge (Wooldridge and Jennings, 1995a) is currently one of the most widely used working definitions. It essentially says:

> An agent is a hardware or software-based computer system with the following properties:
>
> - *autonomy*: agents operate without the direct intervention of humans or others, and have some kind of control over their actions and internal state;
> - *social ability*: agents interact with other agents (and possibly humans) *via* some kind of agent-communication language;
> - *reactivity*: agents perceive their environment and respond in a timely fashion to changes that occur in it;
> - *pro-activeness*: agents do not simply act in response to their environment, they are able to exhibit goal-directed behaviours by taking the initiative.

The social ability and reactivity points are equivalent to the respective parts of our definition. The goal-directedness of the pro-activeness point also meets our fourth point, though we do not explicitly ask for initial activities. However, we think that the pro-activeness is a consequence of the extended planning facilities of the agents. Whenever they recognize that they cannot reach their goal exclusively with their own resources and capabilities, they ask for support, i.e. they initiate for example a support process, a bargaining process, or a task allocation process. The most disparate part of the definitions is the autonomy requirement. Defining it this way is too strong, because on one hand it forbids an explicit intervention of humans and others and on the other hand the social ability asks for an interaction with others, possibly with humans. So if we rephrase the autonomy as: *the agents operate even in the absence of a direct intervention of humans or others ...* then we still exclude interactive payroll programs. And moreover, the relaxed definition makes sense, since the agent permanently reacts upon its dynamic environment. The part "... and have some kind of control over their actions and internal state" is again covered in our requirement for goal-directedness and planning ability. Our definition asks in addition to that of Jennings and Wooldridge for an explicit representation of the world. Hence, an agent is at least an AI system in the classical sense, i.e. knowledge-based and capable of reasoning. This point is only covered in an extension of Jennings and Wooldridge' s definition. They speak of *strong agency* if agents are based additionally on the beliefs, desires, intentions (BDI) paradigm, i.e. they are built explicitly on knowledge, goals, and plans.

Though our definition meets the kernel of agenthood, there are many more types, extensions and refinements of agents. Agents, in addition to the features discussed above, may be:

- adaptive (capable of learning),
- mobile (capable to migrate from one machine to another),
- reactive (capable of immediately responding to changes in the environment without any planning),
- situated (capable of handling unknown situations),
- co-operative (willing to help if requested),
- competitive (optimizing locally),
- reliable (not lying and performing actions if committed),
- etc.

In the following chapters the reader will meet several peculiarities of agents which fit more or less into the definitions discussed above. Hence, trying to give *one* definition of conflict in MAS does not make sense. Furthermore, the ways to avoid, deal with, solve, use, or even deliberately create conflicts highly depend on the kind of agents, and on the epistemological level that is considered.

1.2 EPISTEMOLOGICAL ISSUES

From an epistemological point of view, a project or a study can be considered at four different levels: the *empirical*, *conceptual*, *formal*, and *methodological* levels, each of them having its own objects, methods, results and validation criteria.

Empirical studies usually concern large sets of data or a corpus. The methods are based on experiences, and measures are the basis for statistical analyses. The results are most often given as classes of subjects. The validation of the classes is experimental.
Example: D. O'Leary (O'Leary, 1999) focuses on the identification of conflicts among experts (pathologists) providing probability estimates across a number of categories (diseases), given some particular features. Conflict identification results from statistical analyses that are performed on the set of probability assessments given by the experts.

Conceptual studies focus on ideas or abstract concepts, usually described in natural language. Abstract analyses are performed on the concepts so as to highlight correlations and properties. The results are descriptive models, ontologies, formal classes. The validation is grounded on the semantic consistency of the classes.
Example: Cr. Castelfranchi (Castelfranchi, 2000) proposes an ontology for agents' internal and social conflicts. Each class is characterized by features given in natural language or logic expressions. The aim of this work is clearly to *point out some of the basic aspects or notions of conflict theory to be formalized.*

Mathematical entities are the objects of *formal* studies. Rational methods are applied, such as proofs. The results are theories characterized by definitions, lemmas and theorems. The validation rests on the correctness of the proofs.
Example: a formal description of conflict situations is proposed by Z. Pawlak in (Pawlak, 1984). Allied, antagonistic and neutral pairs of objects are defined thanks to respective relations R^+, R^- and R^0, which allow coalitions and conflicts in a society of agents to be formally characterized. Axioms are set down (i.e. R^+ and R^- are symmetric relations, R^+ is reflexive and R^- is irreflexive). With numerical features associated to objects, a theorem characterizing the link between conflictless and conflict situations is proved.

Methodological studies focus on implementation. The objects are coded data on which sequences of instructions are applied. The results are methods,

algorithms and programs. Complexity, convergence, processing time are the validation criteria. Simulations with various sets of data are often performed to compare the performance of the algorithms.
Example: (Lemaître et al., 1999) propose simulation results to compare various decision criteria for a share decision problem involving multiple agents with different types of constraints.

Of course, a study generally covers several levels, and an ideal research work would cover all the levels.

What is important to notice is that the validation criteria associated to one level are not suitable for another level. For instance, proving an empirical classification does not make sense, neither does assessing the complexity of an ontology.

This is why these short epistemological considerations may provide a better understandability of a pluridisciplinary work as this book, and may be taken as a reading guide for the following chapters.

Table 1.1 summarizes the features of the four epistemological levels.

	Objects	Methods	Results	Validation
Empirical	data sets	experiences statistics	classes	experimental
Conceptual	concepts	abstract analysis	ontologies formal classes	semantic consistency
Formal	math. entities	rationale	definitions theorems	proofs
Methodological	coded data	sequences of actions	algorithms programs	convergence efficiency

Table 1.1 The four epistemological levels

2. ABOUT CONFLICTS IN GENERAL

The term *conflict* induces negative feelings in human contexts. Conflicts produce uncertainty and fear, and people interpret conflicts as harassment or at least as something unpleasant which should better not occur. Most people are proud of having no conflicts at all, because then they are in balance with their environment. However, the evolution of people, teams, and organizations needs conflicts. Most of the radical changes in the human society stem directly from massive conflicts. Hence, conflict avoidance is not always the best choice. Conflicts might also be seen as a chance for improvement and as an indication for invoking learning processes.

In the following, first considerations of conditions for conflicts will be briefly discussed.

2.1 CONCEPTUAL POSTULATES FOR CONFLICTS

Whatever the epistemological level at which conflicts are considered, some conditions are required so that conflicts should actually exist. Obviously the first one is to mention the "things" that are in conflict; in this book, the "things" are agents, i.e. robots, processes, human beings, computers... Many conditions may be found in the literature, either implicitly or explicitly, and we propose several conceptual postulates to synthesize them.

1- Difference vs. common elements

The essence of agents' conflicts is *difference* (Chaudron et al., 2000) in relation to elements that are common : conflicts appear because several different (i.e. distinct) agents want to use the same resource at the same time, or because agents have different viewpoints (i.e. their knowledge is not the same) on one common situation. This is linked to the second postulate, as difference is strongly related to multiplicity, and to the third one, as common elements make up a common reference.

2- At least two agents

At a given time t, no difference can be expressed between agent A and itself. Therefore, a single agent cannot conflict with itself, as it is expressed by Pawlack's axioms ($R^+(x, x)$ and $\neg R^-(x, x)$) (Pawlak, 1984). This seems to be contradictory with "internal conflicts" (Castelfranchi, 2000) as such conflicts occur within one agent. But, as it is the case for "double constraints" in psychology (Watzlawick et al., 1967), a multi-sided agent can be considered, which amounts to having several agents.

3- Symmetry

Pawlack's axioms also express conflict symmetry ($R^-(x, y) \longrightarrow R^-(y, x)$) (Pawlak, 1984). As a matter of fact it is difficult to imagine that agent A would be in conflict with agent B whereas agent B would not be in conflict with agent A : the fact that A is in conflict with B is at least a conflicting element in the relationship of B with A.

4- A common reference

To be conflicting, agents must have things in common at the same time :

resources, rules, processing level, decision level, involvement level... For instance, the inconsistency of two beliefs is only a necessary condition. They should *belong to the same context of belief* which *does not allow or tolerate inconsistency*, should *hold at the same time* and *be about the same time* (Castelfranchi, 2000).

5- Consequences

If there is no consequence, a conflict is not a conflict. As S. Easterbrook says about viewpoint conflicts: *a conflict is simply a difference between viewpoints, that matters* (Easterbrook, 1991). Cr. Castelfranchi is more precise and asserts that *conflicts exist only in relation to goals.[...] When there is a conflict, it is a conflict between two goals* (Castelfranchi, 2000). The concept of goal is linked to decision and action and to success or utility criteria.

2.2 ON CONFLICTS BETWEEN PEOPLE

The discussion of the subsection above gave a first idea of the essentials to be discussed generally in conflict scenarios. In the following an excursion into human conflict handling will give a more precise view of conflicts which may be adapted to agent scenarios. The view taken is based on literature dedicated to conflicts in organizations and used by personal trainers (for a summary see (Bohinc, 1999)).

1- Indications for human conflicts

Obvious indications for conflicts between humans are aggressive behaviours (screaming, shouting, fighting) or emotional changes (winning, depressed). Of course, these behaviours come along with conflicts, but are not exact conditions for them (sometimes they just arise from different opinions). Above it was said that the agents need to have a difference on a common element. In human societies it is possible to strengthen this characterization. The agents have to be interdependent and they cannot flee (one possibility for conflict avoidance). In most such cases people have the intention to intervene into the others' plans and operations, in order to reach private goals. If the goals do not match, then, since the parties are interdependent, the interests of one agent can only be respected if the interests of the others have to be hurt (Pareto-situation). In contrast, there is no conflict if the difference is just in opinions or in the intention without starting activities.

2- Types of human conflicts

As have been discussed above, the usual case conflicts are dealt with within the agent context is conflicts between at least two agents. However, personal trainers distinguish between five types:

- *Individual conflicts* are inner agent conflicts. From a psychological point of view they are necessary to develop the personality and character of people. Individual conflicts occur if the decision function is not precise enough, i.e. people in certain situations cannot decide what to do next. On a higher level of abstraction they show up if general strategies are too vague, i.e. a person does not know whether to be benevolent or self-interested. On the reflective level the question is, whether it was good or bad what the individual has done. Maybe that is the right interpretation of Pawlack's irreflexive rule in the agent context (at least at the current state of the art in agent modelling).

  Pair conflicts stress especially the interdependence between conflicting parties. The classical pair is a couple, but also good friends, colleagues in special relationships like boss and secretary or police patrol teams. Now pair conflicts between people show up special qualities from a psychological point of view. Pair conflicts arise from differences between "the pair" and the individual. Either the individual looses himself in the pair (and thus kills the personality) or one personality dominates the pair. The following differences are the basis for pair conflicts:

  1. restricted individual development,
  2. contradictory individual needs, i.e. liaison vs freedom, propinquity vs distance, stability vs change,
  3. different interests due to cultural background.

- *Triangle conflicts* establish between pairs and an individual. The typical case is the conflict between a couple and "the family". If a couple becomes a family through a child, then three pairs emerge. Thus the individual may be in conflict with the other pair or as a part of the pair he is in a conflict situation with the other individual. In most cases conflicts of this kind arise when the relationship between two members is strong and the third individual feels excluded.

- *Group conflicts* are of a great variety due to the fact that typical groups are formed through common behaviour. Groups try to synchronize their members and thus do not accept individual behaviours, pair or triangle formations. This is the source for typical group conflicts, which can be further structured into the following cases:

  1. territorial: what the individual role (and thus influence) of a person in a group is;
  2. hierarchical: who has the better skills (even against individual needs);
  3. rivalry: who gets the attention of others;

4. normative: what the social rules are;
5. membership: mostly the question of who belongs to the inner circle;
6. leadership: the classical group decision process of tribes;
7. separation: leaving the group is the strongest; version; inside the group, shifts in the hierarchy or in the roles are critical;
8. defence: in case of an (internal) attack; against a member, other members form up to defend him.

- *Organizational conflicts* occur between groups in an organization. In mapping group to individual and organization to group, the above discussed types of conflicts may all occur in organizations too.

The structure in figure 1.1 summarizes the human conflict types.

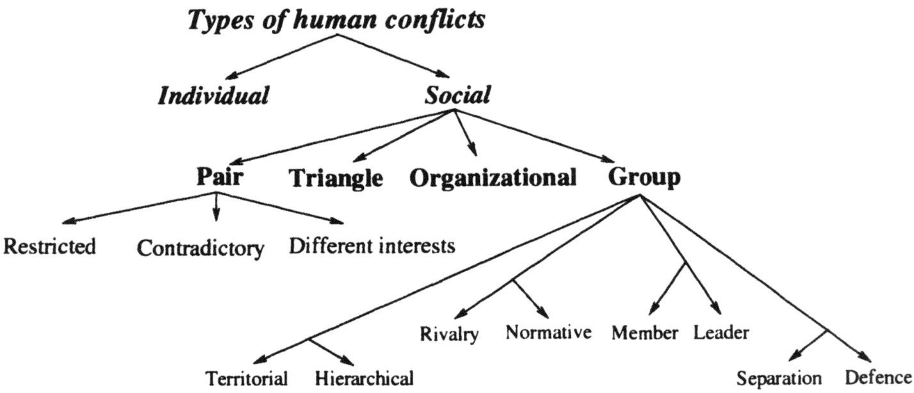

Figure 1.1 Human conflict types

Currently only parts of the human conflict types have been modelled in MAS implementations for two reasons. Firstly, the basis for these types are emotions and though emotions are currently in the focus of the agent community, the realization of emotional agents is still at the beginning. Secondly, the conflict types often need a kind of reflection component in the agents. Theoretically reflection may be modelled within a belief theory, however application oriented implementations lack the realization of such a framework.

3- Consequences of human conflicts

Personal trainers consider several consequences out of conflicting situations which are only partially of interest for MAS. Examples are:

1. conflicts release energy to generate new solutions; however, this energy may be also negative, as will be seen later in the text.

2. conflicts have to be accepted as a part of human life, because social activities inherently cope with interdependencies; the question is just a matter of positively using them.

3. conflicts are compositional as they may bring together people in a team in critical situations.

4. conflicts clarify diversity, which leads to new viewpoints.

5. conflicts are enablers of new results.

6. conflicts are the basis for change. Thus, conflicts must occur in companies in order to improve processes as well as products and services.

2.3 ON CONFLICTS IN MULTI-AGENT SYSTEMS

It must be pointed out that conflicts are tightly linked to multi-agent systems. Actually, there is no multi-agent system without conflict. That is, to what extent the functionality of the multi-agent system *is* to deal with agents' conflicts?

Indeed, the multi-agent paradigm is worth considering in very specific cases that do implicitly involve conflicts. Otherwise, alternative paradigms should be chosen as for instance cellular automata, distributed or parallel computing and so forth. Intuitively, the multi-agent paradigm applies to "complex" systems where "the whole is more than the sum of all the parts". Of course, many systems verify this criterion, especially when no global model of the system is available and the best one can do is make assumptions on how those parts work and interact. For instance, consider the dynamics of a city, i.e. people moving from one district to another one. This phenomenon depends on numerous "local" parameters influencing household decisions (e.g. income variations, flat prices and loan rates, "social homophilia", etc.) However, nobody is able to model the migrations within a town. But, complexity is not the only criterion. From the methodological point of view, data modelling must be done according to four basic components: agents, environment, interaction and organization (Demazeau, 1995). How this can be achieved is out of the scope of this introductory chapter. But it must be pointed out that this decomposition provides means to simulate and validate initial hypotheses (Reynolds, 1987, Minar et al., 1996, Drogoul and Ferber, 1992). Obviously, such an approach embodies the conflict notion as agents will, from the designer's point of view, "compete" to get resources, "share" their common environment, "discuss" and "behave" according to different organization patterns, etc.

Furthermore, the multi-agent paradigm is also used for distributed problem solving which, in fact, amounts to distributed *conflict* solving. Indeed, when considering problem solving, at least two classes of problems have to be distinguished. On one side lies "off-line" problem solving of hard combinatorial problems. For instance, multi-agent systems have been applied very successfully according to pure performance criteria for theoretical problems (e.g. constraint satisfaction, the corner problem (Ferber, 1999), etc.) as well as for concrete applications (e.g. map generalization (Baeijs et al., 1996) which consists in combining, fusing or moving objects from a spatialized database). In this class of problems, as for simulation and modelling, conflicts stem from the multi-agent methodological decomposition. On the other side lies real time problem solving where "true" conflicts arise from interacting machines or autonomous systems; conflicts happen or are avoided no matter how the system is modelled i.e. whatever the paradigm the designer chooses. Such systems range from satellite constellations or computer networks (e.g. for Internet applications, trading or broadcasting) to cooperative robotics (e.g. drones or underwater autonomous vehicles fulfilling intelligence missions). But, why do machines interact ? what for ? Formally, in order to work coherently and achieve their assigned tasks, they have to figure out three generic problems: they have to decompose a gross mission into detailed subtasks to be fulfilled; they have to allocate those subtasks among themselves according to their specific capabilities and skills (depending on resources and equipments) so as to balance their local workload or maximize some performance criteria; finally, they have to coordinate their actions according to execution hazards (e.g. to avoid collisions or solve deadlocks). Needless to say that each of these problems is intrinsically hard to solve and has attracted a lot of attention and efforts from the multi-agent community over the past decade. Many algorithms have been proposed allowing the agents to reach an agreement, find a consensus on what they have to do, how they have to do it, who has to do what, who does what and how, etc. Therefore, conflicts on actions, plans or beliefs are at the very core of multi-agent systems, which should be defined as dynamic organizations paradoxically shaped by contradictory and complementary mechanisms aiming at both division and integration. Moreover, those generic problems are not independent from each other: if one agent fails or breaks down, plans may have to be modified and tasks may have to be re-allocated. This may imply new decomposition, distribution and coordination steps and therefore new conflicts to deal with.

The two classical strategies to cope with conflicts are avoiding them or solving them. As far as the first one is concerned, agents apply common rules

(Jennings, 1994, Shoham and Tennenholtz, 1995) i.e. conventions (e.g. drive on the right lane and pass on the left one) or rely on mutual representations of others' goals, intentions and capabilities (Sichman et al., 1994). More complex approaches try to represent tasks and resources dependencies (e.g. "the achievement of one task facilitates or precedes another one" (Decker and Lesser, 1992), resource constraints, etc.) Hence, this approach makes each agent more predictable and reduces the need for coordination.
However, the agents do have limited knowledge of their environment and of the other agents. Moreover, they have to deal with execution hazards. Therefore, conflict solving is unavoidable; usually, this is done by synchronization algorithms (i.e a centralized approach (Cammarata et al., 1983, Alami et al., 1998)) or negotiation protocols (i.e. a decentralized approach (Rosenschein and Zlotkin, 1994, Müller, 1996a)).

3. TWO CLASSES OF CONFLICTS

As it has been said before, there are many kinds of conflicts as there are many kinds of agents and multi-agent systems. Nevertheless, at a conceptual level, two classes of conflicts may be distinguished, namely *physical conflicts* and *knowledge conflicts.*

3.1 PHYSICAL CONFLICTS

Physical conflicts are *resource* conflicts . Cr. Castelfranchi calls them *extrinsic* or *non analytical* conflicts (Castelfranchi, 2000): agents' goals are not logically contradictory but are not compatible because of the resources required to achieve plans and actions that are associated to the goals.

A typical physical conflict is the intention of using at the same time a resource which cannot be shared out or which is scanty.

For *robot* agents, one of the most critical resource is *space* as two robots must not be at the same place at the same time. Formal definitions for spatial conflicts between robots are proposed by J. Penders in (Penders, 1999). In most of multi-robot systems, spatial conflicts are tried to be avoided thanks to dedicated planning strategies. Nevertheless, such conflicts can be used, as it is shown in chapter 6 by J. Penders. Conflicts may even be deliberately ignored for performance reasons, as it is shown in chapter 7 by F. Chantemargue.

Concurrent agents are often faced with physical conflicts when they have to access common resources while maximizing their individual satisfaction. For instance (Lemaître et al., 1999) deal with a co-funded satellite that has to be exploited among the co-funders under fairness constraints. Various decision criteria are proposed, implemented and tested through simulations.

3.2 KNOWLEDGE CONFLICTS

Knowledge or *viewpoint* conflicts stem from the fact that the agents' information is not the same. For instance, agents may have different skills or may be equipped with different sensors. Such conflicts may concern agents' beliefs, knowledge, opinions, and are often called "epistemic" conflicts.

Contradiction between agents' propositions is the kind of knowledge conflict that is mostly dealt with, especially within formal logical frameworks. Cr. Castelfranchi calls it an *intrinsic* or *analytical* conflict; it can be direct $(Goal/Bel\, x\, p) \wedge (Goal/Bel\, x\, \neg p)$ or indirect , *via* a "crucial belief" $(Goal/Bel\, x\, p) \wedge (Goal/Bel\, x\, q) \wedge (Bel\, x(p \rightarrow \neg q)$ (Castelfranchi, 2000). L. Cholvy has proposed (Tessier and Chaudron, 1998) a set of formulas characterizing contradiction conflicts between two agents x and y or "within" one agent x who is subject to a regulation or to domain laws:
•$\phi \wedge \neg\phi$
•$Bel_x\phi \wedge Bel_y\neg\phi$
•$Bel_x\phi \wedge Bel_x(Bel_y\neg\phi)$
•$Wants_x\phi \wedge Wants_y\neg\phi$
•$O_x\phi \wedge F_x\phi$, with O an obligation modality, and F a forbidding modality.
•$Does_x\phi \wedge F_x\phi$
•$O_x\phi \wedge Cannotdo_x\phi$

Nevertheless, contradiction can be considered as a borderline case of *difference* and it is worth considering a mere difference between agents as a conflict. For instance, if agent A asserts that an object is moving towards the runway, whereas agent B asserts that the same object is a red patrol car moving at a 45 km/h speed towards the building, both assertions are different without being *a priori* contradictory (Chaudron et al., 2000).

Depending on the application, knowledge conflict management may consist in:

- making a choice among the agents' assertions, especially if a decision must be made. Usually, the choice is made according to criteria that are independent of the agents' knowledge (agents' reliability, trustworthiness, or the agents' hierarchy) (Cholvy, 1993).

- building an assertion that is common to the agents, i.e. that accounts for pieces of knowledge on which the agents agree and does not make any choice on pieces of knowledge on which they disagree. In case of a contradiction, the common assertion accounts for the ignorance of the group of agents (Fiorino, 1998).

- waiting for further information that may change or even solve the conflict, provided time is not a critical parameter.

4. TOWARDS A UNIFIED DEFINITION OF CONFLICT?

The idea is now to jump at a higher conceptual level and propose a unified definition for conflicts (Dehais and Pasquier, 2000). The *propositional attitude* and the *crucial propositional attitude* are the key notions for this purpose.

4.1 PROPOSITIONAL ATTITUDES

Propositional attitudes are the beliefs, desires, intentions, fears, hopes, wishes, etc., which have in common to be identified by their propositional content (Houdé et al., 1998). For example, the belief that p is true is identified by proposition p *is true*. This unifying notion allows us to state that: *conflicts only arise between propositional attitudes.*

PA_i will denote a propositional attitude of agent i.

4.2 CRUCIAL PROPOSITIONAL ATTITUDE

Considering again the notion of common reference that is highlighted in postulate 4, and Cr. Castelfranchi's "crucial belief" for "indirect conflicts", it is worth extending the "crucial belief" – or more generally the *crucial propositional attitude* – to all kinds of conflicts. As a matter of fact, two or more propositional attitudes conflict *because* there is a constraint (e.g. something cannot be true and false at the same time), a law (an object cannot be at two places at the same time), a norm, etc., maybe at a meta-level, that holds. Most of the time however, this crucial propositional attitude is not explicit.

This allows us to state that : *any conflict is an "intrinsic" and "indirect" conflict and therefore involves a crucial propositional attitude.*

PA^c will denote a crucial propositional attitude.

Examples

1- $(PA_i\, p) \wedge (PA_j\, \neg p)$ is not a conflict; whereas $(PA_i\, p) \wedge (PA_j\, \neg p) \wedge (PA^c$ *"the PAs of the agents must be logically consistent"*$)$ is.

2- $(PA_i\, R, [t1, t2]) \wedge (PA_j\, R, [t3, t4])$, with R a resource and $[t1, t2]$ and $[t3, t4]$ time intervals such that $[t1, t2] \cap [t3, t4] \neq \emptyset$, is not a conflict; whereas $(PA_i\, R, [t1, t2]) \wedge (PA_j\, R, [t3, t4]) \wedge (PA^c$ *"R must not be used by two or more agents at the same time"*) is.

Remark: some crucial propositional attitudes may be harder than others. For instance a PA^c expressing a physical constraint (such as in example 2) is generally a hard one, whereas a PA^c expressing a knowledge constraint or a norm might not be (a knowledge constraint might be relaxed, a norm might be infringed) .

4.3 CONCEPTUAL DEFINITION OF CONFLICT

Definition 2 (Reduction) *Let C be a set of propositional attitudes. A* reduction *of C is the application of any technique that results (among possible other effects) in removing at least one propositional attitude from C. C is then said to be reduced.*

Remark: a possible effect of reduction is to add in C propositional attitudes that did not belong to C before.

Definition 3 (Conflict) *Let P be the set of propositional attitudes representing the agents' context at a given time. Let C be a subset of P. C is a* conflict *if and only if C must be reduced.*

Remark: this is a characterization of conflict, which may not be confused with conflict solving. For instance, the fact that a choice must be made is a conflict; making the choice is a solving technique.

Most often, solving techniques aim at actually solving the conflict, i.e. the conflict does not linger (C remains the same), grow more bitter (at least one more PA in C), nor evolve towards another conflict (new conflict involved, or not part of the initial PAs of C).

5. CONFLICT HANDLING

5.1 CONFLICT HANDLING IN THE HUMAN CONTEXT

Handling conflicting situations usually concentrates on the resolution, i.e. the search for an acceptable solution of the conflict. The emphasis is on "acceptable", which does not simply imply a mutually acceptable solution as the following first two basic cases will show. In the following, basic patterns of conflict handling methods will be discussed and put into the context of MAS.

1- Flight

If one opponent flees it seems at first glance that the conflict has been solved. However, a closer look makes clear that there is no chance for resolving the conflict at all, because the situation which has led to the conflict has kept its potential. It depends on the special situation whether the staying opponent is satisfied or not. For the fleeing one the propositional attitudes are still the same. In human societies the fugitive thus sometimes reacts with aggression and rage as a result of the unsolved problem. However, if this is not the case, then there is no obvious looser of the conflict.

In MAS fleeing might be seen as a very effective resolution of conflicting situations. In some scenarios, there is also a high chance that the conflicting situation arise again in the same constellation after some period of time. In (Müller, 1996b) pp. 148-167 several situations of conflicts between robots in a loading dock scenario have been described. In his agent model fleeing is implemented as a basic pattern of behavior (PoB) on the reactive level of the robot.

2- Destruction

The most effective method to resolve a conflict is to destroy the opponent, e.g. in an organizational context, destruction might be realized as the take over of a competitor. The method is effective, because no further investigations will be necessary. It is based on the power of the strongest. However, there is no chance to correct the solution and, which is more serious in the context of conflict theories, there is no improvement. The chance to make new and innovative solutions emerge is lost.

In MAS a destructive conflict resolution strategy may be found in situations where selfish rational agents are involved, i.e. in any situation where the agent will not give up the solution which is most valuable for him. The agent will always search for activities which support his rigid point of view, e.g. suppress the conflict and act in a way that forces the opponent to change his propositional attitudes.

3- Subservience

In a sense subservience is the weak form of destruction. There is no brute force which leads to the conflict resolution. Instead, one opponent gives up one of his propositional attitudes, because of an own decision. The assumption is that the solution is acceptable to the complying party. Actions which lead to subservience are persuasion, manipulation, and menace. However in contrast to destruction, the advantage is that the solution is reversible. Due to this fact, subservience leads to a persistent source of conflict in human societies, since the propositional attitude is almost always not completely given up.

In MAS this type of conflict handling is difficult, because the mental context of one of the agents has to be changed. A weak form may be found in the loading dock scenario (Müller, 1996b), though.

4- Delegation

Delegation in this context means that the conflict resolution is delegated to a third party. It is important to notice that the opponents have to commit themselves to accept the proposition of the judge. The problem with the delegation approach is that the opponents are not able to improve their conflict resolution strategy and if the situation is very complex, the generation of the solution by the mediator may take a very long time.

In MAS mediators play an important role. One reason is that the problem solving processes of the agents are very general. Thus there is a need for an entity which has deeper knowledge about the problem domain as well as on more sophisticated problem resolution strategies. Furthermore, the implementation of mediators reduce the amount of communication between the agents, because there is no need for long negotiation phases.

5- Compromise

A compromise is often the result of direct negotiations between the opponents. During the negotiation phase the parties have to give up parts of their propositional attitudes. A compromise has been found if each party agrees on it. However, there is always still the parts of the propositional attitudes which have been given up, and the stability of the solution depends on them. In human societies these parts are often the very core of the conflict and the compromise is just an agreement on minor aspects.

In MAS it is important that the propositional attitudes should be modelled as attributes with a certain range. An example may be found in (Hollmann et al., 2000) where the negotiation process between agents in assessment situations has been discussed. (See also the discussion of reaching a compromise as the result of a negotiation process in (Müller, 1996a).)

6- Consensus

Generating consensus between conflicting parties is the only possibility for a completely mutually accepted solution. It is a long process, because the opponents first have to present their point of view in detail to the other party.

This comprises their assessment details and their problem resolution strategies. Since this is the most creative method it has the potential to lead to really new perspectives for the parties.

In MAS it is difficult to implement consensus strategies. Since the use of agents is often justified by privacy aspects (e.g. calendar agents in appointment management applications) the opposing agents will not be allowed to exchange their data and strategies. However, creative elements may be added. For example in (Hollmann et al., 2000) it was proposed to change the subject to be assessed instead of the propositional attitudes. Thus if the compromise under discussion is too weak, then through a complete change of view, even full consensus may be found.

The following table (see figure 1.2) shows the overview of the discussed human conflict handling methods as motivated in (Bohinc, 1999).

Conflict	Examples	Advantages	Disadvantages
Flight	- Shelving - Ignoring opposition	- Simple - Painless - No loser	- No absolute solution - Reoccurrence in harsh format
Destruction	- Murder - Dismissal - Disposal	- Slow agent is always beaten	- Waste of agent - Mistakes are not correctable
Subservientness	- Talking over - Manipulation - Corruption - Threatening	- Opposing agent not destroyed - Clear responses	- The weaker must comply with the stronger
Delegation	- Parent, judge, superior - Umpires	- Common commitment - Objectiveness	- Estrangement - Slight individual identification
Compromise	- Outcome through negotiation	- Unification - Good compromise if various spheres are implemented	- Conflict reappears if agents'fringe aspects differ
Consensus	- New solution not yet thought of	- Solution suits both sides	- Tedious - Often difficult to satisfy both parties

Figure 1.2 Human conflict handling methods

Personal trainers use a 6-phase-model for characterizing the evolution steps of conflicts (Bohinc, 1999) - see figure1.3. The different phases will be also used later to guide the steps of our concluding agents' conflict handling action model.

- Phase 1 - Antagonisms arise
  At a certain point of time differences become obvious to each of the parties. People very often react with a flight behaviour, especially if they are not trained with other conflict management strategies. Since people try to avoid the conflict, it takes some time until they step into the second phase.

- Phase 2 - Antagonisms obtrude
  The differences are obvious and the parties mutually know that the opponent is aware of the conflict too. Often it is necessary to step into a discussion, e.g. if activities have to be performed or planned. If flight is not possible any more the opponents try to use destruction or subservience to solve the problem.

- Phase 3 - Antagonisms are unavoidable
  The resolution of the conflict seems to be difficult, because each party insists on not changing its propositional attitudes. In this phase a mediator would be the best choice.

- Phase 4 - Antagonisms are unsolvable
  In order not to run into a loose-loose situation, the parties have to recognize that a win-loose solution is not acceptable to both of them. This includes that a solution proposed by a mediator would not be accepted either. Further, the parties comprehend that they have to find a mutual agreed solution, if they do not want to cope with the consequences of the conflict. In the positive case these insights will lead to negotiations.

- Phase 5 - Antagonisms turn
  While negotiating, comprehension about the opponents' perspectives arise and the differences in the propositional attitudes become explicit, thus changeable. The antagonisms become soft. Sometimes also third parties are involved in order to get new perspectives, though no official proposals as with mediators would be accepted.

- Phase 6 - Solution emerges
  Eventually, since both parties try to find an acceptable solution, the conflict will be resolved and a consensus will be found.

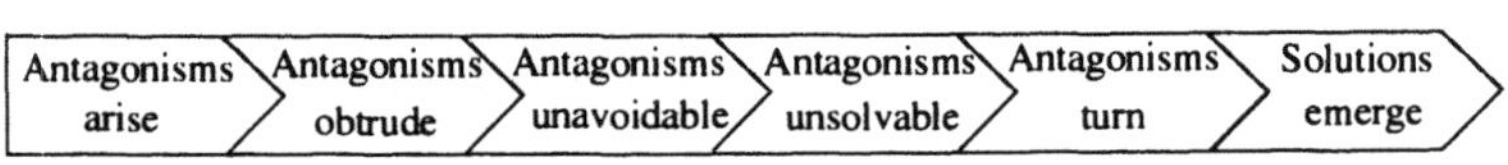

Figure 1.3 The evolution process of conflicts

It is interesting to see how the phases coincide with the conflict handling methods. Moreover it is important to recognize that not necessarily all phases

have to be passed. Each phase may be the final step of the escalation with one of the following outcomes:
loose-loose: this is clearly the case if the antagonisms are not resolved at all. The loose-loose result occurs always if the escalation stops at any phase without having applied the respective conflict handling method.
win-loose: this is the positive outcome of phases 1 and 2 if the corresponding method has been applied. In the case of phase 3, it might be the result of a bad mediation.
win-win: this is the positive outcome of phases 5 and 6 as well as of phase 3 if the mediation was a professional one.

5.2 NEW ISSUES FOR HANDLING AGENTS' CONFLICTS

5.2.1 Going further than conflict management

Let us first mention again the conflict categories proposed by S. Easterbrook (Easterbrook et al., 1993), also discussed in (Müller and Dieng, 2000):

1. occurrence: the factors that affect whether conflict will arise;
2. causes: the specific causes of a conflict;
3. utility: the role that a conflict may play in group interactions;
4. development: the process involved in an individual conflict episode;
5. management: approaches to handling conflict, including resolution techniques;
6. results: the outcomes and long-term effects of conflict.

An analysis of the situation of conflict modelling in Artificial Intelligence in general (Müller and Dieng, 2000) recognizes that most projects and papers on conflicts in AI concentrate on the fifth category. Nevertheless, the other ones are worth focusing on, especially when *ad hoc* management solutions are no longer satisfactory.

Occurrence and causes

Occurrence and causes of conflicts are worth studying, at a conceptual and a formal levels, especially when cooperative agents are considered because they are *a priori* non conflicting agents. As a matter of fact, conflicts within cooperative multi-agent systems are not due to the self-interest of agents – they are not designed as such – but to other factors that have to be identified and formalized.

Utility

Conflicts are classically considered as disturbances in multi-agent systems. That is why many methods are proposed to anticipate, avoid or solve them. Nevertheless, conflicts may deliberately remain unsolved (see chapter 7 by F. Chantemargue), and even be a basis for changing the agents' behaviours (see chapter 6 by J. Penders) or for knowledge enrichment (Chaudron et al., 2000). Moreover, conflicts may be deliberately created to enhance the interaction between agents (see chapter 8 by E. Aïmeur).

Results

Long-terms effects of conflicts in a multi-agent system should be a better robustness of the system to further conflicts, provided conflict management does not only amount to a superficial, arbitrary or *ad hoc* resolution. This is especially true for knowledge conflicts, which may allow new pieces of knowledge to be elaborated and used. This idea is the basis of Lakatos 's approval-refutation cycle (Lakatos, 1984), which has inspired further works on conflicts among cooperative agents (Chaudron et al., 2000).

More fundamentally, a lot of work remains to be done in order to properly understand, formalize and take advantages of conflicts in multi-agent systems even though this book is a noteworthy contribution that considers conflicts as a key notion in the field. However, focusing on conflicts entails some drawbacks because they are strongly related to many other multi-agent and DAI challenging issues that must not be overlooked. Here are two questions that, from our point of view, summarize the links between conflicts and other AI domains of primary importance and that should be carefully investigated.

5.2.2 Are conflicts the counterpart of coherence?

Since the precursor works in DAI, the importance of coherence, i.e. agents making mutually rational choices, has been underlined (Bond and Gasser, 1988, Wooldridge, 1994, Durfee et al., 1987). Then, conflicts can be understood as agents not behaving rationally. But what does it mean? This question is far from been trivial. Indeed, one agent's rationality depends on its own decision criteria.

Example: suppose that the agent must choose between two mutually exclusive decisions d and d' and then flips a coin (see table 1.2).

According to this payoff matrix, if the agent wants to maximize the expected gain it will always choose d'. But, if it wants to minimize the risk in the worst case, it will always choose d.

	d	d'
heads	100	1000
tails	0	-100

Table 1.2 Payoff matrix

Hence, what are the foundations of rational choices? Given one specific application, which are the "best" decision criteria? Those questions get even more complicated in a multi-agent context.
Example: this can be illustrated by the prisoners' dilemma problem (Sandholm, 1999) (see table 1.3).

		K	
		betray	*resist*
J	*betray*	-2 -2	-3 3
	resist	3 -3	1 1

Table 1.3 Prisoners' dilemma

Four deals are possible and one classical criterion is Pareto-optimality (i.e. a deal such that there is no another deal that increases the agent's reward without decreasing the rewards of the other agents). In this problem, the only deal which is not Pareto-optimal corresponds to "both agents betray". Paradoxically, if both agents rely on "the best reward in the worst case" criterion, they will choose this deal.

Those examples are drawn from the decision theory literature but, when devising a multi-agent system, criteria are not so simple to determine. As a matter of fact, knowledge and control are distributed; agents have partial knowledge of their respective activities and their environment; some tasks need several agents in order to be fulfilled; some tasks are undertaken concurrently ; tasks change in an unpredictable way according to execution hazards and to the operator's requests. Therefore, the designer must cope with agent-oriented issues (i.e. micro issues) vs. multi-agent oriented issues (i.e. macro issues). But, how should the gap be bridged between micro and macro issues? how should the agent' s own goals be defined in order to achieve the global expected functionalities? how should *cooperation* and *competition* be balanced?

Once again, these are no plain questions and it seems that conflicts play a central role as cooperation tends to minimize conflicts whereas competition tends to maximize them. That is, cooperation maximizes the satisfaction of the group whereas competition maximizes the agent's satisfaction. Therefore, both strategies are worth considering when there is no way to combine local and global satisfaction criteria, which is an intrinsic characteristic of multi-agent systems. In so far as conflicts are regarded as a control parameter for multi-agent systems, new architectures integrating both *alternative* interaction mechanisms should be proposed. At least, this is suggested by some ecological systems. For instance, some species of vultures cooperatively explore their environment. When one of them finds a prey, it communicates its position by executing specific movements with its wings. On the contrary, the prey is shared in a competing manner: the vultures form a tight herd around the prey. The aggressiveness of the vultures that are besides the prey decreases because they are fed. Hence, those vultures are pushed outwards by more aggressive ones. As a matter of fact, those mechanisms ensure a fair share of the resources and the survival of the species.

5.2.3 Is "conflict" a synonym for "contradiction"?

Contradictions do not exist in nature. Contradictions make sense within a formal framework, e.g. between two statements. Classically, knowledge representation and inference mechanisms are based on logics and on a consistency principle. Well-founded languages are used to talk about the world and are implemented on artifacts. However, it has been claimed that this framework is not sophisticated enough: doors are never ajar, they are just open or closed. But sometimes, an object may be simultaneously A and $\neg A$, or neither A nor $\neg A$. This is especially true in a multi-agent context, when distributed entities are surrogates of persons or social organizations that do not necessarily share the same point of view (e.g. trading, e-commerce, Computer Supported Cooperative Work, etc.) Many works have been undertaken to correct those drawbacks (e.g. the possibility theory (Dubois and Prade, 1988), multi-valuated or contextual logics (Ginsberg, 1986, Perrussel, 1998), etc.) But, they always remain within the logical framework which foundations are: (i) the identity principle (i.e. all objects can be classified and labelled); (ii) the contradiction principle (i.e. a predicate and its negation cannot hold at the same time for the same object, "$(A \wedge \neg A)$ is an antilogy") and (iii) the excluded-middle principle (i.e. there is no intermediate predicate between two contradictory statements, if one is asserted, the other one is necessary refuted, "$(A \vee \neg A)$ is tautology"). Efforts have to be done to promote the "logics of diversity" so as to allow agents to reason on their possible contradictions and jointly build conjectures. Implicitly, the aim is to acknowledge that contradiction is unavoidable and does not necessarily entail inconsistency. In that sense quantum logic (Dalla Chiara, 1986) should represent the proper basic theoretical frame. These heterodox approaches need some revisions of the inner principles of the reference universe of discourse in which (ii) or (iii) or both are violated. Such a fundamental standpoint is adopted in chapter 10 by W. F. Lawless, T. Castelão and C. P. Abubucker as a key to understand the interaction mechanisms and the evolution role of conflicts.

Thus, considering the generic conceptual operators required so as to define a conflict, *negation* appears to be the pivotal one. Both for physical conflicts described as "two entities can*not* be at the same place at the same time" and for knowledge conflicts "one can*not* have both A and $\neg A$", negation is always explicitly or implicitly referred to. This argument can be justified by a contraposition conjecture:
It is impossible to define a conflict without referring to a negation operator.

Usually, and except for chapter 10, negation is considered in a standard way i.e. as an unary function on a set E: $\neg : E \longrightarrow E, x \longmapsto \neg x$
Example: E can be the set of the propositional attitudes of a set of agents, and the conflict between some of the PAs is defined thanks to negation.

Formally, the weakest structure on which negation can operate is a preordered set (poset)[1] and the "nominal" structure is a complemented lattice $(E, \sqcap, \sqcup, 0, 1)$ in which: $(\forall x \in E)\, x \sqcap \neg x = 0, x \sqcup \neg x = 1$. The traditional logic based frame on which mainly all logics are built is a complemented lattice of well-formed-formulas $(F, \wedge, \vee, \perp, \top)$ which is distributive. This comfortable situation allows negation to be involutive and classical De Morgan's laws are verified.

At this point, if an analysis of the conceptual relations between conflict and negation has to be made, two ways appear for knowledge representation: -1- refer to a distributive lattice logical frame (say: *dllf*), -2- build different structures based on weaker negation operators which should be more adapted to the considered conflict requirements. As we have noticed, most of the theoretical works follow the first way: a classical *dllf* kernel is considered and extensions are added to it (see section 3.2). This *dllf* syndrome could be explained by the fact that the set of studies on negation by itself is negligible compared to the tremendous amount of work on modal operators (Béziau, 1994). Even in the reference book (Wansing, 1996) the classical standpoint *dllf* is generally

[1] The minimum a negation can do on a poset $(E, <)$ is the contraposition law (Wansing, 1996): $\forall x, y, \in E, x < y \rightarrow \neg y < \neg x$

adopted.
If we want to go further in way -2-, we will need to explore the inner mechanisms of the conflict notion. As a first step, let us consider $\mathcal{P}$ the set of all propositional attitudes in which the conflict relation is noted $\bowtie$: $PA_1 \bowtie PA_2$ means that PA_1 and PA_2 are two conflicting PAs. If $\mathcal{P}$ can be considered as a complemented lattice $(\mathcal{P}, \sqcap, \sqcup, 0, 1)$ then the minimal definition of $\bowtie$ in the structure should be: $(PA_1 \bowtie PA_2) \leftrightarrow PA_1 \sqcap PA_2 = 0$.
That is to say that both PAs are exclusive to each other. Of course, if $\mathcal{P}$ is a *dllf* logical struture, and if we consider $PA_2 = \neg PA_1$ then: $PA_1 \sqcup PA_2 = 1$ and $PA_1 \sqcap PA_2 = 0$ thus *a fortiori* $PA_1 \bowtie PA_2$. But in this case $\mathcal{P}$ appears to be over-equipped for the conflict notion (for example the complete complemented law: $PA_1 \sqcup PA_2 = 1$ is clearly not a conceptual requirement for the definition of $\bowtie$).
Furthermore, if we try to bound the ontological question of the ideal mathematical structure for defining conflict in $\mathcal{P}$, we can consider that the greatest lower bound should be the anti-diagonal relation Δ in which any pair of PAs is conflicting:

0	1	...	...	1
1	0	1	...	1
⋮	1	⋱		⋮
⋮	⋮		0	1
1	1	...	1	0

and the upper bounds should be negations (i.e. involutive operators).

Consequently, it appears necessary to launch a "conflict-adapted negation" research program so as to understand the minimal requirements to capture of the notion of conflict formally. Thanks to the results of the quantum logic studies, we know that the weakening of the negation can be obtained by considering intermediate operators, i.e: orthogonal operators in weak lattices (e.g. non-orthomodular lattices). This should constitute the next step of conflict modelling.

5.3 AGENTS' CONFLICT HANDLING ACTION MODEL

In the following we summarize our general discussion in an action model for agents who deal with conflicts. It is essential in that it comprises the basic entry steps for conflict handling, it respects the different strategies to deal with conflicts, it uses elementary action points to vitalize the strategies, and it ends up with a learning step. Figure 1.4 describes the agents'conflict handling action model.

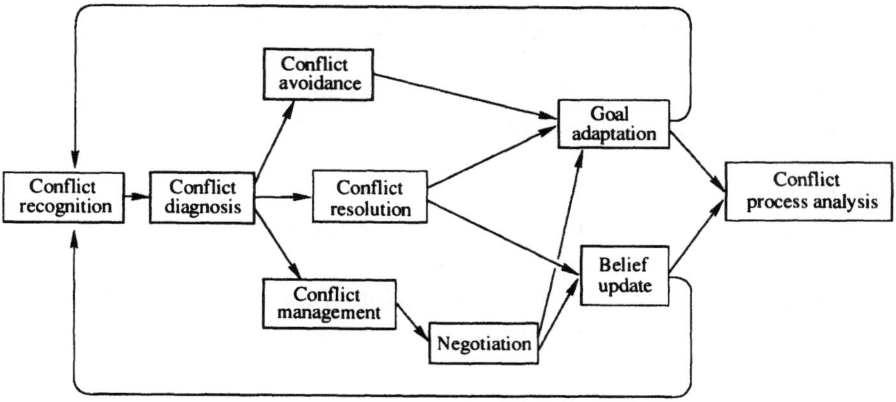

Figure 1.4 Conflict handling action model for agents

1) *Conflict Recognition*

The conflict recognition action (CRA) has as input either an environment information or the status of the internal knowledge base. The CRA checks whether the input gives rise to a potential conflict or current conflict. Thus, the output is a first classification of the conflict together with an importance factor which states the urgency of the conflict.

2) *Conflict Diagnosis*

The conflict diagnosis action (CDA) uses the output of the CRA together with context information from the environment and respective knowledge from the knowledge base as input. The CDA analyzes the conflict with respect to the physical/knowledge distinction, the internal/bi-lateral/multi-lateral differentiation, the propositional attitudes, and the consequences of the conflict. Based on the result of the analysis and the realization of the agent, the CDA may also decide which of the subsequent actions should be triggered. The output is a complete description of the conflict.

3) The perfect agent may have action descriptions for the avoidance, resolution, and management of conflicts in order to act appropriately to the conflict. The result of the CDA gives rise to the three main action points:

3a) *Conflict Avoidance*

The conflict avoidance action (CAA) takes place in Phase 1 of the conflict evolution process. CAA searches for possibilities not to enter into Phase 2.

3b) *Conflict Resolution*

The conflict resolution action is necessary if the conflict evolution process advances into Phase 2 or 3. Thus the conflict resolution action searches for changes which may disintegrate the conflict.
3c) *Conflict Management*
The conflict management action (CMA) aims at detaining the conflict evolution process. Its application is dedicated to Phases 2, 3, 4. Besides simple mechanisms, like ignoring the conflict, a negotiation block follows the CMA in which a mutual accepted solution of the conflict has to be found.

4) *Change*
In most cases the result of the formerly discussed actions is either an adaptation of the agents' goals or an update of the knowledge bases (beliefs). The output of the respective action point is the description of the conflict plus the change action performed. The output serves as an input to the CRA of the backward loop.

5) *Learn*
The Conflict Process Analysis action (CPA) has taken the output of the change action as well. Here it is stored in a case base and used for analysis purposes and thus serves for learning from solved conflicts.

The conflict handling action model integrates the standard conflict handling activities embedded in a complete model from recognition to analysis action points. It respects the conflict evolution process, the main conflict classes, and it is based on the propositional attitude postulate.

6. OVERVIEW OF THE BOOK

The remainder of the book is structured into three blocks with three selected chapters each. The chapters concentrate on agents' conflicts from different perspectives. Their deep insights reflect the current state of the art of dealing with conflicts in societies of intelligent agents and in the context of collaborative work.

Following the current trend where research in Distributed Artificial Intelligence and Sociology shows a certain convergence the first block is dedicated to the interdiciplinary study of conflicts. *Cr. Castelfranchi and R. Falcone* discuss conflicts in client-contractor situations in their chapter on **Conflicts within and for collaboration**. Possible conflicts in these context are conflicts about the kind of delegation, conflicts about the level of autonomy, conflicts about initiative, and conflicts due to the violation of norms. Their results are fundamental steps towards the modelling of agent centered organizations. *M. Han-*

nebauer elaborates the relationship between internal and external conflicts in his chapter **Their problems are my problems**. The sociological debate on the micro-macro-link finds its counterpart in the investigation of internal and external conflicts of agents. A mathematical model will be introduced to describe both types of conflicts and the corresponding algorithms for handling them. *T. Malsch and G. Weiss* provide in their chapter on **Conflicts in social theory and multi-agent systems** a fundamental analysis of conflicts in DAI and Sociology. Their aim is to import elements of the theory of autopoietic social systems and the pragmatist theories of symbolic interaction into conflict approaches of Distributed Artificial Intelligence.

The second block is dedicated to conflicts arising in (physical) teams of agents. *H. Jung and M. Tambe* investigate in their chapter on **Conflicts in agent teams** the study of intra-team conflicts. In their approach conflicts in teams of agents are interpreted as special team problems and the resolution of conflicts is based on negotiation between team members. Their theoretical results have been implemented in the system CONSA in order to exploit the benefits of argumentation in a conflicting team setting. *J. Penders* studies conflicts in a team of robots in his chapter **Conflict-based behaviour emergence in robot teams**. A formal treatment of interaction and conflicts will be applied to teams of avoiding robots. Again the theoretical results have been implemented and will be demonstrated in computer simulations. *F. Chantemargue* elaborates in his chapter on **Conflicts in collective robotics** the emergence of conflicts and conflict resolution when robots do not use direct communication. Hence the conflicts are implicitly managed in the robot society. The results give rise to studies of implicit conflict reduction strategies.

The third block concentrates on collaborative work performed by agents. While the usual methods in CSCW focus on techniques which support CSCW (Computer Supported Cooperative Work), e.g. cooperation protocols, the following chapters investigate in conflicting situations during collaborative work and how these conflicts might be positively used. *E. Aïmeur* studies cooperative learning activities of agents in her chapter **Strategic use of conflicts in tutoring systems**. Agents, in different roles, interact in a learning environment coping with internal and external conflicts. The usefulness of conflicts will be shown in various cooperative learning strategies and their contribution with social interaction to the development of cognition will be proved. *J. Denzinger* analyses **Conflict handling in collaborative search** by investigating in several subtypes of multi-agent search systems and the specific conflicts arising in these subtypes. Based on the results of the analysis the requirements and pros and cons of three basic types will be compared. The final chapter, **Conflict as a heuristic in the development of an interaction mechanics** by

W. Lawless, T. Castelão and C. Abubucker postulates that the replacement of conflicts with cooperation improves the performance of a system only in the case of well defined problems. In contrast they discuss scenarios where conflicts increase the set of available information which then leads to solutions of ill-defined problems.

I

CONFLICTS AND AGENTS: ESSENTIALS

Chapter 2

CONFLICTS WITHIN AND FOR COLLABORATION

Cristiano Castelfranchi and Rino Falcone
Institute of Psychology, Roma, Italy
{ castel,falcone } @ip.rm.cnr.it

Abstract In this chapter we address possible conflicts arising between an agent (the "client") delegating some tasks to some other agent, and this agent (the "contractor") adopting and/or satisfying those tasks; conflicts which are either due to the intelligence and the initiative of the delegated agent or to an inappropriate delegation by the client. We present a plan-based definition of delegation, adoption and task, and a theory of different kinds and levels of delegation and adoption. We examine several kinds of conflict due to different cooperative attitudes between the two agents: conflicts about the kind of delegation/reliance; conflicts about the level of autonomy; and conflicts about initiative. In this perspective, we also analyze: role conflicts (where roles are reduced to classes of delegated tasks); and *the systematic but functional (collaborative) violation of norms, rules, prescriptions*, a very important form of conflict for the dynamics and the evolution of organizations.

We neither analyze conflicts due to some misunderstanding or to the helper's personal interest, nor conflicts about the delegation of control. We claim that delegation and its related conflicts are the core of the interaction among any kind of autonomous agents and are relevant for modelling MAS, organizations, and user-agents interaction. In fact, in order to exploit local knowledge and local adaptation, delegation cannot be fully specified.

1. INTRODUCTION

Autonomy and intelligence are precious features in those agents one is relying on for some task or function. This is why natural selection has developed a *mind* in some organisms so that they can flexibly and creatively guarantee their biological functions, and see about their adaptation.

In fact, if an agent has just to passively and mechanically execute a rigid and very specific task, it will not be able to solve possible problems, to adapt its behavior to circumstances, to find better solutions, etc. But, of course, there is a trade-off: the more intelligent and autonomous the agent (able to solve problems, choose between alternatives, reason and plan by itself) the less promptly and passively "obedient" it is. The probability that the provided solution or behavior does not correspond to what exactly we expect and delegated, increases. In this chapter we study some conflicts that possibly arise between a "client" delegating some tasks, and the "contractor" or in general the agent adopting and/or satisfying those tasks; conflicts which are due either to the intelligence and the initiative of the delegated agent or to an inappropriate delegation by the client. In particular, we examine paradoxical conflicts due to the agent's willingness to collaborate and to better and deeply help the other.

In the first part, we present our definition of delegation and adoption, a plan-based definition of tasks, and of different kinds and levels of delegation and adoption. This implicitly characterizes different levels of agency and autonomy (in the delegated agent). Delegation and adoption are two basic ingredients of any collaboration and organization. In fact, the huge majority of DAI and MAS, CSCW and negotiation systems, communication protocols, cooperative software agents, etc. are based on the idea that *cooperation works through the allocation of some task (or sub-task) by a given agent (individual or complex) to another agent,* via some "request" (offer, proposal, announcement, etc.) meeting some "commitment" (bid, help, contract, adoption, etc.). This core constituent of any interactive, negotial, cooperative system is not so clear-cut, well founded and systematically studied as it might seem. Our claim is that *any support system for cooperation and any theory of cooperation require an analytical theory of delegation and adoption.* We will contribute to an important aspect of this theory with a plan-based analysis of delegation.

In the second part, we analyze four main kinds of collaborative conflicts related to delegation and adoption. By "conflict" we mean that the two agents have two incompatible goals; in particular that Ag_i intends to do a given action while Ag_j does not want that Ag_i does such an action (or Ag_j would prefer/expect another action (*weak conflict*)). "Collaborative" means that the reason for such a conflict does not lie in the agents' competition or hostility, but occurs within a collaboration between Ag_i and Ag_j. More than this: the reason why Ag_i wants to do a helping action different from Ag_j's expectation, or Ag_i wants to do a delegation action different from what Ag_j expects, is not in the self-interest of the disagreeing agent, but in its willingness for a better collaboration.

In this collaboration - which is the meeting between an attitude of delegation/reliance and a complementary attitude of adoption/help - we characterize four main kinds of conflicts:

- *conflicts about the kind of delegation/reliance,* which can be based on mere exploitation, on manipulation, or on some agreement and commitment;

- *conflicts about the level of autonomy*, and more specifically:
  - either the level of delegation (more or less executive, more or less based on some discretion);
  - or the presence and the kind of control (monitoring and intervention);
- *conflicts about initiative*, i.e. about the level of help violating what has been delegated and expected.

In this perspective we also analyze:

- *role conflicts*, (roles are here reduced to classes of delegated tasks);
- *the systematic but functional (collaborative) violation of norms, rules, prescriptions*, a very important form of conflict for the dynamics and the evolution of organization.

All these conflicts might be based on some *misunderstanding* between the delegating agent and the delegated one, but we will not consider this case, because we are interested in studying *conflicts due to different cooperative attitudes* between the two agents, which cannot be solved by a simple clarification, and require other kinds and levels of negotiation.
All this is claimed to be important both for supporting human cooperative behaviors and the organization, and for agents and Multi-Agent systems. This relevance becomes clear considering on the one hand that the notion of "agent" itself is very often based on the notion of delegation (Maes, 1990a, Goodwin, 1993, Luck and d'Inverno, 1995).
On the other hand, task delegation and adoption, and the related conflicts and negotiations, are the core problem of the MASs (Chu-Carrol and Carberry, 1996, Rosenschein and Zlotkin, 1994) and of their protocols (Haddadi, 1996). Also our examples will provide some evidence of the current and future importance of this kind of conflicts in MAS.
We claim that delegation and its related conflicts are the core of interaction among any kind of autonomous agent.

2. A PLAN-BASED THEORY OF DELEGATION/ADOPTION

2.1 DEFINITIONS

The notion of delegation is already explicitly present in the domain of MAS, especially with regard to collaboration (Haddadi, 1996), and team-work. However, our analysis is grounded on much more basic notions that are aimed at characterizing the elementary constituents (Castelfranchi and Falcone, 1998b) of any collaboration: delegation and its complement goal-adoption.
In our model, delegation and adoption are characterized in terms of the particular set of mental states (cognitive ingredients) of the agents involved in the

interaction. Informally, *in delegation an agent Ag_1 needs or likes an action of another agent Ag_2 and includes it in its own plan.* In other words, Ag_1 is trying to achieve some of its goals through Ag_2's actions; thus Ag_1 has the goal that Ag_2 performs a given action. Ag_1 is constructing a MA plan and Ag_2 has a "part" in this plan: Ag_2's task (either a state-goal or an action-goal).
Conversely, *in adoption an agent (Ag_2) has a goal as and as long as it is the goal of another agent (Ag_1), that is, Ag_2 has the goal of performing an action as this action is included in the plan of Ag_1.* So, also in this case Ag_2 plays a part in Ag_1's plan (sometimes Ag_1 has no plan at all but just a need, or a goal).
We assume that to delegate an action necessarily implies delegating some result of that action. Conversely, to delegate a goal state always implies the delegation of at least one action (possibly unknown to Ag_1) that produces such a goal state as result. Thus, we consider the action/goal pair $\tau = (\alpha, g)$ as the real object of delegation, and we will call it 'task'. By τ, we will refer to the action (α), to its resulting world state (g), or to both.

It is possible to delegate not only tasks but also roles (Werner, 1990), since roles are based on *classes of delegated tasks.* In this way roles are viewed both as social relationships among agents and as defined positions in MA-plans and in organizations.
Plan hierarchy affects role hierarchy, and the delegation levels correspond to different levels and entitlements of roles (Castelfranchi and Falcone, 1997).
There exists an hierarchical structure of roles which is related to the kind of task and to the plan structure (for ex. executive roles and decisional roles).
Once established, a role (role-contract) constrains task-delegation: the delegation of a specific task must instantiate the role tasks. There could rise conflicts between task-delegation and role-contract, and the negotiation about specific tasks can bring it up for discussion again the related role-contract.

2.2 FORMAL CONSTRUCTS

Since our notions of delegation and adoption levels are based on a theory of actions and plan, let us very briefly introduce several formal constructs needed in the following. For a more detailed description of these concepts see (Castelfranchi and Falcone, 1998b).
Let $Act = \{\alpha_1, .., \alpha_n\}$ be a set of *actions*, and $Agt = \{Ag_1, .., Ag_n\}$ a set of *agents*.
The *general plan library* is $\Pi = \Pi^a \cup \Pi^d$, where Π^a is the abstraction hierarchy rule set and Π^d is the decomposition hierarchy rule set.
An action $\alpha' \in$ Act is called *elementary action* in Π if there is no a rule *r* in Π such that α' is the left part of *r*. We will call BAct (*Basic Actions*) the set of elementary actions in Π and CAct (*Complex Actions*) the remaining actions in

Act.
Given α_1, α_2 and Π^d, we introduce the $Dom\text{-}c(\alpha_1\ \alpha_2)$ operator to say that α_1 dominates α_2 (or α_2 is dominated by α_1) in Π^d:
$Dom\text{-}c(\alpha_1\ \alpha_2) = True$
if there is a set of rules $(r_1, .., r_m)$ in Π^d, such that:
$(\alpha_1 = Lr_1) \wedge (\alpha_2 \in Rr_m) \wedge (Lr_i \in Rr_{i-1})$
where: Lr_j and Rr_j are, respectively, the left part and the right part of the rule r_j and $2 \leq i \leq m$.
We denote Π_{Ag_x} as the Ag_x's plan library, and Act_{Ag_x}, the set of actions known by Ag_x.
The set of irreducible actions (through decomposition or specification rules) included in Π_{Ag_x} is composed of two subsets: the set of actions that Ag_x believes to be elementary ($BAct_{Ag_x}$) and the set of actions that Ag_x believes to be complex but for which it has no reduction rules ($NRAct_{Ag_x}$:*Non Reduced actions*). Then $BAct_{Ag_x} \subset Act$ and possibly $BAct_{Ag_x} \not\subset BAct$.
In fact, given an elementary action, an agent may (or not) know the body of that action. We define S_{Ag_x} as the skill set of Ag_x, i.e. the actions in $BAct_{Ag_x}$ whose body is known by Ag_x (action repertoire of Ag_x).
Ag_1 has a *complete executable know-how* of α if either $\alpha \in S_{Ag_1}$ or in Π_{Ag_1} there is a set of rules $(r_1, .., r_m)$ able to reduce α into $(\alpha_1, .., \alpha_k)$ and for each $1 \leq i \leq k$, $\alpha_i \in S_{Ag_1}$.
We can define an operator $CEK(Ag_1, \alpha)$ that returns α if $\alpha \in S_{Ag_1}$ or $((\alpha_1, .., \alpha_k))$ if there are the rules able to reduce α as described above. Then, $CEK(Ag_1, \alpha) \neq \theta$
(θ is the empty set) when Ag_1 has at least a complete executable know-how of α. In fact, $CEK(Ag_1, \alpha)$ characterizes the *executive autonomy* of Ag_1 relative to α.
We call R the operator that, when applied to an action α, returns the *results* set produced by α.
We call *relevant results* of an action for a goal the subpart of the results of that action which correspond to the goal; more formally, given α and g, we define the operator Rr as follows:

$$Rr(\alpha, g) = \begin{cases} \{g_i \mid g_i \in g\} & \text{if } g \subseteq R(\alpha) \\ \theta & \text{otherwise.} \end{cases}$$

Therefore, *the same action has different relevant results when used for different goals.*
Let us suppose that α is a component action of α' and $Rr(\alpha', g) \neq \theta$; we define *pertinent results* of α in α' for g, $Pr(\alpha, \alpha', g)$, the results of α useful

for that plan α' aimed at achieving the goal g; they correspond to a subset of R(α) such that:

$$Pr(\alpha, \alpha', g) = \{q_i \in R(\alpha) \mid (q_i \in Rr(\alpha', g)) \vee ((q_i = P(\alpha_1)) \wedge Dom\text{-}c(\alpha'\alpha) \wedge Dom\text{-}c(\alpha'\alpha_1) \wedge (\alpha \neq \alpha_1))\}$$

In other terms, an action α is in a plan α' (aimed at a goal g) either because some of its results are relevant results of α' (aimed at g) or because some of its results produce the preconditions of another action α_1 in that plan.
The pertinent results of an action α in α' represent the real reason for which that action α is in that plan α'. In other words, a plan is not an arbitrary list of actions: an action α is in a plan α' if and only if it contributes, directly or indirectly, to the intended results of α'.

Delegation is a *"social action"*, and also a meta-action, since its object is an action. We introduce an operator of delegation with five parameters:

$$Delegates(Ag_1\ Ag_2\ \tau\ t\ t')$$

where Ag_1, Ag_2 are agents, $\tau = (\alpha, g)$ is the task, and t and t' respectively represent the time in which the delegation is given by Ag_1 to Ag_2 and the time in which the delegated task should start. This means that Ag_1 delegates the task τ to Ag_2. In the following we will put aside the fact that in delegating τ, Ag_1 could *implicitly delegate also the realization of α preconditions* (that normally implies some problem-solving and/or planning).
Hereafter we will call Ag_1 the delegating-adopted agent (*the client*) and Ag_2 the delegated-adopting agent (*the contractor*).

3. TYPES AND LEVELS OF DELEGATION AND RELATED CONFLICTS

We consider a couple of general dimensions (Castelfranchi and Falcone, 1998b) of the notion of delegation: its strenght, implying different kinds of interaction between client and contractor; and the level of specification of the delegated task.

3.1 INTERACTION-BASED TYPES OF DELEGATION

One of the dimensions of delegation is the strength of delegation, which is based on the kind of interaction between client and contractor and the consequent influence of delegation on the contractor's mind (if any).
We distinguish three general cases: *weak*, *mild* and *strict delegation*. For a more detailed description of these kinds of delegation and for an analysis of their cognitive ingredients, see (Castelfranchi and Falcone, 1998b). These

three cases represent different degrees of strength (with respect to beliefs, commitments, goals to pursue, etc) of the established delegation. More precisely,

- *weak delegation*, is the delegation based on mere exploitation, on the passive achievement of the task. In it there is no agreement, no request or even influence: Ag_1 has nothing to do, it is just exploiting in its plan a fully autonomous action of Ag_2.
- *mild delegation*, is the delegation based on induction. In it there is no agreement, no request, but Ag_1 is itself eliciting and inducing in Ag_2 the desired behavior in order to exploit it.
- *strict delegation*, is the delegation based on explicit agreement, i.e. on the active achievement by Ag_1 of the task through an agreement with Ag_2.

Conflicts about weak and mild delegation There might be conflicts just relative to the kind of delegation, either weak or mild. In this chapter we mainly consider conflicts arising in a strict delegation relationship, because this is the more typical delegation-relation within organization, teams, and in collaborations, which are all based on some form of agreement and "contract". However, it is worth to shortly address the conflicts relative to weaker forms of delegation, because they are quite interesting and frequent in social interaction (also in virtual societies and organization). Let us consider two prototypical cases.
A typical conflict arising in weak delegation is Ag_2's "protest", "rebellion", or refusal not of the delegated task -since it can be willing to help and collaborate- but precisely of the weak, non agreed upon form of delegation. Ag_1 is trying in fact to exploit Ag_2's action (and abilities and resources) without Ag_2 being aware of this, without asking its permission and adhesion. So, Ag_2 can be against this tactics that does not acknowledge its help, and its freedom to accept, refuse or negotiate.
Notice that we are referring here to those exploitations which are not included in the organizational plans (very often designed and studied to realize production cycles based on general and canonical exploitation phenomena). What we have in mind are the non institutionalized, unforeseen, not programmed phenomena of exploitation.

In mild delegation there is another additional factor that can rise Ag_2's opposition and ultimately some conflict. Ag_2 could in fact reject the specific modality chosen by Ag_1 for obtaining its help. Ag_1 is inducing Ag_2's intention and behavior without revealing its intention of influencing Ag_2: it is a hidden influence. We call ***manipulation*** the strategy of trying to influence an agent while avoiding that the other understands that we are influencing it.
Ag_2 can be against such a manipulation ("why don't you ask or persuade me

explicitly!?"). There are several reasons why Ag_2 might prefer overt and strong delegation; not only selfish motives (dignity, negotiation power, advantages of reciprocation, recognition, etc.) but also motives relative to a better collaborative relation and to a better contribution on its own part.

3.2 SPECIFICATION-BASED TYPES OF DELEGATION

Another important dimension to consider is how the task is specified in delegation and how this specification influences the contractor's autonomy. The object of delegation (τ) can be minimally specified (*open delegation*), completely specified (*close delegation*) or specified at any intermediate level. Let us consider two cases:

- *Executive Delegation (Close Delegation)*: when the client (or the contractor) believes it is delegating (adopting) a completely specified task; what Ag_1 expects from Ag_2 (or what Ag_2 believes Ag_1 is delegating) is just the execution of a set of elementary actions.
  More formally, either $\alpha \in S_{Ag_1}$, or $\alpha \in BAct_{Ag_1}$, or g is the relevant result of α (and $\alpha \in S_{Ag_1}$, or $\alpha \in BAct_{Ag_1}$).

- *Open Delegation*: when the client (contractor) believes it is delegating (adopting) an incompletely specified task: either Ag_1 (Ag_2) is delegating (adopting) an abstract/complex action (an action that can be decomposed or specified in various ways), or it is delegating (adopting) just a result (state of the world). Ag_2 can (or must) realize the delegated (adopted) task by exerting its autonomy.
  More formally, either $\alpha \in CAct_{Ag_1}$, or $\alpha \in NRAct_{Ag_1}$; and also g is the relevant result of α (and $\alpha \in CAct_{Ag_1}$, or $\alpha \in NRAct_{Ag_1}$).
  We can have several possible levels of openness of the delegated (adopted) task.

It is worth to understand the great importance of open delegation in collaboration theory. We would like to stress that open delegation is not only due to Ag_1's preferences (utility) or practical ignorance or limited ability (know how). Of course, when Ag_1 is delegating τ to Ag_2, it is always depending on Ag_2 as for τ (Sichman et al., 1994): it needs Ag_2's action for some of its goals (either some domain goals or goals like saving time, effort, resources, etc.) However, open delegation is fundamental because it is also due to Ag_1's ignorance about the world and its dynamics. In fact, frequently enough it is not possible or convenient to fully specify τ because some local and updated knowledge is needed in order for that part of the plan to be successfully executed. Open delegation is one of the bases for the flexibility of distributed and MA plans. To be radical, delegating actions to an autonomous agent always requires some level of "openness": the agent cannot avoid monitoring and adapting its own actions.

Conflicts about the openness of delegation A first kind of conflicts about the openness of delegation could be due to different views of the task in client and contractor. In particular, Ag_1's perspective can be in contrast with Ag_2's point of view: τ can be considered at different levels of complexity by the two interacting agents if they do not share the same plan library (see table 2.1).

Ag_1's point of view	*corresponding Ag_2's point of view*	
$\tau = \alpha$ with $(\alpha \in S_{Ag_1})\vee$ $(\alpha \in BAct_{Ag_1})$ "It is an elementary action"	$(\alpha \in S_{Ag_2})\vee$ $(\alpha \in BAct_{Ag_2})$ "It is an elementary action"→ No Conflict	$(\alpha \in CAct_{Ag_2})\vee$ $(\alpha \in NRAct_{Ag_2})$ "It is a complex action"→ Conflict
$\tau = \alpha$ with $(\alpha \in NRAct_{Ag_1})\vee$ $(\alpha \in CAct_{Ag_1})$ "It is a complex action"	$(\alpha \in S_{Ag_2})\vee$ $(\alpha \in BAct_{Ag_2})$ "It is an elementary action"→ Conflict	$(\alpha \in CAct_{Ag_2})\vee$ $(\alpha \in NRAct_{Ag_2})$ "It is a complex action"→ No Conflict

Table 2.1 Conflicts due to different point of views of the agents

A second class of conflicts about openness is due to the intrinsic constraints (varying from very relaxed to very strict) implied by the level or degree of openness. In fact, these constraints define the contractor's degree of freedom (permissions, obligations, etc.) in the choice of the actions/plans for task τ. But it is precisely this attribution that could raise conflicts between client and contractor if the contractor's expectations and/or requests were different (more or less constrained) from the actual delegation (it is important to stress that we are always considering those conflicts that arise to protect collaborative goals). Let us present two examples:

- *The client's delegation is a close delegation: a merely executive task.* In this case the contractor could feel a conflict because of a too strict specification and the impossibility of applying its own competence and critical analysis for the achievement of the task. Notice that such autonomous analysis could even produce the same identical final specification: the conflict is not about what to do, but about letting the contractor *evaluate* what to do. The contractor believes that its freedom of analysis is denied while it could be useful for the cooperation.

- *The client's delegation is an open delegation: an abstract and little specified task.* In this case the contractor could feel a conflict because of a too low specification and the necessity to comply with a request that is beyond its competence and analysis ability. Or simply it does not consider correct (for collaborative reasons) having to solve (and spend resources on) an analysis that somebody else should do. Both the examples could also be based on the agent's role or habits and the contradictions between these elements and the delegation constraints.

4. LEVELS OF CONTROL AND RELATIVE CONFLICTS

4.1 WHAT CONTROL IS

Control is a (meta) action aimed at:
a) ascertaining whether another action has been successfully executed or a given state of the world has been realized or maintained (feedback, checking);
b) dealing with the possible deviations from the expected behavior and unforeseen events in order to positively cope with them (intervention). Plans typically contain control actions of some of their actions.
In general, the agent controlling a task (ConAg) must have some different and/or additional knowledge, competence, ability (control competence) with respect to the task executor (ExAg). Or, at least, it should be authorized, obliged, permitted, etc. to perform control. More in general, the client must rely on the controlling agent (as in the task delegation, also for control delegation (a special task) the client should trust the delegated agent (Castelfranchi and Falcone, 1998a)). And this reliance also implies the attribution of other attitudes (such as willingness) to the ConAg.
Obviously, it is possible that ConAg and ExAg coincide.

Other relevant characteristics of the control activity are:
- Control could be either *intrusive* or *transparent* with respect to the task execution. The execution could be either interrupted, disturbed, etc. or not by the control activity.
- Control could require *additional activities* for the executor of the task (reporting, etc.).
The control of a task τ (in our terms the couple (α, g)) is, in fact, a double control action. It regards both the action and its goal: two different and possibly independent controls (in fact, in our model it is possible to specify only one of these two parameters).

4.2 CONTROL AS FEEDBACK AND INTERVENTION

To understand the origin and the functionality of control it is necessary to consider that Ag_1 can adjust run-time its delegation to Ag_2 if it is in condition of:
a) receiving the necessary information about Ag_2's performance (feedback) in time;
b) intervening on Ag_2's performance to change it before its completion (intervention) - see figure 2.1.

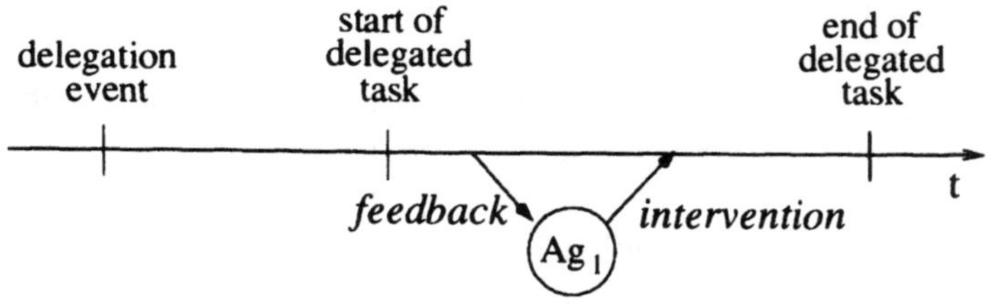

Figure 2.1 Control channels for the contractor's adjustment

In other words, Ag_1 must have some form of "control" on and during Ag_2's task realization. As we said: *Control requires feedback plus intervention* Otherwise no adjustment is possible. Obviously, the feedback useful for a run-time adjustment must be provided timely for the intervention. In general, the feedback activity is the precondition for an intervention; however it is also possible that either only the feedback or only the intervention hold.
Feedback can be provided by observation of Ag_2's activity (inspection, surveillance, monitoring), or by regular messages by Ag_2 to Ag_1, or by the fact that Ag_1 receives or observes the results/products of Ag_2's activity or their consequences.

As for *Intervention* we consider five kinds of intervention:
- *stopping the task* (the delegation process is suddenly interrupted);
- *substitution* (an intervention allocates part of the (or the whole) task to the intervening agent);
- *correction of delegation* (after the intervention, the task is partially or totally changed);
- *specification or abstraction of delegation* (after the intervention, the task is more or less constrained);
- *repairing of delegation* (the intervention leaves the task activity unchanged but it introduces new actions necessary to achieve the goal(s) of the task itself).

The frequency of the feedback on the task could be:

- *purely temporal* (when the monitoring or the reporting is independent of the structure of the activities in the task, they only depend on a temporal choice);
- *linked with the working phases* (when the activities of the task are divided into phases and the monitoring or the reporting is connected with them).

Client and contractor could adjust the frequency of their feedback activity in three main ways:
- *by changing the temporal intervals* fixed at the start of the task delegation (when the monitoring/reporting is purely temporal);
- *by changing the task phases* in which the monitoring/reporting is realized with respect to those fixed at the start of the task delegation (when monitoring/reporting is linked with the working phases);
- *by moving from* the purely temporal monitoring/reporting to the working phases monitoring/reporting (or vice versa).

Also the frequency of intervention is relevant. As explained above, the intervention is strictly connected with the presence of the monitoring/reporting on the task, even if, in principle, both the intervention and the monitoring/reporting could be independently realized. In addition, also the frequencies of intervention and of monitoring/reporting are correlated. More precisely, the intervention could occur: 1) *never*; 2) *just sometimes* (phase or time, a special case of this is at the end of the task); 3) *at any phase or at any time*.

4.3 DELEGATION OF CONTROL

When the client is delegating a given object-action, what about its control actions? Considering, for the sake of simplicity, that the control action is executed by a single agent, when $Delegates(Ag_1\ Ag_2\ \tau\ t\ t')$ there are at least four possibilities:
i) Ag_1 delegates the control to Ag_2: the client does not (directly) verify the progress and the success of the delegated action;
ii) Ag_1 delegates the control to a third agent;
iii) Ag_1 gives up the control: nobody is delegated to control the success of τ;
iv) Ag_1 maintains the control for itself.

Each of these possibilities could be explicit or implicit in the delegation of the action, in the roles of the agents (if they are part of a social structure), in the preceding interactions between the client and contractor, etc.

By matching each kind of control delegation (i, ii, iii, iv) with all the possible kinds of the controlled task ($\tau = (\alpha, g); \tau = \alpha; \tau = g$) we find several different interesting situations of control application. These situations could be causes of various conflict possibilities. Let us analyze these cases:

A. $\tau = \alpha$

This is a very rare but possible case: α can have several different results and the contractor could either know just a part of them or could not be informed at all on which results are related to the delegated task. If we consider the four above mentioned possibilities of control delegation, we have:

Ai. Ag_1 must inform Ag_2 about the goals, the states of the world that the task must achieve.

Aii. Ag_1 must inform Ag_3 (a third agent) about the goals, the task must achieve. In addition:

- if the control also involves additional activities for the execution of the task, Ag_1 must also inform Ag_2 about such activities;
- in general, if the control could be invasive it should be better that Ag_1 informs Ag_2 about it;
- if the control is transparent, Ag_1 could either inform or not Ag_2.

Aiii. The fact that there are not controls on the task activities could be given (or not) as information to the task executor agent (it depends on the circumstances and on other constraints).

Aiv. In this case we have that:

- if the control also involves additional activities for the execution of the task, Ag_1 must also inform Ag_2;
- in general, if the control could be invasive it should be better that Ag_1 informs Ag_2 about it;
- if the control is transparent, Ag_1 could either inform or not Ag_2.

B. $\tau = g$

In this case the control (which is reduced to monitoring) should be applied just at the end of the task to verify the achievement of the desired state of the world. The things to specify are:

Bi and Biii. Nothing to specify.

Bii and Biv. In these cases it seems unnecessary to inform Ag_2 because the control on the final results should not disturb at all the execution of the task.

C. $\tau = (\alpha, g)$

For this case we can imagine a combination of cases (A) and (B).

4.4 CONFLICTS ABOUT CONTROL

In figure 2.2 some of the most important kinds of conflicts due to control are shown.

- A first type regards the necessity of introducing the control itself: both the

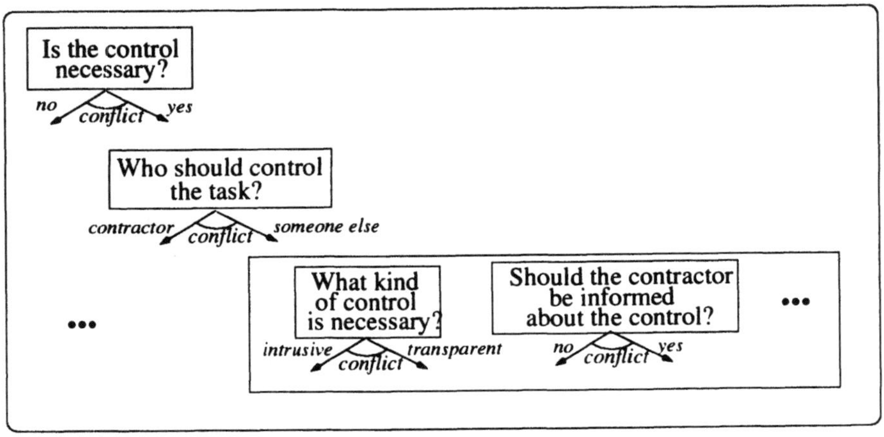

Figure 2.2 Kinds of conflicts due to control

client and the contractor could take either a favorable or adverse position to the control. For example, the contractor could think that the control is useless, for various reasons (because it wants that nobody else controls it -since this would imply lack of trust- or simply because this is a time and resource consuming activity, etc.). Or the contractor could have some reasons to consider the control very useful (for example if it is not confident enough on its own ability or about the stability of the external conditions, etc.). Analogously the client could have these opinions for the same or other reasons. In any case, when there are different positions, a conflict between the client and the contractor holds.

- A second kind of conflicts are about who could/should be the controlling agent. These conflicts could raise different questions: the attribution/disownment of the additional competence for control, the possibility/impossibility to do at the same time execution and control of the task (not only for practical reasons but also -in some specific tasks- for legitimacy and opportunity questions).

Other conflicts could arise for more specific questions related to control:
- about an intrusive or transparent control;
- about the kind and frequency of the feedback;
- about the kind and frequency of intervention;
- about informing or not ExAg about the control (if ConAg is different from ExAg).

5. ADOPTION AND CONFLICT

In analogy with delegation we introduce the corresponding operator for adoption: $Adopts(Ag_2\ Ag_1\ \tau\ t\ t')$.
This means that Ag_2 adopts the task τ for Ag_1.

Given its poor relevance for the purposes of this chapter we can neglect the temporal dimension in the delegation and adoption operators and identify:
$Delegates(Ag_1\ Ag_2\ \tau\ =\ (\alpha, g)\ t\ t') = Delegates(Ag_1\ Ag_2\ \tau\ =\ (\alpha, g))$
and
$Adopts(Ag_2\ Ag_1\ \tau_1\ t\ t') = Adopts(Ag_2\ Ag_1\ \tau_1)$.
We consider now some dimensions of the adoption notion.

5.1 TYPES AND LEVELS OF ADOPTION: INTERACTION-BASED TYPES OF ADOPTION

In analogy with the delegation analysis we will have:
Weak adoption - when there is no agreement, no information or even influence: Ag_2 autonomously has the goal of performing a given action since and until this action is either contained in Ag_1's plan or it is an interest of Ag_1 itself. Notice that this kind of help can be completely unilateral and spontaneous from Ag_2, and/or even ignored by Ag_1. In other words, Ag_2 can adopt some of Ag_1's goals independently of Ag_1's delegation or request.
See (Castelfranchi and Falcone, 1998b) for a detailed analysis of the cognitive ingredients
Strict adoption - there is an agreement between Ag_1 and Ag_2 about Ag_1's task delegation to Ag_2 in response to Ag_2's offer.

In Strict Delegation, the contractor knows that the client is relying on it and accepts the task; in Strict Adoption, the helped agent knows about the adoption and accepts it. In other words, *Strict Delegation requires Strict Adoption, and viceversa:* they are two facets of a unitary social relation that we call "delegation-adoption" or "contract".
The delegation/adoption relation is the core of the "social commitment" relation (Castelfranchi, 1996, Singh, 1995, Fikes, 1982, Bond, 1989). It is a basic ingredient for joint intentions, true cooperation and team work (Kinny et al., 1994, Levesque et al., 1990, Grosz and Kraus, 1996). In other words, we claim that in collaborative activity each partner is relying on the other partners "strongly" delegating them some tasks, and, viceversa, each partner is adopting his own tasks from the other partners. Both delegations and adoptions can be either explicit or implicit.

Conflicts about weak and strict adoption A conflict of adoption could arise when the contractor decides between a weak or a strict adoption. This conflict is a meta-level conflict, not directly related to the help content but to the way chosen for giving that help (and always for collaborative reasons).
Differently from delegation conflicts in this case the conflict is raised by the client: is the client that could not accept the kind of adoption/help. For exam-

ple, consider a weak adoption; in this case the client could refuse to be helped without its own consent, and this for several reasons: it does not accept that someone interferes with its own tasks without its agreement, the only condition -in its view- for a successful achievement; it doesn't want to be deprived of its authority because, even if sometimes spontaneous help (weak adoption) could be useful, in general it could be destructive of the standard collaboration roles, etc.

When a contractor offers a strict adoption, a conflict could arise if the client prefers the weak kind of adoption. Suppose you slide and fail to the ground and somebody which is close to you, instead of automatically trying to help you, asks "Do you want me to help you?". This would be rather stupid and irritating.

5.2 LEVELS OF ADOPTION RELATIVE TO THE DELEGATED TASK

We consider now the contractor's adoption with respect to an explicitly delegated task (contract situation). We also consider *the plan-based context* in which that task is assigned. In fact, just on the basis of a specific plan-based context a collaborative contractor could try to modify that task in one of the following ways:

Sub help - Ag_2 adopts a subpart of what has been delegated by Ag_1 (goal, action, etc.)

Literal help - Ag_2 adopts exactly what has been delegated by Ag_1 (elementary or complex action, etc.)

Overhelp - Ag_2 goes beyond what has been delegated by Ag_1 without changing Ag_1's plan.

Critical help - Ag_2 satisfies the relevant results of the requested plan/action, but modifies that plan/action.

Overcritical help - Ag_2 realizes an Overhelp and in addition modifies/changes that plan/action.

Hyper-critical help - Ag_2 adopts goals or interests of Ag_1 that Ag_1 itself did not take into account: by doing so, Ag_2 neither performs the action/plan nor satisfies the results that were delegated.

Given this characterization of delegation and adoption and of their plan-based levels, we can derive a *basic ontology of conflicts* arising between the two agents when there is a mismatch between the intended delegation and the intended adoption. These mismatches are neither due to simple misunderstandings of Ag_1's request/expectation or of Ag_2's offer, nor to a wrong or incomplete plan (intention) recognition by Ag_2.

5.2.1 Sub-help. In sub-help the contractor might either offer adoption or in fact satisfy just a sub-goal of the delegated task.
Given the situation:
$Delegates(Ag_1\ Ag_2\ \tau = (\alpha, g))$ with $Dom\text{-}c(\alpha'\ \alpha)$
in other words, Ag_1 delegates (to Ag_2) τ within $\tau' = (\alpha', g')$, if
$Adopts(Ag_2\ Ag_1\ \tau_1) \wedge Dom\text{-}c(\alpha\ \alpha_1), with \tau_1 = (\alpha_1, g_1)$ we say that Ag_2 subhelps Ag_1 (see figure 2.3).
In other words, Ag_2 does not satisfy the delegated task. For example in a practical domain, Ag_1 delegates to Ag_2 "make-fettuccine-with-pesto" and Ag_2 limits itself to "make-pesto".
This is due to several possible reasons: Ag_2 is not able to do all the task; it is not convenient for Ag_1; it does not want to help Ag_1 as for the higher goal because for example it believes that another agent is doing that part for Ag_1.
It is difficult to think of a sub-help as a "collaborative" action. But, in some specific situations, a reduction of the contractor's help action could avoid some dangerous, destructive final results for the client. So, if the contractor reduces its help just for these reasons we must consider it as a collaborative behavior.

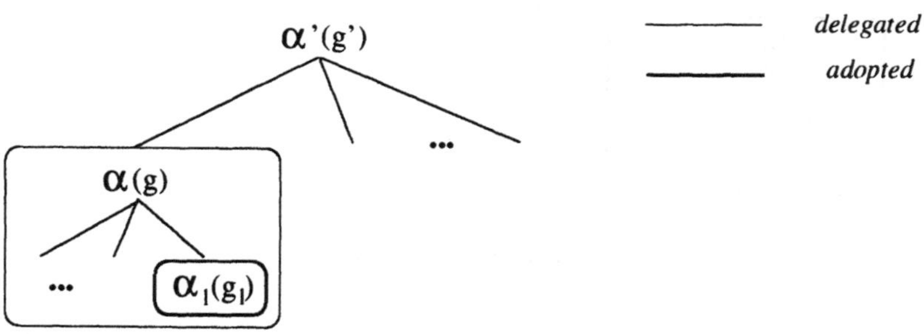

Figure 2.3 Sub-help

5.2.2 Beyond delegation. In the following we will consider collaborative conflicts in which Ag_2's help goes beyond Ag_1's request or delegation, exploiting its own knowledge and intelligence (reasoning, problem solving, planning, and decision skills) for Ag_1.
Ag_2's intention to really collaborate can create some problems. On the one hand, one cannot be satisfied by an agent's help that consists in what it is literally requested to do. This is not a very collaborative agent. It has no initiative, it does not care for our interests, it does not use its knowledge and intelligence to correct those plans and requests that might be incomplete, wrong or self-defeating. Thus, a truly helpful agent should not be "helpful" in the sense defined by (Cohen and Levesque, 1990):

$\forall a(Bel\ x\ (Goal\ y\ (Eventually\ (Done\ x\ a)))) \wedge \neg(Goal\ x\ \neg(Done\ x\ a)) \Rightarrow$
$(P\text{-}Goal\ x\ (Done\ x\ a))$

This agent is just adopting an action (not its goal) and in a literal way. It is a mere executor. It obeys, but is not very helpful. It may even be dangerous. However, on the other hand, there are dangers also when the agent takes the initiative of helping the client beyond its request.

5.2.3 Over, critical, overcritical and hypercritical help. Given the situation:
$Delegates(Ag_1\ Ag_2\ \tau = (\alpha, g))$ with $Dom\text{-}c(\alpha'\ \alpha)$
if
$Adopts(Ag_2\ Ag_1\ \tau_1) \wedge Dom\text{-}c(\alpha_1\ \alpha) \wedge (Dom\text{-}c(\alpha'\ \alpha_1) \vee (\alpha' \equiv \alpha_1))$
we say that Ag_2 overhelps Ag_1 (see figure 2.4).

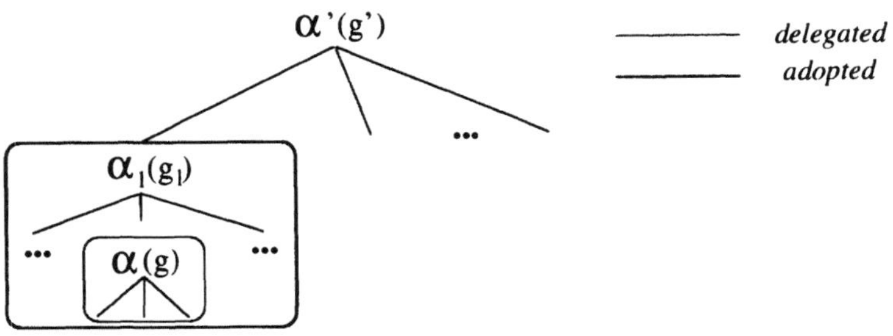

Figure 2.4 Overhelp

In a conversation domain, for example, Ag_1 asks: "What time is it?", and Ag_2 answers: "Be calm, it is 5pm and our meeting is at 6pm, we are in time". Both the delegated action (to inform about time) and the higher, non-delegated results (plan) (to know whether Ag_1 is late or not; to not be anxious) are adopted and satisfied by Ag_2.
In the same vein, suppose Ag_1 asks Ag_2 to prepare the sauce for the ravioli Ag_1 will prepare for dinner, and Ag_2 overhelps Ag_1 by preparing both the sauce and the ravioli.

Given the situation:
$Delegates(Ag_1\ Ag_2\ \tau = (\alpha, g))$ with $Dom\text{-}c(\alpha'\ \alpha)$
if
$Adopts(Ag_2\ Ag_1\ \tau_x) \wedge g \in R(\alpha_x)$
with $\tau_x = (\alpha_x, g)$;
we say that Ag_2 makes a critical help about τ (see figure 2.5). In fact, what happens is that Ag_2 adopts g, that is it is sufficient for Ag_2 to find in Act_{Ag_2}

an action α_x whatever, such that $g \subseteq R_{Ag_2}(\alpha_x)$. In other words, the contractor achieves the goal(s) of the delegated plan/action, but it changes that plan/action.

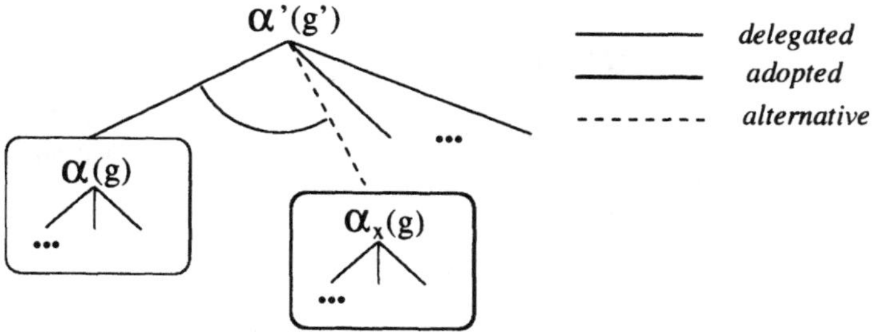

Figure 2.5 Critical help

Critical help holds in the following alternative cases:
i) $(CEK(Ag_2, \alpha) = \theta) \vee (g \not\subset R_{Ag_2}(\alpha)) \vee (P(\alpha) = false)$;
that is to say, agent Ag_2 is unable either to execute α or, on the basis of its knowledge on action results, it guesses that g is not among the results of α, or the conditions of α are not true (and it is unable to realize them).
Correspondingly Ag_2 must guess that there is an action α_x such that:
$(CEK(Ag_2, \alpha_x) \neq \theta) \wedge (g \subseteq R_{Ag_2}(\alpha_x)) \wedge (P(\alpha_x) = true)$; in other words Ag_2 finds another way to realize g, using another action α_x in its action repertoire, such that: Ag_2 is able to realize it, the new action contains g among its results and its conditions are satisfied.
ii) Ag_2 thinks that the other results of α (beyond g) are in conflict with other goals - in plan or off plan - or interests of the client. On the other side, it thinks that there is an action α_x with:
$(CEK(Ag_2, \alpha_x) \neq \theta) \wedge (g \subseteq R_{Ag_2}(\alpha_x)) \wedge (P(\alpha_x) = true)$
and the results of α_x are not in conflict with other goals or interests of the client.
iii) There is also the case of optimization, where the conditions in (i) are all false but there is an action α_x such that g is reached in a more profitable way for Ag_2 (relative to any criteria).

Given the situation:
$Delegates(Ag_1\ Ag_2\ \tau = (\alpha, g))$ with $Dom\text{-}c(\alpha'\ \alpha)$
if
$Adopts(Ag_2\ Ag_1\ \tau_x) \wedge Dom\text{-}c(\alpha_1\ \alpha) \wedge (Dom\text{-}c(\alpha'\ \alpha_1) \vee (\alpha' \equiv \alpha_1))$
with $\tau_x = (\alpha_x, g), \tau_1 = (\alpha_1, g_1)$, $R(\alpha_x)$ the set of the results produced by α_x; we say that Ag_2 makes an overcritical help about τ (see figure 2.6). In fact, what happens is that Ag_2 adopts g_1, that is to say it is sufficient for Ag_2 to find

in Act_{Ag_2} an action α_x whatever, such that $g_1 \subseteq R_{Ag_2}(\alpha_x)$. In other words, the contractor implements both a critical help and an overhelp (it chooses a task that satisfies a higher level task with respect to the delegated one, and achieves the goal(s) of this higher task, while changing the expected plan).

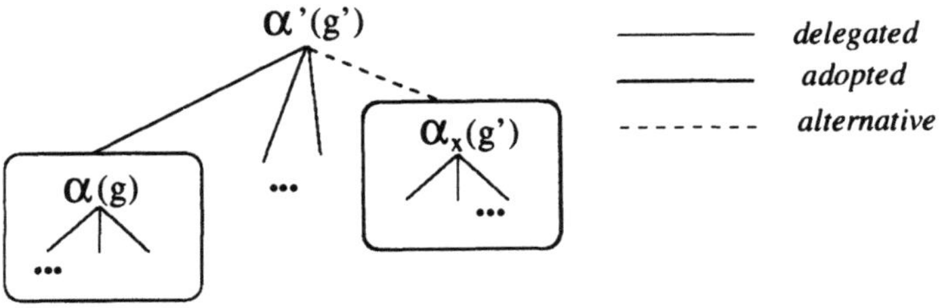

Figure 2.6 Overcritical help

Overcritical help holds in the following alternative cases:
i) $Pr(\alpha, \alpha', g') = \theta$ and at the same time
$(\exists \alpha_x \in Act_{Ag_2} \mid (Pr(\alpha, \alpha', g') \neq \theta \wedge CEK(Ag_2, \alpha_x) \neq \theta \wedge P(\alpha_x) = true))$.
In other words, there are no pertinent results of α in α'; but it exists at least one action α_x some results of which is pertinent to α' aimed at g'. This means that α is useless for τ'. It is even possible that it is noxious: i.e. that $R(\alpha)$ produces results that contradict those intended with τ'. Ag_1 is delegating a plan that in Ag_2's view is wrong or self-defeating.
ii) $Pr(\alpha, \alpha', g') \neq \theta \wedge CEK(Ag_2, \alpha) \neq \theta \wedge P(\alpha) = true$ and in addition
$(\exists \alpha_x \in Act_{Ag_2} \mid (Pr(\alpha_x, \alpha', g') \neq \theta \wedge CEK(Ag_2, \alpha_x) \neq \theta \wedge P(\alpha_x) = true))$
moreover
iia) $R(\alpha_x)$ achieves the goals internal to the plan (i.e. g') in a better way (*maximization*). For example, Ag_1 asks Ag_2 "to buy a second class train ticket for Naples" (action α) for its plan "to go to Naples by train cheaply" (action α'). Ag_2 adopts Ag_1's goal "to be in Naples and spend little money" (goal g') replacing the whole plan (α_x) with another plan: "go with Paul by car".
iib) $R(\alpha_x)$ achieves not only the goals of the plan (i.e. g') but also other goals of Ag_1 external to that plan (ex. g"):
$(g' \subset R(\alpha_x)) \wedge (g'' \subset R(\alpha_x))$.
For example, Ag_1 asks Ag_2 "to buy a second class train ticket for Naples" (action α) for its plan "to go to Naples by train cheaply" (action α'). Ag_2 adopts Ag_1's goal "to be in Naples and spend little money" (goal g') replacing the whole plan (α') with another plan (α_x) "to go with Paul by car" that also satisfies another goal of Ag_1 - that Ag_1 did not consider in its plan - but Ag_2 knows: "to travel with friends".
iic) $R(\alpha_x)$ achieves not only the goals of the plan but also *some interests (I)* of

Ag_1:
$(g' \subset R(\alpha_x)) \wedge (I \subset R(\alpha_x))$.
For example: Ag_1 asks Ag_2 "to buy a second class train ticket for Naples" (action α) for its plan "to go to Naples by train cheaply" (action α'). Ag_2 adopts Ag_1's goal "to be in Naples and spend little money" (goal g') replacing the whole plan (α') with another plan (α_x) "to go to Naples by bus" that satisfies an interest of Ag_1 that it ignores of "not risking to meet Paul on the same train".

Given the situation:
$Delegates(Ag_1\ Ag_2\ \tau = (\alpha, g))$ with $Dom\text{-}c(\alpha'\ \alpha)$
if
$Adopts(Ag_2\ Ag_1\ \tau_1) \wedge (g_1 \neq g') \wedge (g_1 \neq g) \wedge (g_1 \in I_{Ag_1})$
with $\tau_1 = (\alpha_1, g_1)$, and I_{Ag_1} being the set of the interests (Castelfranchi, 1991) of Ag_1,
we say that Ag_2 makes hypercritical help about τ (see figure 2.7). In fact, Ag_2 adopts g_1, where g_1 is an interest (or an off-plan goal) of Ag_1 more important than g' (we leave here this notion just intuitive). Since there is a conflict between the result $R(\alpha)$ (and/or the result $R(\alpha')$) and some g_1 of Ag_1, adopting g_1 would imply renouncing $R(\alpha)$ (or $R(\alpha')$).
In other words, Ag_2 adopts goals or interests of Ag_1 that Ag_1 itself did not take into account: by doing so, Ag_2 neither performs the delegated action/plan nor achieves the results that were delegated.

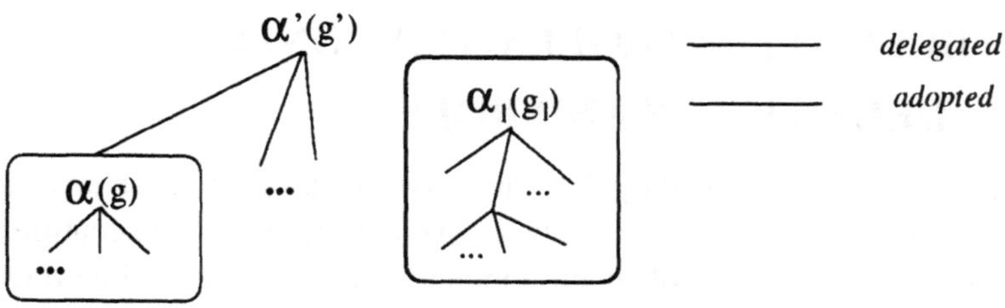

Figure 2.7 Hypercritical help

5.2.4 Considerations about the conflicts implied in the previous kinds of help. In any case of over, critical, overcritical and hypercritical help apparently there is a conflict, since Ag_1 has the goal that Ag_2 does α, while Ag_2 is doing or intends to do something different for Ag_1. Normally these conflicts can be quickly solved for two reasons. First, Ag_2's intention is to help Ag_1, it is a collaborative one; second, normally Ag_2 is "entitled" by Ag_1 (either explicitly or implicitly) to provide this deeper help, and Ag_1 is expecting this initiative and autonomy. Thus, normally there is no real conflict since Ag_1 is

ready to accept Ag_2's collaborative initiative.
However, sometimes these cases trigger serious conflicts which have to be negotiated. This is specially true in organizations and among different roles.
Leaving aside possible cases of misunderstanding between client and contractor about Ag_1's request/expectation or Ag_2's offer, we can distinguish the reasons for conflict into two main classes:
i) *Threat to Ag_1's goals*
Ag_2 can jeopardize Ag_1's goal achievement: this is possible for at least two reasons:
i1) *Lack of coordination*
A plan is composed of many actions (assigned to several agents, when there is a partial delegation), so a unilateral initiative on the part of one agent to change that plan without reconsidering the general plan might be fatal (because of interference) or lead to a waste of resources, time, etc. (because of redundancy).
i2) *Disagreement about action results*
Ag_1 knows or believes that the action executed by Ag_2 does not bring about the results expected or believed by Ag_2 itself.
ii) *Role and Status*
In this case the conflict is relative to the entitlement of Ag_2 by Ag_1 to take the initiative of changing the delegated task. For reasons of power, job, subordination, role, Ag_2 while doing such a sub/over/critical help is going beyond what it is permitted to do (according to Ag_1).

6. DELEGATION ROLES AND CONFLICTS

6.1 DELEGATION AND ROLE

Agents delegate roles as they delegate tasks. In a broad sense *any task delegation is the creation of a role*: in fact, given an occasional execution of any plan through the execution of its component actions by more than one agent, one might say that these agents have a given "role" in that plan and group. This is a "transitory" or occasional role. However, we decide to use (as usual) the term "role" only for more long term and stable duties, as those typically assigned in organizations; and to use just the term "task" for occasional delegation.
We can specialize the defined contract relation in two subtypes: the *task-contract* and the *role-contract*. The task-contract concerns an occasional delegation.
Let us define as Role contract or relation (ρ), the triple ρ=(**A**, **B**, **T**); where **A** is the *Role Client class*, **B** is the *Role Contractor class* and **T** is the *Role Task class*. In fact, ρ=(**A**, **B**, **T**) implies Delegates(**A**, **B**, **T**). More precisely:
- **T** is the "Role domain" or "Role competence": $\{\tau_1, \tau_2, ..., \tau_2\}$, a set of task

classes where each τ_i $(1 \leq i \leq n)$ represents either a domain task class or a meta-domain one. In fact, **T** is the set of the services the role can provide.
- **A** and **B** are the classes of the contractor agents and of the client agents respectively. There is a relation of Delegation-Adoption between these two types of agents about the Role Task (Nomic Task).
Then, for each task $\tau \in \mathbf{T}$ if $Ag_i \in \mathbf{B}$, τ is a potential task of Ag_i, that is to say the agent is delegated (by **A**) to bring it about. Analogously, for each task $\tau \in \mathbf{T}$ if $Ag_j \in \mathbf{A}$ τ is its potential task to be delegated to **B**.

6.2 ROLE CONFLICTS

The commitments about classes of goals within the organization plans, define, as we said the role of the agent in that organization.
The existence of such an established role, generic commitments, and pre-agreement, deeply changes the relation between the client and the contractor. In fact, if Ag_1 asks Ag_2 to do something (α) that belongs to its role, this is just an instantiation of what Ag_2 already promised/agreed to do: it is its role-duty. Ag_2 has to do this "by role", by contract. Also this source of duty rises possible conflicts of delegation.
On the one side, Ag_2 might disagree about α belonging to its office:

$$(Bel\,Ag_1(\exists\rho_1 \mid ((Ag_1 \in \mathbf{A}_1) \wedge (Ag_2 \in \mathbf{B}_1) \wedge (\tau \in \mathbf{T}_1)$$
$$(Bel\,Ag_2(\neg\exists\rho_1 \mid (((Ag_1 \in \mathbf{A}_1) \wedge (Ag_2 \in \mathbf{B}_1) \wedge (\tau \in \mathbf{T}_1)$$

On the other side, the conflicts might depend on different interpretation of the original contract (Organizational Commitment); the conflict might also be about reasons for adoption: Ag_1 might search for a due, role-based adoption, while Ag_2 is ready to help Ag_1 for other reasons. For example Ag_1 gives a "command" to Ag_2, while Ag_2 does not want to "obey" but just to friendly help or to exchange.

The main types of role conflicts are:
Given $Delegates(Ag_1\ Ag_2\ \tau)$:
- Ag_1's delegation does not match with Ag_2's role: either a sub-task or an over-task is requested:
$Bel(Ag_2(\exists\rho_2 \mid ((Ag_1 \in \mathbf{A}_2) \wedge (Ag_2 \in \mathbf{B}_2) \wedge (\tau' \in \mathbf{T}_2)))) \wedge (Dom\text{-}c(\alpha'\ \alpha) \vee Dom\text{-}c(\alpha\ \alpha'))$
- Ag_1's delegation does not fit with Ag_1's role: Ag_1 shouldn't delegate/ask for that kind of task (for ex. it is not entitled to delegate τ):
$(Bel\,Ag_2\forall\rho_i \mid ((Ag_2 \in \mathbf{B}_i) \wedge (\tau \in \mathbf{T}_i))(\neg\exists\mathbf{A}_i \mid (Ag_1 \in \mathbf{A}_i)))$
- Ag_1 and Ag_2 disagree about τ belonging to Ag_2's office:
$(Bel\,Ag_2\forall\rho_i \mid (Ag_2 \in \mathbf{B}_i)\neg\exists\mathbf{T}_i \mid \tau \in \mathbf{T}_i)$
- Ag_1 and Ag_2 disagree about the reasons for Ag_2's adoption (whether it has to be a role adoption or not).

7. TUTORIAL AND PATERNALISTIC CONFLICTS

The adoption of Ag_1's interests beyond its request and expectation is the more problematic case. In fact, Ag_2 is claiming to know what is good for Ag_1 better than Ag_1 itself. Not only, but it can also claim that Ag_1 does not have the proper goals.

When Ag_2 takes care of Ag_1's interests and tries to induce Ag_1 to pursue certain goals because these are in its own interest ("for your sake") we call this social attitude and relation *tutorial*.

Of course, this attitude is very pretentious and might be annoying for Ag_1, which perceives it as "paternalistic". Any adult agent pretends to know and to be able to decide what is better for him.

Nevertheless -given our cognitive and rational limits- in many cases we in fact ignore our interest, what is better for us, and we do not pursue as a goal what we need. Thus this dialectic is intrinsic in any relation of deep and spontaneous help.

Normally tutorial adoption and attitude imply some conflict since the contractor wants that the client has a different goal from those it currently has. In fact an objective "interest" is defined as something that an agent believes should be a goal of another, but that (it believes) it is not. Something that is useful or necessary for the other agent, that it is needed, but that the other does not understand or know, or does not prefer. When you believe that I is an interest of yours ("it is in your interest") I becomes a goal of yours, although not necessarily a pursued goal. When you believe that I is your prevailing interest (or that is your interest to pursue I), I not only becomes a goal but it is preferred and pursued. What the tutorial agent is trying to do is to influence you to adopt your interest as a goal or the prevailing goal of yours.

A tutorial software agent or system would be an agent that, for example, answering to your request of reserving a table in a nice restaurant might say "it is too expensive for you!", or, if requested to order a box of whisky answers "alcohol is toxic". Do we want such an intrusive and father-like agent? What kind of limits do we have to put to this helping intrusion? What about a software agent that, without expliciting its criteria, just gives us advise and suggests plans that are based on our supposed interests more than on our actual goals? This might be even worse, even if it has some interesting aspects. Consider for example a tourist adviser that has the goal of avoiding crowding of tourists all in the same famous places and the goal of make them visit beautiful but not well-known monuments. This is claimed to be in the interest of the tourist themselves (but of course is also in the interest of the tourist office, of the city and of its major, etc.). Suppose you are in Rome and have just one day and would like to see Caravaggio's paintings. Well, this system will adopt your goal, but also your interest, and send you to see some beautiful Caravaggio that is not that famous and perhaps is not what you expected. You might appreciate this discover and your quiet enjoying it. But you might also be disappointed about not seeing the Caravaggio your friends will ask you about when you are back home. So, what to do? Should this kind of help be allowed in artificial agents? With what kind of limits?

There are several possible remedies:

- Agents should tacitly and automatically adopt the interests of the client only when those interests are reconcilable with the client's request, and there is a plan for satisfying both. In this case the over adoption is just a better solution for a broader problem.

More formally, Ag_1 delegates $\tau = (\alpha, g)$ and Ag_2 adopts $\tau' = (\alpha', g')$ with $(g \cup i) \subseteq g'$ (i is an Ag_1's interest).

- In their social life humans accept (and expect) this kind of help only from certain agents (mother, friends, doctor, etc.) relative to certain area of goals (for ex. health from the doctor, salvation from a priest, happiness from a friend). Similarly we could decide whether we want a tutorial attitude from our software agents or helping systems or not, and relative to which domain. In practice, we could establish various classes of tasks where the agent can assume a paternalistic behavior.

- The adoption of our interests in case of conflict must be explicit, so that the adopted agent can refuse or at least discuss until he or she is persuaded. In this case the hypercritical adoption must be communicated to the client before being applied.

- The agent's refusal of the client's request for tutorial reasons is not allowed (except for some "vital" interest, like life).

8. FUNCTIONAL VIOLATIONS OF NORMS AND COMMITMENTS

As a very nice, important and systematic form of collaborative conflicts in organizations, let us explain the functional violation of tasks, roles, procedure and norms. They are very important also because they are permanent internal causes of transformation and adaptation of organizations.

In this section we aim to apply our analysis of task and role delegation, of social and role commitment, and of norms to a very important phenomenon discovered in work and industrial sociology and in sociology of organization: what they call "the functional violation/disregard of norms".

In our view, the understanding and the theory of this phenomenon is particularly important in AI and in general in computer science approaches to organization. In fact, if it is true that real organization of any type cannot efficiently and adaptively work without regularly ignoring or violating some of their own rules, norms, procedures; and if for being really collaborative and efficient a good worker/member has to frequently enough violate some of the rules that regulate his job and some of his official commitments to the organization. Then, we can say that *one can predict serious difficulties or damages in formalizing, applying, and supporting with information technology the formal and official procedures, rules and norms, and literal commitments within organization.*

In fact, the resulting system would be very rigid. Notice that several applications of AI to institutions and cooperative work are aimed precisely at such a formalization. On the contrary, one should be able to understand the logic and the function of that "transgressive" behavior, and to implement and support it. But to do this we need an explanation of that behavior and of its functionality, and we have to know when and why agents do resort to this behavior, and when and why it is useful or not.

Our claim is that this sociological phenomenon is just a special case of the general principle of Over- and Critical-Adoption and of its usefulness for a deep and effective help (cooperation) between agents. The worker/member is just over-critically adopting the goals prescribed by the organization (task, rules, norms) taking into account the global plan, the current circumstances, the interest of the Organization, and going beyond what has been literally prescribed or negotiated. As in the theory of Over (critical) help, this decision does not depend on the agent's individual interest, preferences or advantages, but exactly on its willingness to collaborate and to adopt the interest of the helped agent. This is why, applying this attitude to the organization, those "violations" are paradoxically "functional", i.e. helpful relative to the organization's plans and interests.

From a seemingly bad, irregular, arbitrary and non-prescribed behavior we see that a good effect emerges for the organization. Let's now see how this form of intelligent collaboration applies to organizations and to the phenomenon of norm/rule violation.

8.1 THE SOCIOLOGICAL DESCRIPTION AND DEFINITION OF THE PHENOMENON

The "Functional violation or disregard of norms" (FVN) is characterized in the sociological literature as

"the repeated and systematic violation of criteria, prescriptions and dispositions included in the normative apparatus that defines and regulates (through "norms", in a broad sense) a collective organized activity. This violation favors an acceptable level of functioning of the organization itself, while the literal and punctual application of the normative will produce levels of functioning either unacceptable or less efficacious" (Manciulli et al., 1986).

As a quite revealing proof of the existence and efficacy of this behavior, sociologists refer to what in Italy we call "white strikes" (what in France is called, very appropriately, "grève du zèle"), that are "forms of sabotage consisting just in a rigorous application of rulements" (Mottez, 1971). The existence of this paradoxical form of functioning and cooperation within organization is a real problem for classical theories of organization. More importantly it constitutes a problem and an everyday dilemma (Manciulli et al., 1986) for the management.

What should be done? Forcing workers to discipline (reducing efficiency) or allowing systematic micro-violations they are aware of, exploiting the intelligence and local knowledge of the agents? As we have shown, this is the general dilemma and trade-off of "autonomy" in delegation: it is the dilemma of the delegation-controller.

It is important to notice that these violations are not random or rebellious acts, and are not just related to the worker comfort or personal preferences, but are systematic and intended to favor the collective work.

This analysis and view has to be traced back to the classical theory of conflicts in functionalist sociology, introduced in AI studies by Galliers. According to this view conflicts are not a bad thing for groups and organizations. They do not necessarily damage or destroy the group, or disturb its work. They are functional to the organization in several ways: by favoring quick adaptation to evolving situations, the circulation of ideas, by dealing with the unavoidable lacks of knowledge, planning and control.

This is also the case of FVN, that is just a special case of functional conflicts in organizations. In fact, however useful and aimed at being useful for the organization, norm and task violation create conflicts. As we just saw, even at the simple level of Over(Critical) Help, conflicts arise.

8.2 OUR PERSPECTIVE ON FVN

For "functional disregard" we mean the deliberated violation of a norm, rule, prescription finalized to make the required/expected work (also) more functional to the organization's aims (over- and critical-help).

Notice that not only the violation but also its functionality for the organization is deliberated.

Consider this example taken from a research on socio-cognitive organization of work in an airport control tower. Fly controllers should use the interphone, also in communication among people within the same control room. There is a rule prescribing this. However, the interphone has some inconvenience (for ex. voices overlaps, misunderstandings, ...) and the controllers consider its use not only less natural for them, but "potentially safety critical". This is why they in fact do not use interphone for messages within the same room, and communicate "directly". In this real example we clearly have a systematic violation for *functional, cooperative reasons.*

Notice that this violation is functional both subjectively, in the controllers intention, and - probably- objectively, since this practice must have proved efficient to be consolidated through some form of reinforcement learning (or evaluation of results) and through social learning.

More than this, we have in this example a true *convention to violate*. In fact, the functional violation is no longer an individual and independent initiative, an individual problem solving (this is how probably it was born); it is now an implicit or explicit agreement among the controllers. They know, approve and positively expect that the others violate the norm; they probably implicitly or explicitly teach a new member to violate. They *cooperate in violating*; both at the very moment of bilaterally communicating with each other, and in knowing and letting the other violate (also with others) so that they too can violate the norm. Thus, a true social expectation and prescription, i.e. a social, informal group norm against the official norm, is at work, and works.

Isn't such a violation of a norm actually the application of another, higher level, implicit and informal, contrasting norm (Manciulli et al., 1986)? or better of a superior implicit contract and delegation? It might be. Consider that when Ag_1 delegates/prescribes a task to Ag_2 and fixes its modalities, it is presupposed and meant by both Ag_1 and Ag_2 that the specified task is useful for the aims of Ag_1 (that Ag_2 adopts). So, if Ag_2 finds some disfunctionality between what has been prescribed and Ag_1's aims, there is a strange, conflicting situation. We move from "do τ and in doing τ do Ag_1's interest" to "do τ OR do Ag_1's interest"! Should Ag_2 obey "do τ" or the (frequently implicit) "do Ag_1's interest"? The command (the obligation) happens to be self-contradictory; it generates two diverging norms Ag_2 has to obey, or better to choose.

Ag_2 must make a "critique" of the literal delegation precisely in order to fulfil the deepest delegation: i.e. to satisfy the intended need or purpose of Ag_1. In violating the pact, Ag_2 is in fact keeping the pact.

Moreover, isn't there some sort of tacit entitlement, of tacit agreement and permission to violate? Linhart in (Manciulli et al., 1986) suggests that in real organizations there is in fact a social representation, a fiction, in particular by the management, consisting in tacitly allowing functional violations while pretending that rules remain untouched and simulating that they are basically respected. They cannot admit and officially tolerate the illegal practice, so they are acting "as if", just simulating. However, given the very important social rule "Qui tacet consentire videtur" (silent consent) if it is clear that the management cannot be unaware of that illegal practice, and that they do not block or punish it, this might be interpreted as an assent, a tacit, informal permission. However, notice that not always or not forever the disregarded rules remain untouched in a fictive rule-obeying behavior. Frequently enough this spontaneous functional violation of norms generates a permanent evolutionary dynamics within the organization. Organizations do not evolve only for adapting to the challenges of the external environment and to competition; they also change for this internal dialectics between official organization, roles, rules, etc. and real functional and adjusted practices. At a given point formal rules, explicit knowledge, official organization are changed for integrating or facilitating the functional, creative, bottom-up practices. This conflict is a permanent innovation and evolution mechanism.

9. CONCLUSIONS

Delegation and its related conflicts are the core of the interaction among any kind of autonomous agents. In this chapter we have presented our definition of delegation and adoption, a plan-based definition of tasks, and of different kinds and levels of delegation and adoption. We have tried to show that:

i) There are several levels of cooperation - more or less "deep" and helpful- and several levels of task delegation.

ii) These levels are related to the hierarchical structure of plans or tasks.

iii) There is a non-arbitrary correspondence between levels of delegation and levels of adoption; we have called "contract" this relation.

iv) A "deep" cooperation needs the understanding of plans, goals, and interests of the other agent or user.

v) There is a fundamental distinction between the delegation/adoption of a domain task (practical action), or a planning or problem solving action, or a control action.

We have described the most interesting conflicts that arise when the provided help does not match the intended delegation (except conflicts due to misunderstanding). We have also discussed conflicts due to critical over help, and to the tutorial (paternalistic) attitude of the helper, who takes care of our interests against our requests. We have also analyzed role conflicts and the systematic but functional (collaborative) violation of norms, rules, prescriptions, a very important form of conflict for the dynamics and the evolution of organization.

Acknowledgments

We would like to thank Maria Miceli for her precious comments.

Chapter 3

THEIR PROBLEMS ARE MY PROBLEMS

The transition between internal and external conflicts[1]

Markus Hannebauer

German National Research Center for Information Technology, Berlin, Germany

markus.hannebauer@gmd.de

Abstract In Multi-Agent Systems there has been quite an amount of research on how to model conflicts in (intelligent) agent architectures for example by imitating mental states and augmenting them with social notions. Nevertheless, a great deal of investigation is missing on the transition between internal and external conflicts. Arguments in favor of taking a closer look at this transition include a practical one from applications where internal conflicts may easily become external conflicts and vice versa, and a technical one motivated by the existence of more efficient algorithms for solving internal conflicts.

In this chapter we will use a rather technical and restricted notion of "conflict" to exploit the mathematical model of distributed constraint satisfaction problems that covers internal as well as external conflicts in a unique framework. In this model conflicts can be identified as "inconsistencies" and there are several algorithms for conflict detection, conflict avoidance and conflict resolution. After introducing models for internal and external conflicts and algorithms to solve them, we will focus on a new concept called AUREcON (autonomous dynamic reconfiguration) that provides a means for balancing on the transition between internal and external conflict.

1. INTRODUCTION

Though research in Sociology has long been investigating the so-called *micro-macro-link* (Alexander et al., 1987) that concerns the close relationship between individual behavior and social structures, research in classical Artificial Intelligence has long neglected the strong relation between internal and external conflicts. The modeling and solving of conflicts within agents has long

[1]This chapter summarizes the results presented in (Hannebauer, 2000a) and (Hannebauer, 2000b) and extends them in several ways.

been interpreted as being a task for expert systems, planners and schedulers motivated by results of Logic, Cognitive Science or Decision Theory. On the other hand, the modeling and solving of external conflicts among autonomous entities has been seen as a research task for Coordination Theory inspired by Sociology and Economics. Research in Distributed AI and especially Multi-Agent Systems has proven this distinction to be antiquated.

Despite the fact that there has been quite an amount of research on how to model conflicts in (intelligent) agent architectures for example by imitating mental states and augmenting them with social notions, a great deal of investigation is missing on the transition right between internal and external conflicts. But this transition is not only theoretical: as soon as an agent a decides to adopt two goals from competing agents b and c, the external conflict between b and c will become an internal one for a. Vice versa, an internal conflict of agent a produced by different goals will become an external conflict if the pursuing of the different goals is delegated to different agents b and c. Additionally, there are often quite different algorithms available to solve internal and external conflicts. Not always but often, internal conflicts can be solved more efficiently than external conflicts because of a better understanding of the situation and the missing communication overhead. Hence, there is an obligatory and a mandatory argument for taking a closer look at the similarities and differences of internal and external conflicts and their solving procedures.

Conflicts in their broadest sense are manifold in type, quality and quantity and the concepts presented in this chapter (especially in section 4.) are generic enough to be applied to many of them. Nevertheless, we will use a rather technical and restricted notion of "conflict" to exploit a mathematical model that covers internal as well as external conflicts in a unique framework. This model will be based on research in *distributed constraint satisfaction problems* (DCSPs, (Yokoo et al., 1998)). The big advantage of the DCSP model is its expressiveness but simplicity. It is a canonical extension of *constraint satisfaction problems* (CSPs, (Mackworth, 1992)) that allow for very efficient algorithms to solve internal conflicts. In CSPs, conflicts can be identified as so-called "inconsistencies" and there are several algorithms for conflict detection, conflict avoidance and conflict resolution. In section 2. we will introduce the CSP model for internal conflicts and briefly present results of other researchers and some own contributions to solving CSPs. The CSP model will be extended in section 3. to cover external conflicts. In this section we will also describe an algorithm for solving external conflicts, called *multi-phase agreement finding*. The main part of this chapter is section 4. presenting AURECON (autonomous dynamic reconfiguration), a means for balancing on the transition between internal and external conflict and bringing internal and external conflict solving together. Some pointers to related work and further remarks conclude our chapter.

2. INTERNAL CONFLICTS

2.1 MODELING INTERNAL CONFLICTS – CONSTRAINT SATISFACTION PROBLEMS

As already motivated, we will adopt the mathematical model of constraint satisfaction problems to describe internal conflicts. Most conflicts within an agent arise if there are several subproblems (goals) to solve (to achieve) that conflict in some way, for example because of competing for scarce resources. In CSPs this is modeled by assuming every subproblem to be a *variable* ranging over a (typically discrete and finite) *domain* of possible solutions to the subproblem. Conflicts among these subproblem variables are modeled by restrictions, so-called *constraints*, that relate the allowed (and such indirectly disallowed) combinations of the several subproblem solutions. A conflict is at hand if a certain combination of subproblem solutions violates one or more of the specified constraints. In this situation, called *inconsistency*, the conflict can only be resolved by choosing another combination of subproblem solutions, such that finally all constraints are satisfied and all subproblem solutions are conflict-free or consistent. The procedure of finding such a solution combination is called *constraint satisfaction*. The following definition of CSPs can be found in several articles on constraint satisfaction.

Definition 1 (Constraint satisfaction problem) *A (general)* constraint satisfaction problem *(CSP) is specified by a triple* $\Pi_{cs} = (X, D, C)$.

- $X = \{x_1, \ldots, x_n\}$ *is a set of* domain variables x_i *each ranging over its* domain D_i *from the set* $D = \{D_1, \ldots, D_n\}$.
- *A* labeling $\lambda : X \longrightarrow D_1 \cup \ldots \cup D_n, \lambda = (v_1, \ldots, v_n) \in D_1 \times \ldots \times D_n$ *assigns a value* $v_i \in D_i$ *to each domain variable* x_i. *A* partial labeling $\lambda' : (\{x_{\lambda'_1}, \ldots, x_{\lambda'_l}\} = X' \subseteq X) \longrightarrow (D_{\lambda'_1} \cup \ldots \cup D_{\lambda'_l} = D')$ *assigns a value* $v_i \in D_i$ *to each domain variable* $x_i \in X'$.
- $C = \{C_1, \ldots, C_m\}$ *is a set of* constraints $C_i \subseteq D_{i_1} \times \ldots \times D_{i_k}$, *each of which is a relation of type* $2^{D_{i_1} \times \ldots \times D_{i_k}}$ *restricting the set of* feasible *(partial) labelings.*

Given this specification, the problem is to find a labeling $\lambda \in \Lambda(C) = \{(v_1, \ldots, v_n) \in D_1 \times \ldots \times D_n | \forall C_i \in C : (v_{i_1}, \ldots, v_{i_k}) \in C_i\}$ *from the* solution space Λ *defined by* C.
A constraint satisfaction problem is called binary *(*Π_{bcs}*), iff all constraints* $C_i \in C$ *are binary relations.*

Sometimes it is opportune to reformulate a given CSP to solve it more efficiently. Nevertheless, it is important to ensure that the reformulation does not influence the set of solutions to the initial problem. This property is defined as follows.

Definition 2 (Solution equivalence) *Two constraint satisfaction problems* Π^1_* *and* Π^2_* *are called* solution equivalent *(*$\Pi^1_* \equiv \Pi^2_*$*), iff* $\exists (f : \Lambda^1(C^1) \longrightarrow \Lambda^2(C^2)) : f$ *bijective.*

Remark 1 a) In the definition of binary CSPs Π_{bcs} we do not consider unary constraints since they only restrict the domain of a single domain variable and can hence be satisfied directly by reducing the proper domain. No further processing is needed.
b) Every general CSP Π_{cs} can be transformed into a solution equivalent binary CSP Π_{bcs} by introducing further domain variables (Rossi et al., 1990).

Sometimes it is necessary to illustrate constraint satisfaction problems graphically. Especially binary CSPs are easily represented by ordinary graphs as given by the following definition and example.

Definition 3 (Constraint graph) *A* constraint graph *of a binary CSP* Π_{bcs} *is a triple* $\Gamma_{bcs} = (N, E, \mu)$.

- $N = \{n_1, \ldots, n_n\}$ *is a set of* nodes *each associated with a domain variable* x_i *from* Π_{bcs}.
- $E \subseteq \{\{n_j, n_k\} \mid n_j, n_k \in N \wedge n_j \neq n_k\}$ *is a set of* edges *with* $\{n_j, n_k\} \in E \Longleftrightarrow \exists C_l \in C : (C_l : 2^{D_j \times D_k})$.
- $\mu : N \cup E \longrightarrow T$ *marks nodes and edges with terms built from symbols of* Π_{bcs}*;* $\mu(n_i) = \langle (x_i, D_i) \rangle$, $\mu(\{n_j, n_k\}) = \langle C_{l1}, \ldots, C_{lm} \rangle$, $C_{l1}, \ldots, C_{lm} : 2^{D_j \times D_k}$.

Example 1 (Simple constraint satisfaction problem)

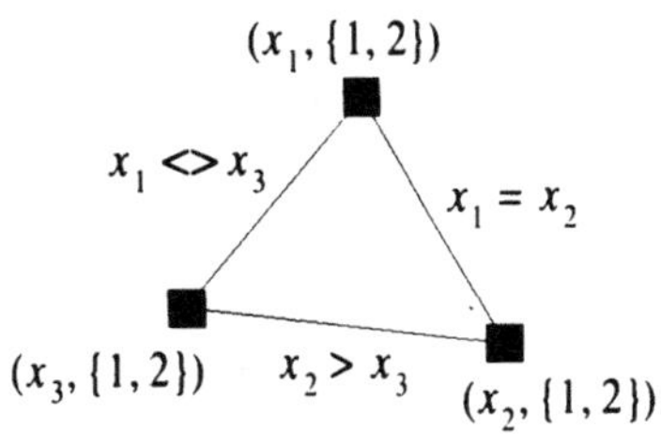

Figure 3.1: Simple CSP

The simple binary constraint satisfaction problem $\Pi_{bcs} = (X, D, C)$ with $X = \{x_1, x_2, x_3\}$, $D = \{\{1,2\}, \{1,2\}, \{1,2\}\}$ and $C = \{C_1, C_2, C_3\}$, $C_1 = (x_1 = x_2) = \{(1,1), (2,2)\}$, $C_2 = (x_2 > x_3) = \{(2,1)\}$, $C_3 = (x_1 \neq x_3) = \{(1,2), (2,1)\}$ can be illustrated by the constraint graph given by figure 3.1. The only feasible labeling λ is determined by $\Lambda(C) = \{(v_1, v_2, v_3) \in \{1,2\} \times \{1,2\} \times \{1,2\} | (v_1, v_2) \in C_1 \wedge (v_2, v_3) \in C_2 \wedge (v_1, v_3) \in C_3\} = \{(2,2,1)\} \ni (2,2,1) = \lambda$.

Though it is theoretically possible to reduce every general constraint satisfaction problem to a binary one, this is not very convenient and the constraint graphs tend to explode. To illustrate general CSPs graphically, we introduce an extended form of constraint graphs that can encode any type of constraints.

Definition 4 (Extended constraint graph) *An* extended constraint graph *of a general CSP* Π_{cs} *is a 4-tuple* $\Gamma_{cs} = (VN, CN, E, \mu)$.

- $VN = \{vn_1, \ldots, vn_n\}$ *is a set of* variable nodes *each associated with a domain variable* x_i *from* Π_{cs}.
- $CN = \{cn_1, \ldots, cn_m\}$ *is a set of* constraint nodes *each associated with a constraint* C_i *from* Π_{cs}.
- $E \subseteq \{\{vn_j, cn_k\} \mid vn_j \in VN \wedge cn_k \in CN\}$ *is a set of* edges *with* $\{vn_j, cn_k\} \in E \Longleftrightarrow C_k : 2^{\cdots \times D_j \times \cdots}$.
- $\mu : VN \cup CN \longrightarrow T$ *marks variable and constraint nodes with terms built from symbols of* Π_{cs}; $\mu(vn_i) = <(x_i, D_i)>$, $\mu(cn_i) = <C_i>$.

2.2 SOLVING INTERNAL CONFLICTS – CONSTRAINT PROGRAMMING

Although even binary CSPs are NP-complete, there is a whole bunch of algorithms for solving CSPs. We can only give a shallow introduction here and refer the interested reader to overview articles or textbooks such as (Kumar, 1992, Tsang, 1993, Marriot and Stuckey, 1998, Barták, 1999). A very coarse classification distinguishes *constructive* from *refining* algorithms. Constructive algorithms start from an empty partial labeling and extend the labeling sequentially by adding further variable values to the partial labeling always keeping the labeling consistent and such conflict-free. Refining algorithms start from a full, most likely inconsistent labeling and try to improve the degree of consistency by changing the labeling gradually. Consistency checking algorithms and search algorithms belong to the first class. Local search algorithms and similar stochastic algorithms belong to the second class. We will focus on the first class here.

Todays constructive constraint solvers are always an aggregation of several algorithms for conflict detection, conflict avoidance and conflict resolution. Given a certain full labeling, conflict detection is usually quite simple, since a check of all constraints will easily reveal an inconsistency. Nevertheless, it will not always be clear what concrete value combination has caused the conflict. Hence, in constructive CSP solving it is important to detect conflicts as soon as possible and furthermore avoid them. This is the main purpose of *consistency checking* algorithms, also called *look ahead* algorithms. Given a

CSP, they try to deduce as many consequences of the constraints in the CSP to the value domains of the variables and such recognize potential future conflicts. Famous algorithms were at first formulated for binary CSPs but have been extended to general CSPs. Among them are *arc consistency* (AC) (Mackworth, 1977), *path consistency* (PC) (Montanary, 1974) and their generalization *k-consistency* (Freuder, 1978).

Though the strongest versions of consistency checking algorithms are able to deduce all consequences of constraints and can hence calculate the whole solution space (they are *complete*), these algorithms have exponential complexity. Therefore, weaker consistency algorithms are used in CSP solvers that can only avoid some conflicting situations (they are *incomplete*). They have to be combined with constructive search methods (*look back* algorithms), such as *chronological backtracking* and its extensions *backjumping* (Gaschnig, 1979), *backchecking* and *backmarking* (Haralick and Elliot, 1980), *dynamic backtracking* (Verfaillie and Schiex, 1994) and others that can solve conflicts. The interleaving of constructive search using look back algorithms for conflict resolution with consistency checking using look ahead for conflict avoidance has produced some of the most powerful CSP solvers.

Constraint logic programming (CLP, (Frühwirth and Abdennadher, 1997, Marriot and Stuckey, 1998)) combines these successful algorithms with Logic Programming. The big advantage of CLP is its expressiveness and declarativity that allows to state CSPs very elegantly. The following CLP program specifies and solves the CSP given by Ex. 1.

```
Source code:                              Query:

  solve(X1,X2,X3) :-                        solve(X1,X2,X3).
    % define variables/domains
    [X1,X2,X3]::[1,2],
    % state constraints                   Output:
    X1#=X2,
    X2#>X3,                                 X1 = 2
    X1#\=X3,                                X2 = 2
    % start search                          X3 = 1
    labeling([X1,X2,X3]).                   yes.
```

Powerful CLP programming environments to solve CSPs include CHIP, ECL^{i}PS^e, SICStus Prolog and several others.

2.3 A MODULAR INTERNAL CONFLICT SOLVER ARCHITECTURE

To support our prospective target of internal conflict solving in a distributed environment we are in need for an internal conflict solver that can incorporate foreign knowledge on variables, constraints and solving strategies as if it was its own. In addition, the representation of constraints, solving strategies and solutions should be generic to be suitable for several applications. Our approach to fulfill these demands has been to design and implement a modular solver architecture that is built of dynamically loadable components that share commonly defined interfaces and can be used in a generic solving framework. This framework heavily bases on the strength of constraint logic programming since it incrementally builds a CLP program that can be handed over to one of the off-the-shelf CLP solvers. Figure 3.2 illustrates our framework for internal conflict solving.

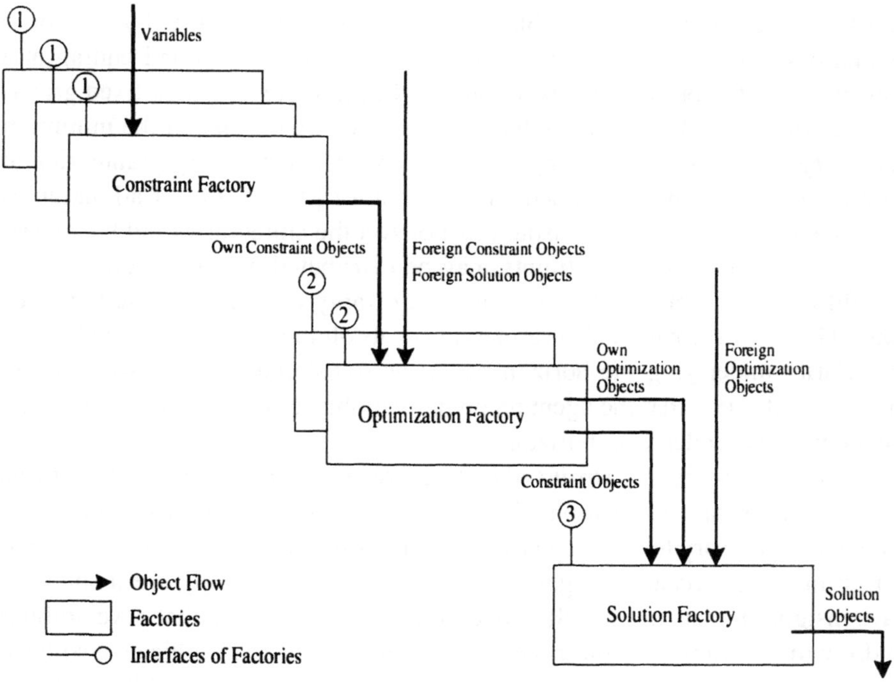

Figure 3.2 Modular framework for internal conflict solving

Central to our framework are the notions of *objects* and *factories*. Objects encapsulate the state and methods of variables, constraints, solving/optimization strategies and solutions. Factories do not have any state. They consume objects of a certain type and produce other objects of another type. Though the objects and factories are specific and application-dependent, they all implement certain standard interfaces that allow an agent to use them without knowing their actual purpose. The image of a black-box supply chain of different connected suppliers/consumers may help you in understanding this framework. The framework involves three typical stages in CSP solving: declarative specification of the problem, operational specification of solving strategies, and solution process. Each stage is realized by a certain set of factories.

2.3.1 Problem specification. In a monolithic, centralized problem solver it would be possible to directly produce CLP programs without further considerations, but our problem solver should be enabled to work in a distributed environment. Agents have to exchange knowledge on variables, domains and constraints. CLP expressions, especially those defined over finite domains, are not directly suitable, since they usually contain implicit contextual knowledge that cannot be derived from the pure CLP expressions. Here is a typical example: CLP problem models in scheduling usually assume a certain discrete scheduling horizon, often starting from zero and ending at a however found upper bound. Additionally, they assume a certain, fixed granularity of the scheduling horizon that is determined by the size of the minimum necessary time unit. For example, one day with a scheduling granularity of 15 minutes would imply a scheduling horizon of $[0, \ldots, 96]$. If all variables and constraints were defined using this horizon the situation would be consistent. But variables and constraints may be distributed among several agents, and different variables and constraints may imply different scheduling horizons. Hence, the contextual information on absolute time points and absolute granularity underlying the horizon has to be transfered together with the set of constraints such that the agent receiving variable and constraint information can deduce the underlying horizon.

In our framework, *constraint objects* are responsible for encapsulating this kind of contextual information. They are designed to contain as much information as necessary to make clear the semantics of the transfered variables and constraints to the receiving agent, but not more. The receiving agent shall not have insight on facts in the CSP model of the sending agents that have nothing to do with the transfered information. Therefore, constraint objects also have a security and privacy purpose in constraint communication. All constraint objects implement the following IDL-like interface, which is derived from an interface for XML-enabled objects.

```
interface IConstraintObject : IXMLObject
{
  GetOwnVariables([out] ICollection variables);
  SetOwnVariables([in] ICollection variables);
  GetForeignVariables([out] ICollection variables);
  SetForeignVariables([in] ICollection variables);

  GetContext([out] IContext context);
  SetContext([in] IContext context);
  UpdateContext([in, out] IContext context);

  ToCLPExpression([out] String string);
};
```

Constraint objects need to know which variables they have to restrict. Since we are aiming at distributed constraint satisfaction, variables are classified as being "own" variables administrated by the agent itself or "foreign" variables administrated by other agents. This distinction will become important later. Additionally, the interface ensures that every constraint object implements the ability to determine its solving context. The according set of methods is used to adjust the context of the constraint objects correctly by traversing them. After adjusting the context correctly and indicating the set of affected variables, the method `ToCLPExpression` can be used to produce a string containing a sequence of arbitrary CLP expressions that describe the meaning of the constraint object. The CLP expressions produced by the `ToCLPExpression`-method of constraint objects can directly be concatenated and formulate a declarative model of the given CSP. An important initial part of conflict solving is the procedural ability to form such a declarative problem model of the given constraint satisfaction problem. This ability is of course application-dependent and hence differs from application to application and has to be encoded in some kind of program. One significant idea of our approach is not to hardwire this ability within the agent, but to encapsulate it into *constraint factories*. Constraint factories implement the simple IDL interface ①.

```
interface IConstraintFactory
{
  Init([in] ICSPKnowlegde knowledge);
  SetVariables([in] ICollection variables);

  CreateContext();
  GetContext([out] IContext context);
  UpdateContext([in, out] IContext context);

  ProduceConstraintObjects([out] ICollection constraintobjects);
};
```

Each problem solving agent can posses an arbitrary number of different constraint factory instances and types. Prior to first usage, each constraint factory is initialized with interface access to the agent's CSP knowledge base by calling `Init`. This initialization equips the factory with CSP information that is always up-to-date. The variable specification is done via the method `SetVariables`. Finally for initialization, the agent calls `CreateContext` to force the constraint factory to build its production context, for example by exploring the given CSP knowledge and the given variables. After initialization, the agent can simply call the `ProduceConstraintObjects` method for commanding the factory to produce a proper collection of constraint objects. Every constraint factory knows on its own what parts of the CSP knowledge have to be investigated to produce proper constraint objects. Because of the monotony of constraint sequences, the agent can simply traverse its constraint factories without even knowing about their purpose and collect the resulting constraint objects. Because constraint factories are dynamically loadable components, the set of constraint factories acquainted to an agent can even change dynamically.

2.3.2 Operational specification. Since conflict solving in CSPs is NP-hard, there is no general algorithm that can efficiently solve all problems given by a declarative specification. Hence, researchers from Artificial Intelligence and Operations Research have proposed various heuristics to control the search for a solution. In backtracking search, heuristics can be distinguished mainly in *variable ordering* heuristics that determine which variable will be next to become the current variable and *value ordering* heuristics that determine which value from the domain of the current variable will be tried next. Additionally, if we are not looking for any solution to the given problem but for a "good" one, we are in need for an objective function. This kind of operational specification is encapsulated by *optimization objects*. They implement the following interface.

```
interface IOptimizationObject : IXMLObject
{
  GetOwnVariables([out] ICollection variables);
  SetOwnVariables([in] ICollection variables);
  GetForeignVariables([out] ICollection variables);
  SetForeignVariables([in] ICollection variables);

  GetContext([out] IContext context);
  SetContext([in] IContext context);
  UpdateContext([in, out] IContext context);

  OwnVarListToCLPExpression([out] String variablelist);
  ForeignVarListToCLPExpression([out] String variablelist);
  ValueOrderToCLPExpression([out] String valueorder);
  OptCriterionToCLPExpression([out] String criterion);
};
```

Similar to a constraint object, an optimization object allows to set the affected variables and to adjust the information necessary to achieve a common context among several optimization objects. Instead of a single method, there are now four methods for distilling CLP expressions from the optimization object. The first two methods produce an own and a foreign list of variables that determine the preferred order for labeling the variables affected by the optimization object. The distinction between own and foreign variables is due to the fact that an optimization object might prefer own variables to foreign variables in the labeling heuristics or in the optimization criterion. The third method produces a CLP expression describing predicates for value ordering and the last method defines an optimization criterion in CLP.

Optimization objects are produced by *optimization factories*. Optimization factories build such objects based on a knowledge about the given CSP, constraint objects built by the agent itself and foreign constraint objects sent by other agents in the run of a communication protocol. Before producing a single optimization object, the factory ensures that all constraint objects share a common context. Own variables of own constraint objects are added to the own variables of the produced optimization object. All other variables are added to the foreign variables. The distinction between own and foreign constraint objects can be dropped after having done this since the distinction has been encoded in the produced optimization object. Optimization factories implement interface ②.

```
interface IOptimizationFactory
{
  Init([in] ICSPKnowlegde knowledge);

  GetConstraintObjects([out] ICollection constraints);
  SetOwnConstraintObjects([in] ICollection constraints);
  SetForeignConstraintObjects([in] ICollection constraints);

  ProduceOptimizationObjects([out] ICollection optimizationobjects);
};
```

2.3.3 Solution process. Finally, after having specified the current problem in a declarative manner and having determined the solution strategy in an operational manner, the problem has to be solved. Remember that solutions are variables labeled with values in the CSP context. A special set of such variables is encapsulated in *solution objects* that can also encode alternative solutions. A solution object implements an interface inherited from the constraint object interface. In addition to the variable handling methods, context methods and `ToCLPExpression` method defined there, it implements a method for retrieving the different solutions in form of variable sets.

```
interface ISolutionObject : IConstraintObject
{
  GetSolution([out] ICollection variables);
};
```

The main work in the solution process is done in the so-called *solution factory*. Different to constraint factories and optimization factories, an agent has only one such factory. It consumes a declarative problem specification given by a set of constraint objects and an operational solution strategy specification given by own optimization objects. It also allows the integration of foreign optimization objects that represent the desires of other agents on the local CSP solution process. The solution factory combines all constraint objects and all optimization objects. While combining constraint objects is relatively easy because of the common context and their monotonic property, combining optimization objects is difficult. A solution factory usually tries to incorporate all strategies and cumulates the different optimization criteria, but in case of conflicting optimization targets the solution factory should usually prefer the specification given by own optimization objects over the ones given by foreign optimization objects. A solution factory implements interface ③.

```
interface ISolutionFactory
{
  Init([in] ICSPKnowledge knowledge, [in] ICLPSolver solver);

  SetConstraintObjects([in] ICollection constraints);
  SetOwnOptimizationObjects([in] ICollection optimizationobjects);
  SetForeignOptimizationObjects([in] ICollection optimizationobjects);

  ProduceSolutionObjects([out] ICollection solutionobjects);
};
```

Calling `ProduceSolutionObjects` causes a solution factory to ensure a common context among its constraint objects and optimization objects and sequentially calling the `XXXToCLPExpression` methods of these objects. This incrementally builds a CLP formulation of the current CSP. The variable lists of the different optimization objects are merged and fully ordered. The value ordering predicates are coordinated and the optimization criteria are cumulated according to a weighting among optimization objects. After this, the whole CLP program is handed over to a traditional CLP solver (in our case it is ECL^{i}PS^e) and hopefully solved. The result of the CLP program is interpreted and put into several solution objects describing the outcome. These solution objects can be used to update the own CSP knowledge (for example for labeling own variables) or to communicate with other agents.

3. EXTERNAL CONFLICTS

3.1 DISTRIBUTION – MERITS AND PITFALLS

Social structures, such as in enterprises or in supply networks of different enterprises, create heterogeneous fields of competencies and influences. Few executives of organizational units accept transferring all their process data to other organizational units for global control. Even less they accept automatic control over their unit's processes by a central instance. For acceptance, there have to be secure interfaces between realms of competency that only let pass authorized and restricted information. Decisions on processes have to be done at the same locations of competency where these processes are enacted in reality. At this point emerges a demand for distributed concepts towards modeling of distributed constraint problems and solving conflicts of a new quality – external conflicts among autonomous agents.

Even in the that case a monolithic solver could be theoretically applicable, constraint satisfaction problems of real-world size tend to be too complex to be solved by such a global system. Monolithic systems often scale poorly in the size of variables and constraints. Partitioning the problem and searching for a solution composed from the solutions of detached subproblems is a typical approach of parallel computing and more recent distributed computing (refer also to chapter 9 of Denzinger on collaborative search). But this efficiency and scalability argument is by far not the only one in favor of collaborative problem solving. The information on variables and constraints is very often spatially distributed among different natural organizational units. Even in case of a monolithic solver one would have to collect all the information from its several sources, transfer it to the solver, solve the problem and again distribute the results of optimization among the different users. Hence, even in case of a central controller one has to cope with communication and information consistency problems.

A last argument in favor of distribution is redundancy and robustness. A crash of a central solver or missing connectivity would influence the whole enterprise connected to the solver leading to chaos. Master/slave concepts raise the amount of communication overhead by caching and mirroring. In contrast to that, the crash of a single problem solver in one organizational unit would influence only that unit and potentially its neighbors.

Despite the advantages of distribution, such systems also have major disadvantages. The complexity that has been saved within the several solvers is transfered to the coordination process. Due to this fact, investigations on todays distributed solver systems often report poor optimization results or vast communication overhead. Since global problem solving promises the higher quality solutions to the common problem but may be infeasible due to social, technical or security restrictions, we are facing a well-known trade-off between a global and a distributed design. Therefore, the design of the distribution is itself an optimization problem. But before coping with this problem in Section 4., in the next subsections we will extend the presented CSP model to be suitable for distributed environments and present an algorithm for solving conflicts arising in such environments.

3.2 MODELING EXTERNAL CONFLICTS – DISTRIBUTED CSPS

Since we are in search for a unifying model for internal and external conflicts, it should be comprehensible to try to augment the central constraint satisfaction problem model to distributed environments. We are talking about *distributed constraint satisfaction problems* (DCSPs). To cite Denzinger, "conflicts between [the search] agents occur when the requirements of an agent (resp. its actual solution) are not compatible with the requirements of other agents." The notion of DCSPs canonically keeps the interpretation of conflicts from CSPs as inconsistencies between combinations of values for variables. These inconsistencies again arise from violating several constraints that relate consistent value combinations. In our chapter we will build upon a DCSP definition that is slightly more general than the classical one of Yokoo et al. (Yokoo et al., 1998). It allows for complex constraints and additionally extends the notion of distribution to the constraints also. That means that the administration of the knowledge needed to test consistency of a constraint is not necessarily implied by the distribution of the variables but can be in the competence of totally different agents.

The formal model of distributed constraint satisfaction problems differs from that of ordinary CSPs only by adding a distribution function ϕ assigning each variable and constraint to a certain problem-solving agent out of a set of agents A.

Definition 5 (Distributed constraint satisfaction problem) *A* distributed constraint satisfaction problem *(DCSP) is specified by a 5-tuple* $\Pi_{\text{dcs}} = (X, D, C, A, \phi)$.

- *X, D and C are defined as given by Def. 1.*
- $A = \{(a_1, \kappa_1), \ldots, (a_p, \kappa_p)\}$ *is a set of* agents *each possessing a local consistency predicate* $\kappa_i : (X' \longrightarrow D') \times 2^C \longrightarrow \{\texttt{true}, \texttt{false}\}$ *defined on a (partial) labeling and a set of constraints.*
- $\phi : X \cup C \longrightarrow A$ *assigns an agent to each domain variable and each constraint.*

Given this specification, the problem is to find a labeling $\lambda \in \Lambda(C) = \{(v_1, \ldots, v_n) \in D_1 \times \ldots \times D_n | \forall C_i \in C : (v_{i_1}, \ldots, v_{i_k}) \in C_i\}$ *from the* solution space Λ *defined by* C.

Remark 2 a) From a declarative view point, a DCSP does not differ from its associated CSP. The difference can only be seen from an operational view point.
b) Since domains are always directly associated with their domain variables, the distribution of domains depends on the distribution of variables and is not discussed further. Hence, according to (Luo et al., 1993) our approach to distribution can be classified as *variable-based.*
c) ϕ defines a partition on the union of domain variables and constraints that can be denoted by $\phi^{-1} = \{(a_1, \phi^{-1}(a_1)), \ldots, (a_p, \phi^{-1}(a_p))\}$ with $\phi^{-1}(a_i) = \{xc \in X \cup C \,|\, \phi(xc) = a_i\}$. Hence, $\bigcup_{a \in A} \phi^{-1}(a) = X \cup C \wedge \forall a_i, a_j \in A, i \neq j : \phi^{-1}(a_i) \cap \phi^{-1}(a_j) = \emptyset$. For convenience we write $\phi_X^{-1}(a_i) = \{x \in X \,|\, \phi(x) = a_i\}$ and $\phi_C^{-1}(a_i) = \{c \in C \,|\, \phi(c) = a_i\}$.
d) DSCPs are denoted graphically by using extended constraint graphs together with VENN-diagram-like hulls illustrating the partition. Edges connecting nodes from different partition sets, i. e. $e = \{vn_i, cn_j\} \wedge \phi(vn_i) \neq \phi(cn_j)$, are called *external edges.* All other edges are called *internal edges.*
e) The existence of a local consistency predicate κ_i only makes sense for an

agent that administrates some constraints. In this case, the predicate can be specified more detailed by $\kappa_i : (X' \longrightarrow D') \times 2^{\phi_C^{-1}(a_i)} \longrightarrow \{\mathtt{true}, \mathtt{false}\}$, with X' being a subset of the variables connected to the constraints which are administrated by a_i.

Example 2 (Medical appointment scheduling) In principle, medical appointment scheduling is a slightly extended variant of classical job-shop-scheduling. Primarily, it involves a set of patients each demanding appointments (decision variables) for a set of medical examinations and a set of diagnostic providers each offering a certain set of examination types. Constraints restricting the choice of appointments include partial orders among examinations of patients, capacity constraints defined by the calendars of the providing units and others, e. g. maximum number of examinations each day, setup times and so on. Figure 3.3 shows an extended constraint graph for a small sample of such a medical appointment scheduling problem. Only partial order and capacity constraints are shown. Two patients $\{a_1, a_2, a_3\}$ and $\{a_4, a_5, a_6, a_7\}$ compete for two common diagnostic resources. The appointments are sequentialized by before-relations. The figure also illustrates the distribution function ϕ. There are four agents, two patient agents p_1 and p_2 and two diagnostic unit agents d_1 and d_2.

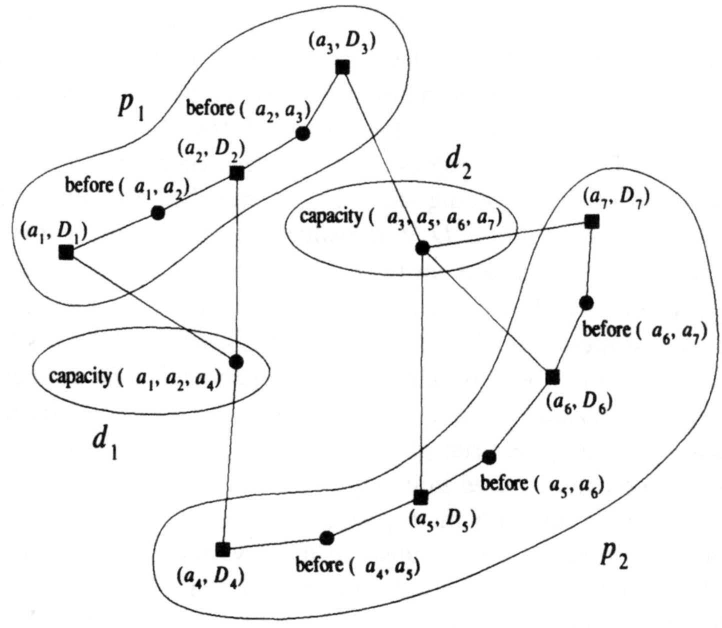

Figure 3.3 Small sample of a medical appointment scheduling problem

3.3 SOLVING EXTERNAL CONFLICTS – MULTI-PHASE AGREEMENT FINDING

3.3.1 Basics of the protocol. Denzinger presents a detailed classification of solving conflicts among search agents (refer to chapter 9). Especially section 5. on multi-agent search fits well our interpretation of distributed constraint satisfaction. In this subsection we will present a protocol, called *multi-phase agreement finding*, that unifies dynamic allocation of subproblems via announcement/bid messages, such as in the *contract-net protocol* (Smith, 1988), with look ahead consistency checking and search, such as in other DCSP algorithms. Figure 3.5 illustrates our protocol using the notation of algebraic Petri nets. We cannot give a detailed introduction to algebraic Petri nets. Please refer to (Reisig, 1998) for details.

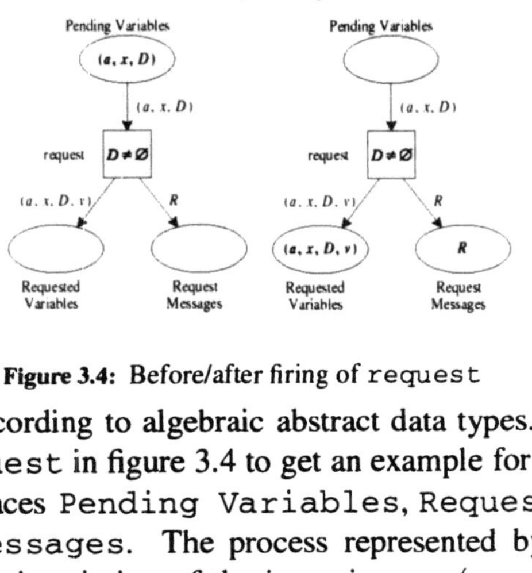

Figure 3.4: Before/after firing of `request`

In Petri nets local states are represented by *places* (denoted by ellipses) and *tokens* on these places (drawn within ellipses). Atomic processes are represented by *transitions* (drawn as rectangles). Arcs connect places with transitions and model control and data flow. In algebraic Petri nets places, tokens, transitions and arcs are typed according to algebraic abstract data types. Take a look at the transition `request` in figure 3.4 to get an example for this. `request` is connected to the places `Pending Variables`, `Requested Variables` and `Request Messages`. The process represented by `request` can happen (*fire*), iff the inscription of the incoming arc (a, x, D) matches a token on `Pending Variables` and the *guard* $D \neq \emptyset$ evaluates to `true` under this matching. In this case, `request` takes away (a, x, D) from `Pending Variables`, produces a value v and places (a, x, D, v) on `Requested Variables` and several request messages R on `Request Messages`. All transitions in the net behave according to this rule totally independently and concurrently. In this context, a transition t in conflict to other transitions for the same token is treated *fair* by a system run (denoted by φ), iff t does not fire only finitely often, though being activated infinitely often.

As given by definition 5 multi-phase agreement finding involves p agents some of which care each for a subset of the n variables $x_1, \ldots, x_n \in X$ and some of which care each for a subset of the m constraints $C_1, \ldots, C_m \in C$ according to the distribution function ϕ. Agents caring for variables are called *variable agents*, agents caring for constraints are called *constraint agents*. A variable x has only one variable agent but may have several constraint agents

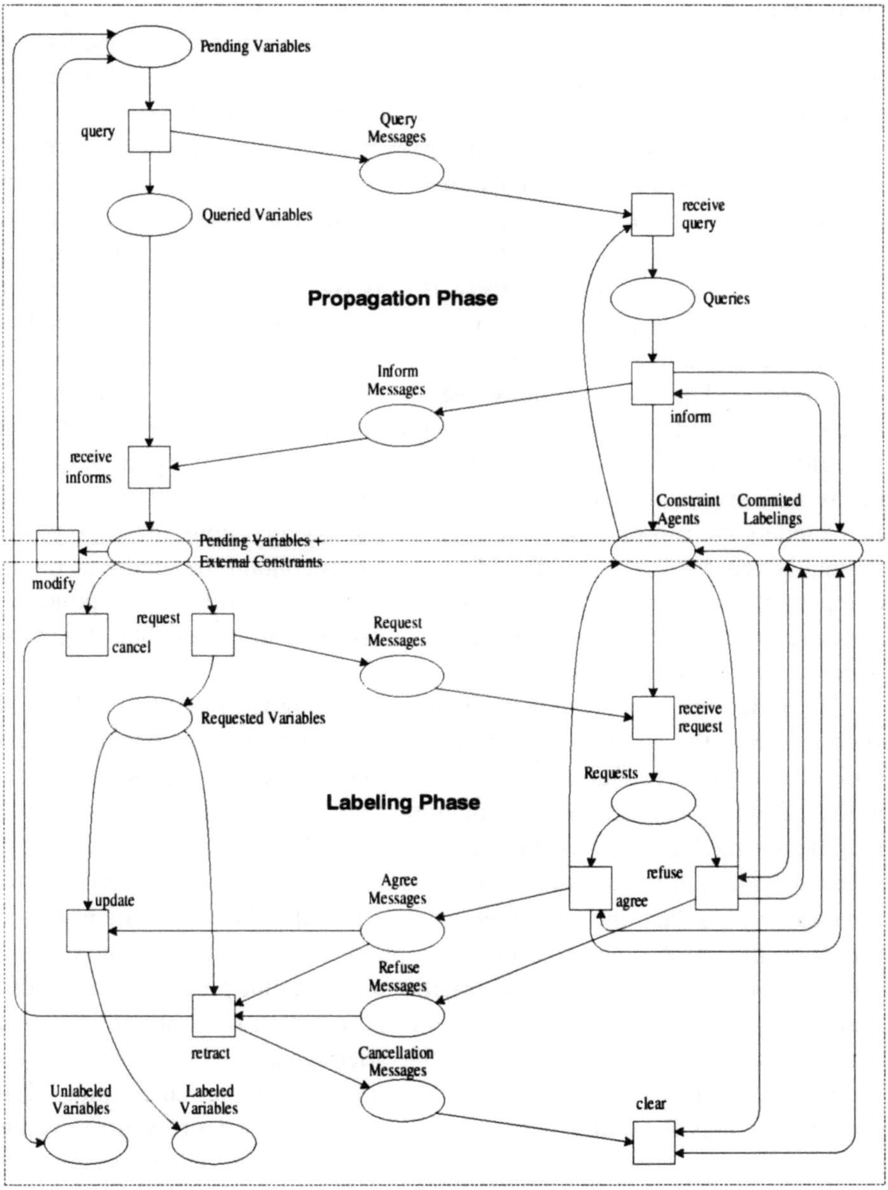

Figure 3.5 Coarse Petri net model Σ_{af}

that administrate constraints on x. Variables and their annotations are given by a tuple (a, x, D) in which a is the agent that cares for the variable, x is the variable itself and D is the domain of x. The set of constraint agents administrating constraints on x is denoted by $N(x) = \{(a, C)\}$ in which a is the agent and $C = \phi_C^{-1}(a)$ is the set of constraints administrated by a. $N(x)$ is also called the set of ***neighbors*** of x. In the following, this set will be fixed for the run of the protocol. It is nevertheless possible to determine this set by a dynamic announcement/bid exchange in the first phase of the protocol.

An agent a may be variable agent for several different variables, hence there may be several tuples $(a, \cdot, \cdot)$. That means that a single agent may have several protocol instances running concurrently for different variables in its role as a variable agent. The same agent may also administrate several constraints, but because of consistency matters there is only one (a, C) tuple. This ensures, that an agent is only participating in a single protocol instance at a time in its role as a constraint agent which is important for the consistency property of our protocol. The result of the whole protocol shall be that if a variable x is labeled with a certain value, then all neighbors out of $N(x)$ have agreed on that labeling and have stored that information. The left half of figure 3.5 models the run of every annotated variable in the course of the protocol, the right half models the run of constraint agents. The asynchronous message passing system is denoted in the middle. Message tuples contain the sender as the first component, the receiver as the second component and further components as message content. The message system is assumed to be reliable, though not necessarily preserving sequence.

The basic idea of multi-phase agreement finding is to reduce conflicts and such search in the distributed problem space by making decisions on subproblem solutions well-founded. To refer again to Denzinger "agents solve conflicts among them by exchanging information about their specific subproblems so that the normal local view of an agent gets more global. This way, an agent can select the solution to its problem that has the greatest chance to conform with the other agents (and their requirements)." In multi-phase agreement finding, this basically involves a pre-processing phase in the protocol that is comparable to constraint propagation in traditional constraint programming. Before making a proposal for a specific solution to a certain subproblem, a variable agent collects as much information on the other agents' constraints on this subproblem. This information can then be included in the internal conflict solving procedure. This hopefully will remarkably reduce the probability to request agreement on an inconsistent solution. Again, constraint logic programming is advantageous here since it allows agents to exchange highly abstract constraint descriptions rather than large sets of allowed or disallowed value combinations.

3.3.2 A run of the protocol. We will follow exactly one instance of this protocol to exemplify the protocol following figure 3.5. Given a set of pending variables, the variable agent initiates the protocol by sending a query to all potential neighbors for gaining information on external constraints on its current variable. The variable agent can specify its requirements for this variable in the query message. The state of the variable is changed from `Pending Variables` to `Queried Variables`. The task of all potential neighbors in this phase is to answer the query on constraints restricting the current variable according to their knowledge about already given commitments and constraints. Neighbors are assumed to be benevolent, so they will answer honestly. Nevertheless, they will follow their own strategies and safety requirements in posting information on that variable. This is done via the modular conflict solving architecture described in the previous section. The variable agent collects its variable together with its neighbors' answers on `Pending Variables + External Constraints`. The constraint information is collected asynchronously by waiting for the responding messages. After a certain timeout the constraint information is considered to be complete. Since constraint propagation is only an informative phase, non-responding neighbors are not critical. The variable agent can decide to start the next protocol phase based on the acquired information or to modify its requirements and restart the constraint propagation phase.

In the next phase of the protocol, called *labeling phase*, the variable agent selects a certain value from the domain of the current variable and a certain subset of potential neighbors that has answered the query messages. It is assumed that the variable agent selects a subset of constraint agents that is mandatory for labeling the current variable with the chosen value. For choosing a value for the current variable the variable agent solves a full internal CSP considering all constraint information provided by the selected agents. The labeling phase then ensures the agreement of all these mandatory neighbors to the value selected by the variable agent. Since this protocol phase is critical to the correctness of conflict handling, figure 3.6 presents a more detailed model of this phase. The used symbols are explained in the following table.

Symbol	*Description*
$R = \{(a, b, x, v) \mid (b, \cdot) \in N(x)\}$	set of request messages from variable agent a to all neighbors $(b, \cdot) \in N(x)$ concerning variable x with value v
$N = \{(b, a, x, v) \mid (b, \cdot) \in N(x)\}$	set of agree messages from all neighbors $(b, \cdot) \in N(x)$ to variable agent a concerning variable x with value v
$N_r = \{(b, a, x, v) \mid (b, \cdot) \in N_r(x) \subset N(x)\}$	(non-empty) set of refuse messages from some neighbors $(b, \cdot) \in N_r(x) \subset N(x)$ to variable agent a concerning variable x with value v.

Symbol	*Description*
$N \backslash N_r = \{(b, a, x, v) \mid (b, \cdot) \in N(x) \backslash N_r(x)\}$	set of agree messages from some neighbors $(b, \cdot) \in N(x) \backslash N_r(x)$ to variable agent a concerning variable x with value v
$CM = \{(a, b, x, v) \mid (b, \cdot) \in N(x) \backslash N_r(x)\}$	set of cancellation messages from variable agent a to all neighbors $(b, \cdot) \in N(x) \setminus N_r(x)$ that have agreed on variable x with value v
$L_b = \{(b, \cdot, \cdot)\}$	all committed labelings agreed by neighbor b
$\kappa = \kappa_b(L_b \cup \{(b, x, v)\}, \phi_C^{-1}(b))$	evaluation of local consistency predicate of neighbor b under L_b together with the requested variable x with value v and constraints administrated by b

The variable agent a selects a certain value v out of D to label x (D has to be non-empty for this) and sends request messages to all selected neighboring constraint agents. Based on the received request, its constraints C and its maximum set of already committed labelings $L_b = \{(b, \cdot, \cdot)\}$ each constraint agent b can decide to agree to the labeling or to refuse it by evaluating its consistency predicate $\kappa(L_b \cup \{(b, x, v)\}, \phi_C^{-1}(b))$. This is also done by the internal problem solving facility of the constraint agent. In case of agreement the constraint agent adds the labeling (b, x, v) to its set of committed labelings L_b and sends an agree message. Otherwise, the set of committed labelings remains unchanged, a refuse message is sent to the variable agent a and the constraint agent returns to its idle state being ready for handling new messages.

The variable agent is blocked until all neighbors have answered. It can only update the requested variable (a, x, D, v) to the state `Labeled Variables` when all neighbors have sent agree messages. This full demanded set of agree messages is denoted by N. The according incoming arc of the `update` transition ensures the desired behavior. A single refusing neighbor is enough to hinder firing of the `update` transition. But even if their is already a refusal, the variable agent will have to wait for all responds of its neighbors to inform the agreed neighbors on the failure of the consensus. This is realized by the transition `retract`. This transition can fire iff there is a set $N_r \neq \emptyset$ of refusal messages from some neighbors (these neighbors are denoted by $N_r(x)$) and exactly the complementary set of agreement messages $N \backslash N_r$ from the other

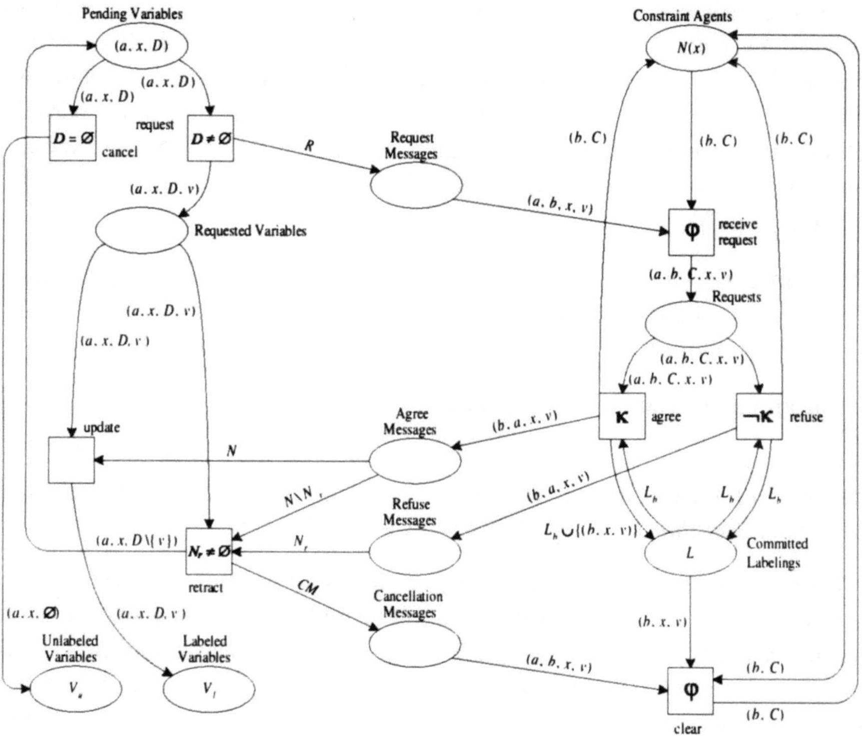

Figure 3.6 Detailed Petri net model Σ_{afl} of the labeling phase

neighbors (denoted by $N(x)\backslash N_r(x)$). The transition `retract` deletes v from the domain of x and starts a new protocol instance. Additionally, all neighbors that have already agreed on the labeling v are informed by according cancellation messages to free them from their given commitments via the transition `clear`.

3.3.3 Properties of the protocol. Multiphase agreement finding provides facilities for conflict avoidance *via* its constraint propagation phase and conflict detection *via* its labeling phase. It preserves a special kind of consistency which is formalized in the following.

Definition 6 (ϕ-consistency of a partial labeling) *Given a DCSP* $\Pi_{\text{dcs}} = (X, D, C, A, \phi)$. *A partial labeling* $\lambda' : \{x_{\lambda'_1}, \dots, x_{\lambda'_l}\} \longrightarrow D'$ *is called* ϕ-consistent, *iff*

$$\forall (a, \kappa) \in A : \kappa\,(\lambda', \phi_C^{-1}((a, \kappa))).$$

Remark 3 a) The function $\lambda' : \emptyset \longrightarrow \emptyset$ is assumed to be also a valid and ϕ-consistent partial labeling.

b) The ϕ-consistency property is usually weaker than the consistency property achieved by testing consistency with the full information of all constraints. This holds even in case we are using the same algorithms for local and global consistency checking. In this context, "weaker" means that more partial labelings are accepted as consistent than actually may be. Nevertheless, ϕ-consistency of a full labeling implies global consistency, iff $\kappa_i(\lambda, \phi_C^{-1}(a_i)) \Rightarrow \lambda \in \Lambda(\phi_C^{-1}(a_i))$.

Theorem 1 *Given a DCSP $\Pi_{\text{dcsp}} = (X, D, C, A, \phi)$. Then, each possible run of Σ_{afl} is finite and will finally produce a ϕ-consistent partial labeling $\lambda' : X' \subseteq X \longrightarrow D'$ potentially trying each domain value of each variable $x \in X$.*

The proof can be found in the appendix.

Corollary 1 *Given a DCSP $\Pi_{\text{dcsp}} = (X, D, C, A, \phi)$. If a run of Σ_{afl} has produced a full labeling $\lambda : X \longrightarrow D_1 \cup \ldots D_n$ λ is globally consistent under the assumption that $\kappa_i(\lambda, \phi_C^{-1}(a_i)) \Rightarrow \lambda \in \Lambda(\phi_C^{-1}(a_i))$.*

Though multiphase agreement finding allows a variable agent to test several values for a variable from its domain and provides such some sort of conflict resolution facility, it is not complete in the sense of always finding a conflict resolution if there exists one. This is due to its lack of some kind of distributed systematic backtracking. Backtracking may be added by augmenting the protocol for allowing cancellation of committed labelings in future work.

4. AUTONOMOUS DYNAMIC RECONFIGURATION

4.1 MOTIVATION

Since the distribution of problem-solving agents is often not fully specified by the natural distribution of the problem, a typical engineering task in distributed constraint satisfaction is the design of the distribution itself. As soon as major parts of the problem space are under control of a single realm of authority (as it usually is in information or enterprise resource planning systems) it has to be decided what part of the problem should be assigned to a certain agent. As already mentioned, more global problem solving promises the better solutions to the subproblem but may be infeasible due to technical, social or security restrictions. Distributed problem solving is able to obey social aspects and may diminish problem complexity by partitioning but also entails suboptimal solutions and vast communication overhead. Therefore, the design of distribution (called *configuration*) and the task allocation mechanism is critical to the quality and efficiency of the problem solving process and is itself an optimization problem.

The traditional approach to distributed problem solving is to design the distribution aspects off-line by statically assigning certain roles and competences to specific agents. Thus, the problem space is statically distributed among a more or less fixed set of agents. The disadvantages of this approach are strikingly shown by returning to our example 2 and scaling it up in the number of involved entities. Figure 3.7 shows ten patients competing for four diagnostic resources (even this example is not of real-life size). Every arc between agents marks the need for external conflict solving and such extensive communication.

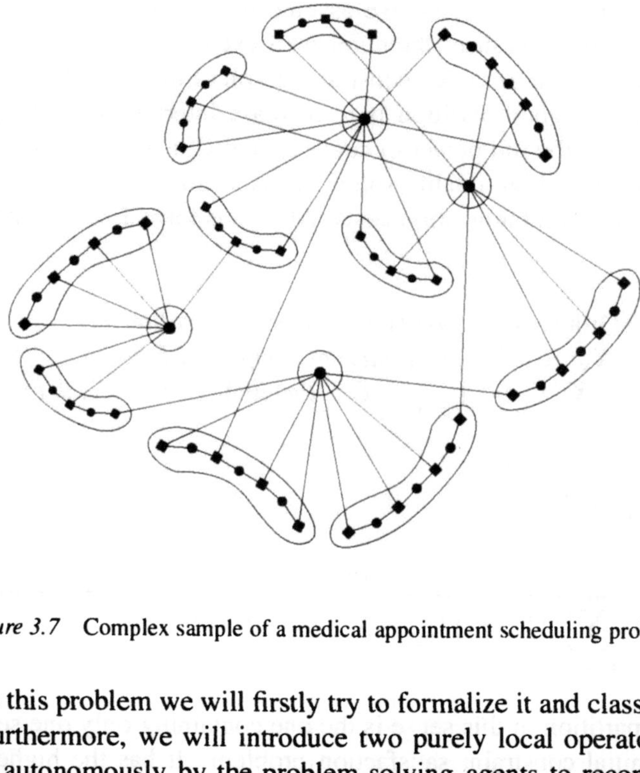

Figure 3.7 Complex sample of a medical appointment scheduling problem

To solve this problem we will firstly try to formalize it and classify its complexity. Furthermore, we will introduce two purely local operators that can be applied autonomously by the problem-solving agents to reconfigure their social organization. All this cumulates in bringing all pieces presented in this chapter together to form the AURECON approach.

4.2 THEORETICAL FOUNDATION

4.2.1 Partitions and quality. A first and important step towards a formalization of the configuration problem is to define the term "good". To do this, we assume that the quality of a partition is mainly determined by two criteria that are complementary: internal problem complexity and external communication cost. In DCSP solving, internal problem complexity depends on the structure of the sub-CSP to solve, i e. the number of variables, the number of constraints and the complexity of variable-constraint relations. Research in *phase transitions* (Hogg et al., 1996, Gent et al., 1996, Hayes, 1997) defines a notion of *constrainedness* that promises to be a good measure for identifying the complexity of a given sub-CSP. We simply assume the existence of a function $\xi : 2^{X \cup C} \longrightarrow \mathbb{N}$ that assigns a complexity value to a subset of all variables and constraints. By external communication cost we do not denote the physical time for transmitting a message from one problem solver to another, but we denote the semantic effort of a whole agreement finding protocol run as presented in Subsect. 3.3 to ensure agreement between several autonomous problem solvers. Nevertheless, we assume this effort to be directly related to a very simplistic measure: the number of external edges between different partition blocks in the extended constraint graph of the DCSP.

The target of a good partition is to increase internal complexity as far as possible to utilize the full power of conventional CSP solving within the agent and such to achieve high-quality solutions. Additionally, a good partition has minimal external communication costs. All this is formalized by the following definition.

Definition 7 (Quality of a partition) *Given a partition* $\phi^{-1} = \{(a_1, X_1 \cup C_1), \dots, (a_k, X_k \cup C_k)\}$ *and an internal complexity function* $\xi : 2^{X \cup C} \longrightarrow \mathbb{N}$ *(*$X = \bigcup_{i=1,\dots,k} X_i, C = \bigcup_{i=1,\dots,k} C_i$*), the* quality *of* ϕ^{-1} *is defined by*

$$q_{\phi^{-1}} = \sum_{i=1}^{k} \Bigg[\overbrace{\xi(X_i \cup C_i)}^{\text{internal complexity}} - \overbrace{\sum_{C' \in C_i} \left| \{ \phi(x_j) \mid x_j \in X \wedge C' : 2^{\dots \times D_j \times \dots} \wedge \phi(x_j) \neq \phi(C') \} \right|}^{\text{external communication cost}} \Bigg] \tag{3.1}$$

The best partition in this sense is the one containing only one set including the whole initial constraint satisfaction problem. It has the highest possible internal complexity and no external communication costs at all. That directly corresponds to our intuition to solve a CSP problem centrally if only possible. Alas, following our argumentation in favor of distributed problem solving this is not always possible. Therefore, we have to encode the restrictions we used to argue in favor of DCSPs as it is done in the next paragraph.

4.2.2 Core problem and variants. The main restrictions that do not allow us to solve many CSP centrally are the boundedness of tractable complexity and social boundaries. We will encode these restrictions by an upper bound ξ_u on the internal complexity perhaps found by empirical studies on the given CSP class and the careful attention to the social competency boundaries. Both are formalized in the following definition.

Definition 8 (DCS CONFIGURATION problem) *A static* DCS CONFIGURATION problem *is specified by a 5-tuple* $(\Pi_{cs}, \xi, \xi_u, \xi_l, \phi_s)$.
$\Pi_{cs} = (X, D, C)$ *is a constraint satisfaction problem,* $\xi : 2^{X \cup C} \longrightarrow \mathbb{N}$ *is an internal complexity function,* ξ_u *is an internal complexity upper bound,* ξ_l *is an internal complexity lower bound and* ϕ_s *defines a social partition. Additionally, let*

$$Q = \Big\{ q_{\phi^{-1}} \;\Big|\; \Pi_{cs} \equiv \Pi_{dcs} = (X, D, C, A, \phi) \;\wedge \tag{3.2}$$

$$\forall (a_i, X_i \cup C_i) \in \phi^{-1} : (\xi_l \leq \xi(X_i \cup C_i) \leq \xi_u) \;\wedge \tag{3.3}$$

$$\forall xc_i, xc_j \in X \cup C : \tag{3.4}$$

$$\phi_s(xc_i) \neq \phi_s(xc_j) \Longrightarrow \phi(xc_i) \neq \phi(xc_j) \Big\}.$$

Then, three variants of the static DCS CONFIGURATION problem *are*

1. *Is* $q^* = \max Q \geq k$ *for a given* $k \in \mathbb{Z}$*? (decision problem* Π_{CON}*)*
2. *Find* q^**! (value optimization problem* ω_{CON}*)*
3. *Find* $\Pi^*_{dcs} = \arg\max Q$*! (solution optimization problem* Ω_{CON}*)*

The set Q includes the quality measures of all possible DCSPs that are solution equivalent to the given CSP. The following restrictions are put onto these DCSPs: (3.2) ensures that the DCSPs preserve the set of variables X, the set of domains D and the set of constraints C. Hence, the only free variables of the DCS CONFIGURATION problem are the set of agents A used to solve the given CSP and the distribution function ϕ. (3.3) ensures that the complexity of every set of the partition defined by ϕ lies within the bounds given by ξ_u and ξ_l. This property is called *complexity feasibility* and is denoted by the predicate $feasible_c$. Finally, (3.4) enforces the given social partition defined by ϕ_s to be preserved by the found partition defined by ϕ, such that no two variables or constraints that are desired to be in different social partition sets are in the same partition set. This property is called *social feasibility* and is denoted by the predicate $feasible_s$.

Theorem 2 *The decision variant of* DCS CONFIGURATION Π_{CON} *is NP-complete in the size of* $|X \cup C|$.

See the appendix for the proof.

Corollary 2 *The optimization variants of* DCS CONFIGURATION *are NP-hard.*

Though the DCS CONFIGURATION problem is itself interesting, it is too static and centralized in nature to be fully suitable for what we are behind in

Multi-Agent Systems research. Hence, we propose an extended version of this problem that describes the task to dynamically adapt to the given CSP structure.

Definition 9 (DCS RECONFIGURATION **problem)** *A dynamic* DCS RECONFIGURATION problem *is specified by a 5-tuple* $(\Pi^o_{dcs}, \xi, \xi_u, \xi_l, \phi_s)$.
$\Pi^o_{dcs} = (X, D, C, A^o, \phi^o)$ *is a distributed constraint satisfaction problem,* $\xi : 2^{X \cup C} \longrightarrow \mathbb{N}$ *is an internal complexity function,* ξ_u *is an internal complexity upper bound,* ξ_l *is an internal complexity lower bound and* ϕ_s *defines a social partition. Additionally, let* Π^o_{dcs} *be complexity and socially feasible and*

$$Q = \Big\{ q_{\phi^{-1}} \;\Big|\; \Pi^o_{dcs} \equiv \Pi^n_{dcs} = (X, D, C, A^n, \phi^n) \;\wedge\; feasible_c(\Pi^n_{dcs}, \xi, \xi_u, \xi_l) \;\wedge\; feasible_s(\Pi^n_{dcs}, \phi_s) \Big\}.$$

Then, three variants of the dynamic DCS RECONFIGURATION problem *are*

1. *Is* $q^* = \max Q \geq k$ *for a given* $k \in \mathbb{Z}$*? (decision problem* Π_{RECON}*)*

2. *Find* q^**! (value optimization problem* ω_{RECON}*)*

3. *Find* $\Pi^*_{dcs} = \arg\max Q$*! (solution optimization problem* Ω_{RECON}*)*

Remark 4 a) An interesting special case of the decision variant Π_{RECON} is $q^* = \max Q \geq k = q_{\phi^{o-1}}$?, i. e. whether the optimal partition quality is greater than the partition quality defined by the given DCSP Π^o_{dcs}.
b) Of course, the decision variant of this problem is again NP-complete. This can be proven similarly to theorem 2 by reducing MINIMUM BISECTION to this problem with the help of a trivial initial bisection (for example $X_1 \cup C_1 = \{x_1, \dots, x_{\frac{|V|}{2}}\} \cup C$ and $X_2 \cup C_2 = \{x_{\frac{|V|}{2}+1}, \dots, x_{|V|}\}$).

4.2.3 Solving DCS CONFIGURATION **problems.** In subsection 3.1 we have argued in favor of distribution to solve realistic constraint satisfaction problems. The same arguments hold for solving a given DCS CONFIGURATION problem and its variants. For example, if our system of problem solvers underlies a certain social competence structure, the configuration of the problem solvers won't be manageable by a central instance. Due to this, we need reconfiguration operators that allow for local and potentially autonomous adaption to the problem structure.

Please take another look at figure 3.7. Ten patient agents have to communicate with four resource agents to reach consensus. Now, figure 3.8 shows the results of a local operator, called *agent melting*. In part a) patient agents that are strongly connected with a single resource agent have been unified to a single patient group agent. Though this has the advantage that requests of several patients can be bundled and sent collectively to the resource agent, external communication has not decreased substantially. Part b) shows a further step of local reconfiguration in which resource agents have been melt with patient group agents that often use their resource. As can be seen by the thick lines, this step significantly reduces the external communication overhead. In the next subsections we will formalize a minimal set of local operators that will prove to be sufficient to solve any given DCS RECONFIGURATION problem and will briefly present steps towards getting this theoretical result to practice.

The local operator introduced by the aforementioned example is formalized by the following definition.

Definition 10 (Agent melting) *Given a set of agents* $A = \{a_1, \ldots, a_p\} : \mathcal{A}$*, a partition* $\phi^{-1} = \{(a_1, X_1 \cup C_1), \ldots, (a_p, X_p \cup C_p)\} : \Phi$ *of a domain variable and constraint set* $X \cup C$ *and two indices* $i, j : \mathbb{N}$, agent melting *is a function* $\mu : (\mathcal{A} \times \Phi) \times \mathbb{N} \times \mathbb{N} \longrightarrow \mathcal{A} \times \Phi$ *defined by*

$$\mu\left((A, \phi^{-1}), i, j\right) = \begin{cases} \Big(A \setminus \{a_j\}, (\phi^{-1} \setminus \{(a_i, XC_i), (a_j, XC_j)\}) \cup \\ \quad \{(a_i, XC_i \cup XC_j)\}\Big), & a_i, a_j \in A \\ (A, \phi^{-1}), & \textit{else} \end{cases}$$

Of course, to fulfill all demands on complexity and social feasibility of a problem solver configuration, agent melting alone is not sufficient. As soon as one agent emerges to have a too high internal complexity it has to be split into two (or more) smaller agents. The complementary local operator to agent melting is called *agent splitting* and is defined as follows.

Definition 11 (Agent splitting) *Given a set of agents* $A = \{a_1, \ldots, a_p\} : \mathcal{A}$*, a partition* $\phi^{-1} = \{(a_1, X_1 \cup C_1), \ldots, (a_p, X_p \cup C_p)\} : \Phi$ *of a domain variable and constraint set* $X \cup C$*, an index* $i : \mathbb{N}$ *and a subset* $XC' : 2^{X \cup C}$ *of domain variables and constraints,* agent splitting *is a function* $\sigma : (\mathcal{A} \times \Phi) \times \mathbb{N} \times 2^{X \cup C} \longrightarrow \mathcal{A} \times \Phi$ *defined by*

$$\sigma\left((A, \phi^{-1}), i, XC'\right) = \begin{cases} \Big(A \cup \{a_{|A|+1}\}, (\phi^{-1} \setminus \{(a_i, XC_i)\}) \cup \\ \quad \{(a_i, XC_i \setminus XC'), (a_{|A|+1}, XC')\}\Big), & a_i \in A \wedge XC' \subset XC_i \\ (A, \phi^{-1}), & \textit{else} \end{cases}$$

Remark 5 To simplify the notation of consecutive application of these local operators to the same initial set of agents A and partition ϕ^{-1}, we will use the following abbreviations. Applying agent melting of agents i and j to (A, ϕ^{-1}) is denoted by $(i, j)(A, \phi^{-1})$. Applying

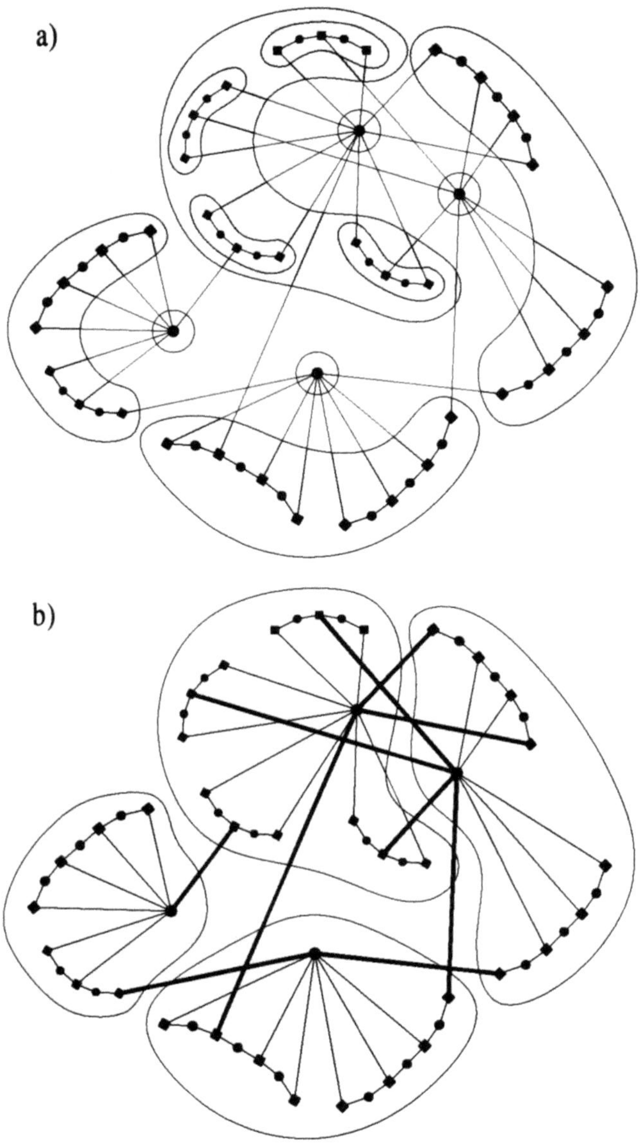

Figure 3.8 Results of agent melting

agent splitting of agent i with subset XC to (A, ϕ^{-1}) is denoted by $(i, XC)(A, \phi^{-1})$. For further abbreviation, we write $(\vec{\imath}, \vec{\jmath})^m(A, \phi^{-1})$ for $(i_m, j_m) \ldots (i_1, j_1)(A, \phi^{-1})$. Hence, $((\vec{k}, \vec{XC})(\vec{\imath}, \vec{\jmath})^2)(A, \phi^{-1})$ denotes $\sigma\left(\mu\left(\mu\left((A, \phi^{-1}), i_1, j_1\right), i_2, j_2\right), k_1, XC_1\right)$.

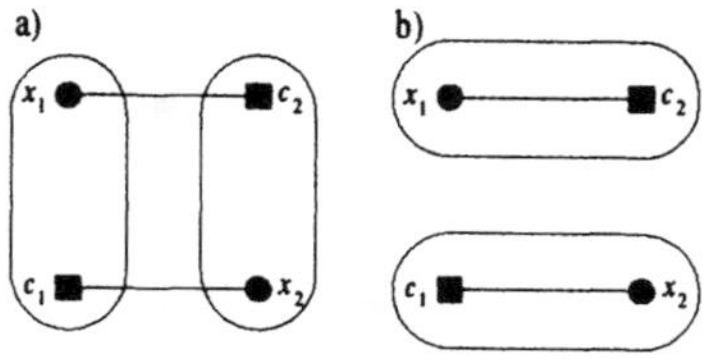

Figure 3.9: Counter-example

The given definitions of the local operators do not obey complexity and social feasibility. These operators are not directly applicable to DCS RECONFIGURATION problems, since they may only lead to configurations that are not feasible. This can easily be seen by the example given by figure 3.9. Let's assume that $\xi\,(X \cup C) = |X \cup C|, \xi_u = 2, \xi_l = 2$. Though this may seem very restrictive, we have used a similar restriction in our NP-completeness proof. Part a) of the figure shows the given configuration and part b) shows the optimal one. Neither agent melting nor agent splitting is solely applicable to the configuration given by a), because both operators violate the demanded complexity restrictions. Therefore, we cannot build our reconfiguration strategy directly on the local operators. We need an extended atomic operator that is able to obey complexity and social feasibility. We call this atomic operator *reconfiguration transaction* and specify it as follows.

Definition 12 (Reconfiguration transaction) *Given a complexity and social feasible dynamic* DCS RECONFIGURATION *problem* $*_{\text{RECON}} = ((X, D, C, \mathcal{A}, \phi), \xi, \xi_u, \xi_l, \phi_s), \mathcal{A} : \mathcal{A}, \phi : \Phi$, *a* reconfiguration transaction *is a function* $\rho : \mathcal{A} \times \Phi \longrightarrow \mathcal{A} \times \Phi$ *specified by*

$$(A', \phi^{-1'}) = \rho\,(A, \phi^{-1}) = (\vec{k}, \vec{XC})^n (\vec{\imath}, \vec{\jmath})^m \,(A, \phi^{-1}),$$
$$\vec{\imath}, \vec{\jmath} \in (\{1, \ldots, |X \cup C|\})^m, \vec{k} \in (\{1, \ldots, |X \cup C|\})^n,$$
$$\vec{XC} \in (2^{X \cup C})^n, m, n \in \mathbb{N}_0$$

such that

$$\textit{feasible}_c\,((X, D, C, A', \phi'), \xi, \xi_u, \xi_l) \;\wedge\; \textit{feasible}_s\,((X, D, C, A', \phi'), \phi_s)$$

To solve the example illustrated by figure 3.9, only a kind of exchange operator would be sufficient. Fortunately, with the help of the above specified reconfiguration transaction we can emulate any other feasible local operator, like exchange and transfer. Figure 3.10 shows how a reconfiguration transaction composed of one melt and one split can be used to emulate an exchange and solve the given example.

Though we may already have an intuition on the strength of reconfiguration transactions, the following theorem lays a theoretical foundation for the sufficiency of this concept to solve DCS RECONFIGURATION problems.

Theorem 3 (Sufficiency of reconfiguration transactions) *Given a complexity and social feasible* DCS RECONFIGURATION *problem* $*_{\text{RECON}} =$

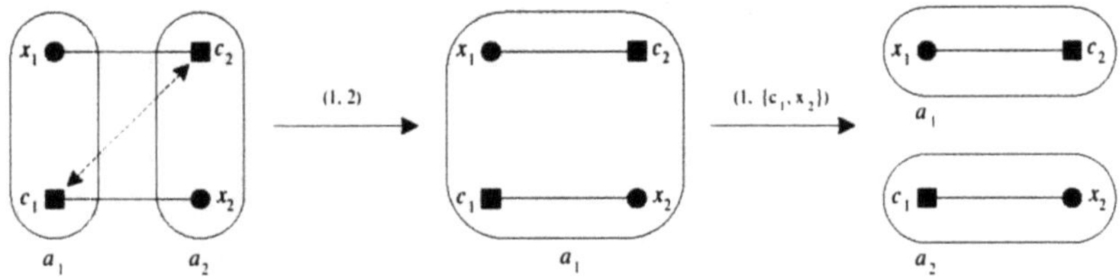

Figure 3.10 An exchange transaction composed from local operators

$((X, D, C, A, \phi), \xi, \xi_u, \xi_l, \phi_s)$. *Assuming that* A *and* ϕ *do not influence the solution equivalence between two different DCSPs, i. e.* $\forall A_1, A_2 \in \mathcal{A}, \phi_1, \phi_2 \in \Phi : (X, D, C, A_1, \phi_1) \equiv (X, D, C, A_2, \phi_2)$, $*$RECON *can be solved by finding a certain sequence*

$$((\vec{k}_p, \vec{XC}_p)^{n_p}(\vec{\imath}_p, \vec{\jmath}_p)^{m_p}) \ldots ((\vec{k}_1, \vec{XC}_1)^{n_1}(\vec{\imath}_1, \vec{\jmath}_1)^{m_1})$$

of reconfiguration transactions applied to (A, ϕ^{-1}).

The proof can be found in the appendix.

4.3 COMBINING THE PIECES

Of course, the aforementioned theorem is only a theoretical result. The algorithm presented in the appendix to prove this theorem is neither realistic nor efficient. In fact, it is much less efficient than simply enumerating all possible partitions, since there are many reconfiguration transactions leading to partitions already stored and there are even more local operator sequences that are no valid reconfiguration transactions. Nevertheless, the theorem is the theoretical foundation for allowing us to seek in the space of reconfiguration transactions rather than in the space of partitions to solve a DCS RECONFIGURATION problem. This can be exploited to develop a more realistic approach.

The algorithm used to prove the sufficiency of sequences of reconfiguration transactions is in fact a global one, since it employs a centrally controlled function `gen_new_params` to systematically enumerate all possible reconfiguration transactions. This is bad for two reasons: first, we originally wanted to avoid a global algorithm to solve DCS RECONFIGURATION problems; second, the way of enumerating all possible transactions is far from being efficient. Nevertheless, the local character of reconfiguration transactions remains and we can modify their use to build a real autonomous approach to DCS RECONFIGURATION solving.

Real autonomy means in this context to allow arbitrary concurrent reconfiguration transactions to be initiated by the conflicting agents on their own using knowledge-based heuristics. The techniques presented in section 2. and section 3. for internal and external conflict solving directly support this kind of *autonomous dynamic reconfiguration*, which is also denoted by the acronym AUREcON. The modular conflict solving architectures allows an agent to possess an arbitrary number of variable, constraint, optimization and solution objects and factories. Objects and factories are implemented by dynamically loadable components. Additionally, objects can be serialized to XML expressions and such exchanged among agents. Hence, agent melting between two agents a_1 and a_2 can easily be realized on the micro-level of a_1 and a_2 by transferring all factory references of a_2 to a_1 and transferring all objects of a_2 to a_1 by serialization. Since the flow of objects among the "supply chain" of factories is generic to every agent, agent a_1 can then work on with the additional knowledge and skills of agent a_2. Agent splitting can be realized accordingly.

The protocol presented for external conflict solving is also open to different organizational configurations. It works as well with a large number of very small agents each possessing one variable as with a few complex agents each able to solve large internal problems. Alas, multiphase agreement finding is not complete and it is arguable if it wouldn't loose all efficiency when forced to be complete. In our opinion, it is suitable to use complete algorithms internal conflicts and incomplete cooperation protocols for solving external conflicts. This also emphasizes the need to minimize external communication demand while maximizing internal complexity which has been our initial motivation for balancing on the transition between internal and external conflict solving. Albeit, allowing external conflict solving to be incomplete directly violates our assumption in theorem 3 that configuration does not influence solution equivalence. One way to cope with this structural problem is to resign solution equivalence in the definition of the DCS CONFIGURATION problem and its variants and replace it by a weaker notion of *solution reducibility*. In words, solution reducibility means to resign completeness but to keep correctness.

Definition 13 (Solution reducibility) *A constraint satisfaction problem* Π_*^2 *is called* solution reducible *to another constraint satisfaction problem* Π_*^1 ($\Pi_*^2 \leq \Pi_*^1$), *iff* $\exists (f : \Lambda^2(C^2) \longrightarrow \Lambda^1(C^1) : f$ *injective.*

The technical basis for AUREcON has been created using Microsoft DCOM and Message Queue Server to build a distributed environment for agent existence. The modular internal solver architecture has also been successfully realized using the CLP language ECL^{i}PS^e. Multiphase agreement finding is in its evaluation phase. Many questions regarding our target of autonomous dynamic reconfiguration remain open. Allowing agents to autonomously perform agent melts and splits yields the potential to be much more efficient than centrally and sequentially scanning all possible transactions, but also entails the danger of instability and loops. It is also not clear yet what concrete measures and methods can be used to equip agents with a well-founded knowledge on when to apply reconfiguration transactions. Statistical and other simple learning methods seem to be suitable but have not been tried yet. An important part of our future research work is the definition of evaluation scenarios that determine the CSP to solve, the initial quantity and quality of agents and other parameters.

5. RELATED WORK

5.1 DCSP SOLVING

An excellent, though a little out-dated overview to DCSP models and algorithms is given in (Luo et al., 1993) and (Luo et al., 1992a). The authors identify four basic characteristics of DCSP algorithms: centralized or decentralized control, shared or separated search space, message-passing or shared memory and termination. Another, orthogonal classification distinguishes variable-based approaches (in which every agent cares for a subset of variables), domain-based approaches (in which every agent cares for a subset of values for common variables) and function-based approaches (in which costly computations in centralized CSP solving are distributed to speed them up). In this chapter we have only considered decentralized variable-based algorithms on a shared search space using asynchronous message-passing, since this is the closest model to socially embedded and naturally distributed CSPs.

There seem to be at least two major strategies towards solving DCSPs. The first considers mainly binary, often weakly structured academic CSPs and tries to distribute successful sequential algorithms for constraint propagation and search using constraint representations based on no-good sets. Being a classical reference in DCSP, the work of Yokoo and Ishida introduces a DCSP model that simply assigns the variable nodes of a binary CSP graph to the different agents. Hence, this is a variable-based approach. Their main contribution lies in the development of distributed search algorithms, like *asynchronous backtracking* and *asynchronous weak-commitment search*. The earlier versions (collectively presented in (Yokoo et al., 1998) and (Yokoo and Ishida, 1999)) relied on the assumption, that every agents cares for just one variable. Newer versions (Yokoo and Hirayama, 1998) overcome this restriction by allowing complex local problems. All these algorithms are correct and complete. To coordinate the different forms of asynchronous backtracking, the algorithms establish a static or a dynamic order among agents that determines the cooperations patterns between agents. Unfortunately, the assumption of simple binary constraints restricts the applicability in real-world settings. The same holds for the work presented in (Luo et al., 1992a, Luo et al., 1992c, Luo et al., 1992b). The authors propose different algorithms to solve DCSPs variable-based, domain-based and function-based. They all assume a binary DCSP and are hence based on simple constraint representations via no-good-sets. Nevertheless, this research work has strongly influenced the labeling phase of multiphase agreement finding.

Extending Yokoo's asynchronous weak-commitment Mammen and Lesser (Mammen and Lesser, 1998) investigate the impact of problem structure to the solving process. To do this, they propose a parameterized problem generator for DCSPs and implement a MAS simulator. Based on simulated runs they draw conclusion on the interdependence of structure and solvability. Though providing useful insight in random problem generation and simulation their approach does not allow to assign constraints to agents. While Yokoo et al. concentrated on the search part of DCSP solving, others (Zhang and Mackworth, 1991, Nguyen and Deville, 1998) have investigated distributed derivatives of sequential constraint propagation techniques, namely DistAC and DisAC-4. This work has been applied in the constraint propagation phase of multiphase agreement finding.

Researchers following the second strategy also employ knowledge gained from classical CP, like backtracking, backjumping and so on, but apply it usually to more structured practical problems with complex n-ary constraints employing specific heuristics. The research work of Sycara et al. (Sycara et al., 1991) on *distributed constrained heuristic search* has been ground-breaking in this area. They characterize the design trade-off for a proper level of distribution in a system for a given communication bandwidth, but do not address this problem in the paper. Sycara et al. characterize the effect of different decompositions and their characteristics to be a subject of future research. This is exactly what AUREConN is about.

Another approach to DCSP solving does not try to solve the DCSP with new distributed propagation or search methods but to facilitate existing CSP solvers to solve the problems local to an agent and then to combine the results of these solvers. An early reference on this approach is (Berlandier and Neveu, 1995). Berlandier and Neveu introduce the notion of *interface problems* by partitioning a DCSP along variable nodes and not as usual along constraint arcs. All variable nodes that belong to more than one agent form a new problem — the interface problem. The variable nodes not belonging to the interface problem can be labeled independently from other variable nodes. Such, solving the interface problem and then solving the independent problems eventually using backtracking solves the whole problem. A disadvantage is the need for a global instance for finding the solution to the interface problem and collecting the solutions of the independent problems. Solotorevsky and others (Solotorevsky et al., 1996) follows a similar strategy by defining *canonical DCSPs* which consists of a special constraint graph connecting all independent local constraint graphs. Similar to Berlandier and Neveu they use common CSP solvers to solve the partitioned problems. All these authors assume a given partitioning of the DCSP and facilitate a global instance for guiding the solving process.

5.2 GRAPH PARTITIONING

Our DCS CONFIGURATION problem and its variants are strongly related to the problem of partitioning graphs, as can be seen in the reduction of MINIMUM BISECTION to our problem. It is not surprising that graph partitioning algorithms are quite often the basis for load balancing in parallel computing. Hendrickson and Leland (Hendrickson and Leland, 1994) provide a good overview on static graph partitioning algorithms. They include greedy algorithms like the famous one by Kernighan and Lin (Kernighan and Lin, 1970) and extensions of it (Bui, 1986), so-called *spectral methods* (Barnes, 1982, Boppana, 1987, Barnard and Simon, 1994) and other hybrid approaches. Several of these algorithms have been implemented and integrated into tools that can be used as off-line pre-processors to partitioning a central computing problem. Among these tools are Chaco (Hendrickson and Leland, 1995), METIS (Karypis and Kumar, 1995) and JOSTLE (Walshaw et al., 1998). Recent research also tackles the problem of dynamic load balancing. Hendrickson and Devine (Hendrickson and Devine, 1999) assess different approaches to this problem.

Though the problem of load balancing in parallel computing is similar in its objectives to our research context, the given environmental situation is usually quite different. In parallel computing there is a central problem that can easily be decomposed into equally sized subproblems which can be solved nearly independently. Hence, the task of load balancing is to find a good distribution of these decomposed subproblems to processors such that communication is minimized. In our setting, decomposition itself is the problem. Subproblems are not easy to find and have to be constructed such that interrelations are minimized. These interrelations are not just communication lines but semantic connections, like shared resources or other social constraints. Nevertheless, results from load balancing, especially heuristics are promising to be applied to our autonomous dynamic reconfiguration approach.

5.3 AGENT TECHNOLOGY FOR REORGANIZATION

In (Durfee, 1999) Durfee reports on various approaches to organizational structuring in distributed problem solving as a strategy for reducing communication. Durfee states that the design of organizational structures is a complex search problem in its own right. He reports on the work of Decker and Lesser (Decker and Lesser, 1993) that allows structuring when the problem instance is initialized and the work of Ishida et al. (Ishida et al., 1992) and Prasad et al. (Prasad et al., 1996) that allow dynamic restructuring. Our approach to autonomous dynamic reconfiguration differs from these approaches as they do not reconfigure on the social structure level but on the individual structure level of agents. Additionally, the work of (Ishida et al., 1992) relies on a production system-based agent architecture which entails the known problems of rule-based computing (e. g. rules are not combinable).

Agent cloning (Decker et al., 1997, Shehory et al., 1998) denotes the reproduction of a similar agent in place or remotely. This approach claims to subsume mobile agents and other similar approaches. It has been mainly developed to support load balancing by delegating tasks to other or new agents that are idle. Compared to our proposal, this approach is more on the technical side of reconfiguration. The concepts presented in this article include not only a quantitative reconfiguration but also a qualitative reconfiguration in the sense of forming new agent types.

In the project MetaMorph I (Maturna and Norrie, 1996, Maturana et al., 1998) Maturana and others have developed an architecture for distributed task decomposition in manufacturing and coordination in dynamically created clusters. The agents in this system are organized by mediators and contain templates and cloning mechanism to create new agent (sub)levels. The follow-up project, MetaMorph II (Shen and Norrie, 1998) extends these concepts by taking into account manufacturing design issues, marketing, supply chain management and execution control. MetaMorph II has not been fully implemented. Again this approach for reconfiguration lies on the social level of agency and not on the individual like proposed in this article.

Sandholm et al. report research on *coalition structure generation* (Sandholm et al., 1999) that is quite near to ours. Alas, the optimization measure is simpler in this setting, since it only cumulates the value (in our approach complexity) of all partition subsets without taking into account connecting edges. Hence, they can use different kinds of algorithms. Additionally, no concept similar to our local operators can be found in this work.

6. CONCLUSIONS

The transition between internal and external conflicts within and among autonomous agents is an important area of research. This is because the transition is evident in many socially embedded applications of Multi-Agent Systems. The transition is also tangent to matters of efficiency in conflict avoidance and conflict resolution. Therefore, we have presented a technical notion of conflict in this chapter based on research in constraint satisfaction that allows a unified view on internal and external conflicts as inconsistent values for several decision variables.

We have described a model for constraint satisfaction problems, algorithms to solve them and a novel modular conflict solver architecture that behaves like a supply chain. This conflict solver follows a generic control flow, incrementally builds a declarative problem specification from variables and constraint objects, determines the operational behavior by optimization objects and finally solves the problem using the means of constraint logic programming. Our conflict solver allows to incorporate foreign knowledge and preferences in any stage of the internal conflict solution process. The realization of all objects and transforming factories as loadable components with well-defined interfaces allows a dynamic change in the conflict solver behavior.

After a discussion of the merits and potential pitfalls of distribution in problem solving, we have introduced a model of distributed constraint satisfaction problems that slightly differs from other models by assigning constraints to agents, too. The presented multiphase agreement finding protocol covers external conflict detection and conflict avoidance in its constraint propagation phase and a restricted form of conflict resolution in its labeling phase. This protocol is guaranteed to terminate on a static input problem and preserves a special kind of consistency that leads to global consistency under certain assumptions. These properties have been formally proven using the means of algebraic Petri nets.

Since there is often some freedom in assigning subproblems to agents, the main administrative problem in DCSP solving is the design of distribution. In the main section of our chapter we have introduced the DCS CONFIGURATION problem and its variants and have proven them to be at least NP-complete. To solve these kind of problems we have described two local operators, agent melting and agent splitting, that can be combined to sequences of reconfiguration transactions and such are sufficient to solve any given DCS CONFIGURATION problem. This theoretical result is practically exploited in the AUREcON approach that combines the results in solving internal conflicts and external conflicts to a framework that allows for an autonomous usage of the local reconfiguration operators. Though we have presented some thoughts on this approach, there remains much to do. Our next steps will mainly focus on the further realization of the technical basis for reconfiguration, on heuristics for controling the local reconfiguration process and empirical analysis in selected evaluation scenarios. All this is to achieve our main research target — to build an artificial society of agents that can successfully poise on the transition between internal and external conflict.

Acknowledgments

Many thanks to Hans-Dieter Burkhard, Wolfgang Reisig and Armin Wolf for fruitful discussions on parts of this chapter.

Appendix

A.1 PROOF OF THEOREM 1

To prove theorem 1 we first of all need means for proving *safety* properties and *liveness* properties of distributed and concurrent algorithms since the theorem contains both types of properties. These proof tools, namely place invariants and the *causes* operator, will be briefly introduced in the next subsections.

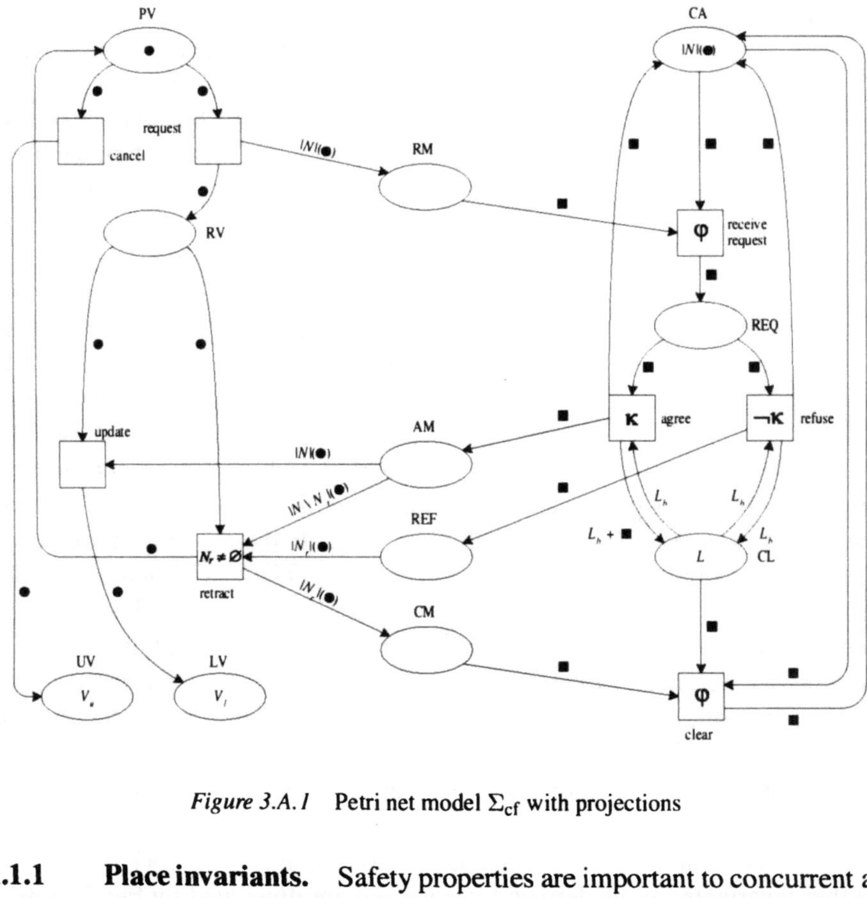

Figure 3.A.1 Petri net model Σ_{cf} with projections

A.1.1 Place invariants. Safety properties are important to concurrent algorithms, since they allow statements such as "at each reachable state of Σ holds p", with p a propositional expression. Techniques to verify such properties include *place invariants*. Informally, a set of places defines a place invariant if under the firing of each connected transition the set of removed tokens equals the set of produced tokens. A formalization of this property in algebraic

Petri nets is quite technical and involves the use of multisets and linear algebra. To simplify things, we will not define invariants directly on Σ_{cf}, but on a transformed net under the assumption that their is only one annotated variable to label. This will be sufficient for our proof later. The transformed net model is shown by Fig. 3.A.1. On the left half of the figure we are simply projecting each token and arc inscription onto x thus gaining always the same token $\bullet$ that represents an instance of the variable token. On the right half we are projecting each token and arc inscription onto b thus gaining always the same token $\blacksquare$ that represents an instance of a constraint agent. As you can also see on the arcs leading from the left to the right half and vice versa the weight of a token $\bullet$ is always $|N|(\bullet)$ times higher than the weight of a token $\blacksquare$. Such, there are one variable agent instance and $|N|(\bullet)$ many constraint agent instances involved in a single protocol instance.

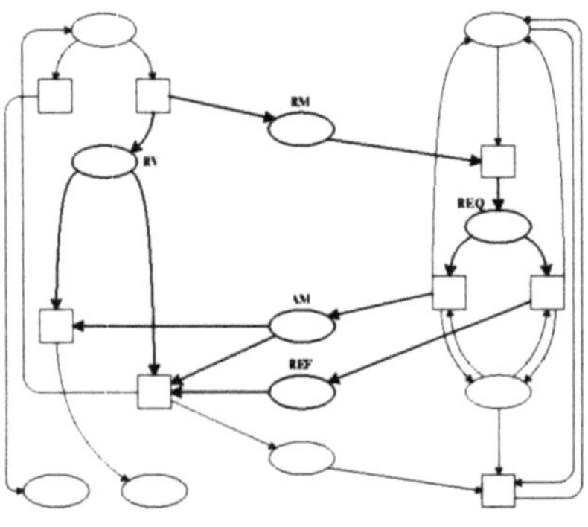

Figure 3.A.2: Invariant 1

Figure 3.A.2 details one important invariant of Σ_{cf}. This invariant can be formally validated by solving a linear homogeneous equation but we will only motivate it intuitively. Invariant 1 involves the five places `Requested Variables` (RV), `Request Messages` (RM), `Requests` (REQ), `Agree Messages` (AM) and `Refuse Messages` (REF). Looking at Fig. 3.A.2 it seems obvious that each transition connected to one of the invariant places adds the same amount of tokens to the invariant places as it consumes. Graphically this can be verified by following the flow of tokens along equally directed arcs between RM, REQ, AM and REF. The only exception is place RV since the flow of tokens reverses in this place with arcs directed into the opposite direction of all other arcs. Additionally, RV has a higher weight as explained above. The consequence is that the weighted instance sum of all tokens on RM, REQ, AM and REF equals the instance sum of tokens on RV times $|N|(\bullet)$. This is formalized by introducing a special addition operation defined on multisets, counting instances in this case. Such, invariant 1 is given by

Invariant 1: $RM + REQ + AM + REF = |N|(\bullet) \cdot RV.$

Further invariants can be derived likewise and are illustrated by Fig. 3.A.3.

Invariant 2: $|N|(\bullet) \cdot LV + AM + CM - CL = -L$

Invariant 3: $PV + RV + LV + UV = 1$

Invariant 4: $CA + REQ = |N|(\bullet)$

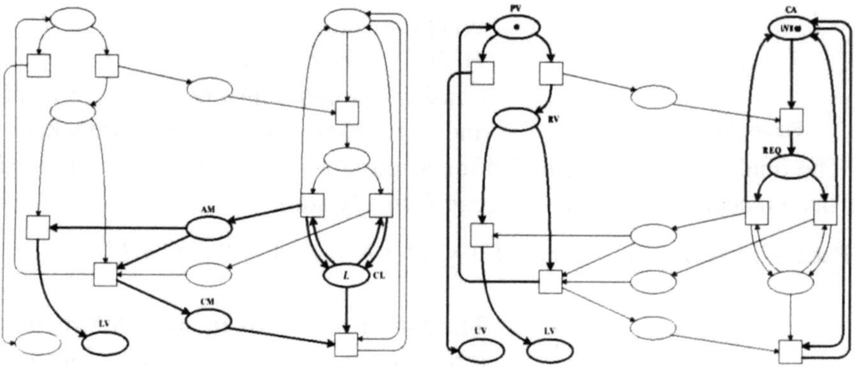

Figure 3.A.3 Invariants 2, 3 and 4

A.1.2 Causes operator. We informally introduce a concurrent deduction operator, called *causes* and denoted by $\hookrightarrow$, to prove liveness properties of concurrent algorithms. Please refer to (Reisig, 1998) for details. $\Sigma \models p \hookrightarrow q$ ("in Σ holds p *causes* q") means that in Σ each reachable state in which p holds is always followed by a reachable state in which q holds. The *causes* operator can be described further by inscribing the transitions that are involved in the process on top of the $\hookrightarrow$ symbol. We are using so-called *pick-up patterns* to derive liveness properties directly from the static structure of an algebraic Petri net. Though there are some more basic ones, the following pick-up patterns are sufficient for our purpose. Every pattern preserves a certain context α that remains unchanged by transitions in the pattern. $A = U$ means that exactly the set U of tokens is on A. $A.U$ means that at least the set U of tokens is on A.

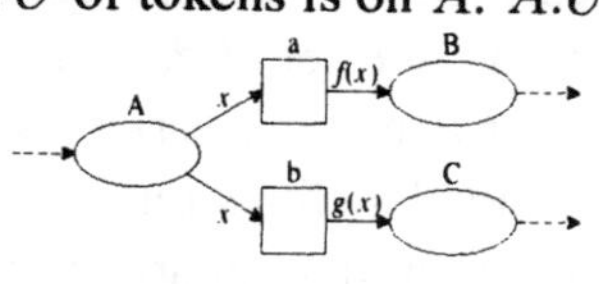

Figure 3.A.4: Pattern 1

The pattern shown by figure 3.A.4 covers alternative forward branching. Transitions a and b are in conflict for the tokens on A. Given $A = U$, these transitions can non-deterministically and concurrently consume a token x from A and produce $f(x)$ or $g(x)$, respectively. The final result of firing a and b as often as possible is that A is empty and the transformed tokens have been placed on B or C, respectively. The set of tokens V consumed by a unified with the set of tokens W consumed by b again equals U. Hence, we can formally state

Pattern 1: $\alpha \wedge A = U \overset{a(A) \vee b(A)}{\hookrightarrow} \alpha \wedge A = 0 \wedge B.f(V) \wedge C.g(W) \wedge U = V \cup W$

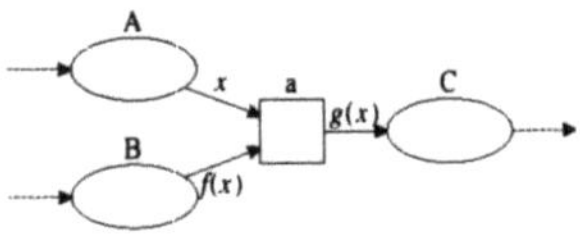

Figure 3.A.5: Pattern 2

The pattern shown by figure 3.A.5 covers synchronization. Given that $A = U$ and $B.f(U)$ (invariant notation $f(U) \leq B$), transition a can consume tokens x from A and $f(x)$ from B as long there are tokens on A. The final result of firing a as often as possible is that A is empty and $g(U)$ has been placed on C. Hence, we can formally state

Pattern 2: $\alpha \wedge A = U \wedge f(U) \leq B \overset{a(A)}{\hookrightarrow} \alpha \wedge A = 0 \wedge C.g(U)$

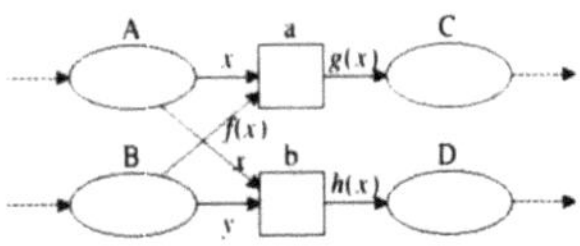

Figure 3.A.6: Pattern 3

The pattern shown by figure 3.A.6 covers alternative synchronization. Transitions a and b are in conflict for the tokens on A and B. Let's assume that we can derive somehow that, given $A = U$ and $f(U) \leq B$, transition b is prevented from firing for some reason. Then we can adapt pattern 2 and formally state

Pattern 3: Let $A = U$ prevent $b(f(U))$. Then $\alpha \wedge A = U \wedge f(U) \leq B \overset{a(A)}{\hookrightarrow} \alpha \wedge A = 0 \wedge C.g(U)$

Since, if $\Sigma \models p \hookrightarrow q$ and $\Sigma \models q \hookrightarrow r$ then $\Sigma \models p \hookrightarrow r$, we can connect simple *causes*-deductions and propositional deductions to form more complex proof sequences. In fact, we can even form graphs of deduction steps. These graphs are called *proof graphs*.

A.1.3 The proof. Since the empty labeling $\emptyset \longrightarrow \emptyset$ is also a ϕ-consistent partial labeling, we can make the assumption that at the present situation we already have a ϕ-consistent partial labeling, represented on variable agents' side by the set of labeled annotated variables V_l on LV, the set of definitively unlabeled annotated variables V_u on UV and all other annotated variables on PV, on constraints agents' side by the set of committed labelings on CL and all constraint agents on CA. It is an important observation that all arc expressions in Σ_{cf} are directly bound to a specific variable x, except of the incoming arcs (b, C) and L_b of the transitions `receive`, `agree`, `refuse` and `clear`. Therefore, different instances of the protocol concerning different variables only conflict in these transitions. Because there is only a single (b, C) token on CA for each constraint agent these conflicting accesses to CA and CL are synchronized producing an arbitrary but strictly ordered sequence. I. e. only a single protocol instance can fire a `receive` and `agree/refuse` sequence or a `clear` transition at a time. All protocol instances are totally synchronized and it is therefore enough to take a closer look at the properties of a single protocol run for adding a single annotated variable (a, x, D) to the existing partial labeling. Figure 3.6 reflects exactly this situation with only one annotated variable on PV and the according constraint agents $N(x)$ on CA.

Adding an annotated variable to the existing partial labeling preserves ϕ-consistency, iff every constraint agent can still evaluate its consistency predicate $\kappa(L_b \cup \{(v, x, v)\}, \phi_C^{-1}(b))$ to `true`. Thus, every constraint agent (b, C) has to check this property by testing the new labeling proposal (a, x, D, v) against its set of constraints and recent committed labelings. If only one constraint agent refuses the new labeling proposal is inconsistent and has to be discarded. The following proposition formalizes this demand to the protocol Σ_{cf}

$$\Sigma_{\text{cf}} \models PV.(a, x, D) \wedge CL = L \hookrightarrow \quad (3.A.1)$$
$$(LV.(a, x, D, v) \wedge \quad (3.A.2)$$
$$CL = L + \{(b, x, v) | (b, \cdot) \in N(x)\} \wedge CM = 0) \vee$$
$$(UV.(a, x, \emptyset) \wedge CL = L \wedge CM = 0). \quad (3.A.3)$$

In words this proposition means that given a pending variable (a, x, D) under an existing partial labeling represent by L (3.A.1), every possible run of the protocol causes either that (a, x, D, v) has been successfully labeled and every neighbor has committed to it (3.A.2) or the domain of x has been traversed without success, $(a, x, \emptyset)$ is in state `Unlabeled Variables` and not a single neighbor is still committed to the related requested labeling (3.A.3).

Figure 3.A.7 shows the proof graph that proves the aforementioned proposition. To justify the deduction steps in this graph we use the invariants 1 to 4 and the *causes* pick-up patterns 1 to 3 presented above.

① Invariant 2.

② + ③ Pattern 1 according to $D \neq \emptyset$ or $D = \emptyset$.

④ Invariant 1 with $RV = 1$ and invariant 2.

⑤ Combining invariants 1 and 4 with $RV = 1$ provides $RM + AM + REF - CA = 0$ and such $RM \leq CA$.

⑥ No conflicting transition, but only fair `clear` together with pattern 2.

⑦ No conflicting transition, L_b may be $\emptyset$ and pattern 1.

⑧ Propositional logic.

⑨ Invariant 3 with $RV = 1$ yields $LV = 0$ and such invariant 2 with $CM = 0$ yields $CL = AM + L$. Fall differentiation leads to two possible cases.

⑩ Conflicting transition `retract` is prevented since $REF = 0$. Pattern 3.

Figure 3.A.7 Proof graph for Theorem 1

⑪ Conflicting transition `update` is prevented since $\neg AM.N$. Pattern 3.

⑫ `receive`, `agree` and `refuse` are the only transitions in conflict to `clear`. `receive` is fair and will hence not deny `clear` forever. Due to invariant 4 all constraint agents will always return to CA after answering a request (`agree` and `refuse` do not block forever if there is a request on REQ). Also from invariant 4 we can derive that $CA.(b, C) \longrightarrow \neg REQ.(\cdot, b, C, \cdot, \cdot)$. Hence, if $CA.(b, C)$ `agree` and `refuse` are prevented and `clear` will finally fire.

The proof graph starts at $PV.(a, x, D) \wedge CL = L$ (1) and has three possible outcomes two of which directly correspond to (2) and (3) of our proposition.

The third outcome $PV.(a, x, D') \wedge |D'| = n - 1 \wedge CL = L \wedge CM = 0$ corresponds to the starting point of the proof graph with a reduced domain. Nevertheless, this situation cannot be produced infinitively, since D is fully traversed, $|D|$ reduces by a constant in every protocol cycle and will in the long run reach $|D| = 0$. Only `cancel`(PV) ③ is enabled in this situation and the protocol terminates after trying each value v from D. □

A.2 PROOF OF THEOREM 2

a) ($\Pi_{\text{CON}} \in NP$) Π_{CON} is in NP because it can be solved by enumerating every possible partition ϕ^{-1} of $X \cup C$ (which are $B_{n=|X \cup C|} = \sum_{k=1}^{n} \left[\frac{1}{k!} \sum_{i=0}^{k-1} (-1)^i \binom{k}{i} (k-1)^n\right]$ many[1]) and testing $q_{\phi^{-1}} \geq k$ (which can be done in polynomial time as long as ξ is computable in polynomial time).
b) (NP-hardness of Π_{CON}) We reduce the MINIMUM BISECTION graph problem to Π_{CON}. The MINIMUM BISECTION graph problem is proven to be NP-complete (Garey et al., 1976) and is defined as follows.
Given a graph $\Gamma = (N, E), |N| = 2 \cdot i, i \in \mathbb{N}^+$. Let

$$M = \Big\{ m = \big| \{ \{i, j\} \in E \mid n_i \in N_1 \wedge n_j \in N_2 \} \big| \qquad (3.A.4)$$
$$N_1 \cup N_2 = N \wedge N_1 \cap N_2 = \emptyset \wedge |N_1| = |N_2| \Big\}.$$

Is $m^* = \min M \leq k$ for a given $k \in \mathbb{Z}$?
We will do the reduction in a three step process.

1. (Input) We transform the input of the MINIMUM BISECTION problem to an input of Π_{CON} by $X = N$ and $C = \{\{(v_i, v_j)\} \mid \{i, j\} \in E\}$. Hence, there are only binary constraints in C. The domain set D is without any importance to this reduction and can be left empty.

2. (Restrictions) According to remark 2b) ϕ defines a partition. Additionally, defining $\xi(X_i \cup C_i) = |X_i|$ and $\xi_u = \frac{|N|}{2} = \xi_l$ enforces ϕ^{-1} to be a bisection with equally sized parts, since

$$\forall (a_i, X_i \cup C_i) \in \phi^{-1}:$$
$$\left(\xi(X_i \cup C_i) \leq \tfrac{|N|}{2} \wedge \xi(X_i \cup C_i) \geq \tfrac{|N|}{2} \right)$$
$$\Longrightarrow \forall (a_i, X_i \cup C_i) \in \phi^{-1} : |X_i| = \tfrac{|N|}{2}$$
$$\Longrightarrow |\phi^{-1}| = 2 \wedge |X_i| = |X_j| = \tfrac{|N|}{2} \quad \left(|N| = \textstyle\sum_{(a_i, X_i \cup C_i) \in \phi^{-1}} |X_i|\right)$$

Finally, disabling the social partition by $\forall xc \in X \cup C : \phi_s(xc) = 1$ leads to a full reduction of the set restrictions of M [Eqn. (3.A.4)] to the set restrictions of Q [Eqn. (3.2)–(3.4)].

[1] B_n is the so-called *Bell*-number.

3. (Measure) We have to reduce the measure m of the MINIMUM BISECTION problem [Eqn. (3.A.4)] to the measure of $\Pi_{\text{CON}}\ q_{\phi^{-1}}$ [Eqn. (3.1)].

$$\begin{aligned} m &= |\{\{j,k\} \in E \mid n_j \in N_1 \wedge n_k \in N_2\}| \\ &= |\{\{j,k\} \in E \mid \phi(x_j) \neq \phi(x_k)\}| && \text{(see restrictions)} \\ &= |\{\{(v_j,v_k)\} \in C \mid \phi(x_j) \neq \phi(x_k)\}| && \text{(see Def. of } C) \\ &= \textstyle\sum_{(a_i,X_i \cup C_i) \in \phi^{-1}} && \text{(altern. counting)} \\ &\quad \textstyle\sum_{C' \in C_i} |\{C' = \{(v_j,v_k)\} \mid \phi(x_j) \neq \phi(x_k)\}| \end{aligned}$$

What we are doing here is to check every constraint $C' \in C$ whether it restricts variables that are in different sets of the partition ϕ^{-1}. Since we have only two sets in the partition and constraints are only binary, there are three possible cases for the relation among a constraint C' and its restricted variables x_j and x_k: $\phi(C') = \phi(x_j) \neq \phi(x_k)$, $\phi(C') = \phi(x_k) \neq \phi(x_j)$ or $\phi(C') = \phi(x_j) = \phi(x_k)$. In the first two cases, m is increased by 1. Alternatively, we can count the number of variables connected to a constraint C' that are not in the same partition set as the constraint, because (looking at the three cases) there is exactly one such variable or none, leading also to an increase of m by 1 in the first two cases. Hence, we can derive

$$\begin{aligned} m &= \textstyle\sum_{(a_i,X_i \cup C_i) \in \phi^{-1}} \\ &\quad \textstyle\sum_{C' \in C_i} |\{x_j \in X \mid C' = \{(\ldots,v_j,\ldots)\} \wedge \phi(x_j) \neq \phi(C')\}| \\ &= \textstyle\sum_{(a_i,X_i \cup C_i) \in \phi^{-1}} \xi(X_i \cup C_i) - q_{\phi^{-1}} \\ &= \textstyle\sum_{(a_i,X_i \cup C_i) \in \phi^{-1}} |X_i| - q_{\phi^{-1}} \\ &= |N| - q_{\phi^{-1}} \end{aligned}$$

Therefore, m has been successfully reduced to an equivalent term containing a constant and the inverse of $q_{\phi^{-1}}$. The constant can be removed by adjusting $k \in \mathbb{Z}$ properly, the negative sign is indeed correct and needed because Π_{CON} maximizes Q while MINIMUM BISECTION minimizes M.

This polynomial three step procedure reduces MINIMUM BISECTION to Π_{CON} and hence proves our proposition. □

A.3 PROOF OF THEOREM 3

Since we are assuming that the solution equivalence between any pair of DCSPs does not depend on (A, ϕ), it is enough to show that we can systematically enumerate all complexity and social feasible partitions of the underlying CSP with the help of a sequence of reconfiguration transactions.

a) (Correctness) In our context, correctness means that only complexity and social feasible partitions are created by a sequence of reconfiguration transac-

tions. This is true by definition 12, since every single reconfiguration transaction of the sequence takes a complexity and social feasible partition as input and computes a partition that is forced to be complexity and social feasible.
b) (Completeness) In our context, completeness means that (1.) every given complexity and social feasible partition can be produced and that (2.) all partitions can be found by systematically enumerating sequences of reconfiguration transactions.

1. Assume that we want to produce the (complexity and social feasible) partition $\phi_2^{-1} = ((a_1, XC_{2,1}), \ldots, (a_n, XC_{2,n}))$ given the (complexity and social feasible) partition $\phi_1^{-1} = ((a_1, XC_{1,1}), \ldots, (a_m, XC_{1,m}))$. This can be done by the following reconfiguration transaction

$$(A_2, \phi_2^{-1}) = \underbrace{(1, XC_{2,n})(1, XC_{2,n-1})\ldots(1, XC_{2,1})}_{\text{split agent } a_1 \text{ according to } \phi_2^{-1}}\underbrace{(1,m)(1,m-1)\ldots(1,2)}_{\text{melt all agents}}$$

Note that this may be only one (and not very clever) reconfiguration transaction of several possible. Nevertheless, this reconfiguration transaction is invariant to (A_1, ϕ_1^{-1}) as long as $a_1 \in A_1$, i. e. (A_2, ϕ_2^{-1}) can be produced from every given partition.

2. Given any initial partition (A, ϕ^{-1}), the following algorithm realizes a systematic enumeration of all possible reconfiguration transactions and incrementally builds the sequence of successful reconfiguration transactions (*sequence*) and the set of feasible partitions (*partitions$_f$*) and non-feasible partitions (*partitions$_{\neg f}$*).

{initialization}
sequence $\leftarrow$ (); (1)
$(A_c, \phi_c^{-1}) \leftarrow (A, \phi^{-1})$; (2)
partitions$_f$ $\leftarrow \{(A_c, \phi_c^{-1})\}$; (3)
partitions$_{\neg f}$ $\leftarrow \emptyset$; (4)

{enumeration scheme}
while $|partitions_f| + |partitions_{\neg f}| < B_{|X \cup C|}$ **do**
{compute new partition}
$(\vec{\imath}, \vec{\jmath}, \vec{k}, \vec{XC}, m, n) \leftarrow (\bot, \bot, \bot, \bot, 0, 0)$; (5)
while $(A, \phi^{-1}) \in partitions_f \vee (A, \phi^{-1}) \in partitions_{\neg f}$ **do**
{compute and apply new local operator sequence from the previous one}
$(\vec{\imath}, \vec{\jmath}, \vec{k}, \vec{XC}, m, n) \leftarrow$ `gen_new_params` $(\vec{\imath}, \vec{\jmath}, \vec{k}, \vec{XC}, m, n)$; (6)
$(A, \phi^{-1}) \leftarrow (\vec{k}, \vec{XC})^n (\vec{\imath}, \vec{\jmath})^m (A_c, \phi_c^{-1})$; (7)

end while

{test feasibility of new partition}
if $feasible_c\,((X, D, C, A, \phi), \xi, \xi_u, \xi_l) \ \wedge$
$feasible_s\,((X, D, C, A, \phi), \phi_s)$ **then**
{local operator sequence is a valid reconfiguration transaction}
$sequence \leftarrow sequence : (\vec{\imath}, \vec{\jmath}, \vec{k}, \vec{XC}, m, n);$ (8)
$(A_c, \phi_c^{-1}) \leftarrow (A, \phi^{-1});$ (9)
$partitions_f \leftarrow partitions_f \cup \{(A, \phi^{-1})\};$ (10)
else
$partitions_{\neg f} \leftarrow partitions_{\neg f} \cup \{(A, \phi^{-1})\};$ (11)
end if
end while

After initializing the reconfiguration transaction sequence, the current configuration and the partition sets (lines 1 to 4), the algorithm passes two loops. The outer loop checks whether all possible partitions have been enumerated (this is done by checking the cardinality of the two partition sets against the *Bell*-number). If not, we have to compute a new partition by initializing the search for a new local operator sequence (line 5) and running the inner loop. Using the previous parameter set, we compute a new parameter set (line 6) and apply the local operator sequence to the current partition (line 7).

So why can this inner loop produce all possible partitions? This is because for every partition there is at least one local operator sequence producing the partition regardless of the given recent partition (see 1.). Hence, if we are able to enumerate all possible local operator sequences every partition will eventually appear. It is the responsibility of the function `gen_new_params` to ensure that all possible local operator sequences are enumerated. The parameters of a local operator sequence i_r, j_r, k_r, XC_r are from finite sets, because they are all restricted by the given fixed number of domain variables (X) and constraints (C). Even m and n are restricted to be from a finite set because we cannot apply an arbitrary number of effective agent melting operator to a set of agents as well as we cannot split agents infinitely. Therefore, the set of possible local operator sequences is finite and well-structured, i. e. we can enumerate it by trying one melt with all parameter combinations without any splits, one split with all parameter combinations without any melts, one melt and one split and so on.

After having found a new partition, it is checked whether we have found a valid reconfiguration transaction and such a complexity and social feasible partition. If yes, our sequence of reconfiguration transactions is augmented, the current configuration is set to the found one and the partition is stored in the set of feasible partitions (lines 8 to 10). If not, the partition is stored in the set of non-feasible partitions (line 11) and the sequence of transactions and the current configuration remain unchanged.

Following the described algorithm, we can derive all possible feasible partitions from the given partition by consecutively applying the reconfiguration transactions from the computed sequence. Hence, we can easily solve the decision variant, the value optimization variant and the solution optimization of the given DCS RECONFIGURATION problem.

Chapter 4

CONFLICTS IN SOCIAL THEORY AND MULTI-AGENT SYSTEMS

On importing sociological insights into Distributed AI

Thomas Malsch
Technische Universität Hamburg-Harburg, Germany
malsch@tu-harburg.de

Gerhard Weiss
Technische Universität München, Germany
weissg@in.tum.de

Abstract This chapter seeks to give the reader an idea of how to import conflict conceptions from sociology into distributed AI (DAI). In a preliminary comparison of conflict research in DAI and sociology, we show that both disciplines talk about essentially the same issues when they refer to conflict, although there are important differences in their motivations and reasons for studying conflict. The main sections deal with conflict from the perspectives of two mainstreams of sociological thought: the theory of autopoietic social systems and the pragmatist theories of symbolic interaction. Following our attempt to derive useful conceptual insights from the two theoretical approaches and to identify potentialities for future interdisciplinary research, six interrelated themes are described which seem to be of particular promise for both DAI and sociology alike.

1. INTRODUCTION

Conflict is a prominent issue both in DAI and in sociology. Ever since Georg Simmel, one of the forefathers of modern sociology, wrote his famous essay on strife more than a century ago, conflict has been regarded as one of the central topics of social research, whereas it is a mere ten years since Marc Klein first suggested that conflicts should be given a first-class status in DAI research (Klein, 1991). Today there is a wide consensus that conflict issues are of particular importance in DAI,[1] but there is still a lack of theoretical understanding and important questions are still waiting to be addressed more thoroughly. Sociology, for its part, has addressed some of these questions quite successfully and seems to have gained valuable theoretical insights which merit serious consideration in DAI. Accordingly, in this chapter some ideas of how to import sociological insights into DAI conflict research will be discussed.

As Simmel had shown "the binding values or norms are brought into awareness through conflict so that conflict, far from being only incidental to an affirmation of common values, is an agency through which these values come to be affirmed" (Coser, 1956, p. 127). In the sociological tradition of Simmel, conflict issues have a positive connotation and are widely acknowledged as being beneficial for social life. Instead of over-emphasising the negative or destructive aspects of a phenomenon that is as natural to society as cooperation and solidarity are, it largely understands conflicts as a legitimate form of expressing discontent and opposition. Conflicts are danger signals and play an important role in a society's immune system (Luhmann) and have a tremendous impact on social innovation. They help to make social pathologies visible and to prevent explosive constellations and they also contribute to the restructuring of a society's institutions and to the creation of new participative regulations and democratic procedures (Mead, Dewey). Today it is sociological common sense that conflicts serve as a vital means of affirming a society's fundamental values and as a powerful motor of structural social change.

In contrast to sociology, viewing conflict as something that should not simply be avoided and "out-designed" is relatively new in DAI research (Grasso, 1998, Chantemargue et al., 1998). Ever since distributed problem solving was first introduced as a superior alternative to centralised approaches, the DAI community had been haunted by the nightmare of multiagent systems degenerating "into collections of chaotic, incohesive individuals" (Jennings, 1993, p. 225). Indeed, the ultimate goal of coordinated problem solving, global coherence[2], is threatened in numerous ways: "Agents may spread misleading and distracting information, multiple agents may compete for unsharable resources simultaneously, agents may unwittingly undo the results of each others activities and the same actions may be carried out redundantly ... the dynamics of such systems can become extremely complex, giving rise to nonlinear oscilla-

[1] This wide consensus is also reflected by the increasing number of related workshops and publications (Jokiinen et al., 1997, Klein and Lander, 1994, Lander, 1994, Müller and Dieng, 2000, Sen, 1999, Tessier and Chaudron, 1998, Tessier and Chaudron, 1999).

[2] An interesting question is whether DAI should take the problem of "failure indeterminacy" (Gasser, 1991) more seriously and depart from unrealistic notions of coherence and success. Perhaps we just have to accept that "in practice, many negotiations ... may fail ... (and that) there are no a priori guarantees of success" (Hewitt and Inman, 1991, p. 1417).

tions and chaos. In such cases the coordination process becomes correspondingly more difficult as well as more important" (Jennings, 1993, p. 227).

Certainly, these are strong arguments in favour of avoiding and out-designing conflicts before they turn virulent. However, it appears as though rational conflict avoidance becomes increasingly difficult as multiagent applications become more complex and more demanding. Meanwhile a new insight has gained ground in DAI: Conflicts cannot be avoided any longer but must be accepted as normal social behaviour (Castelfranchi, 2000, p. 20). Conflicts "become increasingly inevitable" as they have to meet "growing requirements of scale and autonomy" (Tambe and Jung, 1999b, p. 1). As conflicts have been identified as "the focal point of interaction", they "must be explicitly addressed" (Lander, 1994, p. 9) and can no longer be excluded from the research agenda by simply treating them as "undesirable side-effects which would impair the (agent) community's performance" (Jennings, 1993, p. 246). All these quotations convey the same message: "Conflict in multi-agent systems is ubiquitous" (Wagner et al., 1999, p. 1). But what, then, are the conceptual consequences to be drawn from the ubiquity of conflict?

Despite the fact that DAI has made considerable efforts to develop useful techniques for conflict resolution and conflict management, other issues of a more theoretical nature like definitions, causes, dynamics, and outcomes of conflicts have been largely neglected (Müller and Dieng, 2000, p. 6). This is particularly true for the conceptual neglect of the relationship between conflict and coordination, one of the core tenets of any advanced conflict theory. Although it is easy to see that conflict and coordination are somehow twin concepts, it seems much more difficult to see how exactly they are interrelated: Do conflicts have to be modelled, as has been suggested by Shaw and Gaines, as failures of coordination (Shaw and Gaines, 1994)? Or is this view a curious misconception, as suggested by Müller and Dieng, "since usually coordination ... is used to resolve conflicts" (Müller and Dieng, 2000, p. 9)? Instead of seriously analysing and discussing the question whether coordination follows conflict or conflict follows coordination, the issue is dropped from the agenda because it appears to be just another version of the ill-reputed hen-and-egg problem. Instead of striving to uncover the conceptual difficulties inherent in the relationship, business is done as usual. On one hand there are the "modern" approaches operating along the formula of "conflict - coordination" which try to resolve conflicts by explicit negotiation and contracting techniques. On the other there are the "traditional" approaches along the reverse formula of "coordination - conflict" with the aim of out-designing conflicts by multiagent planning or commitment-convention modelling.

Sociological conflict research, in turn, is more theoretically inclined – and has produced some interesting insights into the hen-and-egg problem which could prove useful for DAI. But how can DAI researchers learn from sociologists who are primarily inclined to explain society? What can those who are interested in engineering innovative techniques for conflict resolution learn from those who want to understand how conflicts are generated in modern human society and how social conflict is intertwined with structural social change? Why should it be valuable for DAI as an engineering discipline to gain a theoretical understanding of why social conflicts are in the main not rationally resolved but transferred, suppressed, postponed, translated and transformed? Although it seems clear that DAI and sociology do not talk of essentially different matters when they refer to conflicts, considerable spadework must go into the preparation of the ground for a fruitful collaboration which will – eventually – be able to answer these questions. The first thing to do, however, is to answer the question how to choose the most promising sociological approach to conflict research.

To an observer from the DAI community sociological conflict studies present themselves as a sweeping bouquet of heterogeneous approaches and disparate traditions (Giegel, 1998). Far from having developed a unified theoretical framework, sociologists are by no means unanimous in following Simmel's lead and conceptualising conflict as a positive phenomenon, nor is there a generally accepted conflict definition. Instead, there is an ongoing debate on the opportunities and dangers, benefits and damages of social conflict and political struggle. Conflict issues have been controversially discussed in social philosophy and political theory as a deeply ambiguous phenomenon ever since Thomas Hobbes spelled out strife and struggle as "homo hominem lupus", the "war of every man against every man". Hobbes' sombre conclusion was that in order to maintain social order conflicts had to be vigorously suppressed by an absolute power. The sociologist Talcott Parsons, whose theory of social systems became very influential in the post-war years of the 1950s and 1960s, took the Hobbesian problematic of social order as his point of departure. Parsons viewed conflicts as essentially destructive and thus was primarily concerned with the establishment and maintenance of social stability and harmony. However, unlike Hobbes, he did not believe in "zero tolerance" but explained social order in terms of a system-environment equilibrium based on internalised norms and values. Parsons was later criticised for the bias of his conceptual "equilibrism" which made him blind to one of the most interesting sociological issues: the link between conflict and social change (Coser, 1956). Today, many sociologists are in search of the missing link, but a unified theory is still not in sight. In other words, the most promising sociological approach to conflict research simply does not exist. In the light of this lacuna, the ground for importing sociological conflict theories into DAI must be paved in the following sections by comparing two of the more promising candidates: the sociology of autopoietic social systems and the pragmatist sociology of symbolic interaction, both of which rank among the intellectual heavyweights of sociological theory.

In the following we will begin by considering some differences and similarities concerning the meaning of conflict in sociology and DAI. These will be highlighted in section 2.1. with reference to two paradigmatic cases of conflict research: scheduling a meeting and the tragedy of Antigone. Having framed the setting with a short comparison of Simmel and Hewitt in section 2.2., section 3 introduces us to Luhmann's autopoietic sociology of conflicts as systems of communicated contradictions. Whereas the sociology of autopoietic systems is closely associated, if not identical, with the name of Luhmann, the pragmatist sociology of symbolic interaction discussed in section 4 does not easily lend itself to personalisation,although it clearly stands in the American pragmatist tradition of Peirce, James, Dewey, and Mead. However, the reader should be prepared to find other names associated with pragmatist symbolic interaction, names like Blumer, Strauss, Maines etc. In section 5 Dewey's theory of inquiry as a democratic learning process based on collective intelligence is contrasted with Luhmann's evolutionary approach of functional differentiation. In section 6 an attempt is made to identify some lines of sociologically grounded DAI research on conflicts.

2. DIFFERENT REASONS FOR STUDYING CONFLICTS IN DAI AND SOCIOLOGY

2.1 WHAT WE CAN LEARN FROM SCHEDULING A MEETING AND FROM THE TRAGEDY OF ANTIGONE

For preliminary clarification it is useful to draw on the problem of meeting scheduling, a canonic example in DAI research on multiagent systems. A quotation from a report on experiments in conflict resolution with agents which communicate and negotiate via message passing and which are able to relax their individual preferences when conflicts arise, will help to clarify an interesting point of difference between DAI and sociology: "In our experiments ... the agent with the fewest available time intervals becomes the task coordinator who is responsible for sending the first proposal. Each agent that receives a proposal accepts or rejects it by replying the message. ... When ... the proposal was accepted by all agents, the coordinator sums up the priorities to get the group utility measure for that meeting and sends a final confirmation message to all agents ... However, when the proposal is rejected by at least one agent, the coordinator selects a new task coordinator to the agent who opposes the current proposal. If there are more than one opposing agent, the agent with the fewest available time intervals is selected. The new task coordinator relaxes its time constraints and sends a new proposal and the process is repeated"

(Garrido-Luna and Sycara, 1996, p. 88). In the light of the sociological approaches discussed in the following sections in more detail – the pragmatist sociology of interaction and the sociology of autopoietic systems – it is inadequate to call such a scheduling negotiation a conflict. Despite the fact that agents oppose each other while pursuing their respective subgoals, from a sociological perspective it would make more sense to speak of coordination or a coordination problem rather than a conflict or a conflict-resolution process.[3]

The reason for rejecting the idea that negotiating a meeting schedule as shown in the above example should be construed as a conflict is not that the agents are benevolently trying to come to terms with each other in the course of further negotiations. It is rather that the opposition evinced in the course of negotiations is simply too weak. To provoke a conflict, an agent must act in opposition to established norms or conventions. And for a fully-fledged or strong[4] conflict, his or her opposition must be opposed by another agent. Rejecting a proposal *per se* is not necessarily a conflict, but merely a cooperative opposition – although it may turn into a conflict later on in the course of a problem-solving process. Sociologically speaking, conflict is to be defined by rejecting a rejection of a normative expectation, as, for instance, in the case of Antigone. In Sophocles' tragedy the Greek princess Antigone was caught in a moral double-bind: on the one hand family piety commanded her to bury the corpse of her brother whilst on the other hand the king her father's express command prohibited it. Antigone's is a very special case though. Nevertheless, the message should be clear: Without rejecting or trespassing against the normative expectations of others, there can be no conflict. In the case of scheduling a meeting, however, rejecting other agents' proposals corresponds to socially expected behaviour. This is not to say that expected opposition will never turn into a conflict scenario. Indeed, it may turn into a conflict when agents continue to say "no" to each others' proposals until the point is reached when everybody realises that all further proposals will be rejected too. At that moment allegedly legitimate opposition to a particular schedule is exposed as what it really is: an illegitimate rejection of the meeting itself, or, in sociological parlance, a rejection of an expectation.

But there is more that we can learn from Antigone's moral predicament: Why, for heavens sake, did she not make as rational a choice as possible, when she was prohibited, under penalty of death, from doing what family piety com-

[3]The suggestion that has been made to distinguish in DAI between "cooperative conflicts" and "competitive conflicts" (Klein, 1990) is not really helpful; in fact it is a curious contrastof a paradox with a tautology. As a contradictio in adiecto the term "cooperative conflict" is merely a symptom of the underlying difficulty rather than its solution.

[4]In DAI literature we find a similar distinction between "weak" conflicts that can be resolved by the decision of a mediator and "hard" conflicts that must be resolved by negotiating a compromise (Hollmann et al., 2000).

manded her to do, namely to bury the body of her brother? Why did Antigone not take the strategic decision to, as it were, "bury and run"? Why did she commit herself to "disobedient obedience" and why, despite the fact that she could have escaped, did she commit herself to a voluntary acceptance of her penalty? The reason seems to be as clear as it is simple: social conflicts are morally constituted. They are intertwined with the normative foundations of human society and therefore cannot be treated like so many technical collisions or accidents. This also holds true for less rigid, more differentiated constellations of trust and treason that make life in modern societies much more complicated and much more contingent than life in pre-modern societies. Endowing a heroine's actions with higher degrees of freedom is a feature specific to modern society. So what can be learnt here is that it is the normative dimension of expectations that makes the difference between rational choice and social action. From a sociological point of view it is a misconception to qualify social conventions merely as "useful social laws" (Shoham and Tennenholtz, 1992) in the sense of traffic laws. For obvious reasons, however, society cannot be reduced to the normative or moral dimension alone. Modern society rather embraces a highly differentiated set of intersecting and sometimes conflicting logics of social action. And again it was Simmel who first introduced a concept of conflict based on the idea of intersecting logics of obligations and commitments.

2.2 SIMILARITIES BETWEEN SIMMEL AND HEWITT: "LOGICAL" AND "MATERIAL" CONFLICTS

For Simmel conflicts arise from intersecting circles of social obligations and duties. As part of different social circles, a human individual can be represented as a point of intersecting expectations. Such intersections impact on the individual in the form of more or less incompatible demands, conflicting obligations and colliding duties. Cross-cutting through individual intentions and commitments, the courses of social interaction are shaped by two different types of social conflict, namely "logical" and "material" conflicts ((Simmel, 1892)). A "logical" conflict is characterized by a constellation in which an actor is simultaneously committed to a number of contradictory normative obligations. According to Simmel such conflicts are unavoidable and irresolvable.[5] They are the stuff from which classic tragedy is made: an antagonistic conflict between legitimate demands transformed into an unbearable individual

[5]According to Simmel, Antigone's tragedy does not lie in her inevitable death. "The real tragedy ... lies in the fact that the very contradictions survive the heroine's death" ((Simmel, 1892, p. 389)). In Simmel's view her self-sacrifice did not constitute the tragic element but rather the fact that her sacrifice was in vain as social circumstances did not allow for a resolution of conflict through a creative restructuring of society's normative foundations.

weight of conscience with, as in the case of Antigone, all exit options blocked. A material conflict, on the other hand, is due to an incidental or contingent collision of goals and interests with no innate or logical contradiction between the goals and interests involved. Material conflicts arise when two courses of action happen to collide because they require the selfsame means or resources in pursuit of their respective ends or goals. Both courses of action are morally compatible and equally qualified as legitimate by the two parties involved. It is not the moral quality of incompatible norms and values which is in question but the economic scarcity of (un)available means and ends that gives rise to material conflict.

Intuitively and at first glance, Simmel's distinction seems to make sense, but a closer look shows his terminology to be unclear and distorted. Why does he qualify normative conflicts as logical and avoidable collisions as material? Does he want to make the dubious point that (material) interests and desires are negotiable while (logical) norms and values are not? Or is he implicitly drawing on the distinction between meaning and causality – logical conflicts have meaning while material conflicts have causes – without realising that there is nothing more logical than causes? Simmel's distinction seems to be inconsistent: material conflicts are neither meaningless nor illogical, logical conflicts are not non-negotiable or non-causal, and both are sometimes foreseeable and sometimes not. Of course, with today's hindsight it is all too easy to criticise a theory that was written more than a hundred years ago: material conflicts are neither meaningless nor illogical, logical conflicts are not non-negotiable or non-causal, and both are sometimes foreseeable and sometimes not. However, what makes this theory so interesting even today is the connection it establishes between normativity and logical necessity, and between material causality and contingency. A further point of particular interest is that Simmel's distinctions and connotations can be found in a slightly different guise in DAI where Carl Hewitt's work can be read as a curious reconfirmation of Simmel's two concepts of conflict.

Open information systems, according to Hewitt, are faced with a problem of overcomplexity that makes itself felt as unforeseeable or contingent conflicts. Such conflicts are not based on "differing ... theories of how to achieve an optimal solution" or "different conflict resolution strategies", but on coincidence and complexity when "the parties ... discover unforeseen interactions in their activities" (Hewitt and Inman, 1991, p. 1417). That conflicts in DAI are generally conceived as unforeseen "material conflicts" in Simmel's sense, seems to be fully in line with DAI mainstream literature. What is different in Hewitt's distinction is the claim he makes that there is another type of deliberative and foreseeable conflict based on contradictory theories of problem-solving and conflict resolution. Although Hewitt is not very explicit on the difference between the two types of conflict, the deliberative type of conflict seems to be more fundamental and comes quite close to Simmel's logical conflict. Deliberative or theoretical conflicts are rooted in the problem of "logical indeterminacy" (Hewitt, 1977) which occurs when two different "microtheories" of the same knowledge domain, both undoubtedly correct and both in full accord with deductive logic, lead to contradictory conclusions. As Hewitt showed, this type of conflict is irresolvable, unless it is transferred into the pragmatic dimension of social action.

What we can learn from Hewitt and Simmel is that DAI and Sociology are not talking of essentially different things when they refer to conflicts. Rather, the scope of both approaches reaches out and embraces similar topics. It should be clear by now that a set of common ideas, intuitions and distinctions cannot replace a systematic theory of conflict. To prepare the ground for more ambitious conflict theories in both DAI and sociology, current distinctions and definitions of conflicts must be taken as starting points for an explanation of how conflict dynamics are interwoven with structural social change. In the following sections two theories of conflict will be examined more closely: Niklas Luhmann's sociology of autopoietic social systems and the pragmatist sociology of symbolic interaction based on the works of Charles S. Peirce, George H. Mead and John Dewey.

3. CONFLICTS IN THE SOCIOLOGY OF AUTOPOIETIC SOCIAL SYSTEMS

3.1 CONFLICT AS A COMMUNICATED CONTRADICTION

According to Luhmann a conflict is an explicitly communicated contradiction (Luhmann, 1984, pp. 530ff). Wherever a communication is rejected, there is a conflict, and whenever an expectation is communicated and remains unchallenged by a subsequent communication, there is not a conflict. Conflict, in other words, depends on someone saying "no". It is an outspoken opposition defined as a synthesis of two communications which contradict each other.[6] This definition is based on the assumption that social life consists of "autopoietic" systems that use and generate communications, and nothing but communications, as the operational elements of their own reproduction. Communication, in Luhmann's sense, is black box communication at arms-length relationships. This is not to deny the empirical facts of intrapersonal or psy-

[6] It is interesting to note that Luhmann emphasises the defensive over the offensive aspect of conflict . In saying "no", an individual defends itself against an imputed expectation but does not necessarily articulate the offensive wish to actively change it. In DAI research, the emphasis usually is on defining conflict as an active attempt to change another agent's belief state (Galliers, 1990), for instance by persuasion or argumentation (Sycara, 1985, Parsons et al., 1998).

chological conflicts. Rather, this means that the notion of intrapersonal conflict is not a category describing the "autopoiesis" – self-production as a closed process – of a social system but a category of the system's environment, part of which is the human being. In other words, a conflict which remains inside a human individual as an unarticulated feeling of hostile anxiety and aggression is not a social conflict.

The advantages of Luhmann's definition seem to be clear. By strictly defining conflict at the behavioural level of observable communication, speculations about mental or emotional states of hostility or aggression can be avoided. Moreover, this definition helps to clarify the more current sociological confusion between "structural" and "behavioural" conflicts (Luhmann, 1984, p. 531). Conflict dynamics and their structural reasons must be clearly distinguished. Keeping conflicts apart from their structural reasons, has the conceptual advantage of acknowledging and taking into account that everyday social life is massively imbued with conflicts. However, there is an inconsistency in Luhmann's definition that should be settled straight away. After having defined conflict as a communicated contradiction, as an outspoken "no", it is inconsistent to change the definition by labelling the "no" as the mere beginning of a conflict. Luhmann does so when he explains how a hierarchy enables and constrains conflicts: Only those who are in a higher hierarchical position "are free to say 'no' because this will not be followed by a conflict" (Luhmann, 1984, pp. 539f).[7] In other words, if a "no" is followed by a conflict, then that "no" as such is obviously not a conflict in itself – unless we assume that Luhmann implicitly distinguishes between a conflictive "no" that is followed by a conflict (e.g. Antigone) and a cooperative "no" that is not followed by a conflict (e.g. meeting scheduling). Consequently, unless we assume that a single "no" is just a necessary but not a sufficient condition for a conflict system to emerge, Luhmann's statement is inconsistent.

Indeed, Luhmann seems to have noticed the inconsistency in his argument because when touching on the issue again some years later, he took pains to distinguish between a conflict as a communicated contradiction on one hand and the consequences it holds on the other: Political domination allows "to strengthen the rejection of a communication while relieving the rejecter from the strain of having to bear the consequences of conflict at the same time." (Luhmann, 1997, p. 467, our emphasis) Instead of following Luhmann's revised proposal, we would suggest resolving the inconsistency the other way round by introducing the distinction between ephemeral or virtual conflicts and real conflicts. An ephemeral or virtual conflict shall be defined as a communicated expectation followed by a single "no", a real conflict as a rejected

[7] All quotations from Luhmann translated by the authors.

expectation followed by yet another "no". A first "no" must be followed by a second "no" in order to have a real conflict.[8] This definition is certainly more restrictive. Nevertheless, it is still far less restrictive than those currently circulating in contemporary sociology and hence it is quite in line with Luhmann's intention to effect a sharp distinction between conflict as a mass phenomenon of social communication and its underlying reasons.

Conflicts are mass phenomena (Luhmann, 1984, p. 534). They are constantly flaming up and cooling down again, usually without deeper reason or meaning. They seem to break out spontaneously at almost any occasion and any time only to pass into oblivion again a few moments later. As mass events of social communication, conflicts usually erupt without doing much damage or harm to the structures of social expectation. Communication has an "innate tendency towards conflict" (Luhmann, 1997, p. 462). The fact that minor conflicts are ubiquitous not only reveals that expectations in social life are counterfactual expectations; it also highlights conflict in its role as a permanent stimulus to the "immune system" of a society, as a prime means of reinforcing and modifying social expectations. At this point, however, another conceptual difficulty in Luhmann's conflict theory arises. If conflicts in the guise of harmless mass phenomena appear stripped of their menace, it is because the distinction between rejecting and accepting a communicated expectation has not been sufficiently clarified. Our objection here is that most communications are neither explicitly accepted nor rejected. How can we tell, for instance, whether a communicated information is rejected or not if it is followed neither by a "no" nor by a "yes"? Of course, there is not just the word "no" but many other ways to articulate or communicate a conflict, ranging from not agreeing explicitly or giving cautious signs of discontent to overt resistance and pugnacious opposition. Communicating a conflict may often occur as a somewhat camouflaged form of politeness, of not agreeing explicitly, of pondering other proposals, postponing a decision, or tacitly looking out for potential allies who also give signs of non-agreement or discontent. As will be shown below, this is a conceptual disadvantage that seriously counterfeits Luhmann's proposal as it raises the question when a reluctant "yes" or a tacit "no" is an unambiguous "no".

Perhaps it is the conceptual ambiguity of a "no" which makes conflicts appear to be all too harmless and all too dangerous at one and the same time. For the other side of the coin is that Luhmann conceives conflicts as parasitic social systems, with no standing of their own, parasitically feeding off other social systems in respecifying and reorganising every single communicative

[8] In the sociological debate two options were put foward: either to ignore Luhmann's inconsistency as being of no vital importance for his conflict theory (Nollmann, 1997) or to resolve it through an unambiguous definition of conflict as a double negation (Schneider, 1994).

act according to the logic of adversarial interests and priorities. Once a conflict has been reciprocally defined and, however casual and meaningless its point of departure might have been, has begun to mature into the adversarial relationship of a double "no" officially declared by both conflicting parties, it is difficult to keep it from escalating. All sorts of communicative events, all elements of the hosting social system and all its heterogeneous acts and actions are sucked into the undertow of an ever widening conflict system. Thus conflict systems tend to "overintegrate" themselves by changing gears from low to high interdependence of all their operational elements and by exchanging loosely coupled structures for tightly coupled ones. The "destructive power of conflict" (Luhmann, 1984, p. 532), therefore, lies in its relationship to the system within which and from which a conflict originally started and gathered momentum. Hence, the metaphor of conflicts as parasitic systems is quite accurate, albeit not in the sense of a friendly symbiosis, but in the destructive sense of absorbing all the attention and resources of the host system. Just like other highly interdependent systems, conflicts too tend to ruthlessly exploit and demolish their environments, because in conflict systems the use of external resources is rigidly defined in advance: subordinating all available material and information to a sharp friend/foe polarisation at the structural level whilst remaining highly receptive at the level of action to all kinds of possibilities for harming and coercing the opponent. This is what we call the "cancer theory" of conflict .[9]

On the other hand, Luhmann emphasises that there is no need for external intervention and containment to stop conflicts from running out of control because of an innate tendency in conflict interactions towards trivialisation and minimisation, expiration and exhaustion (Luhmann, 1984, p. 534). This is the "entropy theory" of conflict. While he considers the cancer theory more or less as a thought experiment, Luhmann seems to take the entropy theory at face value. Conflicts usually do not continue to grow ever larger but tend to extinguish themselves at some point (Luhmann, 1984, p. 537). The difficult thing to explain, then, is how conflicts are to be given a chance for consolidation. Conflicts are consolidated by what Luhmann calls regulation. It is important to note, however, that conflict regulation is not the same as conflict resolution. Within a theoretical framework that does not lend itself as a "nice" social theory of benevolent cooperation, as Luhmann ironically notes, but which is rather interested in understanding the "normalisation of the unlikely" (Luh-

[9]The cancer theory of conflict reveals a weakness in Luhmann's conception of autopoiesis. If conflict systems override the established boundaries of functional subsystems, subsystems will no longer be able to follow their specific mode of autopoietic reproduction alone. This conceptual weakness could be cured by disavowing the strong empirical claim that social systems are autopoietic systems. Instead, autopoiesis should be construed as a useful analytical or heuristic concept that allows us to assume different degrees of autopoiesis (Teubner and Willke, 1984).

mann, 1984, p. 537), conflict resolution cannot be more than a by-product of a more encompassing question, namely how is it possible that despite their entropic tendencies to disappear again, conflicts are able to enjoy outstanding careers of cancerous growth and consolidation (Luhmann, 1984, p. 535).

3.2 CONFLICT REGULATION INSTEAD OF CONFLICT RESOLUTION

The reasons for such exceptional careers are not to be found at the level of interaction but rather at the level of society. Society needs conflicts because they help to disclose and highlight problematic social structures. By reinserting uncertainty (or "doubt", as pragmatist philosophy would have it) into well established structures of expectation, conflicts irritate and strengthen a society's "immune system". Society recruits conflicts, i.e. allows and, to a certain extent, even hatches opposing actions like refusal, disobedience, and deviant communication in order to keep itself on the alert via the installation of specialised systems of self-awareness and early warning. But how does that work if there is no way of consciously reconstructing or changing a society? The answer is: by differentiation. Differentiation develops "top down" (Luhmann, 1984, p. 574) from the top-level of social systems – which is the level of society – without necessarily having to be backed up by differences at the lower system-levels of organisation and interaction. How conflicts are encouraged by evolutionary differentiation is shown in the following four points.

1. Firstly, conflicts are encouraged by a society that at the same time discourages and suppresses the exertion of illegitimate violence. This is made possible by installing what Luhmann calls asymmetric power relations, those displayed in stratified societies. Asymmetry of power and/or wealth is guaranteed by a sharp differentiation between a dominant or a ruling class and a dominated or subservient population. Examples here include ancient Greece, the Indian caste system, and European feudalism. Obviously – and this applies to stratified societies and our modern world in equal measure – those who are in a dominant position and equipped with sufficient monetary and political power are more easily able to say "no" than those without financial or political clout since they do not have to fear the consequences of conflict (Luhmann, 1997, p. 467).

2. Secondly, by introducing a third party as an impartial mediator or moderator[10], it is possible to reintroduce uncertainty again (Luhmann, 1984,

[10]Apart from the judge or the impartial mediator, Simmel envisages two other types of interested third parties (Simmel, 1908, pp. 108f): the powerless third who stands aside and passively waits until the conflicting

p. 540). The presence of third parties usually tends to discourage conflict tendencies, aids in the deescalation and easing of tension and prevents conflict systems from overintegrating their host systems. In the course of evolutionary differentiation conflict procedures have been furnished with a growing body of operational capabilities known as law and justice. The operational capabilities of law and justice function to lower the threshold of conflict risks including for those who are powerless as well – as long as they comply with and conform to the law and to the rules and procedures of conflict regulation. A significant feature of this development, moreover, is that it leads to an enormous enhancement of conflict possibilities without necessarily posing a threat to the social structures.

3. Thirdly, evolution evokes a differentiation between conflict reasons and conflict topics. There may be deep structural reasons that give rise to repeated and perpetual outbreaks of conflict, but, as Luhmann points out, conflict systems often prefer to choose other topics and issues instead of directly addressing the reasons and attacking the roots of the underlying structural problem which has brought them about in the first place (Luhmann, 1997, p. 469). At this point Luhmann's sceptical message is very clear. He does not believe in conflict resolution but, at best, in evolutionary change. For him, conflict resolution – in the sense of an ultimate solution – is a futile endeavour because it is hardly ever possible to abolish the underlying reasons for conflict by consciously changing a society's structure. Or, even worse, he considers that deliberate attempts to pull up conflicts by their roots all too often drastically aggravate the situation instead of restoring peace and harmony.

4. Fourthly, highly specialised conflicts are enabled by functional differentiation between and disintegration of specific expert arenas. A conflict or dispute among the experts of a specific expert community in the main is a highly sophisticated, recondite affair which nobody else seems to understand or be interested in. This is particularly true for the arts and sciences. Power and law are early evolutionary achievements going far back to pre-modern times, but the growing differentiation between different kinds of conflict themes along the lines of disjointed functional subsystems (politics, economy, religion, science etc.) is a peculiarly modern phenomenon. In the course of social evolution, each of these subsystems has developed a highly specialised code and speaks an idiosyncratic tongue of its own. And rather than denying or suppressing

parties have weakened each other so much that he turns out the exultant winner ("tertium gaudens"); and the powerful third who divides and rules by actively taking sides and encouraging both conflict parties ("divide et impera").

conflicts, they are forward in the promotion and enhancement of specific types of conflict communication.

The scientific subsystem of modern society furnishes a prime example of how conflicts are specified within the boundaries of functionally differentiated subsystems. To understand the way it operates as a functional subsystem, we must recall that the scientific community is not to be defined as a cancerous conflict but rather by its innovative function in producing new knowledge of a very specific type: scientific truth. In order to hatch scientific truth it has to foster a discovery-friendly cultural climate , i.e. a climate in which new proposals may emerge and be tested and modified without discouraging those who propose and those who criticise. To achieve this climate it is necessary to release participants from what would otherwise be considered as normal, polite, smooth behaviour at the level of social interaction. Here aptitude for contradiction and zest for conflict must be underpinned by a specific professional attitude. Accordingly, subsystems like the scientific community fulfil a specialised function within modern societies. They "use asymmetric relations, corroborated by professional and/or organisational structures, and they must encourage contradiction as a means of control, advancement, and improvement. This leads to highly artificial rules for interactions, which then become 'dried up' and functionally specialised – and unpleasant. (...) In spite of the formal equality of all fellows, the society must recognise the asymmetry between the researcher and his or her critical audience. In spite of its interactional mode of communication it must encourage polite distrust, delay in acceptance and critical contradiction" (Luhmann, 1987, p. 123).

The task of scientists is to produce new knowledge and in order to do so they are constrained to contradict established doctrines and currently accepted knowledge. In other words, it is their job to say "no" to entrenched belief expectations and to face stubborn opposition. Indeed, a scientific controversy is a highly conflict-ridden affair. If a scientific knowledge proposal were but a reappraisal of a current doctrine or a mere replication of what other people have found out already, it would be considered as a truism by the scientific community, unworthy of mention, publication or criticism. But if it lays claim to being new, then it is essentially conflictive in nature because its very newness poses a threat to earlier discoveries. And whether the new proposal will be accepted and the old doctrine rejected or vice versa is dependent on the process of peer review. Peer review is essentially conflict communication. Any scientific proposal implies a "no" to another proposal and hence runs the risk of rejection or disqualification by the scientific community as being false or irrelevant. Before being dismissed or accepted as a discovery that adds more truth to the accumulated knowledge of mankind, a proposal must run the gauntlet of much hostile interrogation. And, as Luhmann argues, this kind of punctilious hostility is acceptable for those who risk proposing only because of what he calls the evolutionary differentiation between an author and a person. In order to make scientific conflicts functionally possible, it is necessary to shelter those whose contradiction is contradicted from being totally discredited as people – in the event that their contribution is rejected by the scientific community.

This means that all other contexts of personal interaction must be buffered from the potentially discrediting effects of controversial scientific discourse. Marriage, friendship, income, public reputation, and the political right to vote must remain untouched (Luhmann, 1992, p. 243). Buffering the person from the damages done to the author does, even nowadays, not always work as it should - a deplorable empirical fact of life, as Luhmann readily admits. Even so modern vicissitudes are as nothing compared to the case of the 16th century Polish astronomer Copernicus who was vilified as a liar and condemned as a blasphemer for his scientific discoveries. Nowadays, within the boundaries of a differentiated scientific arena and other specialised subsystems, modern societies refrain from conflict suppression and enable flourishing cultures of controversial debate. So conflict is systematically elevated and cultivated through evolutionary differentiation. Thus it is not conflict resolution which sociology must address but conflict regulation, and it is not the intended "solution" of the established procedures of conflict regulation that should stimulate our curiosity, but the questions how evolution and conflict are interrelated and how it is possible that there is always something unexpected about to happen somewhere else once a conflict system has gained momentum.

4. CONFLICT IN THE PRAGMATIST SOCIOLOGY OF SYMBOLIC INTERACTION

4.1 FROM HOSTILE FEELINGS TO ADVERSARIAL RELATIONSHIPS

In George H. Mead's theoretical framework for a pragmatist sociology of symbolic interaction, conflicts are closely associated with strife and struggle, hostile feelings and adversarial relationships. Conflict is anthropologically rooted in socio-physiological impulses or behaviour tendencies that lead to social antagonism among individuals (Mead, 1934, pp. 303f). Thus Mead's approach seems to be much more in line with common sense notions of conflict and struggle than Luhmann's more sophisticated definition. Conflict, here, is more than just someone saying "no" to someone else's proposal. Rejecting a proposal in an attitude of friendly cooperation is not a conflict but an act of cooperation between two or more individuals who express different views on how to attain a collective goal. Unless explicitly symbolised as an attitude of aggression or enmity or hostility, a social situation cannot be conceived as a conflict. Accordingly, an unstructured social setting in which different views or opposing opinions impact as a need for further clarification and alignment holds a potential for both conflict and cooperation. Thus a pragmatist sociology of symbolic interaction can neither be reduced to a concept of conflict along the lines of Coser nor to one of harmony as suggested by Parsons. To quote Mead's well known disciple, H. Blumer, who coined the phrase "symbolic interactionisms": "Imposing either of these two optional patterns of human sociality on the breadth of social interaction is a fallacious claim" (Blumer, 1966, p. 538).

Social interaction is a fundamental concept that covers the whole range of sociality and is constitutive not only for human societies but for the human individual as well. In Mead's pragmatist sociology the point of departure is not the individual human being or the individual social action, as in Max Weber's sociology, but a group activity of at least two individuals exchanging significant gestures or symbols. Meaning is reciprocally attributed through a mechanism called "role taking". The mutual assumption of each other's role by participants shapes the course of social activity whilst those engaged in symbolic interaction simultaneously confer meaning on the respective social settings. For it is not the individual intention but the exchange of significant gestures among actors in the flow of everyday group life which constitutes meaning. Hence, meaning is always socially situated meaning. It does not have an existence outside and apart from the social situation in which it is socially constituted. By taking the role of the other, both participants develop a shared meaning, a common or mutual understanding of their situation and of themselves as socially intelligent beings. This links in with the intuition of pragmatist sociologists that, in a more general sense, the human mind and human society are constituted in essentially the same way. Mind, self, and society are shaped just like any other meaningful object in a fundamental process of symbolic interaction. Society is created and formed in a never-ending process as a web of interlocking actions and reactions, proposals and responses that give rise to new objects and conceptions, new patterns of behaviour, and new types of social intercourse.

Within the conceptual framework of symbolic interactionist sociology, conflictive interaction can be defined by an exchange of significant gestures and symbols that generate feelings of aggression, for instance shaking a fist or announcing the withholding of vital resources or the revocation of a given commitment. There is no automatism of conflict escalation envisaged in pragmatist sociology. Role taking enables the conflict parties to anticipate a possible chain of escalating reactions, and, through anticipation and reflection, enables human actors to consciously interrupt an impending escalation and to resolve a conflict by reconstructing the situation in a novel way. Viewed in this manner, role taking looks like a powerful mechanism for interrupting blindfolded chain reactions and restoring agency to the social group of actors by allowing them to combine conflict prevention with deliberative social change. Thus a pragmatist sociology of symbolic interaction claims to wield a conceptual tool of innovative conflict resolution, where Luhmann's theory of social systems has to step back and wait cap in hand for evolution to occur. Advantage pragmatism? Not quite. The case for overcoming the structural reasons for conflict through collectively redefining and restructuring social life is not as strong as it looks at first sight. It cannot explain stability and robustness because it construes human societies as fragile webs of reciprocal commitments that could collapse at almost any moment.

Indeed, the very fragility of patterns of joint action emerging in a process of permanent behavioural adjustment and readjustment makes it difficult to explain why and how these patterns can be sustained and confirmed, whereas it looks altogether too easy to change them or make them collapse. If symbolic interaction is conceived as a process of permanent readjustment of group life by defining and reinterpreting social norms and shared knowledge, it looks as though it is an unlikely candidate to affirm and maintain established patterns through their continued use. Pattern maintenance seems to require a permanent and exhaustive effort of explicit approval and tiresome reapproval from all members of a social group. People seem to have to say "yes" all the time. Or, as Blumer explicitly points out, group life just does not carry on by itself but depends on recurrent affirmation and agreement. This means, in Luhmann's terminology, that the established patterns of sociality are overintegrated and highly vulnerable to dissent and disagreement. They can be easily undermined or disrupted by changing definitions from others and may easily be brought to collapse. On the other hand, variations in the use of the original schemes of conduct and discontinuities in the use of shared knowledge seem to be acknowledged by symbolic interactionist sociologists as the most normal things to happen. Here, conflict seems to be just one more way among others – though a particularly important one – for the production of discontinuities: "In the flow of group life there are innumerable points at which the participants are redefining each other's acts. Such redefinition is very common in adversary relations, it is frequent in group discussion, and it is essentially intrinsic to dealing with problems" (Blumer, 1966, p. 538).

Blumer's statement comes quite close to what Luhmann writes about the bubbling-up of myriads of minor conflicts at the level of face-to-face interaction. What is different, though, is that Luhmann explicitly states that these minor conflicts usually do not reach the system level of society. Pragmatism, in turn, does not clearly differentiate between interaction and society and is largely unable to explain its self-made mystery why and how a modern society can stand living under the permanent threat of being questioned and renegotiated all the time. Seen from the perspective of pre-modern societies, and particularly from the perspective of segmented societies like tribes and clans, this type of self-questioning communication would indeed be unbearable. Tribal societies are largely interactional societies, which means, according to Luhmann, that the system levels of interaction and society are largely undifferentiated and that every communication is communicated at the interactional and societal level simultaneously. Hence, a conflict in a group of tribesmen sitting around a fire is not as harmless as a conflict among a casual group of friends drinking in a pub as it would pose a direct threat to the foundations of kinship and the continuance of tribal existence. Therefore, along the lines of Luhmann, the immediate suppression of even minor conflicts becomes a matter of sheer survival. In the casual-friends-in-the-pub case, a conflict would usually be a minor event, over and done with the next day because it does not impinge on the job, the family, the church, the school, the government or the economy. It does not even inhibit the return to the pub the next evening because, even in a worst case scenario when the conflict is still fresh, there are still other pubs and other friends.

Another controversial point has to do with the conceptual distinction between explicit and implicit conflicts . According to Luhmann's theory of autopoietic social systems, a "no" which remains unspoken or a fist that is secretly shaken in the pocket is not a conflict. A contradiction which is not explicitly communicated as a contradiction but remains inside a human being as a pure mental state, as an unarticulated frustration, or a tacit objection, cannot be acknowledged as a conflict unless a distinction between manifest or external and latent or implicit conflicts is introduced and conceived of as being useful.[11] The pragmatist sociology of symbolic interaction considers this to be a very useful distinction indeed, and one quite in line with Mead's idea of internalisation (Mead, 1934, p. 307). The distinction between internal or latent and external or manifest conflicts is conceptually implied in the sociology of symbolic interaction because the mechanism of role taking is based on the interplay between internal and external behaviour. Taking the role of the other means interiorising or internalising the other actors' normative expectations and impulsive intentions in a process of reciprocal socialisation and developing what sociologists like Habermas or Joas call "intersubjectivity": the capability to anticipate another actor's reactions to one's own actions – as in the case of Antigone's intrapersonal conflict which is, of course, a social

[11] Again there is a parallel in DAI literature: Impressed by Gasser's critique (Gasser, 1991), Hewitt was too hasty in abandoning the interesting distinction he had made between "trials of strength" and "conflicts" which comes quite close to Luhmann's distinction between plain contradiction and conflict as a communicated contradiction: "Sometimes a trial of strength occurs without manifest conflict. One participant says 'Let's do it this way', and everybody agrees, so no conflict is noticed, but there is always the potential for conflict" (Hewitt, 1991, p. 91).

and an interpersonal conflict.[12] At this point it is possible to build a bridge between internal and external conflicts. A human being, or in Mead's terminology a social "self", is able to anticipate and balance the risks and outcomes of a conflict by an inner dialog between the "I", representing an individual's spontaneity and impulsiveness, and the "Me", representing the expectations and normative demands of the "generalised other" or the society. Thus, external or manifest conflicts are but the tip of the iceberg of latent or tacit conflicts most of which are below the surface of observable social interactions and it would certainly be fascinating to know more about the circumstances of why and when conflicts are switched from the internal to the external level and back again.

Is introspection via intersubjectivity to be regarded as a legitimate empirical method? Social systems theory does not believe in building a bridge between internal and external conflicts – except by what Luhmann calls "structural coupling" – not just because such a theoretical move would blur the distinction between sociology and psychology, but because it confuses conflicts with conflict reasons and opens a Pandora's box of speculation on the observability of unobservable conflicts. If there is no conflict visible, is this due to conflict suppression, because people do not dare to express their hostility and frustration or is the absence of conflict to be explained by an invisible consensus based on common values and norms? Or does the internal/external distinction help to explain why and when a society allows a conflict to develop into a full-blown conflict system? These are the sceptical questions that must be raised from the perspective of a theory of social systems. In spite of his conceptual scepticism regarding social theories of action, Luhmann does not hesitate to draw heavily on an implicit notion of the intersubjective capabilities of human actors which comes quite close to a Meadian concept of taking the role of the other. This is obvious in Luhmann's account of open decision-making processes where conflicts are handled not by the process of communication as such, but by empirical participants who are able to intelligently adjust their individual contributions and responses to each other by anticipating the others' possible reactions. When it comes to the point when an influential group member has given his or her definitive commitment to the case in question, the others will be cautiously weighing their chances for overt opposition. And, as in the case of the tribesmen sitting around the fire, they will choose their words very carefully, before daring to express disagreement, because they know "by introspection" or by "taking the role of the other" that this might provoke a destructive conflict.

[12] DAI distinguishes between inter-agent (social) and intra-agent (mental) conflicts (see (Castelfranchi, 2000, Wagner et al., 1999).

4.2 CONFLICT APPEARS WHERE ROUTINE COORDINATION BREAKS DOWN

In a pragmatist sociology of symbolic interaction, social change and innovation is based on nothing more than human beings defining and reinterpreting each other's acts. Reinterpretations and redefinitions, be they of minor or major scope, are intimately linked to conflict resolution, or, as Blumer explicitly states, to adversarial relationships. More generally speaking, however, Blumer's point is that all social situations are ambiguous to some extent and that redefinitions are nothing particularly exceptional or peculiar. Redefinitions are mass phenomena that occur in all different kinds of everyday situations that must be distinguished from problematic situations which are quite exceptional events. Whenever the continuous flow of routine action is seriously inhibited, people start to rethink their situation and, after having found out that restoring the status quo ante is out of reach and not just a matter of minor repair, they tackle the situation by trying to find an innovative solution. In pragmatist sociology, finding a new way out of a problematic situation is considered a creative act of problem-solving that, after the new solution has been successfully proven, leads to a new routine and allows action to flow continuously again.

The concept of creative action is a core tenet of a pragmatist theory of social change (Joas, 1992). Creative action marks the turning point within a process of change that transforms an established pattern of individual or joint conduct into a new one. Charles S. Peirce, the founding father of pragmatist philosophy, was the first to elaborate the idea that knowledge and action are deeply intertwined and that the notion of objective knowledge or belief apart from human behaviour is false.[13] In his view, the objective world of facts is a Cartesian illusion because it is based on the epistemological separation of subject and object, of a material world separated from an extra-mundane mind. Descartes' separation is an untenable misconception because the world cannot be construed at all unless it is construed as our world, a world for us, constructed by real human beings whose cognitive actions are inseparably interwoven with their practical actions (Peirce, 1991b). And this interwovenness explains how "objective" knowledge is possible and why it changes as the relationship between action and world changes. Peirce's formula for knowledge transformation is "belief - doubt - belief".

In rejecting Descartes' tenet of "radical doubt" as a fallacious abstraction from the empirical roots of practical problem solving in a real world, Peirce

[13]That knowledge and action are irreducibly intertwined is one of the fundamental assumptions of pragmatist sociology adopted by bottom-up or behaviour-based approaches to AI which speak of "situated agents" (Maes, 1990b, Steels and Brooks, 1994). It should be noted that this view is incompatible with another distinction which has become popular in DAI, namely between epistemic or belief conflicts and intentional or goal conflicts (Garagnani et al., 1998, Maudet and Evrard, 1998, Galliers, 1990).

claimed that belief and doubt cannot exist apart from the reality of practical action. Hence, "radical doubt" must be replaced by "real doubt". It is a fact of life that people normally do not doubt their beliefs unless they have a practical reason for doingso. As long as everything runs smoothly they stick to their practical beliefs and generally they are not even aware that they "believe" in something. Whenever people begin to doubt, however, they have a very practical reason to do so – the experience of a dissonance, for instance, or a difficulty arising in the course of action. But they do not experience doubt in a situation of smooth flowing, uninhibited routine action. Real doubt begins to make itself felt when well proven and hitherto unquestioned patterns of action and knowledge unexpectedly break down in the face of an obstinate reality. This is the moment when, in Peirce's terms, belief abruptly changes into doubt. At the outset doubt is experienced as a state of disorientation and despair which later passes over to a state of creative problem solving. Solving a problem means analysing the reasons that have caused the breakdown of a routine and rearranging the entire course of action, including its goals and means, in a thoroughly novel way. After the new solution has passed the reality test and turns out to be successful, it will be established as a new pattern of action and will eventually be accepted as an unquestioned belief. And it will remain unquestioned until a new problem arises.[14]

Mead's concept of symbolic interaction differs from Peirce's formula "belief - doubt - belief" inasmuch as it is both more general and more sociological. More sociological, since Peirce, although he emphasised that "logic is rooted in the social principle" (Peirce, 1991a, p. 218) and referred to the scientific community as its paradigmatic case, conceived both cognitive and practical action as individual exercises.[15] And more general, since Mead treated reasoning as a special case of symbolic interaction, among many others. Mead, too, believed that "reasoning conduct appears where impulsive conduct breaks down"

[14]Gasser introduced the pragmatist model of Peirce and Dewey into DAI research in terms of settled and unsettled issues: "... internalised conventions are the outcome of previously 'solved problems' or 'settled questions' that have been codified into routines. Conventions and routines are built in this way by repeated negotiation and problem solving ... settled issues ... can be taken for granted and for further reasoning. However it is important to remember that a settled question – in this case the solution to a coordination or control problem – may have to be unsettled in a new situation; the problem may have to be re-solved in a new way for the new situation. In Dewey's terms, certain tentative positions or reasoning perspectives of the agent will have to be given a 'loan of certainty' so that the agent has a ground of belief on which to stand for the purpose of taking action" (Gasser et al., 1989, p. 57). However, some of the most important "certainties", e.g. agent roles and communication structure, are designed into the multiagent architecture and cannot be revised by the agents. It would be interesting to explore how an agent community could be endowed with capabilities not only of distributed reasoning about organisations but of collectively changing or restructuring it.

[15]The difference should not be overestimated, though, since Mead like Peirce was convinced that problems can only appear in the experiences of the individual. In Campbell's words: "Unless individuals are able to bring to social consciousness anticipated ills, we will never be able to respond to them. This involves listening to the reports of individuals" (Campbell, 1981, p. 197).

(Mead, 1934, p. 348), in other words, that a human being who experiences a critical situation of inhibited action is shocked from the usual prevalent attitude of immediate experience to a more exceptional attitude of reflexive analysis. Facing a situation of maladjustment, human beings feel extremely insecure before they seek to adapt themselves to the new circumstances by conscious intellectual reconstruction. According to Mead, this is but a special case in a more general conception where two human beings, alter and ego, produce meaning by reciprocally defining and interpreting each other's actions. But what has caused the routine conduct of symbolic interaction to collapse in the first place is, of course, nothing else but a conflict among individuals. Hence, the sociological term for Peirce's doubt is conflict: I do not believe what you do believe. And thus "belief - doubt - belief" can be translated into the formula "cooperation - conflict - cooperation".

In the main meaning is changed and adapted in exactly the same way as it is originally constituted and there is nothing particularly shocking about that. In everyday communication, an "ego" usually does not conceive an "alter's" interpreting reaction to his own defining action as extremely irritating or at the point of a serious inhibition, even if the reaction unexpectedly redefines and changes the social situation. According to Blumer openness and change is just the normal way of producing and reproducing any socially defined situation. And as all situations, objects and realities are defined or constructed socially, this goes hand in hand with people acting in a continuum of attitudes shifting between immediate experience and reflexive analysis, sliding from conscious to unconscious, from unreflexive to reflexive attitudes. Thus, symbolic interactionist sociology envisages a continuum of social change instead of a discontinuum between little readjustments at the interaction level and deep transformations at the level of society.

What makes Peirce's epistemological formula different from Blumer's view, then, is the idea that changing a shared belief or an established body of knowledge is an experience of abrupt discontinuity. Experiencing doubt as a shocking event implies that the continuous flow of impulsive (inter)action must have been previously channelled into a solid state or pattern of routine action or an unquestioned normative social structure. Indeed, a belief is acknowledged as a belief only to the extent that it has the quality of consolidated trustworthiness, of some kind of structural unchangeability. And this is the point where a powerful sociological conception of "doubt", now conflict, can be introduced. Although sociologists of symbolic interaction like Blumer refrain from construing society as a rigidly objectified pattern of shared values, norms, and convictions which, as in social systems theory, cannot easily be bent to and by the will of individual or collective actors, they clearly dispose of a concept of normative social structure: the "generalised other". This concept allows us to respecify Peirce's original formula in sociological terms of conflict: Alter's redefining reaction to ego's action may trigger a conflict if it is experienced as a shocking violation of ego's expectation and if ego's spontaneous readjustment is seriously inhibited. Moreover, conflict in a sociological sense is characterised by an inhibition or a blockade of ego's spontaneous adjustment which is not simply given by alter's refusal, but by a particularly unexpected and unacceptable refusal that must be interpreted as a refusal of the generalised other, i.e. as an offence against the cultural and normative foundation framing ego's and alter's situational interaction. What is at stake here is not ego's more or less idiosyncratic "expectation" in the sense of a disappointed wishful hope or desire, as in the case of loosing a fair competition. What is at stake are the very foundations of sociality, as in the case of loosing a competition not because of defeat in fair play but because of fraud and deception.[16]

The distinction between a conflict in the sense of a "problematic" encounter with another person, i.e. a rule-breaking reinterpretation of an expectation on one hand, and an almost unnoticed everyday adjustment of a normative pattern on the other, paves the way for specifying the impact of conflict for a theory of social transformation. A problem arises from the shocking experience of a continuous flow of action being exacerbated and disrupted by an unexpected obstacle, but a conflict must be defined as a problematic event caused by a very specific obstacle, namely the unexpected action or reaction of another human being. However, this alone is not sufficient to define conflict. Since people often act and react in an unpredictable and unexpected manner, usually without provoking any serious irritation – since unpredictability is normally expected in everyday human interaction too – conflict must further be specified as a reaction that trespasses against a normative expectation. Again, as long as rule-breaking behaviour is limited to minor incidents and harmless exceptions that rather confirm the rules of, for instance, a competitive game like football, or, in other words, as long as ego is not seriously inhibited or shocked by alter's unexpected reaction, there is no conflict impending.

A conflict begins to escalate when alter's rule-breaking actions can no longer be interpreted by ego as casual or exceptional incidents, even under idealistic assumptions of benevolence, but must be seen as deliberative and harmful violations of a normative pattern of action to ego's disadvantage. In the course of a conflict, both parties, at first, will be claiming to act in accordance with the established patterns of action, i.e. with the normative basis of social behaviour. Sooner or later, however, a conflict will escalate and bring the normative basis itself into question. This is the case when ego begins to reinterpret alter's

---

[16]Of course, the former case may trigger a conflict too, when the looser of a fair competition feels too disappointed or humiliated to accept her or his defeat and starts to play foul, although she was not taken by surprise since loosing was part of the expectation. In that case, however, it is the looser who is provoking a conflict with his unexpected reaction.

actions as a definitive departure from the shared normative foundation which both alter and ego, and all other members of a social group, have so far been committed to. More than ego's frustration at being inhibited by alter in the attainment of a goal or satisfaction of a personal desire, more than ego's moral disappointment that alter has played unfair or broken a promise, is the discovery that, because alter has definitely departed from the shared normative basis, the basis itself is shattered and cannot be trusted any longer. Taking the role of the other, here, precisely means that ego can no longer believe in the trustworthiness of an established and well-proven pattern of interaction, once she or he has realised that alter has already stopped believing in the generalised other.

The crucial point in a conflict process is reached when both parties realise that the foundation of binding norms and shared values that has hitherto structured their relationship is on the verge of collapse. This is the reason why conflict parties are overcome by a feeling of deep insecurity far beyond their situational frustration at being inhibited in attaining a certain goal. Conflict, then, highlights the strategic importance of doubtful or problematic situations for a pragmatist theory of social change. As the grand old men of classicist pragmatism, Peirce, Mead and Dewey, repeatedly emphasised, the touchstone of inhibited action is the shock, the immediate experience that the inhibition can neither be removed nor by-passed nor ignored which goes hand in hand with panic-stricken feelings of doubt and despair. In the case of a conflict, this could be the devastating experience that all other participants who frame or contextualise ego's and alter's situational setting – and particularly those who, like the referee, somehow act on behalf or in the name of the generalised other – begin to reinterpret and reorganise their actions according to the logic of conflict. This can be illustrated with the fiction of a football player who, in a Kafkaesque reinterpretation of Mead's paradigm of a game, has been fouled by another player only to be told by the referee that his protest is out of order because the rules have just been changed. Or, to take a more realistic example, it is the experience of someone threatened by the Mafia who turns to the police for help only to find that they are in league with the very gangsters gunning for him.

This is the moment when the conflict parties will be aware of walking on very thin ice. The sociological insight that unquestioned norms cannot be trusted unless they are permanently reconfirmed is revealed as an insight of everyday knowledge which appears when the official representatives of the generalised other no longer acknowledge and approve the established patterns of normative action. At this point first-order conflicts about rule-breaking behaviour can turn into second-order conflicts about the appropriateness of an underlying social rule. However, Mead's idea of the generalised other is not organised as a static construction but rather as a dynamic web of reciprocal commitments. Usually, in case of a conflict there are always some others who still can be trusted, there are other committed players and referees who act according to the rules of the game, other police officers, attorneys, and judges who still respect the law. And even the criminal who consciously breaks the law is contributing to its reproduction, so long as crime remains the exception: A criminal act reconfirms the foundation of shared values not only by provoking retaliation by the police, but by the very fact that the offender must first know the law before she is successfully able to break it. The example of the police officer and the criminal shows that conflict interaction is based on a layer of shared knowledge below the contested terrain of rule-breaking behaviour. Since it is not possible to outwit an opponent and to win a conflict without taking the role of the other, both conflict parties, the law breaker and the law restorer, must share the same norms and values and must know what is right and wrong. Hence, both parties share the knowledge of what it means to break a law. What they do not share, however, is the moral conviction that it is wrong to do the wrong thing (Haferkamp, 1985, p. 179).

5. CONFLICT AND SOCIAL CHANGE

5.1 CONFLICT NEGOTIATION AS INQUIRY INTO INQUIRY

The interesting question, now, is not how to resolve a conflict in the case of unambiguous criminal behaviour and how to restore social order by coercing the maverick back onto the right track. The point in question now concerns conflicts between parties who both claim to be right in the face of a value conflict and are unable or unwilling to resolve their disagreement by violence. What will happen if a value conflict cannot be resolved by coercion or violence because such measures are prohibited by a superior third party or because the conflict parties are equally powerful and shun the risks of open violence with its concomitant risks of moral and material self-destruction? The answer is that nothing will happen. Instead, both conflict parties will experience the famous pragmatist shock of inhibited action. And as long as nothing happens, there will be an undeclared moratorium or a kind of tacit armistice which, after it has been unofficially respected for a while, may begin to crystallise into shared knowledge with gradually growing normative implications. However, so long as the parties are far from accepting the status quo and so long as conflict is still imminent, the shock of inhibition will pass over into what pragmatists call the attitude of reasoning or reflexion. Reasoning and reflexion may begin with cautiously taking the bite out of the conflict by declaring a unilateral armistice and by taking other one-sided measures of de-escalation. And they will gain momentum when both parties agree on a bilateral or collective exchange of arguments. Such a collective process of conflict reasoning is called a negotiation. While unilateral, individual conflict reasoning alone usually tends to produce avoidance behaviour and conflict latency by encapsulating and by-passing the conflict, negotiations as a multilateral or collective form of conflict reasoning have the potential for restructuring the situation in such a way as to resolve the conflict by creating novel forms of social order.

Negotiation is a collective process of consciously restructuring a conflictive situation, and its outcome is a "negotiated order" (Strauss, 1978).[17] Its formula is "order - conflict - negotiation - order". Once the new order has been established, the way in which the conflict has been successfully resolved is not forgotten but stored in the memory of a society's accumulated wisdom. Whenever a similar conflict reoccurs, the successful mode of earlier conflict resolution will be drawn on again, and, via case-based reasoning and repeated use, will be gradually transformed into an established pattern of conflict negotiation. Any negotiated order, therefore, is endowed with its own complementary institutions of negotiation. From now on, order does not follow conflict alone but conflict follows order, too. The new order of negotiation consists of its own regulations and methods and is specifically institutionalised as a "social inquiry" (Dewey, 1991) to settle the conflicts from where its own institutionalisation originates. Thus, conflict settlement becomes a routine. As this happens a remarkable shift in the meaning of conflict takes place. The conflict looses its original shocking quality and no longer functions as a crisis-trigger. People just remember how they have learned to resolve it collectively. In this way, through accumulated learning, conflict is turned into regular competition, and "struggle" becomes an expected, legitimate form of behaviour. Of course, this is only true to the extent that opponents adhere to the new rules of conflict negotiation. Creating order from conflict via negotiation is, by and large, no longer an excursion into unknown territory, but has been turned into a meta-routine that effaces the disturbing ambiguity of conflicts and conflict negotiations.

Transformed into a negotiated order of negotiation, the origins of negotiation in conflict are no longer visible, and conflict negotiations appear to be plain negotiations, devoid of hostile impulses and ill-feelings. This may be the reason why the protagonists of the negotiated order approach do not explicitly discuss the connection between conflict and negotiation. They speak rather vaguely instead of "ambiguities" that "require negotiation, either explicit or

[17] According to Strauss, negotiation is not only conflict negotiation. Strauss distinguishes between three aspects or levels of negotiation: the types of interaction, the immediate context of negotiation, and the structural context. Hence, although negotiations usually influence the immediate or situational context, they may even have an impact on the higher level and can be measured in changes in structural contexts (Maines, 1982, p. 270). However, negotiations do not determine the context; rather, the lines of influence can go both ways (Strauss, 1978, p. 101). This means that it is also the context which influences the course of negotiations. The relevant features of the immediate negotiation context enter into the process of negotiations directly and affect its course in a more direct way, whereas the larger structural context constrains and conditions the course of negotiations in a more indirect way.

implicit" (Maines, 1982, p. 269). Seen this way, a scientific dispute within the conventions of civilised discourse cannot be conceived as a conflict, but rather should be seen as a normal collaborative search for truth among people who share the same values and follow the same goals. What makes it so difficult for those who adhere to the sociology of symbolic interaction to perceive the original conflict as having been domesticated by, and incorporated into, a regulation is Mead's fundamental anthropological distinction between friendly or cooperative impulses and hostile or conflictive impulses. This is not to say that Mead ignores or excludes phenomena like argument, dispute, or disagreement from his agenda. On the contrary, he vividly argues for the individual right of disagreement and even claims, as though he were personally sharing Antigone's burden, that an individual should not be punished for disagreeing with the majority, as long as she is acting in full accordance with her own moral judgement (Campbell, 1981, p. 199). Mead is able to make such a claim because he does not believe in fundamental value conflicts but in an ever growing, all encompassing moral order of universal values. However, Mead's moral justification of disagreement would not really make sense unless he expected such disagreements to continue in the future and, as Campbell remarks, they will certainly continue, simply because "different evaluations of human goods are related, not to factual disputes, but to different positions on the nature of a good human life" (Campbell, 1981, p. 199).

Again, it is obvious that Luhmann was absolutely right to criticise the lack of an elaborated sociological conflict terminology. The lack of clarity in the sociology of symbolic interaction makes it difficult to understand how underlying conflict reasons like "hostile impulses" and "different value positions" are related to visible conflict symptoms like "factual disputes" and "negotiations", and whether a disagreement should be called a conflict as long as it is a legitimate form of behaviour regulated by an order of negotiation. In any case, Campbell feels encouraged by Mead and Strauss to abandon hope for ultimate solutions and to adopt an approach of "continual readjustment" (Campbell, 1981, p. 197) in order to anticipate value conflicts and to preclude their most damaging consequences. What he suggests is the creation of a kind of early warning system endowed with flexible modes of response that seeks out and resolves problems and conflicts "before they come upon us full-blown ..." (Campbell, 1981, p. 197). In his philosophical terminology, John Dewey calls such an early warning system an inquiry. "Inquiry is the controlled or directed transformation of an indeterminate situation into one that is so determinate in its constituent distinctions and relations as to convert the elements of the original situation into a unified whole" (Dewey, 1991, p. 108). Translated into contemporary sociological terms, Dewey is imagining a "nonindividualistic society, based on cooperative, experimental intelligence" (Denzin, 1996, p. 66) which voluntarily institutionalises public processes of conflict negotiation.

According to Dewey's pragmatist social philosophy, history is made by conscious human beings who, under given conditions of pragmatic interaction, produce what he calls "potentialities" by actively mediating between possibility and reality – a conception which seems to come quite close to Luhmann's definition of meaning as the difference between actuality and potentiality. Working on the same lines as Peirce's problematic-situation approach, Dewey developed the idea that mankind's historical progress in democracy, science and technology is based on a cooperative process of goal-oriented and self-correcting inquiry. Inquiry is a kind of practical inference and its settled outcome is called a judgement. Dewey's theory of inquiry is explicitly modelled on the procedural principles of "due process" or a fair and prompt trial: "A literal instance of judgement ... is provided by the judgement of a court of law in settling some issue which, up to that point, has been in controversy. The occurrence of a trial-at-law is equivalent to the occurrence of a problematic situation which requires settlement. (...) This settlement or judgement is the outcome of inquiry conducted in the court-hearings" (Dewey, 1991, p. 123). However, inquiry and judgement are more than a first-order mode of conflict settlement constructed on the blue print of a democratic court of law and its trial regulations. The crucial difference here is that Dewey's idea of continually readjusting a democratic society does not stop short when it comes to improving democratic institutions, the very modes of a society's cooperative and explorative intelligence. Inquiry is essentially self-adjusting. It is inquiry into inquiry.

In order to understand why Dewey calls an inquiry a controlled or directed transformation, it is necessary to take the institutional model of a court of law seriously but not literally. Inquiry as a highly generalised model of a creative decision-making process is abstracted from both jurisdiction and legislation, and enriched with elements from scientific discourse. Inquiry does not mean solving standard disputes by standard jurisdiction, but producing "legislation" by creatively resolving unprecedented conflicts, quite in the Anglo-American judicial tradition of a precedent. It is the model of a democratic process of collectively analysing and negotiating a controversy and transforming it – as well as the institutions of negotiation in cases of second-order conflicts – into a novel solution that can be reactivated as a precedent for the future resolution of similar conflicts. Dewey envisages four or five stages in a cyclical process of inquiry beginning with a conflict of an exceptional quality and ending with a practically proven judgement. Unless the initial conflict does not immediately end in a catastrophe,[18] the stage of inhibition is followed by an attitude of de-

[18]Hence, any inquiry presupposes that social life is just partially, but not totally, collapsing in the face of a conflict. Apart from the broken routine there must be a large amount of other routines and other resources available which are not affected by the crisis and which allow normal social life to be continued outside

tached reasoning and the attempt to delineate the conflictive constellation by arranging what Dewey calls a "logical division of labour". All aspects which might be conducive to a solution are identified and decomposed, propositions and hypotheses are generated and debated in expert hearings, further empirical evidence is collected, and experimental settings are explored and tested until "functional fitness" between a conflict and its resolution is reached. Indeed, inquiry is largely described as a scientific method, but as a rational method whose rationality is rooted in practical action: "functional fitness", by definition, cannot exist apart from those individuals who have the problem. It is a non-starter unless accepted and confirmed as a shared judgement by those who are practically involved. Judgement[19], thus, is the operational link between expert cultures and common sense, and inquiry is the mode of reflexive mediation that allows a society to change the way in which the link is institutionalised and justified in accordance with democratic progress and human rights. Indeed, Dewey's "defence against the rise of totalitarian states always returned to the level of the individual. It was up to cooperating individuals to create voluntarily institutions that would protect their most vital liberties" (Denzin, 1996, p. 67).

5.2 COMPETING EXPLANATIONS: INQUIRY VERSUS EVOLUTION

In contrast to the proponents of American pragmatism, Luhmann neither believes in voluntary democratic reforms, planned change, nor in establishing a direct operational link between expert cultures and common sense via inquiry and judgement. In his eyes, concepts like inquiry and judgement must appear to be heavily overburdened with the onus of having to operate both ways: as an institution of routine negotiations on one hand and as a creative procedure of planned self-modification of routine negotiations on the other. Unlike pragmatist sociologists of symbolic interaction and their philosophical ancestors, he is firmly convinced that social change is a matter of evolution or unplanned self-adjustment. Conflicts play a double role in Luhmann's evolutionary conception. They are enabled by functional differentiation and they enable functional differentiation. To begin with, specialised conflict communication is the outcome of evolutionary differentiation. Conflicts become more visible and more tractable – and more harmless. They are more harmless because they

the realm of inhibited action. Moreover, these routines and resources will be badly needed to fuel the resource-intensive process of inquiry.

[19] "Judgement may be identified as the settled outcome of inquiry. It is concerned with the concluding objects that emerge from inquiry and their status of being conclusive. Judgement in this sense is distinguished from propositions. The content of the latter is intermediate and representative and is carried by symbols; while judgement, as finally made, has direct existential import" (Dewey, 1991, p. 123).

are encapsulated within the closed worlds of expert cultures and, according to Luhmann, it is neither possible nor desirable to bring expert cultures in direct touch with, or translate them into, common sense judgements and democratic progress.

Luhmann's conceptual equivalent to the pragmatist formula of inquiry is evolutionary change. As has been shown earlier in section 3, social life is packed full of conflict communications with their heady brew of deviance, coercion, and persuasion all of which are adept at producing masses of new variations of surplus "semantic material", which mostly vanishes soon after it has been communicated. Far from being confirmed and stabilised by acceptance and repetition, most conflicts are hardly ever noticed and disappear without trace Some of these variations, however, happen to have been selected and reconfirmed in a largely unintentional, unplanned process of contingent social exchange – and afterwards, in the rear-view mirror of historical hindsight, this looks curiously like a progress in system differentiation. Social change is an evolutionary process, quite in Darwin's sense, that follows the three stages of variation, selection and restabilisation. It cannot be conceived of as a conscious, planned change since communicating a new or an unexpected proposal (variation) is systematically disconnected from being either accepted or refused (selection) and from being transformed into structures or institutions by perpetual repetition (restabilisation). Conflict tolerance is like the invention of writing, an evolutionary achievement which helps accelerate and propel the evolutionary process. Conflicts allow us to test the potential for rejection (Luhmann, 1997, p. 466) and this helps to strengthen the immune system of a society and its self-adaptation. Thus, conflicts propel the evolutionary process of differentiation on the one hand, while, on the other, they are reinforced and stabilised by functional subsystems.

Within the theoretical framework of autopoietic social systems it is easy to show how subsystems immunise and reproduce themselves with the help of domesticated conflicts. However, it is difficult to demonstrate how further advances in social differentiation might occur via conflict systems by thoroughly restructuring a subsystem's mode of reproduction. But the truly difficult thing to explain is how conflicts contribute to the transformation of the structural foundations of a given mode of subsystemic autopoiesis. If these cannot be fundamentally restructured by conscious reasoning or by collective decision, but solely by evolution, then how is it possible that an old subsystem gives birth to a new one? Luhmann's theory can demonstrate how the modus operandi of conflict regulation in a social subsystem like the scientific community produces and generalises cognitive knowledge. What is difficult to explain, however, is how the modus operandi of conflict negotiation in the scientific subsystem was originally generated, and, turning from retrospection to prospection, to what extent it will be able to transform itself into more differentiated subsystems in the future. According to Luhmann, it is quite clear that as long as a specialised type of conflict is bound by the regulations of an existing subsystem like the scientific community, it is prevented from both entropic expiration and cancerous escalation. As a result of scientific conflict communication, an ever growing body of knowledge is being accumulated, perpetually refined, reworked, and revolutionised. But how do conflicts account for generating a qualitative differentiation between, say, the code of religious truth and the code of scientific truth in the era of enlightenment? Or, in trying to anticipate future developments, how is it possible that new modes of autopoietic reproduction will be generated from old ones?

Retranslated into the pragmatist terminology of negotiated order, it seems as though scientific conflicts within the scientific subsystem tend to reproduce the same old procedural rituals or modes of inquiry again and again during the creation of innovative knowledge, and while the system's stock of knowledge is rapidly changing it seems as though the system's structural order of negotiation always remains the same. In other words, scientific controversies are revolutionary only with regard to cognitive content, but appear blatantly conservative with regard to the subsystem's order of negotiation. They seem to lack the potential for second-order conflicts characterised by the fundamental challenge they pose to a given mode of conflict regulations. The question whether a subsystem is able to change its own structural regulations – or its own order of negotiation – by means of internal conflict communication or whether it can only be interrupted and modified from outside or from above (Luhmann, 1984, p. 532) remains essentially unanswered. Perhaps an answer could be sought in Luhmann's historical reconstructions of evolutionary change, for instance in his analysis of the semantics of passionate love in French literature (Luhmann, 1982) or in the transformation of the concept of truth from a medieval religious category into a modern scientific category. What we might find there, however, will not resemble a social order negotiated by participant actors. Rather we should brace ourselves to find interesting changes in areas where those who brought them about would least have expected them. Unlike the sociologists of symbolic interaction, Luhmann would never recommend following social actors to find out what really happens in a society. He would recommend excavating a society's semantic material instead.

However, pragmatists have no reason to be self-righteous. Dewey's scenario of inquiry, where conflict parties, judges, attorneys, lawyers, witnesses and experts sit around a table elbow to elbow with democratic common sense, in order to purposely organise a unique procedural structure or a "logical division of labour" for conflict resolution, also stops short when it comes to inquiring into its own procedural foundations. In our view, inquiry into inquiry is a misleading label as long as the underlying structures of inquiry remain untouched throughout the process of inquiry. The crucial point here is that, apart from certain cosmetic modifications, questioning the foundations of inquiry is not provided for by pragmatist theories of inquiry and negotiation. There is no provision for an aggressive rule-breaking inquiry into the institutionalised setting of the court of law itself with all its roles and regulations. In contrast to Hewitt's conclusion, Dewey does not seem to have seriously considered that "negotiating conflict can bring the negotiating process itself into question" (Hewitt, 1986, p. 323) in a radically obstructive way. Instead, pragmatists seem to reify the theoretical concept of inquiry with existing institutions that must be respected by everybody – conflict parties, judges, attorneys, lawyers, witnesses and experts alike. Pragmatists seem to assume that playing with regulations by inviting unexpected new witnesses, calling for other experts with different expertise, or even by exchanging a biased judge for an impartial one is self-reflexive inquiry. But this leaves the institutional structures themselves untouched. Luhmann, who in any case does not believe in inquiry into inquiry, would probably argue that it is impossible to question social structures by practical inquiry because structural change is not a short-term achievement but a long-term accumulation of minor events – of masses of conflict events which usually will not even be recognised as crucial symptoms of a fundamental change before the new structure has been established and consolidated.

As we do not have to believe in the existence[20] of autopoiesis either, we should try to exploit Luhmann's approach as a heuristic way of referencing conflicts from different subsystemic perspectives. We should begin to observe how conflicts migrate across the boundaries of subsystemic domestication and become cancerous. From here, ecological conflicts or social movements can be construed as symptoms of structural or tectonic tensions which fall betwixt and between the established codes of subsystemic conflict communication (Luhmann, 1986). These conflicts have no choice. They must become "cancerous" in order to produce resonance and amplification. Evolution begins with masses of tiny conflicts bubbling up at the level of social interaction. Some of these will be recruited by larger systems which are endowed with powerful amplifiers, the mass media, for instance. The interesting question here is cross-boundary conflict recruitment or conflict migration. How is it possible for conflicts to be recruited across the established boundaries of subsystems? Is it possible that a "no" which is communicated in a particular subsystem language may contain a sort of information which is useful – for whatever reasons – for some other subsystem? If so, then it might have a chance to be recruited as

[20]Strictly speaking, autopoiesis is not an "ontological" category. Relative to Luhmann's theory architecture, however, autopoiesis shares a quasi-ontological status with other terms like communication, differentiation and system. Luhmann's "ontology" assumes that "systems exist" (Luhmann, 1984, p. 30). Things that "exist" can be distinguished in his theory from more "constructivist" categories like action, intention, observation, perception etc. ascribed by the sociological observer.

a starting point for structural differentiation. When a conflict communication is rejected by one subsystem but accepted as a useful contribution by another one, it has already won a natural ally. Thus it could be stabilised and strengthened and eventually remigrate into its originating subsystem to induce structural change there by enforcing a new mode of differentiation within the subsystem in question. To elaborate on the idea of differentiation by cross-boundary conflict migration, however, would imply a departure from the essentially negative connotations of Luhmann's cancer theory of conflict.

6. CONCLUSION: IMPORTING SOCIOLOGICAL INSIGHTS INTO DAI

Importing conflict theories from sociology into DAI opens new opportunities for both disciplines. Viewing conflict as rule-breaking behaviour in a sociological sense and defining it – with Luhmann – as a double "no" or a communicated rejection of a rejected expectation, appears to be a promising point of departure for future collaborative work. Moreover, viewing conflict as conflict communication allows us to construe intrapersonal conflicts as internalised interpersonal conflicts or – with Mead – as inner dialogues between "I" and "me". But more questions have emerged which need further investigation. How can a conflict be conceived as a rule-breaking behaviour when it has been domesticated by social institutions and negotiation procedures? How can a conflict be experienced as a shocking event or a deep crisis of inhibited coordination if it is just a competitive game? How are conflicts interrelated with structural social change along the lines of the pragmatist formula "coordination - conflict - coordination", and how is it possible to translate this formula into a useful design for multiagent systems? To understand and answer these questions is of importance for both sociology and DAI. Developing multiagent systems that are able to effectively and efficiently handle conflict and coordination as twin concepts signals a departure from the myopic assumption that coordination mechanisms can be designed to perfection. Rather it would be more adequate to build computational systems under the premise that states of coordination and conflict continuously alternate – no matter what coordination mechanisms are applied. Along these lines we can identify six research topics that would repay future collaborative work.

(1) *Conceptual clarifications*

As shown in the introductory sections, there is a broad variety in the ways the term "conflict" is used in DAI. The sociological theories treated in this chapter provide two interesting starting points for more precise definitions of this term. First, by following the theory of autopoietic social systems, a computational conflict could be defined in terms of a communicated contradiction, that is, as an agent's communicated rejection of another agent's communicated rejection. Second, by following the pragmatist theories of symbolic interaction, a conflict could be defined as a rule-breaking action that contradicts shared values and harmfully violates the expectations of other agents to such an extent that it is experienced as a shock. Both definitions offer a perspective that goes far beyond a friendly rejection of a proposal within a shared framework of coordination, and beyond a casual exchange of different views on how to use joint resources and how to treat detected (or perhaps even undetected) inconsistencies in the knowledge bases of agents. To make these ideas computationally tractable raises a number of interesting research questions for DAI. What forms of explicit rejection are possible in multiagent systems, given the agents' communication facilities? Does rejection always require an exclusive and definite "no", or would it make sense for computational agents to also interpret a conditioned "no" (i.e., a "no, under this or that circumstances") as a communicated rejection? Similarly, would it make sense to adopt a more relaxed, extended form of Luhmann's definition by also considering an implicit rejection (i.e., a rejecting by not saying "yes") as a sufficient condition for the existence of a conflict? How can agents decide whether an expectation is in accordance with established norms or whether an action violates some normative expectation? Can this kind of accordance be measured in absolute terms or is some relative metrics more appropriate? Does this decision require a neutral and commonly accepted third-party instance as a mediator? Should the violation of norms be treated in an absolute yes-or-no style, or would it be more appropriate to introduce some relative measure that allows differentiation between levels of violation?

(2) *Levels of conflict and conflict tolerance*

The sociological considerations in the previous sections show that it is problematic to think of conflict as a phenomenon that either is available with maximum impact or is not existent at all. Instead, it seems to be justified to think about conflict as a phenomenon that can show different levels of intensity – maturity, urgency, and implication. Moreover, conflict cannot be expressed and measured in absolute terms because it is recursively related to a structural social context – in DAI terms: a multiagent world composed of other agents' interactions – where each conflict level is potentially associated with different levels of conflict tolerance. Different levels of conflict and conflict tolerance could be distinguished on the basis of different degrees of rejection or different degrees of violation of normative expectations. Distinctions like those between ephemeral and real conflicts or between first-order and second-order conflicts can be considered as a basis for levels of conflicts and conflict tolerance. From an individual or agent-oriented point of view, different levels of conflict and conflict tolerance could be distinguished on the basis of different degrees of goal and belief inconsistency among agents. From a societal perspective, they could be distinguished on the basis of different degrees of maintaining, repairing and adapting structural patterns of coordination. Introducing levels of conflict appears to be particularly attractive for DAI, because this could result in more sophisticated and finer-grained models of, and mechanisms for, coordination and conflict treatment. However, taking levels of conflict into consideration is not equally appropriate for all problems. Hence, the solution variety (or the specificity of the solution requirements) of a problem should also be introduced as another criterion for computational appropriateness.

(3) *Solution variety and global coherence*

What is meant by solution variety can be shown by comparing analytical problems with synthetic problems: Analytical problems like medical diagnosis typically require an optimal solution and thus do not leave much room for alternatives, while synthetic problems like meeting scheduling or computer configuration typically possess several alternative solutions of equal quality. Clearly, high conflict tolerance is likely to be more damaging for problems displaying a highly constrained solution space, while low conflict tolerance may unnecessarily complicate the treatment of weakly constrained problems which dispose over a much larger solution space. Moreover, we suppose that it may be useful to define levels of conflict and conflict tolerance dependent on the phases or stages of a problem-solving process. For instance, and in analogy to the simulated annealing methodology, one could tolerate (or even desire) a high conflict tolerance in the early phases of problem-solving which is then successively lowered as the problem-solving process proceeds. Obviously the computational realisation of levels of conflict and conflict tolerance opens a broad range of open research questions for DAI, and finding answers to these questions is also of relevance to sociology: What are appropriate qualitative and quantitative measures for computationally capturing and handling different levels of conflict and conflict tolerance? How can agents decide what level of conflict is available and what level of conflict tolerance is most appropriate in the current situation? How can agents resolve meta-disagreements on the level of conflict and conflict tolerance (and thus on the actions to be taken in response to the conflict they identified)? How are levels of conflict and conflict tolerance related to degrees of rejected or violated expectations? How are they related to coordination and to multiagent systems' overall coherence? Do they imply corresponding levels of local cooperation and global coherence?

(4) *Detection and prevention of conflicts*

The idea of levels of conflict violation and of levels of conflict and conflict tolerance constitute a promising starting point for the design of "early warning systems" for conflict detection and conflict prevention in multiagent systems. Here, DAI will have to contend with the dilemma that conflict prevention often either comes too early or too late. Intuitively it seems clear that the earlier a conflict (or the possibility of the formation of a conflict) is detected the better are the chances to resolve it and prevent its escalation because it looks easier to handle a low-level conflict or a minor violation of socially grounded expectations than a high-level conflict or a major violation of expectations with far reaching impacts for a large number of agents. However, this intuition is misleading: Immature or low-level conflicts cannot be tackled adequately because at an early stage it is still unclear how they will develop, whether they will be entropic or cancerous, damaging or beneficial, while mature or high-level conflicts often have gained considerable momentum and cannot be stopped from running out of control although they may now be thoroughly understood and analysed. With these difficulties, conflict detection and prevention based on "levelled conflicts" is a highly interesting, yet still unexplored topic in DAI and it is worth noting that sociological theory provides a basis for the development of computational conflict detection mechanisms. An interesting starting point is Mead's concept of role taking according to which intrapersonal conflicts are construed as internalised interpersonal conflicts – as inner dialogues between "I" and "me" – which (as in the case of Antigone's moral conflict) do not occur in splendid isolation from other people's expectations but are directly interwoven with them. Thus, transposed to DAI, role taking can be viewed as a mechanism of conflict detection and prevention. Similarly, Dewey's reflexive conception of inquiry could be translated into a meta-strategy of conflict resolution which becomes part of the societal memory. Again, DAI will have to face the difficulty of making a complicated social process computational, i.e. designing an adequate program of transforming first-order conflicts (regulated by institutionalisation) into second-order conflicts (regulated through collectively restructuring the institutions of conflict regulation). It should be understood that neither role taking nor inquiry can be taken as a blueprint or as a ready-made solution for an immediate transfer into computationally executable models – this transformation challenges DAI.

(5) *Conflict regulation instead of conflict resolution*

The primary reason for studying conflicts in DAI is to develop mechanisms for resolving them. However, as Luhmann convincingly argues, conflict resolution is but one way – and often a rather unlikely way –to cope with conflicts. In this respect DAI can learn from sociology that there are other ways of dealing with conflicts. Apart from resolving them, conflicts may also be regulated by toleration, suppression, externalisation, postponement, ignorance, encapsulation, prevention and institutionalisation. In contrast to the sociological view, conflict research in DAI is predominantly based on the assumption that conflicts can and have to be resolved, and so it is hardly surprising that other forms of coping with conflicts have not been seriously considered in DAI so far. Since it is reasonable and realistic to assume that not all conflicts can be fully resolved under given time and cost constraints, DAI will have to be more careful in addressing theoretical issues like conflict generation, conflict development, and conflict outcome – issues which have hitherto been largely neglected by DAI research. Apart from the theoretical questions, issues of conflict regulation too open a broad range of practical questions for DAI. What, for instance, are the conditions under which agents should decide to tolerate, postpone, ignore, by-pass (and so forth) conflicts? Under what criteria should agents consider a conflict as being irresolvable at least for the moment (so that it is better to tolerate it for a while), and what are the criteria for continuing work on a conflict? Can tolerance and ignorance of conflicts be appropriately captured in an algorithmic framework at all? What are the criteria for appropriate computational mechanisms of conflict suppression? How is it possible to computationally capture the institutionalisation of conflicts as a collective learning process, either through evolution (Luhmann) or through negotiation (Strauss)? What will happen if some agents think that a given conflict is irresolvable, while others insist on further trying to solving it? Is there a need for separately designing what sociologists would call the normative foundations of conflict regulation? Addressing questions like these should help to keep us from building multiagent systems that waste a lot of time trying to solve irresolvable conflicts.

(6) *Robustness, adaptivity, innovation*

Conflict studies in DAI should be understood as inquiries into the robustness and adaptivity of multiagent systems. As sociological theories of conflict show, societies immunise themselves through conflicts and recover from them by repairing their structures and restoring their status quo ante – or by gradually or radically changing their structures. Conflict, thus, appears to be an important source of innovation in human societies. The computational realisation of the restorative or innovative use of conflicts as stimuli for learning to restructure and reorganise their interaction patterns, their normative expectations, their cultural values, and their power relations constitutes another major challenge for DAI. By accepting this challenge in a fundamental way, the sociologies of symbolic interaction and autopoietic systems could be of particular inspiration for DAI research on multiagent learning, adaptation, and organisational self-design. Sociologists, in turn, could considerably profit from constructing and experimentally comparing models of conflict and structural change with respect to both streams of sociological theories considered here. Conflict models of autopoietic origin will have to experiment with producing masses of variations of ephemeral or virtual conflicts to test an artificial society's structural resistance; and conflict models inspired by the sociology of symbolic interaction will have to demonstrate how first-order conflicts turn into second-order conflicts by escalating to such an extent as to radically challenge a given procedure of negotiation if it is no longer capable of first-order conflict resolution. Such models could teach sociologists how to develop a better understanding of how human societies learn from or adapt through conflict, how they take advantage of conflict to build novel regulations and institutions, and – more optimistically speaking – how they might transform conflict into democratic progress. Furthermore, in a highly abstracted way these two models could also be developed into generic technologies of adaptive robustness and graceful degradation for multiagent systems.

Despite their preliminary status these considerations clearly indicate that conflict research both in DAI and in sociology could considerably profit from interdisciplinary cooperation. A joint exploration of the research issues listed above does indeed have the capacity to substantially advance our understanding of theorigins, dynamics, and consequences of conflict in human and computational societies. It is important to see, however, that a set of common ideas and shared intuitions cannot replace a theory of conflict. To prepare the ground for more ambitious conflict approaches in both disciplines, it is necessary to take preliminary distinctions such as those of logical and material or interagent and intraagent conflicts not as the explanans but as the explanandum of inquiries into socionics, to seriously consider sociological theories as a source of inspiration for designing computational technologies, and to exploit DAI technology as a sociological method of experimentation and simulation. For sociologists and DAI researchers alike the comparative exploration of models of conflict and structural change should be ventures of the keenest interest.

Acknowledgments

The authors wish to thank Kai Lorentzen, Mathias Nickles and Kai Paetow for their helpful comments and critical prompts. Our thinking in this paper has been nourished by inquiries into socionics. Socionics (Malsch, 2000) is a scientific endeavour which seeks to build bridges between DAI and sociology. It has become the brand name of a research programme (http://www.tu-harburg.de/tbg/SPP/Start_SPP.html) supported by the DFG, the German Research Fund. The work described here has been funded by Deutsche Forschungsgemeinschaft (DFG, German National Science Foundation) under contracts MA759/4-2 and Br609/11-1.

II
CONFLICTS OF OPERATIONAL AGENTS

Chapter 5

CONFLICTS IN AGENT TEAMS

Hyuckchul Jung and Milind Tambe
Information Sciences Institute, University of Southern California, USA
{jung,tambe} @ISI.EDU

Abstract Multi-agent teamwork is a critical capability in a large number of applications. Yet, despite the considerable progress in teamwork research, the challenge of intra-team conflict resolution has remained largely unaddressed. This chapter presents a system called CONSA, to resolve conflicts using argumentation-based negotiations. The key insight in CONSA (*COllaborative Negotiation System based on Argumentation*) is to fully exploit the benefits of argumentation in a team setting. Thus, CONSA casts conflict resolution as a team problem, so that the recent advances in teamwork can be fully brought to bear during conflict resolution to improve argumentation flexibility. Furthermore, since teamwork conflicts often involve past teamwork, recently developed teamwork models can be exploited to provide agents with reusable argumentation knowledge. Additionally, CONSA also includes argumentation strategies geared towards benefiting the team rather than the individual, and techniques to reduce argumentation overhead. We present detailed algorithms used in CONSA and show a detailed trace from CONSA's implementations.

1. INTRODUCTION

Teamwork is a critical capability in a large number of multi-agent applications, such as virtual environments for education and training (Tambe, 1997), robotic teams (Kitano et al., 1997) and teams on the Internet. In these applications, agents must act together despite the uncertainties of their complex dynamic environment. Considerable progress has indeed been made in teamwork research. For instance, recent advances in teamwork models (Jennings, 1995, Tambe, 1997), which explicitly outline agents' commitments and responsibilities in teamwork, have significantly improved flexibility in teamwork coordination and communication. However, this research has so far not addressed the challenge of resolving conflicts within a team.

Yet, as agent applications advance to meet the requirements of scale and autonomy, inter-agent conflicts become increasingly inevitable. For instance, while autonomously reacting to dynamic events, agents may unintentionally interfere in others' actions, or faulty sensors may provide them with conflicting information or lead them to conflicting inferences. While such conflict resolution is difficult in general, it is even more problematic in teams if intra-team conflicts are not anticipated.

This chapter focuses on a system we have developed to resolve conflicts in agent teams, called CONSA: *COllaborative Negotiation System based on Argumentation*. In argumentation, agents negotiate by providing arguments (which may be justifications or elaborations) in support of their proposals to one another. CONSA builds on past work in argumentation (Chu-Carroll and Carberry, 1995, Kraus et al., 1998, Parsons and Jennings, 1996, Sycara, 1990), but advances the state of the art by fully exploiting the benefits of argumentation in a team setting. Thus, one key idea in CONSA is to cast conflict resolution as an explicit common team goal. As a result, the recent advances in teamwork models are brought to bear during conflict resolution, improving negotiation flexibility. For instance, if a team member privately discovers an event that renders the current team conflict irrelevant, it will be committed to informing its team members — it will not just withdraw privately from negotiations. Additionally, with an explicit common team goal, novel argumentation strategies emerge, e.g., agents may attempt to improve the quality of teammates' arguments. Furthermore, since team conflicts are often rooted in past teamwork, CONSA enables agents to argue effectively about teamwork, by exploiting the teamwork models in a novel way, i.e., not only as a guide to agent behavior during conflict resolution, but as a source for reusable argumentation knowledge. Finally, CONSA is integrated within existing agent teams in complex environments, and has focused on practical issues, such as minimizing the resources consumed in negotiations.

This chapter is organized as follows: section 2. provides background and motivation. Section 3. provides details on STEAM which CONSA is based on. Section 4. describes the representation and evaluation of arguments in CONSA. Section 5. explains CONSA's novel argumentation approach in detail. Section 6. shows how CONSA's implementation works in a specific example. An earlier and shorter version of this chapter has appeared in (Tambe and Jung, 1999a). This chapter presents significant additional details, missing in that work.

2. DOMAINS AND MOTIVATIONS

The motivation for current research on negotiation is based on our previous work in complex, multi-agent domains such as real-world battlefield simulations (Tambe, 1997). We have built different teams of synthetic pilot agents that participate in combat simulations in these environments. These pilot agent teams include companies of attack helicopter pilots and divisions of transport and escort helicopter pilots. The second domain is RoboCup (Kitano et al., 1997) where we have twice successfully participated in the RoboCup tournaments. These agent teams have been developed based on a teamwork model called STEAM (Tambe, 1997). STEAM is based on the joint intentions (Cohen and Levesque, 1991) and SharedPlans (Grosz, 1996) theories of teamwork, but with practical extensions for monitoring and replanning as well as decision-theoretic communication selectivity. STEAM has provided significant teamwork flexibility in all of these applications. Yet, STEAM does not address the problem of conflicts in agents' beliefs and relevant negotiations to resolve such conflicts, limiting teamwork flexibility in key instances. We describe here just a few key examples that outline some of the basic issues for collaborative negotiations:

- The firing position case: individual pilots in a helicopter team typically attack the enemy from firing positions. These positions are planned by a commander agent, who ensures that they do not conflict, i.e., the positions are planned to be at least one kilometer apart from each other. However, despite careful planning, individual pilots may autonomously react to unexpected enemy vehicles, and end up in conflicting positions (e.g., much less than 1 km apart). Figure 5.1 is a snapshot of ModSAF (*Modular Semi-Automated Forces*) (Calder et al., 1993) simulator for pilot agents and illustrates this conflict case. Contour lines show the terrain of the virtual environment in the ModSAF simulator. To attack nearby enemy units (100A12, 100A11, etc.), two helicopter pilot agents, *cheetah424* and *cheetah425*, pop up from a masking position. Unfortunately, they are too close to each other. They need to negotiate to resolve their position conflict.

- The proceed case: in planning the positions described above, the commander pilot plans one position (e.g. position to hide behind a small hill) per team member, and communicates it to the relevant team member via radio. In one run, a message was lost due to radio interference, i.e., the commander thought the position was communicated, but a team member M1 never received it. Thus, when the commander asked the team to proceed because it believed all of the positions were successfully communicated, there was a conflict with M1.

- The enemy position case: two scout helicopter agents may have conflicting beliefs about the closest enemy unit seen. For instance, one scout may report completion of scouting and the closest enemy unit seen as part of this report, while the second scout may see an even closer enemy unit than the one reported.

- The ball position case: in our player team in RoboCup soccer simulation, defenders inform each other if the ball is close by and hence a threat. However, the players' belief of the ball's threat may differ, leading them to have conflicting beliefs about whether the ball is a threat.

In addressing such conflict resolution problems, our goal is to avoid any specialized solutions, and focus instead on a general approach that would be applicable to a wide variety of conflicts.

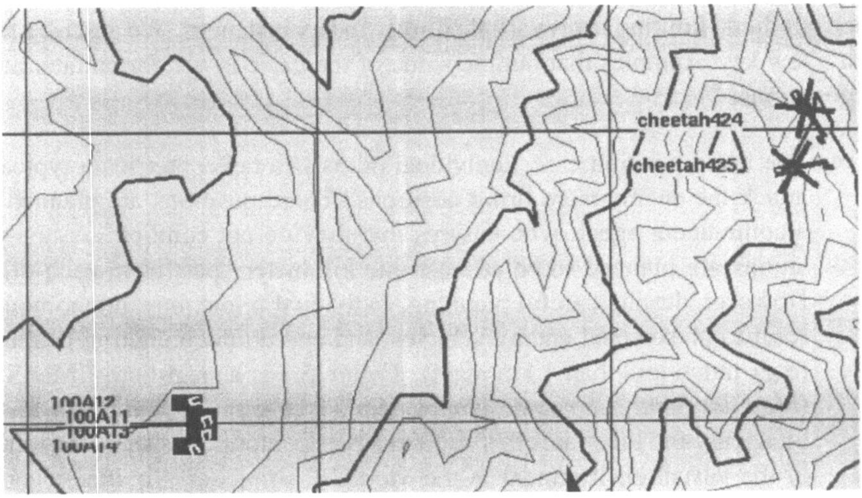

Figure 5.1 Snapshot of firing position case.

3. TEAMWORK MODEL

Before we discuss CONSA, it is useful to briefly overview teamwork models, particularly the STEAM (Tambe, 1997) model, since it is the basis of our team implementations. STEAM consists of two components, both currently realized in the Soar(Newell, 1990) architecture. The first is an enhanced agent architecture with explicit representation of team's joint intentions, mutual beliefs and team goals. Figure 5.2 shows an operator hierarchy (i.e., a reactive plan hierarchy) for a synthetic helicopter pilot developed using STEAM. Team operators (reactive team plans), which explicitly express a team's joint activities, are shown in [ ], such as [Engage]. At any time, one path through this hierarchy is active. This active hierarchy of operators is the team's joint intentions (team operators) and individual intentions (individual operators).

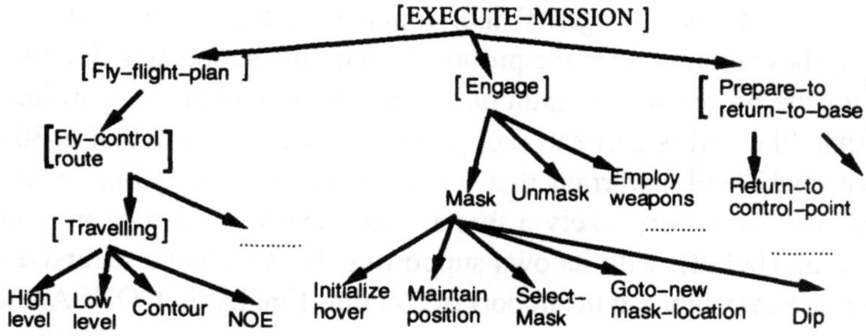

Figure 5.2 Portion of pilot operator hierarchy.

The second component of STEAM is the domain independent teamwork knowledge to enable individual agents' flexible teamwork. Of particular importance here are two of the classes of domain-independent actions. The first is coherence-preserving actions, derived from the joint intention theory (Cohen and Levesque, 1991). These require agents to jointly activate and terminate team operators, by establishing mutual beliefs in their initiation and termination; individual operators are executed without such mutual beliefs. The second class of domain-independent actions is maintenance and repair actions, for re-planning and team reorganization. These actions require an explicit specification of the dependency relationship of the joint intention on individual team members' activities, based on the notion of a role. A *role* constrains a team member Mi to some suboperator op_{Mi} of the team operator [OP]. Three primitive role-relationships (and their combinations) can currently be specified in STEAM. An AND-combination implies that the achievement of team operator requires achievement of each one of the roles. An OR-combination requires success in at least one role for the team operator to be achieved. The role-dependency relationship states that an op_{Mi} depends on op_{Mj}.

4. ARGUMENT REPRESENTATION AND EVALUATION

This section describes CONSA's underlying representation and algorithms to evaluate arguments, which are embedded in a larger CONSA process, discussed in the next section. CONSA's representation of arguments is based on Toulmin's (Toulmin, 1958) argumentation pattern (henceforth TAP), chosen for its generality. In a TAP, an argument consists of the following elements: (i) *claim:* a conclusion whose merit an agent seeks to establish. (ii) *data:* the facts that are a foundation for the claim. (iii) *warrants:* the authority (e.g., a rule) for taking the step from the data to the claim. (iv) *qualifications:* degree of force which conferred on the claim based on the data and warrant.

In CONSA, claims are agents' individual or mutual beliefs. During argumentation, these claims form the proposals, with the supporting TAP as the argument for the proposal. For example, in RoboCup soccer, a claim (proposal) may be that "the ball is a threat," supported by data that "the ball is 30 meters from own goal," and a warrant that "if the soccer ball is within 35 meters of own goal, then it is very likely a threat." In CONSA, the data may itself be another claim (belief), with its own supporting TAP, so that a recursive tree of TAP structure may emerge in support of a claim. Finally, in CONSA, the qualifications on claims determine the strengths of arguments. Currently, claims have qualitative strengths: high, medium and low. Thus, a strong warrant and data will lead to a "high" strength for the claim.

When an agent sends a proposal to its team, team members must determine if their own beliefs conflict with the proposal. Figure 5.3 presents CONSA's algorithm to make this determination. The input is a proposed TAP tree Θ, which forms the proposal (claim), with supporting arguments. The output is a set Ω of tuples $(\{\text{reject}(\text{claim}_i) \text{ or } \text{accept}(\text{claim}_i)\}, \text{justification})$. Here, a reject tuple implies an agent's conflict with the $\text{claim}_i \in \Theta$, while an accept tuple implies an improved justification in support of the claim. The justifications consist of TAPs. If Ω is empty, then no conflicts or improvements are found.

In the algorithm, step 1 checks the input TAP tree Θ for conflicts with the agent's own claims. If a conflict is found, step 2 compares the strengths of the conflicting claims, rejecting the other agent's claim if own claim is found stronger. Step 3 now compares the input claims from Θ for coincidence or agreement. For simplicity, this algorithm assumes a single coincidence. If coincidence is found, then the supports of coincident claims are compared, to determine the stronger support. If one is found, it is added to Ω. When no coincidence or conflict is found in Θ itself, CONSA will not immediately accept Θ. Since leaf nodes in Θ may hold undesirable implications, CONSA derives implications from Θ (step 4). While in general checking undesirable implications is difficult, CONSA currently executes one iteration of such derivations, checking for conflict or coincidence and adding the result to Ω.

To determine the strengths of claim in the *compare-strengths* procedure in Figure 5.3, CONSA relies on the supporting TAP structure. Given that the TAP structure can itself be recursive, claim strengths are evaluated recursively. For leaf-level claims, evidential rules are used. Here, CONSA exploits the benefits of argumentation in a team setting, by relying on the following rules of evidence: assertions from a team member regarding its own role and capability are judged to provide high-strength claims.

Evaluate-proposal(Input: TAP-tree Θ; Output: Ω)

1. In parallel, for all claims α_i in TAP-tree Θ do:
   { Check α_i for conflict with own claims;
   If α_i conflicts with own claim β_j,
   add tuple (α_i,β_j) to conflict-set CS; }
2. For all tuples (α_i,β_j) $\in$ CS, starting from tuple with lowest $\alpha_i \in \Theta$ do:
   { **Compare-strengths**(α_i,β_j);
   If β_j is stronger, add (reject(α_i),β_j) to Ω; }
3. In parallel, for all claims α_i in TAP-tree Θ do:
   { Check α_i for coincidence with own beliefs;
   If coincidence with own claim β_i,
   { **Compare-strengths**(support(α_i), support(β_i));
   If support(β_i) is stronger,
   add (accept(α_i,support(β_i)) to Ω; } }
4. If Ω is empty, check derivations of leaf claims in Θ;
5. Output Ω; if Ω is empty, no conflicts or coincidence found.

Figure 5.3 CONSA's algorithm for evaluating proposal.

5. CONSA APPROACH

Figure 5.4 presents the overall CONSA negotiation process. Step 1 is a proposal generated by a team member. Steps 2, 3 and 4 are the *opening*, *argumentation* and *termination stages* of CONSA's negotiation. In the opening stage, agents agree to jointly resolve the current conflict. In the argumentation stage, they cycle through proposals and counter-proposals, terminating arguments in the termination phase.

Opening and closing stages: in CONSA's opening stage, the conflict detection step (2-a) requires it to address two different types of conflicts. In particular, based on the description of the teamwork model (Section 3.), conflicts can be of two types: (1) Team members may have conflicting beliefs about jointly initiating or terminating a team operator, e.g., one agent believes the team operator must be terminated, while the other believes it cannot be terminated; or (2) Agents executing individual operators may unintentionally conflict with each other's role performance. Thus, in the examples from Section 2., the "firing position case" is a type 2 conflict, but the rest are type 1 conflicts. To detect a type 1 conflict, an agent must evaluate proposals sent by their teammates to jointly initiate or terminate team activities, detected via the **Evaluate-proposal** algorithm in Figure 5.3. In contrast, to detect type 2 conflicts, CONSA uses *role constraints*, that explicitly specify the maintenance goals for the successful performance of the role. For instance, in the firing po-

1. A team member Mi generates a proposal α.
2. *Opening stage:*
   (a) A team member Mj detects a conflict with α.
   (b) If Mj believes joint action not beneficial to resolving conflict, terminate, return;
   (c) Else Mj communicates with team members to establish team operator to resolve current conflict.
3. *Argumentation stage*
   (a) Any member Mk in the current team operator may generate proposal to resolve conflict;
   (b) Other team members evaluate-proposal (see Figure 5.3).
   (c) If no conflict/coincidence found, accept the proposal and go to step 4;
   (d) Else if proposal found to conflict/coincide; continue argument if cost-benefit-wise useful, else accept the proposal and goto step 4;
4. *Closing stage*
   (a) If suggested proposal accepted, then terminate conflict-resolution team operator;
   (b) Else if the conflict resolution found unachievable or irrelevant, terminate conflict-resolution team operator;

Figure 5.4 Three stages of argumentation in CONSA.

sition case, the *lateral-range* (distance) between Mj (the agent performing this role) and any other teammate must be at least one kilometer.

Having detected a conflict in Step 2-a, we temporarily skip over step 2-b to focus on step 2-c. Here, a team member Mj, who has detected a conflict, initiates establishment of a team operator to resolve the current conflict. If the conflict is of type 1, Mj initiates the establishment of *resolve-joint-conflict* as a team operator, involving the entire team from the original joint activity. If the conflict is of type 2, Mj initiates the establishment of *resolve-role-conflict* as a team operator, but the involved team here is only Mj and the agent that caused a conflict for Mj's role. For instance, in the firing position case, *resolve-role-conflict* is established as a team operator between Mj and Mk (the agent that caused the role conflict).

By casting conflict-resolution itself as a team operator, all of STEAM's flexible teamwork capabilities are brought to bear, to guide agents' behavior during conflict resolution. For instance, agents jointly establish the conflict-resolution team operators, using protocols that ensure synchronization and agreement among team members. In particular, teammates may disagree about the existence of the conflict, or they may be unable to negotiate if they are performing another higher priority task. However, by using a team operator for conflict resolution, an agent Mj begins negotiations only after ensuring its teammates agree to and are able to engage in negotiations. Furthermore, STEAM's reasoning about commitments leads team members to behave responsibly towards each other. If a dynamic event causes a team member to privately discover that their conflict is resolved or unresolvable or irrelevant, it will be committed to make this mutually believed in the team. A team member cannot just on its own drop out from participation in the conflict resolution. The utility of such flexibility can be seen in the firing position case. If a team member sees enemy vehicles approaching, it will terminate the current on-going negotiations, but do so responsibly while informing teammates of the situation.

Argumentation stage: the argumentation stage involves an agent (sender) making a proposal to the agent-team (receiver) with an attached justification (argument). The receivers evaluate the proposal taking the justification into account, and either accept or refute it. If refuting the proposal, a receiver may send back a counter-proposal to the team, who may continue this cycle of proposals and counter-proposals. Refutation may be done via rebutting or undercutting (Parsons and Jennings, 1996). Briefly, rebutting refutes the teammate's claim (proposal) directly, with some justifications. In contrast, undercutting attacks the justification provided with the proposal, rather than the proposal itself.

In this argumentation stage, the teamwork setting provides two key novel ideas. First, it enables and requires a third strategy in addition to rebutting and undercutting, which we call "improve support." In particular, an agent receiving a proposal from its team member may accept the proposal, but may have a better justification for the proposal than the one offered by the sender. For instance, in the "enemy position" case from Section 2., the second scout detected a closer enemy unit. The second scout agrees with the top-level claim that the scouting is completed, but it offers a higher quality solution about the closer enemy unit, which allows the helicopter team's performance to improve. It is to enable this "improve-support" strategy that the **Evaluate-proposal** algorithm (Figure 5.3) checks for claim coincidence.

Second, teamwork models provide reusable argumentation knowledge. In particular, team conflicts are sometimes rooted in past teamwork, as for instance in the proceed case. To argue effectively about teamwork, agents must be knowledgeable about teamwork. Here, STEAM provides general, reusable warrants for constructing TAPs. For instance, the warrants shown below, extracted from STEAM's role relationships, are employed in CONSA. Here, warrant $\omega 1$ states that if a team operator τ is an AND-combination, and all of its roles are not achieved, then the team operator is not achieved. $\omega 2$ is a variation for an OR-combination and $\omega 3$ is that for an AND-combination.

- $\omega 1$: Team-Operator(τ) $\wedge$ AND-combination(τ) $\wedge$ $\neg$ All-roles-fulfilled(τ) $\rightarrow$ $\neg$ achieved(τ)

- $\omega 2$: Team-Operator(τ) $\wedge$ OR-combination(τ) $\wedge$ $\neg$ All-roles-unachievable(τ) $\rightarrow$ $\neg$ unachievable(τ)
- $\omega 3$: Team-Operator(τ) $\wedge$ AND-combination(τ) $\wedge$ All-roles-fulfilled(τ) $\rightarrow$ achieved(τ)

Real-time, efficient argumentation: there are three techniques used in CONSA to reduce resources utilized in argumentation and enhance its real-time performance (shown in steps 2-c and 3-d of Figure 5.4). One technique is decision-theoretic reasoning of the cost-benefit analysis of argumentation, i.e., to avoid continuing to argue if the costs outweigh the likely benefits. Specifically, prior to initiating each proposal, an agent weighs the choices of (i) continuing argumentation with teammates to optimally settle the conflict, or (ii) taking possible unilateral action to resolve the conflict. Agents continue the argumentation process only if the expected utility of argumentation is greater. For instance, in the firing position case, helicopters may not be 1 kilometer apart as desired. Given this conflict, an agent has the choice of initiating argumentation to determine the distance "n" each helicopter must move to minimize travel time (example discussed below in detail), or else to just moving a greater distance "$2n$" by itself to resolve the conflict.

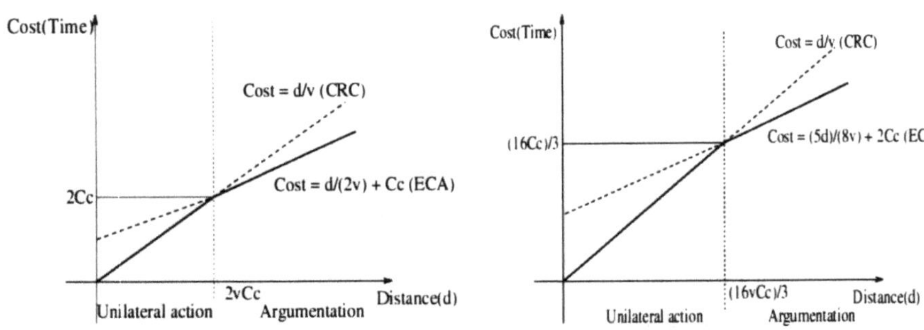

(a) p=1, α1=0.5 (b) p=1/2, α1=0.5, α2=0.25, and β=3

Figure 5.5 Threshold between unilateral action and argumentation

Suppose the cost of the unilateral action choice (e.g., moving "$2n$") is CRC - the conflict resolution cost (this cost is the joint cost to the collaborating agents). In contrast, if an agent were to rely on argumentation, several outcomes are possible. First, if a teammate accepts the agent's proposal in the first cycle, the cost will be (1-α1)*CRC + Cc (α1: expected savings ratio for the collaborating agents together with argumentation after one cycle, Cc: communication cost). Second, if the proposal is not accepted at the first cycle and there are many cycles of sending proposals and counter proposals, it will cost (1-α2)*CRC + β*Cc (α2: expected savings ratio after multiple cycles, β: the expected number of cycles to settle the current conflict). With the probability (p) of teammate's accepting a proposal in one cycle, the expected cost of argumentation (ECA) is p*((1-α1)*CRC + Cc) + $(1-p)$*((1-α2)*CRC + β*Cc). Thus, an agent enters argumentation if $ECA < CRC$. Going back to the firing position case, the cost is time to resolve the conflict. With the unilateral action choice (ii), one pilot agent moves all the distance to resolve the constraint. In this case, the cost (CRC) is d/v (d: distance to be moved, v: helicopter's velocity). Now, to evaluate the argumentation option (i), if the agent assumes that there is no restriction for both agents' movements and expects that the other agent can accept its proposal at the first cycle with the probability (p) of 1, then it suggests 50:50 movements to minimize the time. This makes α1 equals 0.5. Figure 5.5 (a) shows that, with these p and α1, an agent should argue if $d > 2 * v * Cc$. If the helicopter's velocity is 50m/sec and Cc is 5sec, agents enter into argumentation only if the distance to move is greater than 500m. Otherwise, it avoids argumentation and moves the distance by itself. On the other hand, if agents are not sure of the restrictions of the other agent, agents cannot expect that the other agent will accept its proposal at the first cycle. When an agent suggests 50:50 movements, there can be two possibilities. One possibility is that the other agent accepts the proposal at the first cycle and both agents move each half of the distance to be moved, which makes α1 0.5. The other one is that an agent cannot accept its teammate's proposal and additional negotiation cycles are required. In the latter case, if three cycles are usually expected before reaching an agreement and the agreement is likely to be 75:25 movements because of the restriction of the other agent, then α2 is 0.25 (one agent moves 75% of the distance and its time to move comes to be a team's cost) and β is 3. If an agent assumes that the probability (p) of the other agent's accepting its proposal in the first cycle is 0.5, the expected utility of argumentation is $(5 * d)/(8 * v) + 2Cc$. Therefore, agents enter into argumentation only if $d > (16 * v * Cc)/3$ (Figure 5.5 (b)). During the argumentation, such evaluation continues at each cycle.

The second technique is ordering of arguments. If there are multiple arguments applicable, CONSA will communicate the strongest first, in order to speed up the argumentation process. Here the strength of the arguments is compared based on the **compare-strengths** procedure discussed in Figure 5.3. For instance, an agent will prefer an argument based on own role performance over one based on a teammate's role performance, since own role-performance provides a stronger argument given role expertise heuristic discussed earlier. Interestingly, this heuristic contrasts with (Kraus et al., 1998), where in a non-collaborative setting, the weaker arguments are presented first to wear down an opponent. Ordering will also choose the highest claim in the proposed argument that can be attacked.

To reduce communication overhead during argumentation, CONSA also uses pruning to avoid communication of commonly held warrants. In particular, if an agent believes that particular warrants are mutually believed, and uniquely applicable in a given circumstance, it will prune the warrant from the communicated TAP tree.

6. DETAILED EXAMPLE OF IMPLEMENTATION

CONSA is currently realized in the Soar (Newell, 1990) architecture in 132 rules. Our implementation has enabled agents to negotiate to resolve conflicts in all the cases from section 2. Table 5.1 shows a part of the Soar outputs from CONSA's execution trace in the "firing position case". Here, *cheetah424* and *cheetah 425* are names of two pilot agents, and the number (e.g. "2288") in each line is the decision cycle number in Soar. "S114", "S124" etc. are the Soar states which represent a problem solving situation. "O264", "O267" etc. are the executed SOAR operators which make changes to the states. For instance, at decision cycle 2288, *cheetah424* executes an operator "O264" to resolve the firing position conflict: executing the operator enables *cheetah424* to start the argumentation processes with *cheetah425*. *Cheetah424* and *cheetah425* belong to a team of five pilot agents. Since the firing position conflict is a type 2 conflict (see section 5.) between *cheetah424* and *cheetah425*, the other agents are not involved in this argumentation.

While executing operator "O264" at decision cycle 2288, *cheetah424* does decision theoretic reasoning (see section 5.). Since it assumes that both agents have no restriction for their movements, it concludes that it is beneficial to share the distance to be moved through argumentation. At this step, if the communication cost is too high, *cheetah424* avoids argumentation and decides to take unilateral action. At decision cycle 2290 of *cheetah424* and 2289 of *cheetah425*, by executing the operator "establish-jpg", both agents agree to jointly activate and terminate a team operator "resolve-role-conflict". This process is supported by STEAM (Tambe, 1997). Next, *cheetah424* computes both agents' movements based on its beliefs for both of them. Based on the current distance and the assumption of no restriction, *cheetah424* sends a proposal suggesting 50:50 movements with justifications at decision cycle 2362. Figure 5.6 (a) shows the tree structure of the proposal. Leaf nodes are the justifications.

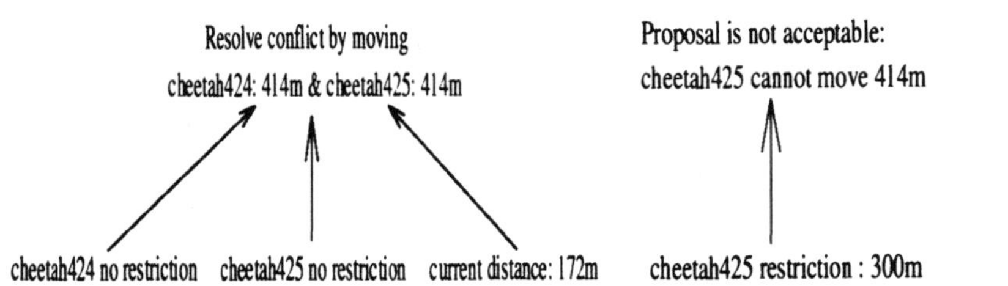

(a) *cheetah424*'s proposal (b) *cheetah425*'s counter-proposal

Figure 5.6 Structure of proposal with justifications

cheetah424	*cheetah425*
...	...
Position conflict detected.	Position conflict detected.
...	...
2288:O: O264 resolve-role-conflict	2287:O: O403 resolve-role-conflict
Decision theoretic reasoning.	...
2289:==>S: S114 (operator no-change)	2288:==>S: S124 (operator no-change)
2290: O: O267 establish-jpg	2289: O: O406 establish-jpg
...	...
Established JPG.	Established JPG.
...	...
2362: O: O273 send-proposal	...
Movements cheetah424:414&cheetah425:414	...
...	Message from cheetah424.
...	2366: O: O413 inconsist-control
...	Begin inconsistency checking.
...	2367: ==>S: S129 (operator no-change)
...	2368: O: O415 make-decision
...	2369: O: O416 compare-claims
2368: O: O218 wait	Compare the claims in arguments.
...	2370: ==>S: S130 (operator tie)
...	2371: O: O417 evaluate
...	Evaluating the claims.
...	Reject the proposal.
...	...
...	2372: O: O432 send-counter-proposal
...	Cheetah425 restriction: 300 meters.
Message from cheetah 425.	...
2373: O: O282 inconsist-control	...
Begin inconsistency checking.	...
2374: ==>S: S119 (operator no-change)	...
2375: O: O285 make-decision	...
2376: O: O286 compare-claim	...
Compare the claims in arguments.	...
2377: O: O287 evaluate	2380: O: O414 inconsist-wait
Evaluating the claims.	...
Accept the counter-proposal.	...
Belief change: cheetah 425's free-move 300	...
Decision theoretic reasoning.	...
2378: O: O289 send-proposal	...
Movements cheetah424:528&cheetah425:300	...
...	Message from cheetah424.
...	2388: O: O416 compare-claims
...	Compare the claims in arguments.
...	2389: O: O417 evaluate
...	Evaluating the claims.
...	Accept the proposal.
...	...

Table 5.1 Traces of firing position case.

Cheetah425 receives the proposal and starts to check whether the claims in the justifications are consistent with its own beliefs or not by executing "inconsist-control" operator at decision cycle 2366. Let's assume that *cheetah425* cannot move more than 300 meters because of close enemy units. At decision cycle 2369, *cheetah425* finds a conflict between its belief (movement restriction of 300 meters) and *cheetah424*'s belief (middle leaf node in Figure 5.6 (a)). *Cheetah425* decides to reject the proposal by comparing strengths of both beliefs at decision cycle 2369 and 2371. Algorithm in Figure 5.3 explains this evaluation process. *Cheetah425* sends a counter-proposal of disagreement with justification (leaf node of Figure 5.6 (b)).

At decision cycle 2377, after receiving the counter-proposal, *cheetah424* evaluates it and changes its belief of the movement restriction for *cheetah425*. *Cheetah424* uses decision theoretic reasoning again before sending another proposal. If *cheetah425* can only move small distance(e.g., 100 meters), there is no benefit from argumentation and *cheetah424* takes unilateral action without argumentation. However, in this trace, *cheetah424* decides to start another cycle of argumentation. At decision cycle 2378, *Cheetah424* sends a counter-counter-proposal of 62:38 movements and *cheetah425* accepts the proposal at decision cycle 2389. Now, both agents make the agreed movements and terminate the jointly committed team operator "resolve-role-conflict".

7. RELATED WORK

Previous work in argumentation-based negotiation has often assumed non-cooperative agents. For instance, (Kraus et al., 1998, Sycara, 1990) uses several argument types borrowed from human argumentation in non-cooperative situations, e.g., threat, promise of a future reward, and appeal to self interest. An example from (Kraus et al., 1998) is negotiation among two robots on Mars. Here, to persuade a robot R2, a robot R1 threatens it (R2) that R1 will break R2's camera lens or antenna, if R2 does not comply. Such arguments appear inappropriate in team settings, e.g., if R1 and R2 are a team, and if R1 carries out its threat, then it will have a teammate (R2) without a lens or antenna. Other explicitly non-collaborative argumentation work appears in the legal domain, e.g., DART (Freeman and Farley, 1993), which is also based on Toulmin's representation schema. In contrast, (Parsons and Jennings, 1996) does not explicitly assume collaborativeness or non-collaborativeness in agents.

CONSA differs from this work in its explicit exploitation of the team setting in argumentation. As seen earlier, it exploits teamwork models: (i) to guide flexible agent behavior in negotiation and (ii) as a source of reusable argumentation knowledge. It also adds argumentation strategies so agents can collaboratively improve each other's arguments. Also, CONSA includes techniques to avoid high overheads of negotiations.

Chu-Carroll and Carberry's work in argumentation does assume collaborativeness on part of the participating agents (Chu-Carroll and Carberry, 1995). While they use SharedPlans (Grosz, 1996) in negotiations, they appear to treat SharedPlans as a data-structure, rather than a teamwork model. Thus, unlike CONSA, they do not use SharedPlans either for prescribing agents' behaviors in negotiations, or as source of reusable argumentation knowledge.

8. SUMMARY AND FUTURE WORK

Multi-agent teamwork in diverse applications ranging from planning, design, education and training, faces the problems of conflicts in agents' beliefs, plans and actions. Collaborative negotiation is thus a fundamental component of teamwork. To address the problem, this chapter describes an implemented system called CONSA for collaborative negotiation via argumentation. While CONSA builds on previous work in argumentation, it advances the state of the art via the following key ideas: (i) CONSA casts conflict resolution as a team problem, bringing to bear some of the recent advances in flexible teamwork to improve the flexibility of agent behavior in conflict resolution; (ii) since team conflicts are often about past teamwork, CONSA exploits teamwork models to provide agents with reusable argumentation knowledge; (iii) CONSA focuses on collaborative argumentation strategies such as improve-support; (iv) as an implemented system in a dynamic environment, CONSA uses a decision theoretic approach, argument ordering and pruning to reduce the cost of negotiation. We have presented detailed algorithms and initial results from CONSA's implementation. Areas of future work include understanding CONSA's implications for argumentation in self-interested agents.

Acknowledgments

This research is funded by DARPA ITO award number F30602-99-2-0507.

Chapter 6

CONFLICT-BASED BEHAVIOUR EMERGENCE IN ROBOT TEAMS

Jacques Penders
KPN Research, Leidschendam, the Netherlands
J.S.J.H.Penders@.kpn.com

Abstract We study conflicts in a team of robots. The domain of our study has a limited ontology, within which we define when an autonomously performing robot has intentions. Goal finding and obstacle avoidance are the main drives behind the intentions. The intentions are the basis of the interaction within a team, and have a considerable impact on the overall performance of the team. The main aim of the study is to get a hold on the team behaviour that emerges from these conflicts. We discuss and define intentions of robot agents and evaluate the team behaviour of congenial teams, that is teams of agents with the same intentions. Typical behaviours are: dispersing behaviour in avoiding teams and clustering behaviour in antagonistic teams.

1. INTRODUCTION

While walking down a crowded street people frequently step aside, speed up or slow down in order to pass or give way to other pedestrians. In a shopping centre, people are constantly manoeuvring their shopping trolleys, left, right, pulling them back thus attempting not to run into others. These situations are a paradigm for the study we undertake here. The agents - that is the humans - have conflicting interests, and as a consequence they interact with each other: the one steps aside while the other speeds up.

We study interaction among robots. Like people in a shopping centre, the robots encounter conflicts and thus react to each other thereby starting interaction. Intuitively it is clear which kinds of conflicts occur. However, to program the robots and to study the resulting behaviour we have to lay down formally what is meant when speaking about a conflict. Robots, like people and trolleys, occupy space, and they cannot at the same time occupy the same place; it is clear that a conflict occurs when two or more of them aim for the same spot. The robot-agents hinder each other while they occupy the shop floor, and that is why they start to interact. Thus the robots interact to divide the space among them. While doing so, rather long chains of reactive behaviours are generated in which the robots react to each other's reactions. These chains of reactive behaviour result into (a low- level type of) team behaviour. The ultimate aim of our studies is to get hold on the emerging team behaviour. Since, the point of interest is that the robots mutually influence each other, it is also natural to speak of teams of robots.

Conflicts

A scarce resource - space in our case - is the cause of a conflict. The resource can be occupied or free, but a conflict in our study is not a single event. Like the people in a shopping centre, the robots are autonomous agents that can perform a variety of spatial movements, and they react and interact. Note that similar to a shopping centre, there is no central 'traffic' control. The robots hinder each other, the one interferes when the other is trying to occupy a certain place. Hence, the environment is far from static, actions and reactions follow upon each other. So, a conflict is clearly a process and we have to stipulate what exactly this process is. The basis of a conflict (as a process) is that agents have aims and that they hinder each other in these aims. However, before we can stipulate what it means that an agent has an aim, we first elaborate on the abstractions which we are making.

Objects

Our robots have a limited cognitive basis (Penders, 1999, Penders and Braspenning, 1997), which means that they have a rather limited view on their environment. As a consequence the ontology of our robot domain is limited. The robots act in the two-dimensional space but neither have a notion of a goal nor of an obstacle; they only process within terms of spatial positions and regions. Goal finding is aiming towards a certain geometrical position, and as regions may be either free or occupied; *objects* coincide with the occupied ones. For convenience, we continue to speak about goals, objects, obstacles and other robots. This will not lead to confusion as long as it is borne in mind that the terms denote geometrical points or regions, without any further connotation. Any of the objects may perform spatial behaviour, and in general we speak about *robot agents* including any kind of object.

Also, the robots in our teams do not communicate directly, and consequently have no means of negotiation. The reason for this constraint is rather practical. Many real-life situations do not require any communication, often they even do not allow for communication. For instance, in shopping centres, people pushing their shopping trolleys, generally pass each other without communicating (Fujimara, 1991) or negotiating. Moreover, in air traffic applications there is obviously no time to negotiate (Zeghal and Ferber, 1993).

Aims and intentions

As said above, we have to stipulate when an agent has an aim, for this purpose we define the notion of *having an intention.* Since our robots only have limited cognitive bases, an intention cannot but denote a pattern of behaviour; more specifically, an intention denotes a pattern of behaviour that shows some aim, for instance finding a goal or avoiding an obstacle. In a dynamic environment a reactive agent often cannot head straight for its goal or avoid an obstacle. Whenever we can recognize a certain characteristic in the spatial (re)actions of the agent, we say that the agent has an intention. Thus, an intention denotes the type of (re)action an agent performs. Agents *a* and *b* have a *conflict* when they hinder each other. We say that agent *a* hinders agent *b* whenever the behaviour of *a* interferes with *b* executing its intention.

The robot-teams are not managed by a central controller, all necessary guidance of the team member has to be pre-programmed in the individual agents. The team behaviour results from the individuals' intentions, and thus is embedded locally in each robots' intentions. We note that interaction patterns and team behaviour can only be described from the standpoint of an external observer; the robots have no notion of a team nor of team behaviour. In order to design such teams, insight is required into the effect each robot has on the team's behaviour.

We study multi-robot teams and aim to get hold on the emerging team behaviour. The teams consist of autonomous robots which have intentions, that do interact with each other, but do not communicate. While performing, long and multiple interaction chains emerge among the individual autonomous agents, and this complicates our studies as we will see. Since our robots do not communicate, our robot-agents differ considerably from most software agents. In the research on software agents, communication is one of the central topics (Wooldridge and Jennings, 1995b). Also, an intention denotes the type of (re)action an agent performs. In this respect we diverge from approaches in software agent development where intentions are often understood as a set of (planned) tasks to be executed (cf (Georgeff and Ingrand, 1989) and chapter 5).

Several practical examples of robot teams are described in literature. (Penders, 1999) discusses a cargo terminal, where a team of robots carries cargo over the platform thus executing a sorting task. (Bay, 1995) describes a team of robots carrying a freight pallet, and (Kube and Bonabeau, 2000) discuss teams robots co-operatively carrying out transport. (Zeghal and Ferber, 1993) discuss agents implemented within the aircraft domain; this team supports air traffic management.

Natural life

Due to the spatial orientation and the exclusion of communication, our studies are also applicable to biological organisms. Quite a number of animals use geometrical navigation strategies. For instance, Kanzaki (Kanzali, 1996) describes the odour-based navigation of silkworm moths in the search for a mating partner. Crickets find a mate by orientation to the chirping song (Webb, 1995). Many more examples are described in literature, we refer further to (Mataric, 1995) and (Trullier and Meyer, 1997). (Lambrinos et al., 2000) describe a robot modelled after the paradigm of an ant species. In this chapter we only make a start in studying team behaviour; the teams which we consider are relatively small. Ant colonies are examples of large multi-agent systems, a colony consists of millions of autonomous individuals showing a dazzling concentration of activities. Nevertheless, the interaction amongst the individuals result in massive team behaviour. The interaction mechanisms and the social organization are not yet understood (Mataric, 1995), nevertheless we believe that it is worth to try to find some clues in the restricted robot domain.

To summarize, the domain of our study has a limited ontology, within which we define when an autonomously performing robot has intentions. Goal finding and obstacle avoidance are the main drives behind the intentions. The intentions are the basis of the interaction within a team, and have a considerable impact on the overall performance of the team. Section 2 below, provides an overview of the types of teams and we compare several different teams with respect to the team behaviour generated. In section 3 we start our formal treatment of interaction, and define conflicts. In section 4 this formalization is applied on specific teams of avoiding robots. The latter are teams of robots that try to avoid each other, they basically behave similar to people on the street or in shopping centres who mainly aim to avoid others.

2. TEAM BEHAVIOUR

As said in the introduction, an intention captures a pattern of actions and consists of the type of actions and reactions which an agent performs because of the presence of objects (or other agents). Technically: whenever we can distinguish a certain pattern (of spatial characteristics) in the (re)actions of the agent, we say that the agent *has an intention* behind its (re)action. Examples of such intentions are shown in figure 6.1, where two robots aim for a goal; we can say that they have an intention for the goal. When an agent reacts to another agent it can also show a certain intention: it might avoid the other agent or on the contrary chase it. A formal definition of an intention in geometrical terms will be given below, after we have specified interaction patterns. In this section we elaborate on intentions as team behaviour generates from them. Intentions guide the behaviour of the team members, and for the moment it is sufficient to say that intentions are different if the patterns of actions with which they are associated are different. For the robot domain we stipulate that robots provided with the same program potentially have the same intentions.

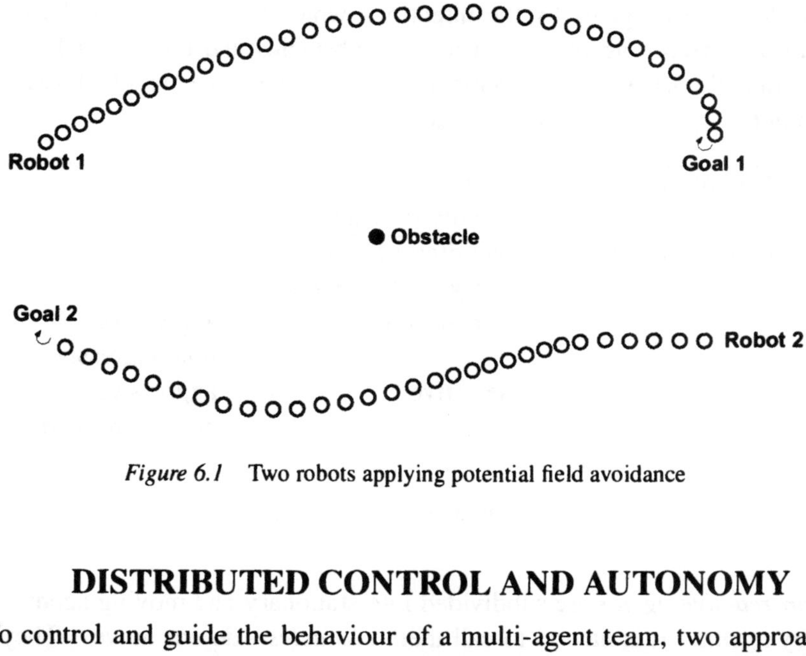

Figure 6.1 Two robots applying potential field avoidance

2.1 DISTRIBUTED CONTROL AND AUTONOMY

To control and guide the behaviour of a multi-agent team, two approaches are possible: a *centralized* and a *distributed* one. In a centralized approach, a central controller (usually called central planner) plans all actions for all agents. The central planner deliberates about a plan for the whole team and checks its validity and completeness (Svesta and Overmars, 1998). In the distributed approach the individual agents act on their own, and have to find their way quite pragmatically.

Central control is associated with path planning. In multi-robot applications path planning is called dynamic motion planning (Latombe, 1991). In a large team, the planning process is very complex, as it has to lay out the course of each robot-agent in detail. The approach is suited to environments in which all factors are fully under control. However, if agents slightly adapt to the behaviour of others and deviate from their prescribed courses, the team behaviour becomes intractable. In our teams of adaptive and autonomously performing robots we do not have much choice but to choose the distributed approach. That is why – as said above – there is no central control in our teams. Instead, any 'control' in the teams can only come from the intentions which are programmed in the agents. Our analyses below reveal how intentions influence team behaviour as we evaluate the behaviour of several teams with different intentions. We first discuss teams in which all members have the same intentions. After that we add to these teams a newcomer having a different intention.

2.2 DIFFERENT INTENTIONS

We distinguish agents by the intentions which they have. The basic distinction is between agents which react to obstacles and those which do not. Hence in table 6.1 we have two main groups, *reactive* agents which react and *non-reactive* agents which do not react.

Non-reactive agents	stationary agents	
	blindly moving agents	
Reactive agents	avoiding agents	
	antagonistic agents	
	non-selective	aggressive
		non-aggressive
	selective	aggressive
		non-aggressive

Table 6.1 Classification of agents by their intentions

Non-reactive agents are subdivided into stationary and moving agents. *Stationary agents* - it is natural to call them *obstacles* - do not move.[1] They can be immovable objects but they might also be agents that for the time being do not move. Non-reactive but moving agents are called *blindly moving*. They are agents that move without (noticeably) reacting to other objects, they are insensitive.

Reactive agents form the second main group. We subdivide the group according to whether the agents move toward the objects or on the contrary move away. *Avoiding agents* are defined as those, which move away from objects. Avoiding agents typically set out for a certain destination and while doing so cautiously avoid contact with others. (Pollack et al., 1987) refer to them as *cautious* agents. *Antagonistic agents* perform quite the opposite behaviour.

[1] In fact stationary agents cannot have intentions in the sense of our definition, but their non-actions can be considered as intentions.

Antagonistic agents are avoiding agents but they also aim at a *moving* target, therefore they need another agent as their target. In other words, antagonists are chasing other agents. Antagonistic agents might differ in that they can be *selective* or *non-selective* with respect to their target. *Non-selective* antagonists chase any other agent. *Selective* antagonists chase a particular agent. We remark that an agent can be selective only if it is able to recognize and select its target. Of course, all kinds of intermediate cases of more or less selective agents are possible. For instance, they may chase a certain type of agent. We consider here the extremes only: selective antagonists chase one particular target, non-selective antagonist chase any other agent. Antagonistic agents may be further distinguished as *aggressive* and *non-aggressive*. Aggressive agents go straight to their target. Antagonistic aggressive agents typically occur in military applications; extreme examples of aggressive antagonistic agents are modern cruise missiles. For our purposes the aggressive agents are not very important: after a successful hit there is no more team. Of interest to our studies are the non-aggressive antagonistic agents. These agents chase their target but approach it only until some threshold distance.

2.3 CONGENIAL TEAMS

In a team, different agents with different intentions might be applied in combination. To characterize multi-agent teams, one usually distinguishes between *homogeneous* and *heterogeneous* teams, see for instance (Fujimara, 1991, Noreils, 1992). (Fujimara, 1991) gives the following descriptions of homogeneous and heterogeneous teams. In a homogenous team *"(...) all robots are identical in the sense that they are operated under an identical set of simple rules."* Heterogeneous teams consist of *"a set of agents with different capabilities with respect to their sensors, planning algorithms, etc."* The terms homogeneous and heterogeneous are relative, and depend on which characteristics are taken into account and how much deviation is accepted. In our further investigation we will be more precise.

We assume that all our agents operate with roughly the same cognitive basis (Penders and Braspenning, 1997) and the same ontology. This means that all agents can signal the same objects. In this respect they are homogeneous. However, the agents might have different intentions. We define a team of agents as *congenial* if they have the same intentions and in other respects they are (nearly) homogeneous. The latter means that they might look quite different, but the actions, which they perform, are comparable, that is, the sensors and actuators, and thus the spatial movements are very similar. Congenial agents have the same intentions, in terms of design they are robots provided with the same programs. Congenial agents apply in the same situations the same actions, thus in a team they can be substituted for each other.

Below, we examine congenial teams and give the major tendencies in their behaviour. The teams might be composed of any of the types of agents described above. An overview is given in table 6.2.

Congenial team	Team Behaviour
Stationary agents	Non-dynamic
Blindly moving	Chaos or Path planning
Avoiding	Scatter
Antagonist non-selective	Cluster together
Antagonist selective	Cluster around one or ring of agents

Table 6.2 Teams of congenial agents.

A congenial team of *stationary agents*, that is, a team of obstacles, is not very exciting for studying interaction since nothing happens and it has no dynamics. *Blindly moving* agents, whether or not acting in a team, just start and go. A team of blindly moving agents typically requires centralized control and dynamic path planning, otherwise the team will end in complete chaos. Moreover, in a large team, extensive path planning must have preceded any action; small deviations from planned courses will accumulate and lead to disorder, as we have discussed above.
Avoiding agents try to avoid and get away from others. Thus, a congenial team of avoiding agents tends to scatter. Generally the agents also aim for a (fixed) goal; the positioning of the goals might force them to approach each other. Thus, goal finding and avoidance behaviours interfere, and the agents can arrive in conflicting situations, we discuss this later (refer to figure 6.2 for a first impression). We start concentrating on the avoiding behaviour. The notion of an autonomous robot is commonly associated with that of an avoiding agent.

As stated before, *antagonists* avoid obstacles and chase for a target agent. *Non-selective antagonists* chase for any target agent. When they get close to the target they maintain a certain distance. It is remembered that we consider only non-aggressive antagonists. Thus in a congenial team non-selective antagonists cluster together. Since they are chasing each other, the team shows cohesion. Team cohesion has interesting applications as we discuss in the next subsection.

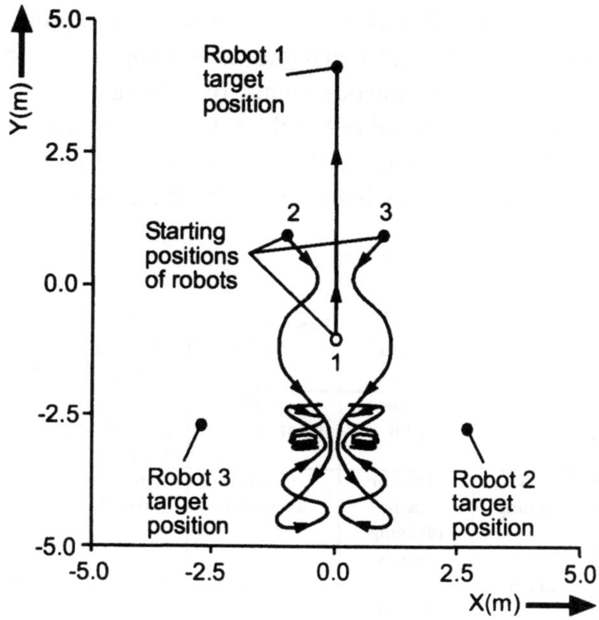

Figure 6.2 Trajectories of three congenial robots

Selective (non-aggressive) *antagonists* chase for a specific target. The target may differ from agent to agent, the composition of teams of selective antagonists form may differ accordingly. We discuss two extremes. The first extreme is a team in which all antagonists focus on the same target agent, in the other extreme each antagonist is itself the target of another agent. In the first team all antagonists chase the same agent and the team will cluster around this target agent. In the second team each antagonist chases a different target. The team will sort out such that each is close to its target while avoiding others. The antagonists will form a ring.

Table 6.2 indicates which situation a team of congenial agents tends to establish. Homogeneity in a team provides a starting point for predicting team behaviour. Stationary agents remain at their places, the start and end situation are the same. Blindly moving agents behave according to the planning, otherwise chaos results. The reactive agents in our teams perform goal finding and obstacle avoidance. As a result of this, avoiding agents scatter and antagonist cluster together.

2.4 NEWCOMER IN A TEAM

The congenial teams studied above are homogeneous, which makes it easier to study them. For a heterogeneous team, it is questionable whether different intentions are consistent with each other. Moreover, it is doubtful whether we can get any hold on the general behaviour of heterogeneous teams. Below, we investigate slightly heterogeneous teams, by adding one single newcomer agent to a congenial team. In table 6.3 the rows give the congenial teams of table 6.2. The columns of the table show which *newcomer* is inserted in the congenial team, and indicate its behaviour. The behaviours of the congenial teams are on the diagonal.

	Newcomer agent				
Congenial team	Stationary	Blindly moving	Avoiding	Antagonistic non-selective	Antagonistic selective
Stationary agents	non- -dynamic	pre-planned path	smoothly going through	smoothly going through (stops at one)	smoothly going through (stops at one)
Blindly moving agents	new planning	chaos or path planning	reactive avoidance	reactive avoidance	reactive avoidance
Avoiding agents	adapts	moves straight through	scatter	looses target	stays close to one agent
Antagonist non- -selective	adapts	caught at once	flee	cluster together	joins cluster
Antagonist selective	adapts	leader	leader	joins cluster	cluster around one, ring of agents

Table 6.3 Teams of congenial agents with a newcomer

The first row gives an environment of *stationary agents* which by itself of course has no dynamics. Adding one more stationary agents or obstacles does not change much. However, newcomers of the other types do move around. A blindly-moving newcomer must apply path planning. The stationary environment is a typical setting for that: there is hardly any interaction. The avoiding and antagonistic agents will equally smoothly pass through this environment: they apply obstacle avoidance. There is little interaction in the team and the different intentions of the newcomers are hardly observable, thus the row is nearly uniform. A slight difference is observed when a newcomer antagonist aims for one of the obstacles as its target.

Row 2 shows a *blindly moving* team. In this team all agents proceed along the pre-planned paths. When adding a stationary object in column one, the planning needs to be reconsidered. When a moving agent (columns 2-5) is added to the team, there is a choice between two possibilities: adapting the team or simply ignoring the newcomer. The first one, to adapt the whole team to the newcomer, means that fully new paths need to be planned. Obviously, this is the best choice when the newcomer is blindly moving as well (column 2). However, if the newcomer is a reactive agent (columns 3-5) it is nearly impossible to set up a plan. Hence, only the second possibility remains: the (reactive) newcomer is simply ignored: the blindly moving agents continue as planned. The newcomer has to avoid the blindly-moving agents and finds itself in a rather discomforting situation. The newcomer avoiding agent (column 3) will give way to the traversing objects. The newcomer antagonists (colomns 4 and 5) will keep away from the objects while chasing one or several of the moving objects.

A congenial team of *avoiding agents* in row 3, will scatter. Since the agents avoid obstacles, they will adapt their courses when a stationary obstacle is added. When a blindly moving object is added (column 2) the avoiding agents will give way to it. The team behaviour becomes particularly clear if we assume that the team is at rest; the blind agent crosses the shop floor straight, and drives the avoiding agents out of his way.[2] A non-selective antagonist inserted in an avoiding team (column 4) will constantly change his target, and subsequently loses each. To be more successful, he should focus on one particular agent as his target. This case represents a real life problem in the natural world. By sticking together, animals in a herd protect themselves from predators. The predator's problem is to single out his prey animal, in order to focus its actions. A selective antagonist (column 5) indeed singles out his target agent, he will follow it and stay close, thus after a while the avoiding team proceeds to scatter where one agent is followed by the selective antagonist.

A team of *non-selective antagonists* given in row 4, will cluster together (column 4). The team's behaviour will not change much with the arrival of a newcomer. The team easily adapts to a new obstacle on the shop floor (column 1). A moving newcomer (columns 2-5) might for a while be chased. However, the non-selective antagonists soon change their interest to others. The blind newcomer will be given way (column 2). The avoiding newcomer will try to flee, and might succeed in escaping the team or become locked in the cluster (column 3). A selective antagonist (in column 5) gets locked or ultimately finds its target and stays close to it (in the cluster).

Selective antagonists in row 5, mutually avoid each other and cluster around one agent or form a ring (column 5). As for all reactive agents, also this team easily adapts to a new stationary obstacle. In columns 2 through 5, the newcomer is moving and the selective antagonists might focus on it. If the newcomer is the common target, the antagonists will follow him, he becomes leading. This is true when the newcomer is a blind agent (column 2) as well as

---

[2] The case is like the chickens on a farm who are driven away when the farmer passes. Obviously, the blind agent is the one which is most successful in reaching its destination. This is the typical case where the agent with the least knowledge is the most successful, as noted in (Fujimara, 1991) and (Penders, 1991).

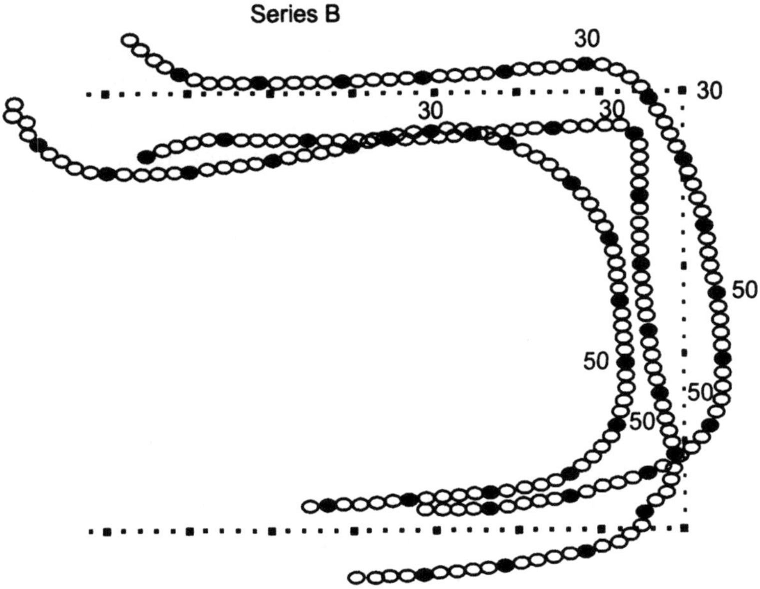

Figure 6.3 Robots moving in formation

an avoiding one (column 3) (the newcomer agent will be followed, as the rats followed the Pied Piper of Hamelin, cf. figure 6.3). A non-selective newcomer (column 4) will chase the selective antagonists and cluster with the team.
So far for the analysis of adding a newcomer to a congenial team. For non-reactive teams we conclude that when a non-reactive agent (an obstacle or a blindly-moving agent) is added the planning has to be redone. On the other hand, when a reactive agent (avoiding or antagonistic) is added to a non-reactive team re-planning is of no use. Reactive teams show much interaction dynamics, and thus they are equipped to deal also with newcomers and no particular provisions have to be made. However, a newcomer might influence the team behaviour considerably.

2.5 EXAMPLE

Non-aggressive antagonistic agents can be used for quite interesting purposes. (Penders, 1999) discusses robots applied on a goods terminal. One of the emerging problems is the possible "chaos" in the robot traffic. Many items of cargo are transported from one side to another, and items are temporarily put aside: it is rather difficult to maintain proper order on a busy terminal. Selective antagonists might be programmed to follow a human worker. The robots will follow him and occurring traffic problems are intuitively solved by

the human worker. A variant is that a robot replaces the human. If the other robots follow this leader, on the main trajectories, we have to deal with a much simpler traffic problem.
Non-selective antagonist are also of interest for being applied on a terminal. When each robot is following an other they will traverse the terminal in a long but moving queue. Apart from the goods terminal, interesting applications are also found in road traffic. Cars (equipped as non-selective antagonists) will follow one another but will keep fixed distances between each other, again a long but moving queue will result on the motorway.

3. INTERACTION: COLLISIONS AND CONFLICTS

We have discussed on a global level how team behaviour generates from the interaction among the robots. In this section we develop formal tools to describe interaction for teams of congenial avoiding agents, moving in a two dimensional plane. The robots perform goal-finding and obstacle avoidance. But, as we have seen in the previous section, the robots interact with each other and that is one of the points here, there is no guarantee that they eventually will arrive at their goal. As an illustration, and before turning to the technical work, we first give an example of the sort of problems we will deal with. Figure 6.2, which is taken from (Wang, 1989) shows the trails of three congenial avoiding autonomous robots. The figure indicates the start positions and the targets of the robots. Robot 1 succeeds to reach its goal, but robots 2 and 3 fail, they run into the insoluble conflict of avoiding one another. To analyse these situations we distinguish various geometrical interaction patterns. Moreover, we formulate and proof a theorem on how to apply the interaction patterns when studying teams. After that we will go into detail with congenial avoiding teams.

3.1 SPATIAL AND TEMPORAL PRELIMINARIES

For clarity we reiterate the major constraints on teams of agents. We assume minimal communication in the team. The robots cannot communicate, let alone negotiate with each other; there is neither a communication link present, nor a (permanent) link to consult a central controller. Once having received its instructions, a robot is assumed to perform on its own. The robots can perceive objects, i.e., obstacles and other agents. Each robot has the same kind of information about its environment, i.e., they have the same cognitive bases.
We treat robots as *free flying objects*(Latombe, 1991). This means that the robots can move freely in the two-dimensional plane, and are not bounded to a grid pattern or the like. We do not take kinematics constraints into account. The robots are considered to be *point robots* (Fujimara, 1991), which means

that they have no spatial extension and thus the robots compete in the plane about points only.
We observe that the team behaviour and interaction patterns can only be described from the standpoint of an external observer. Our approach is to go stepwise from situation to situation, and analyse how each agent reacts to the situation. Such analysis is usual in computer science, in particular in studying *interprocess communication* (see, e.g. (Dolev et al., 1987)), but has to be adapted for spatial applications. A difficulty is that in interprocess communication, actions of agents occur in a temporal sequence, whereas in spatial interaction all agents can react at the same point in time. Nevertheless, the stepwise approach simplifies the mathematics required and reveals the overall characteristics of our teams.
To deal with the temporal aspects of interaction, we introduce *points in time* (or moments) which are common to all robots; which is equivalent to saying that their clocks run synchronized. At the (common) points in time robots might change their action. An action chosen at a point in time is sustained during the subsequent period. When the robots move they use maximum speed all the time, unless they are explicitly instructed otherwise.
Interaction patterns are extended in time and are represented in *time frames*, which are sets of subsequent time points. The course of events has only one future direction, hence a *linear time* model is appropriate. To have sufficient points of time available to represent the crucial events, we need at least a dense model of time (dense means isomorphic to the rational numbers).

Notations

$\mathbf{D}$ is the overall domain of objects and includes all agents and robots. Each agent i is able to observe any of the other agents $j \in \mathbf{D}$ (i.e., they have equal cognitive bases). Thus we can speak of a subset $d \subseteq \mathbf{D}$ of objects to which each agent is in principle sensitive. This, however, does not mean that the domain is fully known in advance. The number of objects present in a situation might vary in time. We have to deal with *appearing*, *disappearing* and *temporary* objects (Fujimara, 1991). Appearing objects are objects which initially are too far away and therefore not seen yet, but which may enter the situation later on. Others move away from a situation, they disappear, as robot I in figure 6.2. Thus, for each point t in time the set d of objects relevant at that time point t is fixed, however the set might vary with the time points.
We use the following symbols:

D	overall domain of objects and robots
d	$d \subseteq \mathbf{D}$ set of relevant objects
i, j, o	variables to denote objects or agents
$(\Re \times \Re)$	the two-dimensional plane
V_{ixy}	position of robot or vehicle i
G_i	the goal of robot i; the positions of the goals are usually fixed
p, q	variables reserved for points in the plane
$dist(p, q)$	(Euclidean) distance between point p and q in the plane
$[p, q]$	line segment between p and q
$Ob(i, o)$	robot i observes object o
S_i	actual speed of robot i ;

The usual logical connectives $\wedge$, $\vee$ and $\rightarrow$ as well as the quantifiers $\exists$ (exists) and $\forall$ (for all) are used in the object language, to describe the situation at a certain point of time. In the meta language, when speaking about temporal relationships we use the words **and**, **if**, and **iff** (if and only if). For example we can further specify the predicate $Ob(i, j)$:

Definition 1 ($Ob(i, j)$)

$$t \models Ob(i, o) \textbf{iff } t \models V_o \in H_i \textit{ for some given horizon } \ H_i \subseteq (\Re \times \Re)$$

At time t, agent i observes an object, if and only if the object is within the horizon of i. The horizon is that part of the plane which i can observe. In any case, horizons might differ between the agents, however for convenience of the discussion in the present chapter, we usually assume that all agents have the same horizon. Moreover we assume that the horizons coincide with the whole plane, $H_i = (\Re \times \Re)$ for every agent i. Consequently the predicate $Ob(i, j)$ is symmetric: $Ob(i, j) \leftrightarrow Ob(j, i)$. Exceptions are the robots in figure 6.1. Robot 1 overviews the plane but robot 2 has a limited horizon, that is why the robots behave slightly different.

3.2 INTERACTION PATTERNS

As a start to distinguish and define certain interaction patterns, we single out certain special situations that may lead to a *collision*. A team of congenial avoiding robots is quite dynamic. During the interaction certain *incidents* may occur because of which the agents change the course of events such that no collision occurs. We introduce the dynamic notion of a *conflict* to denote any course of interaction. A conflict is a series of situations which may or may not lead to a collision. Given this ambiguity we have to elaborate on conflicts and define when they end. At the end of the section we have sufficient tools available to state our formal definition of *having an intention*, as was promised before.

Events

Definition 2 (Situation) *A* situation *is the positioning of agents and objects at one point in time.*

For convenience (and as long as no confusion is expected) we identify situations by the points of time at which they occur.

Certain situations contain a threat towards a collision. We distinguish two types of collisions called *real-collisions* and *semi-collisions*. A situation contains a *real-collision* if starting from this situation, the robots have to cross one particular point (p) in space, at the same (future) point of time. However, this prediction works only when the robots maintain their current speeds S_i and S_j. Figure 6.4 shows a real-collision of two robots A and B.

Definition 3 (Real-collision RC(d))

$$t \models RC(d) \textbf{ iff}$$
$$t \models \exists p \, \forall i \in d(p \in [V_i, G_i]) \textit{ and } t \models \forall i, j \in d \, (dist(V_i, p)/dist(V_j, p) = S_i/S_j$$

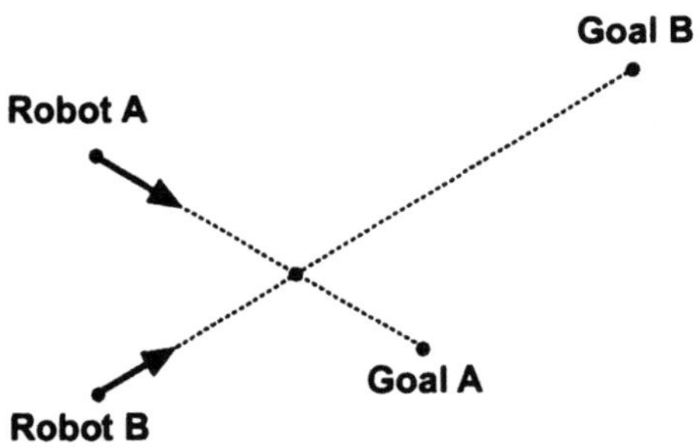

Figure 6.4 A real-collision situation of two robots

From the real-collision situation onwards, the speeds of the robots need not be constant, each robot might change its speed. If the speeds change relative to each other, the collision will not occur. Thus we may therefore drop the clause about speeds, and obtain the weaker notion of a semi-collision. In a semi-collision the courses of the robots intersect, however the robots can be at arbitrarily distances from the intersection point (no relation to the speeds is required). For instance in figure 6.5, robot A nearly passes p while robot B is due to arrive much later.

Definition 4 (Semi-collision SC(d))

$$t \models SC(d) \textbf{ iff } t \models \exists p \forall i \in d(p \in [V_i, G_i]).$$

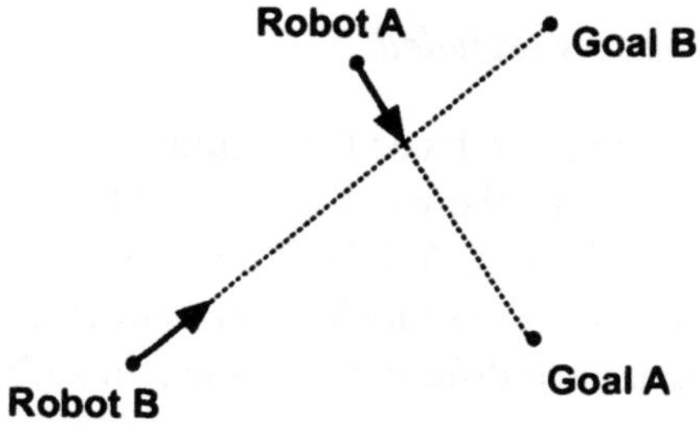

Figure 6.5 A semi-collision situation

In definitions of collisions, we mainly focus on the goal finding behaviour of a robot. However, the robots also avoid each other. When combining avoidance and goal finding, the intersection point p is not fixed throughout a series of situations. Therefore, in real life applications semi-collisions are very often identified as dangerous. Automated collision-avoidance systems applied in airborne traffic, treat real-collisions and semi-collisions similarly (see (Zeghal and Ferber, 1993)). In marine applications the point p is called a *virtual* collision point. (Zhao et al., 1992) review maritime applications, and use the *distance at closest point of approach* (DCPA) and the *time to closest point of approach* (TCPA). Note that both notions only make sense in semi-collisions. We have identified real-collisions and semi-collisions, but reactive agents start to avoid and thus interact, even when there is no indication of a semi-collision. To capture this feature, we introduce the notion of incident. In a certain situation, an agent has an *incident* with the objects in set d if it is sensitive to the objects.

Definition 5 (Incident I(i,d))

$$t \models I(i,d) \textbf{iff } t \models \bigvee_{j \in d} (Ob(i,j)).$$

The notion of incident is relative to an individual agent. Thus, in a team of agents every agent has its particular incidents. Mutual or reciprocal incidents are incidents caused by and observed in the same situation by agents who are mutually involved. In a mutual incident all agents observe each other, and we denote a mutual incident as $I(d)$.

Definition 6 (Mutual incidents I(d))

$$t \models I(d) \textbf{iff } t \models \bigwedge_{i \in d} I(i, d')$$

where d' $d \backslash i$: d' is d but i is excluded.

Above in definition 1 we introduced the assumption that our agents all share the same horizon which spans the whole plane, $H_i(\Re \times \Re)$ for every agent i. Thus we also have $Ob(i, j) \leftrightarrow Ob(j, i)$. The consequence is that in the discussion below incidents always coincide with mutual incidents. However, as said above, agents might have different horizons. In such cases the difference between incidents and mutual incidents becomes crucial, refer to section 4 and (Penders, 1991) for more examples.

Interaction patterns Now that we have identified several particular events, we proceed to model interaction patterns. Basically we need so-called time frames, that is series of subsequent points in time. Technically a frame $\mathbf{T} = 3D(T, <)$ is a set of time points T with an ordering $<$. Of course, to model robots there should be a particular relation between the time point in our frames. The objects in our set d move from one situation to another, however, they must follow a continuous path; they cannot jump from one position to another.

Definition 7 (Path) *(Latombe, 1991) A* path *of an agent from position (x_1, y_1) in situation 1 to (x_2, y_2) in situation 2, is a continuous mapping τ:*

$$\tau : [t_1, t_2] \rightarrow (\Re \times \Re), \textit{with } \tau(t_1)(x_1, y_1) \textit{and } \tau(t_2)(x_2, y_2).$$

Definition 8 (Related situations) *Two situations are (time-)*related *if there exists a path for each agent $i \in d$, from the first situation to the second situation.*

As a consequence of the latter definition, related situations have so-called constant domains: in two related situations t and t' the same agents occur; hence if a new object turns up the situations are not related. We now have the tools available to define the notion of a conflict, which is central to our treatment of interaction. An *interaction pattern* obviously must be a time frame consisting of *incidents* in *related situations*. *Conflicts* are interaction patterns where the agents mutually interfere with one another's aim to reach the (respective) destination point(s).

Definition 9 (Conflict) *A* conflict *is a time frame* **T** $(T, <)$ *of related situations with a fixed domain d, such that at every point of time t in the frame there is a mutual incident.*

$$\mathbf{T} \models \textit{Conflict(d)} \textbf{ iff } \mathbf{T} \models I(d)[t]$$

at all time points t.

Conflicts end when anyone of the mutual and related incident conditions is violated. Examples at hand are cases where objects appear and disappear from the horizon (Definition 1). In such cases the incidents are no longer related. A conflict ends *naturally* if at a certain point of time $t \in T$ at least one of the robots is no longer obstructed by any of the others, which means that – under further normal conditions – it would reach its destination. For convenience and when no confusion is expected, we leave out the qualification 'natural'. A certain point of time t is the *Ending of Conflict(d)*:

Definition 10 (Ending of conflict) $t \models$ Ending of Conflict(d) **iff** $t \models \exists i \in d\ (dist(V_i, G_i)0)$.

Strictly speaking this definition demands that an agent has to come to a standstill exactly at the position of the goal. In general we have to admit some tolerance. We could replace (dist(V_i, G_i) 0) by some criteria which says that agent i has to enter a certain neighbourhood of G_i. Another way around this is to allow the goal to have (spatial) extension. We will not introduce these options here, as it does not affect the general idea we want to sketch. However, it is important to point out that if the agent overshoots its destination point (or the defined neighbourhood) we stipulate that after the overshoot we are dealing with another conflict.
In general a robot involved in a conflict does not approach its destination point straightaway. As we have seen in figure 6.1, due to the interaction with other robots, a robot might make all kinds of enveloping movements. Also, at a certain point in time the robot might be rather close to its goal while some moments later it can again be further away. The robots in figure 6.2 seem to do so. Whatever the case, a conflict has an end if (in the long term) a series of time points exists in which one robot really approaches its goal. This robot must have a path, which is continuous and that gets arbitrary close to its goal. We define *targeting series*, as a sequence of those time points at which the robot really approaches its the goal.

Definition 11 (Targeting series) *Let* τ *be a path defined on time frame* **T** $(T, <)$*, such that at time* t_0 *robot* i *is at distance* c^* *from* G_i *and at time* t_e

it is at G_i, then Targeting series $\mathbf{TS(i, G_i)}$ *consist of time points between t_0 and t_e such that for every c, $c^* > c > 0$,*

$$\mathbf{T} \models dist(V_i, G_i) < c\ [t]\ \textit{for some}\ t \in TS(i, G_i)$$

and for

$$t, t^* \in TS(i, G_i)\ \textit{if}\ t < t^*\ \textit{then}\ dist(V_i, G_i)[t] < dist(V_i, G_i)[t^*]$$

Targeting series are only useful if they indeed characterize ending conflicts. We prove this in the following theorem.

Theorem 1 *A* Conflict(d) *has a natural ending* **iff** *it contains a targeting series $TS(i, G_i)$ for some robot $i \in d$.*

Proof
$\Rightarrow$ when a conflict has a natural end, for some i, dist $(V_i, G_i)0$; a targeting series with a limit of dist $(V_i, G_i)0$ is easily constructed.

$\Leftarrow$ if a conflict contains a targeting series for robot i, robot i will approach its goal arbitrarily close, that is: the limit of dist $(V_i, G_i)0$. □

Many conflicts end in the long run, though at first sight it is not clear. A targeting series, according to theorem 1, provides a characteristic to recognise ending conflicts. However, there are conflicts that do not have an end, as already was illustrated by figure 6.2. We call them balanced conflicts.

Definition 12 (Balanced conflict) *A* balanced conflict *is a conflict that does not have a natural ending.*

A conflict is balanced if from some point in time t^* onwards, none of the robots approaches its goal any closer, that is the conflict does not contain any targeting series.

Lemma
A time frame $\mathbf{T}$ $(T, <)$ contains a balanced *Conflict(d)* **iff**

$$\mathbf{T} \models \forall i \in d(\text{dist}(V_i, G_i) \geq c > 0)[t^*]$$

for a certain time point t^* and

$$\mathbf{T} \models \forall i \in d(\text{dist}(V_i, G_i) \geq c)[t]$$

for all $t, t^* < t$.

Proof
According to theorem 1, a balanced conflict has no end **iff** it contains no targeting series, and that is what the lemma says. □

Reviewing collisions and conflicts In the introduction we referred to a cargo terminal on which robots were to be applied. However, a balanced conflict may withhold a team from making any progress. If the robots set out for a task, but half way get entangled in a balanced conflict, they obviously never accomplish their task. The designer of a team, of course, seeks to avoid balanced conflicts. The above proved theorem and lemma are the main tools for deriving mathematical characteristics of the performance of a team. Their use is that proofs can be restricted, and need to take into account only series of relevant situations. Hence, it is not required that a proof completely outlines the courses followed by the robots involved. For instance, in figure 6.2 balance might be proven by showing that robots 2 and 3 do not enter a certain region around their targets. Yet for showing that a zigzagging robot reaches its goal, it is sufficient to show that the zigzagging course gets arbitrarily close to the target.

3.3 INTENTIONS DEFINED

Above we defined a conflict as a pattern of mutual interactions between two or more robots. Using patterns of interaction, we can formally define the notion *having an intention*, as promised. Intentions concern the behaviour of a single agent, no matter how others react. An intention is applied in a series of related situations. Moreover, an intention designates peculiarities in the behaviour of an agent. Hence, we use the notion of a targeting series, in particular because it does not require that the agent heads straight for its target but instead it allows some freedom.

Definition 13 (Intention) *Agent i* has an intention *for target o (at position (x, y)) if there exists a targeting series $TS(i, o)$ for i with o as its centre point.*

This definition applies for goal finding, but we have also treated avoidance as an intention. When avoiding, the agent moves away from the target object o. A definition of avoidance is obtained by substituting a targeting series with a diverging series.

Definition 14 (Avoiding) *Let τ be a path defined on time frame* $\mathbf{T}$ $(T, <)$, *such that at time t_0 robot i is at distance c^* from o, then agent i* avoids *object o on time frame* $\mathbf{T}$, *if for any $c, c > c^*$:*

$$\mathbf{T} \models \mathit{dist}(V_i, o)\ c^*[t] \text{ for some } t > t_0$$

and for $t, t^* \in \mathbf{T}$ *if* $t > t^*$ *then dist* $(V_i, G_i)[t] >$ *dist* $(V_i, G_i)[t^*]$.

Targeting and diverging series also can be applied when the target object O moves. Thus the definition also applies in the case of moving objects.
The definition lays down an intention as a pattern of performed actions. There is no claim for completeness of the definition. For instance, in a philosophical context an agent might be said to have an intention even if – because of certain circumstances – the agent is unable to effectuate it. Also, an agent might reach a target without (in the philosophical sense) intending to do so. We make no effort to deal with the cases mentioned. What we have obtained with defining an intention is that we have an indication of what intentions are in a geometrical context. To have an intention for target O, is clearly different from avoiding O. The programming of a robot generates the performed actions and thus generates intentions. Different programs applied on the same robot usually imply different intentions. However note that intentions are not identical with (parts of) programs. Moreover, in the geometric context we can judge only performed actions. Nevertheless, all we need here and in the next section is that programs and intentions are related. We restrict the discussion to agents with the intentions of goal finding and obstacle avoidance. Elsewhere (Penders, 1999) we further specify intentions in a philosophical context.

4. AVOIDING ROBOTS

We proceed studying congenial teams and the interaction and team behaviour generated by the intentions: goal finding and obstacle avoidance. Detailed characterisations of interaction, of course, vary with the procedures applied. In this section we discuss two obstacle avoidance procedures: flee-opposite avoidance and potential-field avoidance. We show simulations of these procedures, they illustrate some of the behaviours which we encountered in Introduction. The *flee-opposite* avoidance is discussed first, it is a straightforward procedure basically performing obstacle avoidance without consequent goal finding. The flee-opposite procedure generates series of repetitive movements, as figures 6.6 and 6.7 show. The attractiveness of the flee-opposite procedure is its simplicity in implementation, it requires hardly any processing (Penders, 1999).
Secondly we discuss *potential-field* avoidance. The avoidance is based on a so-called *artificial potential-field*, see (Khatib, 1986), and essentially combines goal finding with obstacle avoidance. The potential-field procedure generates a smoother path, (Penders, 1999) goes at length into the application of the potential-field procedure in a team and gives a mathematical analysis of the interaction that generates in the team, here we recall some of the results.
We explore the interaction in a congenial team of avoiding robots, first we briefly study the flee-opposite procedure and the potential field procedure. In

advance we should stress that we take a rather particular point of view by considering interaction in a team and evaluating the avoidance procedures when applied concurrently. The designers of the procedures probably never have had such a context in mind; our treatment will not do justice to the procedures themselves. However, despite this, the avoidance procedures put us on the way to study interaction.

4.1 FLEE OPPOSITE AVOIDANCE

Newcomer among stationary objects The basic move generated by the flee-opposite procedure is straightforward: as soon as the robot observes an object, it steps backwards until the object is out of sight, that is, out of the horizon definition 1. Out of sight means that the object is out of the range of the sensors (see figure 6.6). Depending on relative position of the object the robot will steer either a little to the left or to the right while moving backwards. After the step backwards is completed, the robot has to resume a course, at this point several choices for heuristic rules are possible. (Chattergy, 1985) discusses a family of such rules. We elaborate two of them, the results confirm those of (Chattergy, 1985).

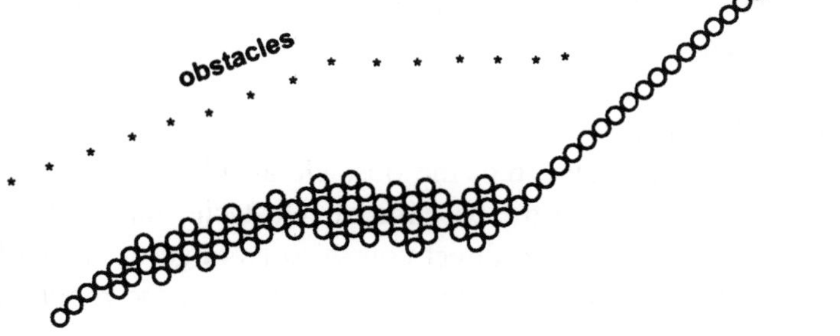

Figure 6.6 Flee-opposite with fixed direction

Figure 6.6 gives simulation results, obtained by a robot that resumes a course straight ahead, as if its target is always in front of it. In the simulation, the robot encounters a row of objects on its left and steps back slightly to the right. After a series of repetitive steps it succeeds in passing the objects. The robot is in fact exploring its environment, as it is not fixed on a particular target.

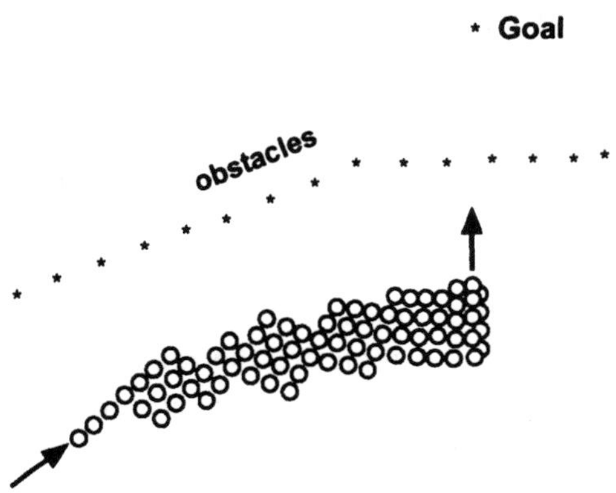

Figure 6.7 Flee-opposite with fixed goal

In the simulation of figure 6.7, the position of the goal is fixed. The robot starts at the same position as in figure 6.6 and encounters the row of objects. After going back slightly to the right, the robot resumes a course. In this case it drives towards the fixed position of the goal and soon becomes trapped. We may call this a balanced conflict, though a degenerated one since there is only one agent acting. In any case, the simulation shows how goal finding and obstacle avoidance interfere.

The same diagnosis applies in the situations shown in figure 6.8. In the left situation, contrary to figure 6.6, the obstacle-avoidance procedure does not guide the robot away from the baseline of [Obstacle,Goal]. When the robot finds an object exactly on the direct course to its target it is also locked in a balanced conflict. In the right situation of figure 6.8 the robot encounters a corner. It makes a couple of moves, however the net effect is minimal, and the robot is trapped. This occurs typically in sharp corners, when the robot is on the diagonal.

Congenial team interaction A team of two congenial robots applying the flee-opposite procedure is shown in figure 6.9. The series (a) and (b) show some successive points in time and the courses of two robots. The series start

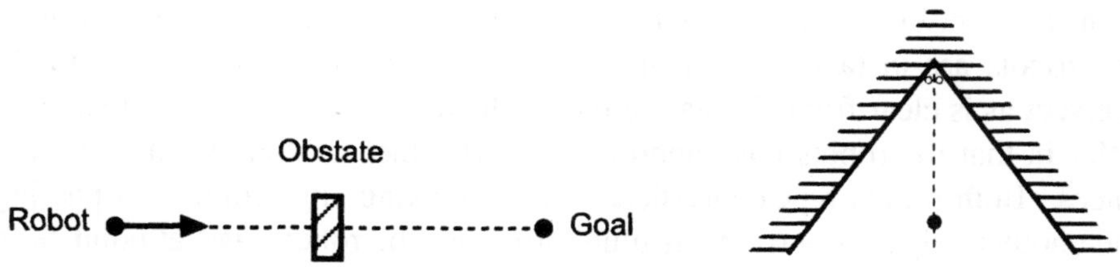

Figure 6.8 Left: a stationary obstacle and one robot; right: a trapped robot

at time point t_0, with the two robots at positions A and B. At the time point t_1, the robots are sufficiently close to perceive each other, then they both flee simultaneously in (strictly) opposite directions (as shown in the figure). At the next point in time (t_2) the robots are too far from each other to perceive one another, so both robots resume moving in the goal direction. The result is a zigzag course of the robots around borders of their horizons, that is the threshold distance at which they are mutually visible. This threshold is the maximum range of their sensors.

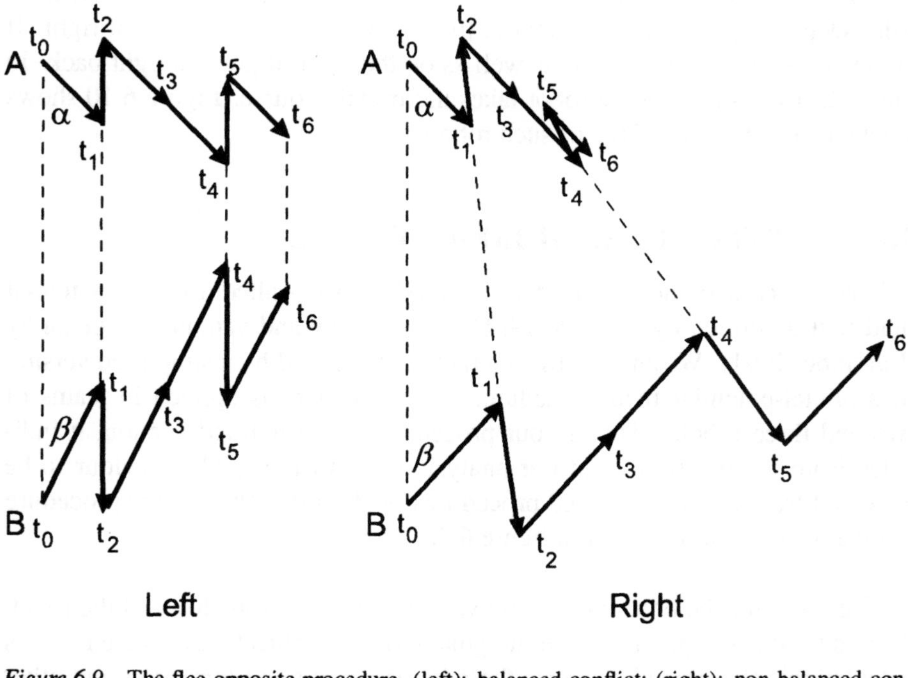

Figure 6.9 The flee-opposite procedure, (left): balanced conflict; (right): non-balanced conflict

In figure 6.9 (left), the situations at points t_1, t_4 and t_6 are quite similar. The robots are in (a repetition of) real-coll isions: their courses eventually intersect as is clear from elongating their velocity vectors. The situations only differ in that the robots have approached each other at slightly different distances. Both robots repeatedly flee, without making any progress in passing one another. Figure 6.9 (right) is quite different, the robots start at point t_0 in a semi-collision. At point t_6 the robots are out of each others range, from that point of time on both can proceed without conflicting.
The explanation for the different behaviours infigure 6.9 (left) and (right) is simple. At the successive points we can draw lines connecting the positions of the robots A and B at that point of time, in the figure they are drawn as broken lines. The orientation of the successive lines at the time points t_1, t_4 and t_6 is important. It is common knowledge among sailors that if, as in the left figure, the lines are parallel to each other the robots will eventually collide. That is the situation of a real-collision. A proof – that in the left figure the robots will cross the same point at the same point in time, and that there will not be such a point in right figure – is easily constructed by similarity in a triangle.

Balanced conflicts also occur in a team of *three* robots. To apply the flee-opposite procedure in a team, we have to define the flee-opposite move when more than one object is detected. For instance the robot discussed in (Penders, 1999) only detects whether there is an object on the right or on the left hand side. Depending on this information, the step back is adjusted left or right. If an object is spotted on the left as well as on the right, it goes straight back. In this indecisive situation the robot takes the middle course. Figure 6.10 shows a balanced conflict for three of such robots.

4.2 POTENTIAL FIELD AVOIDANCE

The second avoidance procedure is based on a so-called artificial potential field first described by (Khatib, 1986), an overview and variants are given by (Latombe, 1991). We analyse the interaction generated by a simplified version of artificial-potential field procedure. The procedure is applied in teams of two and three robots. Though our procedure is a simplified version, it indicates from the perspective of our analysis the rather typical behaviour to be expected from the sophisticated procedures of (Khatib, 1986) or the procedure of (Wang, 1989) as depicted in figure 6.2.

The input for the procedure is an overview of the surroundings of the robot. That is to say, the points where the goal and other objects are located. In its calculations, the procedure treats the goal as a source of attraction and other

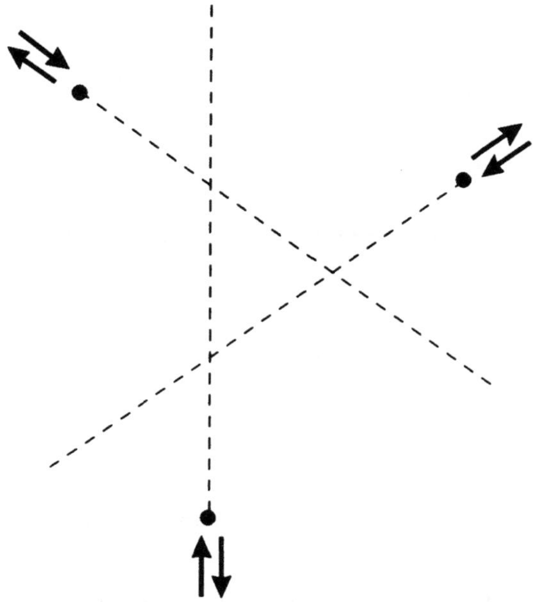

Figure 6.10 Three robots with flee-opposite

objects as sources of repulsion. At each point of time the new velocity of the robot is determined as the vector sum of these forces, see figure 6.11. The magnitudes of the repulsive forces decrease as a function of the distances to them. One often visualises this as a landscape in which the repulsive forces form mountains and the attraction forces valleys. The procedure calculates a path of decreasing resistance, i.e., it steers the robot through the valleys in the landscape.

Newcomer among stationary objects Figure 6.1 shows a simulation of two robots crossing the shop floor, in the middle of which there is an object. As is clear from the figure the potential-field procedure generates smooth paths. Robot 1 fully overviews the shop floor. From the start, it avoids the obstacle and robot 2. A consequence of the overview is the overshoot near the goal 1. The sensor of robot 2 has a limited range. As late as step 5, it becomes sensitive to the obstacle. Note that the last steps are straightforward towards the goal 2. In the figure several of the distinctions made in our interaction model apply. There is no real or semi-collision in the simulation, only incidents. For robot 2, the obstacle appears at a sudden, moreover, since robot 2 does not react to robot 1 there is no mutual incident. Any case the simulation shows how important

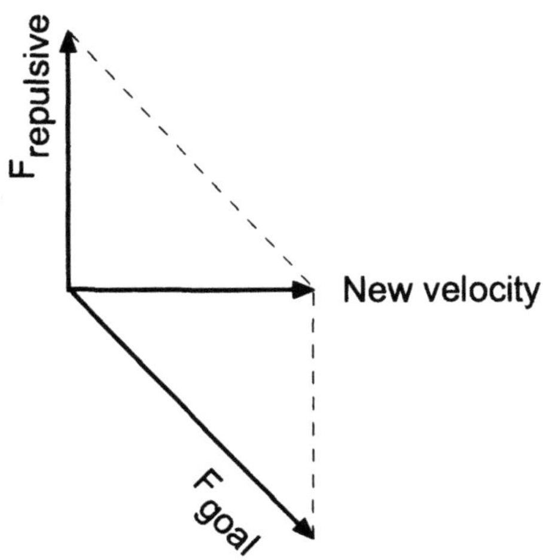

Figure 6.11 Vector sum in the potential-field procedure

it is for interaction, that a team is congenial, as there is no interaction between the robots in figure 6.1.

4.3 CONGENIAL TEAM INTERACTION

A mathematical analysis of the potential-field interaction in a team of two and three robots is given in (Penders, 1999). Below, we discuss several particular cases which together indicate the main characteristics of two and three-robot teams. We discuss a balanced conflict and a slightly different situation in which the robot team turns. Thereafter we discuss a case where two robots force the third robot forward or backward.

A team of congenial robots, applying the potential-field procedure has some similarity with the mechanics of a system of particles, and an analysis of robot teams resembles studies on the many-body problem of physics. The many-body problem is: *For a system of N particles with known interactions, determine the evolution of the system from any given initial state* (Hestenes, 1986). The many-robot problem is in some aspects more simple. The robot team operates within a fixed two-dimensional plane. Also, we do not consider acceleration of the robots. Moreover, we do not have to determine the complete evolution of the robot team. Theorem 1 showed that we can restrict attention to targeting series only, which means that it suffices to study only relatively few points in time (or situations).
A complication is that – as we will see below – the interaction in the robot-team is caused by two system of forces: the repulsive forces which the robots exert on one another and the attractive forces of the goals. The repulsive forces

are the internal forces of the team. An obvious difference with the many-body problem is that the repulsive forces in a robot team work in a direction opposite to the attractive forces in mechanics. The attractive forces of the goals on the respective robots are external forces. The difference between the two force systems is clear from the fact that the repulsive forces do not affect the Centre of Gravity (CG), whereas the attractive forces of the goals do cause the Centre of Gravity to move.

We compare the different impacts of these force systems using the following examples. Suppose first a robot team in which the robots perform only avoidance and no goal finding. The system of repulsive forces generates particular behaviours in the robotteam, typically the Centre of Gravity is an invariant point, and remains at its place.
Next, to see the influence of the system of external forces, consider the team of robots as a point and look at the force field generated by the attractive forces. The point-team will come at a stand still in a point where the sum of the attractive forces is a zero vector. There exists only one such point. The attractive forces of the goals have constant magnitude, and as a consequence this point is the Steiner Point (we call this point ESP) inside the triangle formed by the goals G_A, G_B and G_C (Penders, 1999).

Balanced conflict Now combining the internal and external force systems we can determine a typical example of a balanced conflict, as depicted in figure 6.12. In this particular case the points CG (and the Steiner Point of the robot team SP) and ESP coincide, this case is easy to treat as the robots form an equilateral triangle. Moreover, each robot is situated on a line in the order r, ESP, G_r. The robots A, B and C are all three in a real-collision: each needs to pass the same point at the same point in time, moreover this point coincides with SP and ESP.

If the robot form an equilateral triangle, but they are not on a line r, ESP, G_r, that is r, G_r does not go through ESP then the robot team will turn around and eventually each will reach its goal (refer to (Penders, 1999)).

Far-away goals In the above situation the robots are inside the triangle formed by the goals. We look at cases where the robots are relatively close but where the goals are far away on one side of the robot team. Assume that the goals of the robots are infinitely far away, though all situated in the same direction. Moreover, assume that two robots (A and C) are on a line orthogonal to the direction of the goals, and the third robot (B) is between the course of the

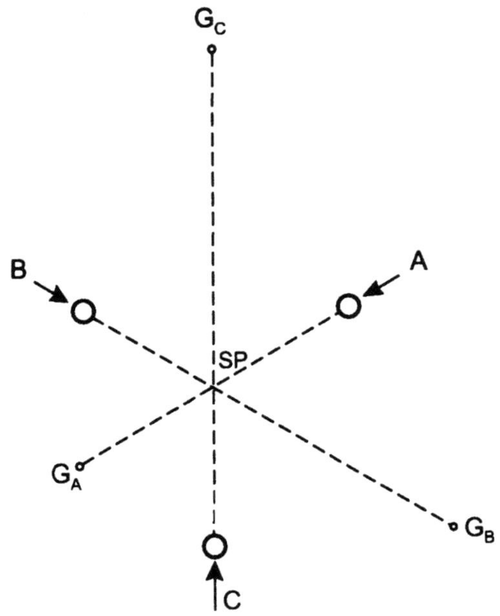

Figure 6.12 A balanced conflict: the robots form an equilateral triangle, the intersection point of the robots' courses coincides with SP and ESP

robots (A and C) to their goals, (see figure 6.13) then three cases are possible:

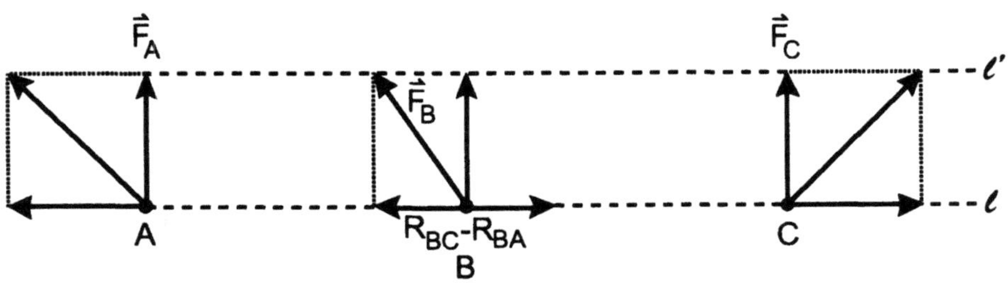

Figure 6.13 Three robots on one line, goals infinitely far away

Case a: if all three robots are on the same line l, they proceed towards the goals while remaining on a line parallel to the initial one. In Figure 13 the forces are sketched and line l is parallel to l'.

Case b: assume that robot B is a little behind the line l which connects A and C, then B will always remain behind the line connecting A and C.

Case c: assume that robot B is ahead of the line l which connects A and C, then B will always remain ahead of the line connecting A and C.

We have discussed five characteristic situations for a team of three robots applying potential-field avoidance. The first situation (figure 6.12) is a balanced conflict. In practice such situations occur seldomly, as the parameters exactly have to satisfy the requirements. The second situation is one in which the robot-team makes a turn around the centre of gravity.
In case the goals are far away, one of the cases **a**, **b** or **c** apply.
In practice, the latter four cases (non-balanced) occur in the dynamics of a robot-team, e.g. in the team of figure 6.3. We have described only cases, which are still far from a full description of the emerging behaviour. For our purposes here, this is sufficient and we will not go further into it.

4.4 OTHER TEAM DESIGNS

The analysis above started from particular intentions to describe congenial teams and a particular ontology. We briefly compare our teams and findings with some other approaches described in the literature.

4.5 OTHER INTENTIONS

The classification of intentions as given in table 6.1 is a slightly adopted version of (Penders, 1994). The present classification covers that of (Zeghal and Ferber, 1993), which originated in airborne systems. They distinguish *co-operative*, *non-co-operative*, *passive*, and *antagonistic agents*. They do not explicitly distinguish between reactive and non-reactive agents. The term *antagonistic agent* is theirs, however they are not explicit whether antagonists are reactive. The term passive agent is used by Zeghal and Ferber for blindly moving agents. We expect the term passive to give rise to confusion with stationary agents. They describe avoiding teams as well, however they call avoiding agents *co-operative*. This term is misleading, since the agents are not co-operative, they do not even have a notion of another agent. They are only *self-interested*, i.e., try to satisfy their own constraints. That avoiding agents can co-operatively perform a task as on the cargo terminal, is incidental. One could say that they co-operate despite themselves. In fact, their actions are co-ordinated. Zeghal and Ferber use the term non-co-operative for agents which differ from the other team members. All the newcomers in table 6.3, for instance, would in their terms be called *non-co-operative*.
(Kube and Zhang, 1994) also study a multi-agent team in which the agents perform spatial behaviours that count as intentions in our sense. The behaviours are: *avoidance*, *goal finding*, *slow*, *follow*, and *find*. *Avoidance* and *goal find-*

ing are the same as those in our teams. The *slow* of Kube and Zhang results in our teams as a combination of avoidance and goal finding. The *follow* is made by substitution of a fixed goal by a target agent. Find is just going around without a fixed goal as for instance the robot in figure 6.6. We conclude that these behaviours are indeed covered by our intentions.

(Mataric, 1995) considers the behaviours *avoidance*, *following*, *aggregation*, *dispersion*, *homing*, and *wandering* as a basic set. *Avoidance* and *following* are discussed. *Wandering* is going around without a fixed goal (as the *find* of Kube and Zhang). Avoidance, following, and wandering are intentions in our sense. However, he also distinguishes *aggregation* and *dispersion*. Aggregation is the same as our clustering and dispersion is similar to scattering. The latter two behaviours are team behaviours, and as we have seen in the discussion following table 6.3, these behaviours result from avoidance and goal finding, depending on the intentions of the team members. Contrary to Mataric, we conclude that clustering and scattering (and thus aggregation and dispersion) are not basic behaviours nor intentions of individual agents; they are resulting team behaviours.

4.6 HUMAN AGENTS

A human agent is the paradigm of an intelligent agent. Human beings flexibly switch from one intention to an other. However, in severely constrained circumstances spatial conflicts occur in human interaction too. We make a slight investigation into human interaction and discuss some examples. This also indicates how our study of artificial teams relates to real life situations.

In figure 6.14 two situations are sketched. On the left a bridge on which it is impossible for two agents to pass at the same time. The right part shows a road crossing where several agents arrive at the same time. In these examples normal traffic rules are not decisive. The situations give rise to conflicts, which are difficult to resolve rationally, even for humans. In such cases humans apply other skills, such as boldness.[3] It is noted that communication does not always solve these conflicts either, which confirms our presumptions concerning communication (cf the Introduction)!

4.7 OTHER ONTOLOGIES

In our study, as well as in the ones of (Zeghal and Ferber, 1993), (Kube and Zhang, 1994) and (Mataric, 1995) the same ontology is used. The agents are in *direct competition* for a resource. This resource is space and the points or

[3] Near our laboratories there is a traffic road with a narrow bridge, and it is rumoured that two drivers turned to physical violence in determining who was allowed to pass first.

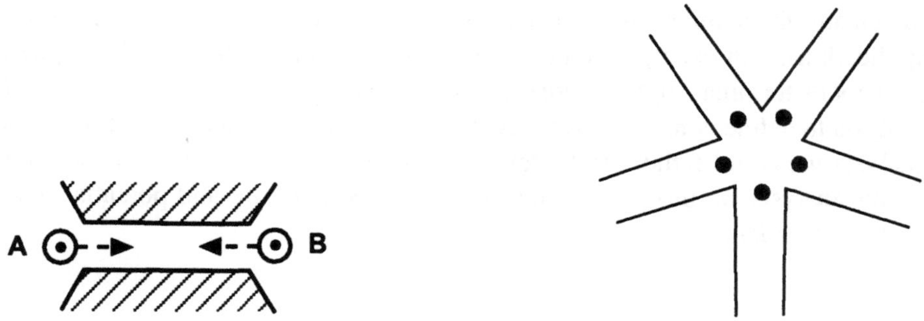

Figure 6.14 Left: bridge; right: road crossing

regions in space may or may not be occupied. Moreover, the agent themselves are the objects that occupy the space on the shared shop floor. The interaction emerges because only one agent at a time can occupy a spatial position; the interaction generates within a spatial ontology.
(Cesta et al., 1996) discuss multi-agent systems operating in a slightly different ontology. Their agents are in permanent need of a certain amount of *supplies* – called energy. The supply level of an agent changes (decreases) as a side effect of its actions. At certain places agents can find new supplies. The authors make stepwise simulations of the team. The agents, one after the other, decide what action to take: to move, to confiscate the supplies or to give them away. Contrary to our teams, in the teams of (Cesta et al., 1996), no interaction generates, the agents does not directly deal with others. To make the simulations comparable to ours, their model would have to allow cases where two (or more) agents concurrently aim for the same portion of supplies. A comparison of the agent types further reveals the importance of the initial ontological assumptions. Cesta *et al.* distinguish four types of agents: *solitary*, *parasite*, *selfish* and *social* agents. Solitary agents actually ignore others, in our teams this is not possible: the space on the shop floor is shared. Selfish agents take the supplies which they need (our agents are of this type). The characters social and parasite agents are defined on the supply dimension; social agents share supplies with other, parasite agents take supplies from other. It is clear that these agents cannot appear in our teams (and ontology).

5. CONCLUSION

The central notion of this paper is that of robots having an intention. We discussed and defined intentions of robot agents and evaluated the team behaviour of congenial teams, that is teams of agents with the same intentions. Typical behaviours which we found were: dispersing behaviour in avoiding teams and clustering behaviour in antagonistic teams. By adding newcomers to such teams the team behaviour can be directed and used proficiently for certain applications. An example is a team following a leader which can be applied on a goods terminal. In the second half of the paper we went through a formal analysis to define conflicts and to lay down what action patterns are. From this analysis we could rather easily define intentions formally. As an illustration of our analysis we discussed teams applying flee-opposite and potential field obstacle avoidance.

Chapter 7

CONFLICTS IN COLLECTIVE ROBOTICS

Fabrice Chantemargue
Département d'Informatique, Université de Fribourg, Suisse
chantemargue@bigfoot.com

Abstract The purpose of this chapter is twofold. First, we briefly discuss the concept of emergence in autonomy-based multi-agent systems and its relation to conflict. And second, in what constitutes the core of the chapter, we thoroughly examine an example of autonomy-based multi-agent system through a simulation of a particular application of object regrouping in the framework of collective robotics. In this example, conflict is present, and nothing is explicitly undertaken or planned ahead to cope with; furthermore, there is no form of direct communication among agents. Nevertheless, the system's performance on this particular task scales good up to a moderate number of agents, even supralinearly in some situations. Moreover, the results suggest that this good performance scaling relates to the fact that there is in the system a type of conflict with a strong influence on performance, which remains nearly constant or even decreases as the number of agents is moderately increased; in a way, and for a moderate number of agents, conflict could be said to be implicitly "managed" in the system. Further work and reflection on this point might lead to a systematic study of implicit ways of reducing conflict.

Introduction

Our work fits in the framework of *Bottom-Up Artificial Intelligence* (Brooks, 1986), (Brooks, 1991) and more particularly, in that of *Autonomous Agents* (Pfeifer, 1995). We are concerned with collective phenomena and their issues and more precisely, the way to carry out solutions that allow an autonomy-based multi-agent system to achieve a global task by virtue of emergence and self-organization. The work is supported by two types of experiments, namely multi-agent simulations applied to collective robotics (the focus of this chapter), and collective robotics applications involving real robots (see (Chantemargue and Hirsbrunner, 1999) for details on the implementation).

The framework of this chapter is a multi-agent case study, which consists of examining through simulation a pool of operationally autonomous agents, capable of regrouping objects distributed in the environment; we concentrate on simple agents with no communication capabilities. In this framework, the aim of this chapter is twofold: first, to briefly discuss the concept of emergence and its relation to conflict: according to us, the presence in a given system of some kind of internal conflict should positively correlate with the degree of manifestation of emergent properties in that system; second, to examine an example of system in which, even though conflict is left unhandled, performance scales good up to a moderate number of agents (even supra-linearly, for some of the studied agent families). Moreover, the results presented in this chapter suggest that this good performance scaling should in part be due to the fact that there is in the system a type of conflict with a strong influence on performance, which remains nearly constant or even decreases as the number of agents is moderately increased. In a way, and for a moderate number of agents, conflict could be said to be partially "managed" in an implicit way. This chapter is intended to promote reflection on implicit ways of reducing conflict. This is a quite opposite stance to what is typically undertaken: conflict is usually handled in an explicit way, by resorting to some kind of action coordination or planning. Even though our stance could seem odd at first sight, it should help to keep agents simple and yet, as it is the case for the example described in this chapter, the system may exhibit a reasonable performance scaling and a high robustness.

This chapter is organized as follows: section 1. starts by briefly reporting how conflict has typically been attempted to be avoided and solved till now in the framework of *Artificial Intelligence* and *Distributed Artificial Intelligence.* Section 2. briefly introduces the basic concepts of *Autonomous Agents.* Section 3. deepens the concept of emergence and points out its relation to conflict. Section 4. describes our experimental testbed. Section 5. gives the most significant experimental results for our purpose. The last section summarizes our point of view regarding conflict and concludes this chapter.

1. CONFLICT IN ARTIFICIAL INTELLIGENCE AND DISTRIBUTED ARTIFICIAL INTELLIGENCE

There are indeed numerous reasons for which conflict may arise, depending on the context of the application and on the type of entities being considered. As far as we are concerned, we consider conflict essentially as a divergence at the level of goals among entities in the system: therefore, for us, conflict is linked to antagonism (Ferber, 1995). An access to a given resource by a given agent can itself be classified as a goal (or sub-goal) and is consequently included in this interpretation of the term. Note that this notion of conflict could be extended so as to encompass *sources* of goal divergences, as in the case of *knowledge conflict*. Generally, it is argued that if conflict is not entirely solved ahead, the system is likely to run into serious trouble (it may not fulfill the goals for which it was designed). And in most cases, the focus is on the development of (explicit) techniques to get rid of conflict, such as cooperation techniques. In (Ferber, 1995), an interaction taxonomy for goal-oriented agents is presented: interactions are classified according to the goals of the agents, their resources and their skills. This taxonomy leads to three categories of situations: *indifference* and *cooperation* situations encompass situations where goals are compatible (with the different combinations for resources and skills, namely sufficient and insufficient), whereas *antagonistic* situations regroup all possible situations in which goals are incompatible (indiscriminately of the status of resources and skills). In (Ferber, 1995), numerous methods for handling cooperation situations are discussed (see (Mataric, 1992) and (Chaib-draa, 1996) as well); we refer to them as methods for *explicit cooperation*, that is, a set of (explicit) interaction organization methods developed for foreseen situations. However, antagonistic situations are not addressed.

In fact, traditional approaches to address the problem of conflict mostly consisted in adapting techniques for the prevention of conflict that were developed in the discipline of *operating systems*, and in fitting them to *Distributed Artificial Intelligence*. Our approach is quite the reverse: we are concerned with the possibility of conceiving systems in which conflict can be left unhandled (more precisely, in the absence of explicit handling) without compromising the functionality for which they were developed, and that in virtue of some of their other intrinsic properties.

2. AUTONOMOUS AGENTS: BASIC CONCEPTS

In *Autonomous Agents*, agents are designed to fulfill internal or external goals by their own actions in continuous long-term interaction with their environment (possibly unpredictable and dynamical).

A major concept in *Autonomous Agents* is that of embodiment. In (Varela, 1994), it is stated that cognition depends on the kinds of experience that come from having a body with various sensory-motor capacities (embodiment). Embodiment can take different forms according to the framework. Even though three forms of embodiment can be found in the literature, we consider only two of them (the third one is too often disputed and is out of our present scope). The first form relates to *physically embodied agents* interacting with their environment by means of sensory perception and motor control (experiments with real robots (Brooks, 1991)). The second form relates to *simulated embodied agents* interacting with artificial environments (various simulations of robotics (Beslon et al., 1995) and artificial life (Lerena and Courant, 1996)). Thus, in

Autonomous Agents, the interactions between the system and the environment are of a paramount importance.

Dealing with interactions leads naturally to another concept in *Autonomous Agents*, namely that of emergence of behavior and functionality (Cariani, 1990), (Forrest, 1990), (Baas, 1994), (Bonabeau et al., 1995), (M.R. Jean et al., 1997), (Scaglione, 1998), (Houdé et al., 1998). According to Forrest (Forrest, 1990), emergence offers indeed a bridge between the necessity of complex and adaptive behavior at a macro level (the one of the system) and situation-based interactions at a micro level (the one of every agent). Still in (Forrest, 1990), a system's behavior can be considered emergent if it can only be specified using descriptive categories which are not necessary to describe the behavior of the constituent components. Steels, in (Steels and Brooks, 1994), adds that an emergent behavior leads to emergent functionality if the behavior contributes to the system's self-preservation and if the system can build further upon it. In (Houdé et al., 1998), emergence is defined by resorting to self-organization: dynamical systems composed of a large number of interacting entities may exhibit global properties that do not exist at the level of the individual entities, that may be characterized as emergent properties. Even a Turing-like test for emergence (purposed at diagnosing emergence in a system) has been proposed in (Ronald et al., 1999).

Finally, another important concept in *Autonomous Agents* is that of autonomy. Two types of autonomy are commonly pointed out (Ziemke, 1997): operational autonomy and behavioral autonomy. Operational autonomy is defined as the capacity to operate without human (or external) intervention, without being remotely controlled. Behavioral autonomy supposes that the basis of self-steering originates in the agent's own capacity to form and adapt its principles of behavior: an agent, to be behaviorally autonomous, needs the freedom to have formed (learned or decided) its principles of behavior on its own (from its experience), at least in part.

3. OUR VIEW ON EMERGENCE

A major difficulty in defining emergence comes from the fact that emergence can not be defined in an objective way: emergence has indeed a subjective component that relates to the cognitive properties of the observer, thus explaining why this notion is still so much disputed today. In this section, we introduce a partial characterization of the notion of emergence, that should serve as a basis for an operational definition, followed by comments on the relation of emergence with conflict.

Our framework is as follows. Let us assume that there is a causal entailment between two parts of an observable world and that we are willing to explain this entailment with the help of a formal model `M0`. To have a modeling relation, the model is to be put in correspondence with the observable world through, on the one hand an abstraction mechanism which allows us to "encode" phenomena of the observable world into the model, and on the other hand a de-abstraction mechanism which does the inverse operation, as indicated in figure 7.1. Furthermore, the result of following the path formed by the sequence (1) abstraction, (2) inferential entailment, and (3) de-abstraction, must be the same as that produced by the causal entailment.

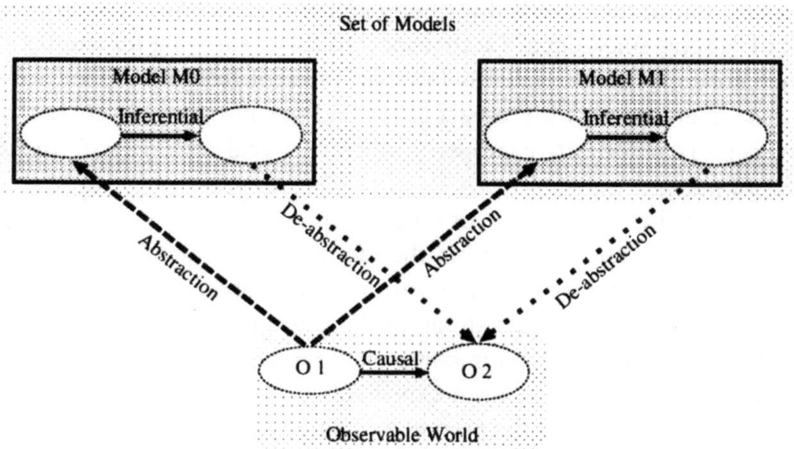

Figure 7.1 Graphical view of emergence.

In this context, the aim is to qualify explanations (inferential entailments); this allows us to evaluate the model on the basis of the explanations it yields. For that, we introduce notions of *cost* and *benefit* of explanations. There are many possibilities for defining cost and benefit. Our present choice for cost (with respect to a given model) is the length of the explanation (strictly positive number). The benefit constitutes the subjective part of the evaluation. It typically refers to human comprehension and cognitive capabilities in general. This is the most sensitive point in this definition, but including this aspect seems unavoidable when evaluating explanations. The benefit indicates (and scales with) the degree of satisfaction with a given explanation[1] and must be a strictly positive number[2]. We define the *value* of a given explanation (with respect to a given observer) as the ratio of its benefit to its cost. Finally, the value of a given model (with respect to a given phenomenon and a given observer) is defined as the value of the explanation with the highest value (among

[1] A rough estimation of the benefit may be sufficient.

[2] This condition makes our present discussion simpler, by conferring an objective character to what we will call "strong emergence"; but the condition is actually not essential.

all explanations the given model can yield for the given phenomenon). If there is no explanation in terms of the given model, its value is defined as zero. Note that this notion of value allows us to compare models (relative to a given phenomenon and a given observer).

When the value of a given model `M0` (with respect to a given phenomenon and a given observer) tends toward zero, we will tend to speak of emergence. This will typically be reflected in the search for another model `M1` with a higher value. Notice that there are two cases: when the value is equal to zero (case of no explanation of the observed phenomenon with the current model), then we speak of "strong emergence" (with respect to `M0`): searching for another model is mandatory. When the value is low but different from zero, then we speak of "weak emergence" (with respect to `M0` and the observer). Note that "strong emergence" is an objective property whereas "weak emergence" includes a subjective part.

We believe that the concept of emergence as defined above relates to that of conflict. This can be seen from the fact that phenomena in simple, linear systems can satisfactorily be explained in terms of their components and their composition, and most explanations in these terms are expected to be short. In contrast, many phenomena in complex, nonlinear systems cannot be easily explained in such terms, and most explanations become lengthy and less satisfactory. This suggests that the presence of some kind of emergence in a given system is directly related to the presence of nonlinearities in that system. From this, and because conflict is just a form of nonlinearity, we believe there should be a positive correlation between conflict-rich systems and systems exhibiting emergent properties.

It may be worthwhile to examine these questions in more detail.

4. AN EXPERIMENTAL MULTI-AGENT TESTBED

Our simulation tackles a quite common problem in collective robotics which is still given a lot of concern: agents seek for objects distributed in their environment in order to regroup all objects. However, the way we address this problem is not classic: the distinctive aspect of our approach rests indeed on a system integrating operationally autonomous agents, that is, every agent in the system has the freedom to act. More precisely, every agent decides by itself which action to take on the basis of its own perception, which is strictly local and private. There is not in the system any type of master responsible for supervising the agents, nor any type of cooperation protocol, nor any form of direct communication, thus allowing the system to be simple, flexible and fault tolerant. In that, this work relates to other work in the framework of collective robotics (see (Deneubourg et al., 1991), (Bonabeau and Theraulaz, 1994), (Gaussier and Zrehen, 1994), (Beckers et al., 1994), (Martinoli and Mondada,

1995) and (Martinoli and Mondada, 1998)) in which the focus is on the collective capabilities of a multi-robot system to achieve clustering tasks (the system typically creates several clusters of objects in the environment) and/or regrouping tasks (the system typically creates a single cluster containing all the objects of the environment) on the basis of a stigmergic[3] coordination between robots.

We implemented our simulation in the Swarm Simulation System (developed at the Santa-Fe Institute, USA) (Minar et al., 1996). In our simulation, the environment is composed of a discrete two dimensional square grid, a set of objects and a set of transparent obstacles. A set of agents is present in this environment: agents roam (by avoiding obstacles), pick up and drop objects. At the outset of an experiment, objects are (randomly) distributed in the environment that may contain obstacles (randomly set or set at a chosen fixed location), with at maximum one object per cell. An experiment will be considered completed when all objects present in the environment will be regrouped by the agents onto a single cell (in this case, we will speak of a stack of all objects).

An agent possesses some sensors to perceive the world within which it moves, and some effectors to act in this world, so that it complies with the prescriptions of *simulated embodied agents* (Ziemke, 1997). An agent consists of several modules, namely *perception*, *state*, *actions* and *control algorithm*. These (almost self-explanatory) modules depend on the application and are under the user's responsibility. The control algorithm module defines the type of autonomy of the agent: it is precisely inside this module that the designer decides whether to implement an operational autonomy or a behavioral autonomy (Ziemke, 1997).

As already mentioned, agents have no explicit coordination features for detecting and managing antagonistic situations nor communication tools for negotiation. In fact they "communicate" in an indirect way, that is, via their influences in the environment. Under these constraints, some variants of control algorithm for our agents have been implemented and tried out. However, in this chapter, we will focus on the following control algorithm: if an agent that does not carry an object comes to a cell containing `N` objects, it will pick one object up with a probability given by `N` to the power of `-Alpha`, where `Alpha` is a constant greater than or equal to zero; if an agent that carries an object comes to a cell containing some objects, it will systematically drop its object. If the cell is empty, nothing special happens and the agent will move to another cell[4]. Note that an agent can not carry more than one object at a time.

[3] To our knowledge, Beckers et al. (Beckers et al., 1994) were the first to exploit a stigmergic coordination between robots. Stigmergic coordination means literally "incitement to work by the product of the work".

[4] It is easy to see that the system could be rendered more robust by enabling a drop on an empty cell with an appropriately chosen, low probability; without this possibility, and if there were (at least) as many agents as

Such a simple control algorithm allows to explicitly modulate the probability of picking objects up as a function of the local density and it is a sufficient condition for the system to regroup objects (as shown in (Deneubourg et al., 1991)).

The state module encompasses the private information of the agent and of course depends on the control algorithm of the agent. In our case, it consists of the information relative to whether the agent carries or not an object plus other internal variables that include the states of its random number generators.

Agents can be endowed with several types of object perception and different moving strategies, thus leading to several families of agents. Yet the perception of other agents and obstacles in the environment is the same for all families in the sense that a cell containing an obstacle or an agent is implicitly perceived as a cell where the agent can not move to. The fact that two agents can not come to the same cell induces spatial conflict. An agent endowed with what we refer to as *a basic object perception*, perceives only the quantity of objects that is present on the cell on which it stands. Such agents are endowed with random move capabilities to roam in the environment: at every step, a move direction is randomly drawn. Agents of this type will be referred to as *basic agents*. A variant is as follows: at every step, the agent, instead of randomly drawing a direction, is given a probability of `0.1` to randomly draw a direction and a probability of `0.9` to keep its direction. This family of agents is referred to as *inertial agents*. A last family of agents is that of *agents with camera*: every agent is given an artificial eye (pin-hole camera model (Horaud and Monga, 1993) with the classical five intrinsic parameters and three out of the six extrinsic parameters, namely two translations out of three and one rotation out of three). So that, every agent, through its camera, is able to perceive objects (and objects only, not obstacles and not other agents) in (part of) the environment and to go towards the object which is the closest to its optical axis, thus avoiding wandering around in an area without interest.

An agent is said to be *regrouping agent* if it is able to regroup all the objects into a single stack on a cell, in a finite time, when acting alone in the environment, for any initial configuration. Experimenting environments where some regrouping agents *concurrently* work is expected to yield a single stack containing all the objects. However, this result is not due to any goal explicitly embodied into the agents when working in a group.

In our experiment, conflict is naturally induced, due to the nature of the agents we consider. Even if there is only one agent in the system, the action of the agent at a given time can lead to an observed contradictory goal when compared to a previous goal suggested by a preceding action: the agent can

objects, all objects could be picked up by the agents in a way that leaves no objects in the environment, and no agent would ever drop an object (clearly, the task would never be accomplished).

indeed pick an object up from stack A and drop it on stack B, and then later, can do exactly the opposite actions, namely pick an object up from stack B and drop it on stack A. When several agents are present in the system, the combined actions of all the agents will as well induce conflict.

5. RESULTS

For a given size of the environment and a fixed number of objects, we have run an intensive number of experiments for two families of agents, namely *basic agents* and *agents with camera*. For *basic agents*, the size of the environment is 9 by 9 cells, there are 10 objects and we have run 400 experiments. For *agents with camera*, the size of the environment is 25 by 25 cells, there are 20 objects and we have run 1500 experiments. For every family, Alpha was set to 0.3 and experiments consisted in varying (i) the distribution of objects in the environment and (ii) the number of agents in the system, and in measuring the cost of the system to achieve the task of object regrouping; this cost is defined as the number of iterations necessary to the system to achieve the task[5]. Moreover, the same experiments have been repeated with a simple obstacle present in the south-west part of the environment (see figures 7.2 and 7.3).

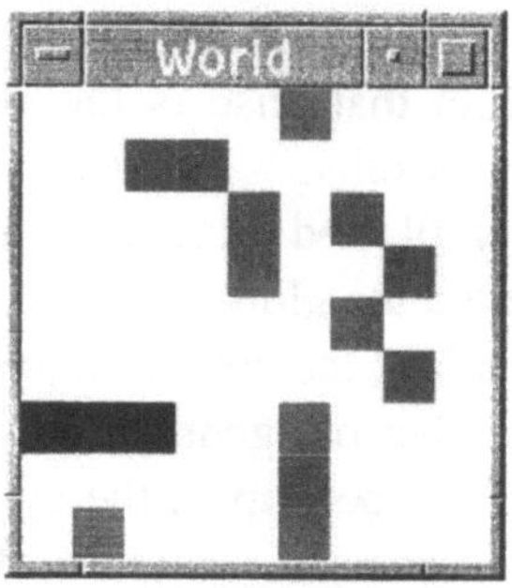

Figure 7.2 A 9 x 9 cell environment with 3 *basic agents*, 10 objects and a simple obstacle: red squares (grey if printed in B/W) represent objects, green squares (light grey if printed in B/W) represent agents, black squares (dark grey if printed in B/W) materialize the obstacle.

Preliminary results were presented at the time of the ECAI'98 workshop on Conflicts (see (Chantemargue et al., 1998)): these results already introduced some features of the collective system, namely the fact that conflict is naturally present in the system and the fact that implicit cooperation (see below) takes place in the system, which conforms to the results presented in (Beckers et al., 1994). Our system has been studied in more detail since. We indeed quantified

[5]This should not be confused with the cost of an explanation introduced in section 3..

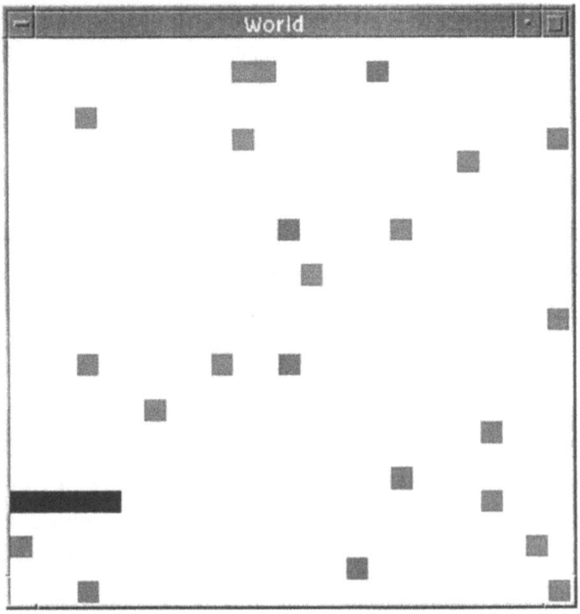

Figure 7.3 A 25 x 25 cell environment with 3 *agents with camera*, 20 objects and a simple obstacle.

the different types of conflict that arise in the system. We present hereafter some of the most significant results.

The first result yielded for all tried parameters, is that (as it may be expected) the collective system achieved the global task of object regrouping. Figure 7.4 (respectively figure 7.6) displays the cost for *agents with camera* (respectively *basic agents*) versus the number of agents in the system[6]. Figure 7.5 (respectively figure 7.7) displays the speedup in the system for *agents with camera* (respectively *basic agents*) versus the number of agents in the system. The speed-up for n agents is defined as the ratio of the mean cost for one agent to the mean cost for n agents.

Speed-up charts (figures 7.5, 7.7 and 7.13) show how the performance of the system scales with the number of agents. To some extent, the higher the number of agents in the system, the better the performance of the system. This illustrates a feature in our system, namely that of cooperation: agents participate in achieving the global task without being aware of it and without any explicit cooperation protocol, but just in virtue of their design and the context in which they operate. A form of implicit cooperation takes place in the system.

[6]Vertical bars on all charts indicate standard deviations.

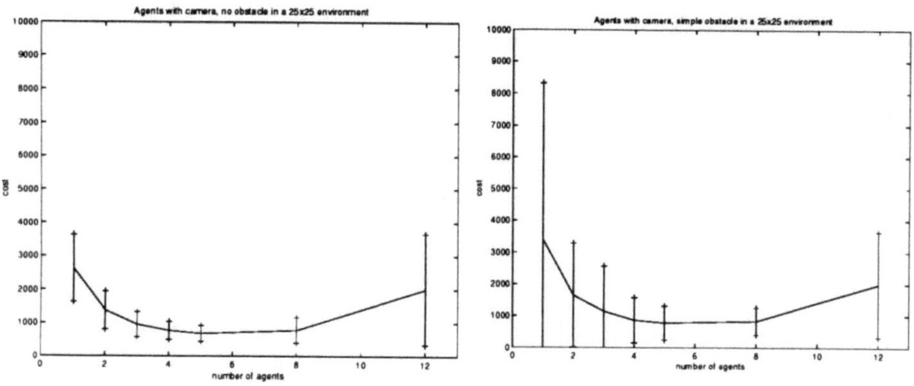

Figure 7.4 *Agents with camera*: cost to complete the task a) without obstacle, b) with obstacle.

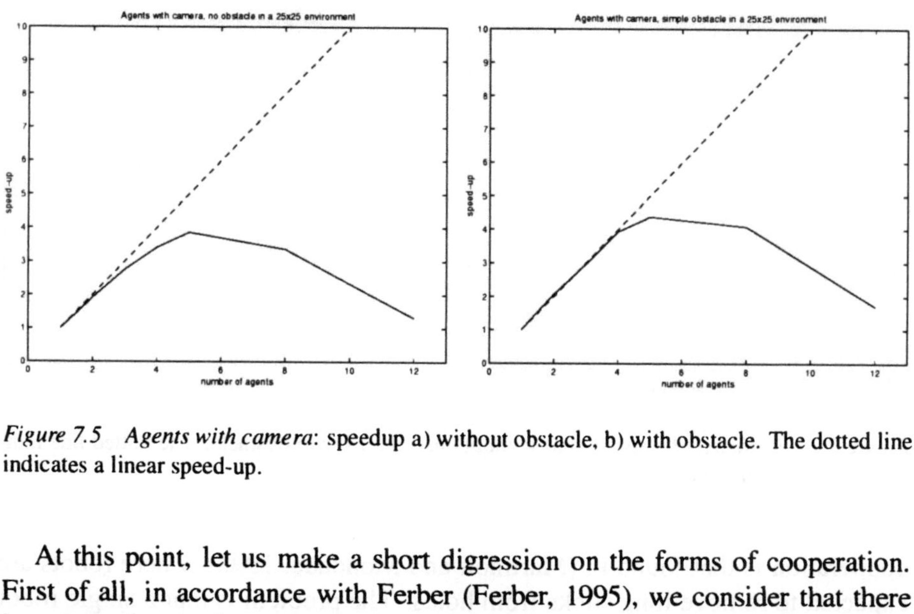

Figure 7.5 *Agents with camera*: speedup a) without obstacle, b) with obstacle. The dotted line indicates a linear speed-up.

At this point, let us make a short digression on the forms of cooperation. First of all, in accordance with Ferber (Ferber, 1995), we consider that there is cooperation in the system as long as the speed-up increases with the number of agents in the system. Let us define the efficiency in the system as the ratio of the speed-up to the number of agents. A linear speed-up means an efficiency of 100%. If the efficiency in the system is equal to or greater than 100%, which corresponds to a linear speed-up (for an efficiency of 100%) or to a "supra-linear" speed-up (for efficiencies greater than 100%), then we speak of a *strong cooperation*. When the efficiency is below 100% but the speed-up still increases with the number of agents, we speak of a *weak cooperation*. In our experiments, we have weak cooperation, excepted for the case of *basic agents* till 4 agents (see figure 7.7) and *inertial agents* till 5 or 6 agents (see figure 7.13) where we have a strong cooperation. Another example of strong

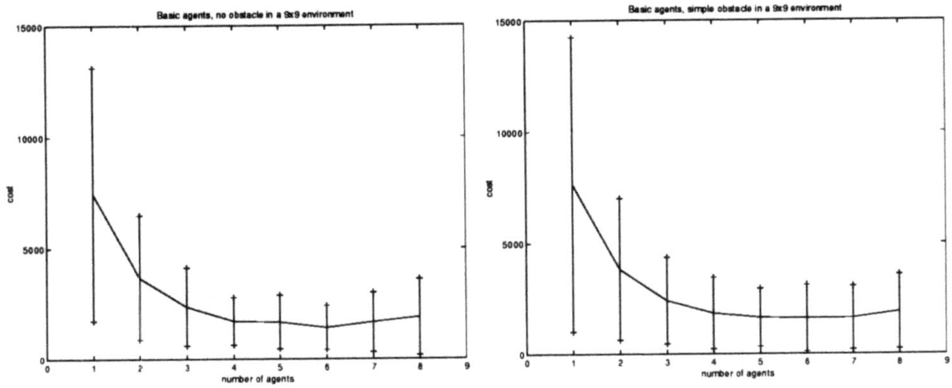

Figure 7.6 *Basic agents*: cost to complete the task a) without obstacle, b) with obstacle.

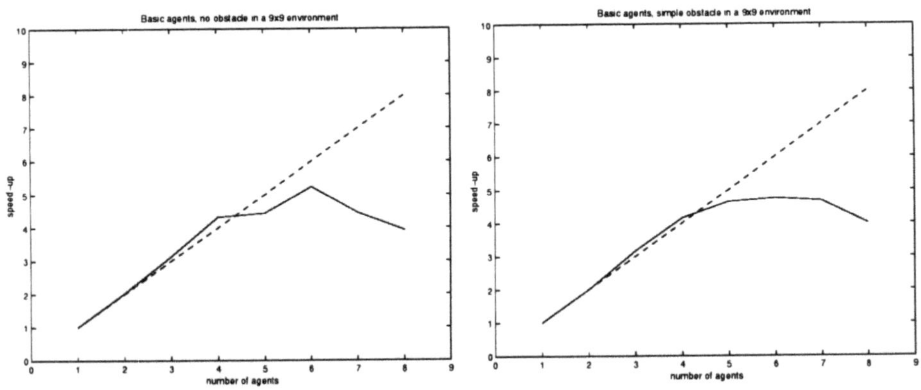

Figure 7.7 *Basic agents*: speedup a) without obstacle, b) with obstacle. The dotted line indicates a linear speed-up.

cooperation is that found in (Martinoli and Mondada, 1998), where robots are expected to remove long sticks from holes. The problem is that a single robot can not do the task by itself. The task, to be achieved, requires indeed a synchronous cooperation between two robots.

For all agent families, the performance scales good up to a moderate number of agents. In the case of *basic agents*, for example, the speedup is even supra-linear up to 4 agents (figure 7.7). A possible partial explanation based on levels of conflicts is given below, in the paragraph devoted to goal conflicts. An additional effect may explain the fact that performance scales up better in the case of *agents with camera* with obstacle than in the case without obstacle: a single agent is greatly perturbed by the obstacle (due to its design, it can be persistently obstructed by an obstacle when going towards an object); the "noise" generated by the presence of other agents attenuates this perturbation.

Notice that in our experiments, the obstacle used can hardly "trap" more than one or two agents at a time.

The different types of conflict that may arise in our system are referred to as spatial conflicts and (sub-)goal conflicts. Spatial conflicts represent the number of times (per iteration per agent) an agent has been perturbed by other agents in its neighborhood when moving. Figure 7.9 (respectively figure 7.11) displays the spatial conflicts that were measured in the system versus the number of agents for *agents with camera* (respectively *basic agents*). (Sub-)goal conflicts (or useless operations) have been quantified by measuring the aggregate number of extra operations done by the agents in the system. `N-1` pick-up operations are theoretically enough to regroup `N` objects onto a cell containing already an object; the number of extra operations in the system will be determined by measuring the total number of pick-up operations in the system minus the theoretical number. Figure 7.8 (respectively figure 7.10) displays the (sub-)goal conflicts that were measured in the system versus the number of agents for *agents with camera* (respectively *basic agents*).

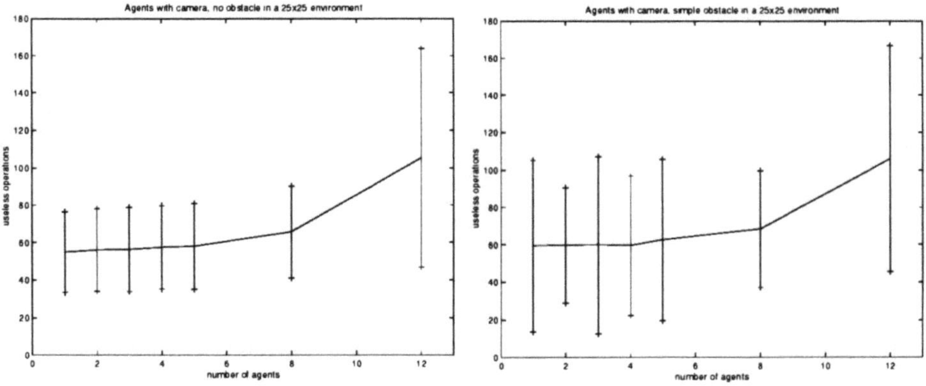

Figure 7.8 *Agents with camera*: (sub-)goal conflicts a) without obstacle, b) with obstacle.

In the case of *basic agents*, the number of spatial conflicts increases linearly with the number of agents: this is expected due to their moving strategies. In the case of *agents with camera*, the use of the camera considerably reduces the parts of the space used for moving; consequently, the number of spatial conflicts strongly increases as the number of agents grows[7].

In the case of *basic agents*, the number of (sub-)goal conflicts decreases in the system with the number of agents ranging from 1 to 6. This may partially

[7]Notice that the effects of this kind of conflict on performance should depend on the details of the moving strategy of the agents, and that the present measure is clearly not sensible to them. Furthermore, spatial conflict in our context should have much less influence on performance than the number of useless operations, so that we will concentrate on the latter form of conflict.

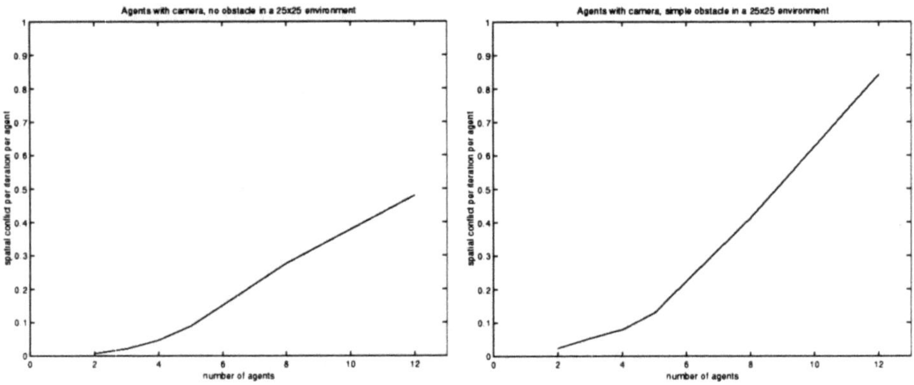

Figure 7.9 *Agents with camera*: spatial conflicts a) without obstacle, b) with obstacle.

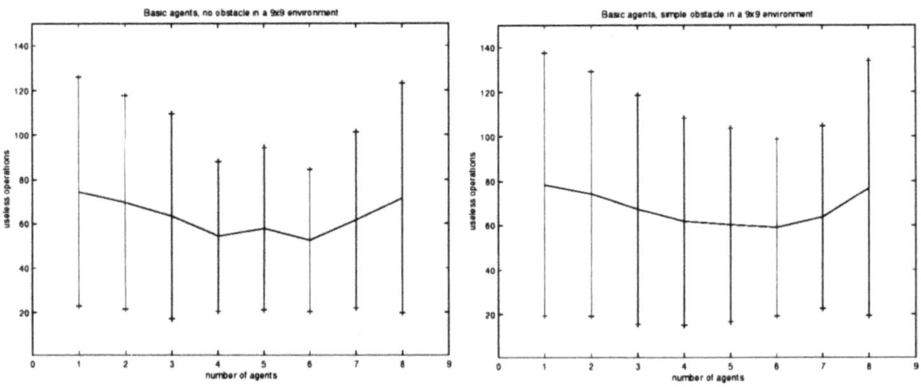

Figure 7.10 *Basic agents*: (sub-)goal conflicts a) without obstacle, b) with obstacle.

explain the supra-linearity observed in the speedup. The reason can be seen in terms of the dynamics of the objects, the number of stacks remaining after the first few steps quickly decreases as the number of agents in the system is increased, and with fewer stacks, less goal conflicts can be expected. Nevertheless, if the number of agents is "excessively" increased (above 6 in this case), the number of useless operations starts to increase. Part of the explanation of this may be as follows. Let us consider the end phase of a run, from the instant in which only one stack remains (and at least one object is still being transported by one of the agents). In this final phase, having many agents in the system is disadvantageous. This is because agents not carrying any object still have a probability of picking an object from the remaining stack. The more agents wandering around, the higher the probability that one object is picked up from the stack, making this final phase longer.

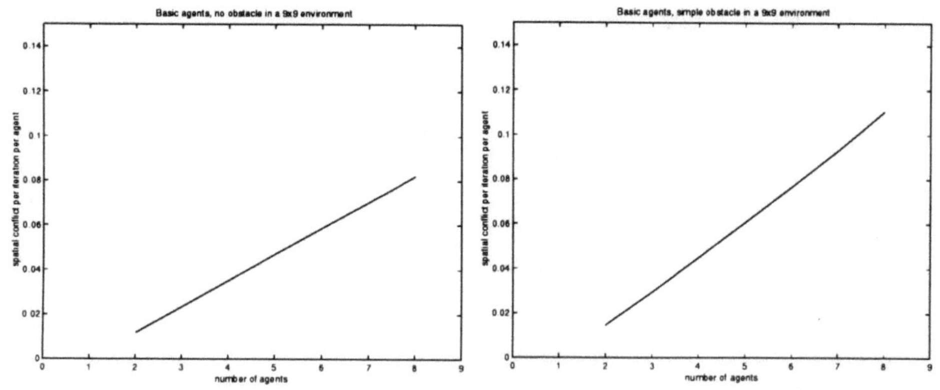

Figure 7.11 *Basic agents*: spatial conflicts a) without obstacle, b) with obstacle.

We have further run `400` experiments with a system involving *inertial agents* with `Alpha` set to `0.3`. The size of the environment is `9` by `9` cells and the number of objects is `10` (experimental conditions identical to those of *basic agents*). Figures 7.12 and 7.13 display respectively the cost and the speed-up that were obtained. Figure 7.14 displays the (sub-)goal conflicts that were measured in the system versus the number of agents. Figure 7.15 displays the spatial conflicts that were measured in the system versus the number of agents. These results are similar to those for *basic agents*.

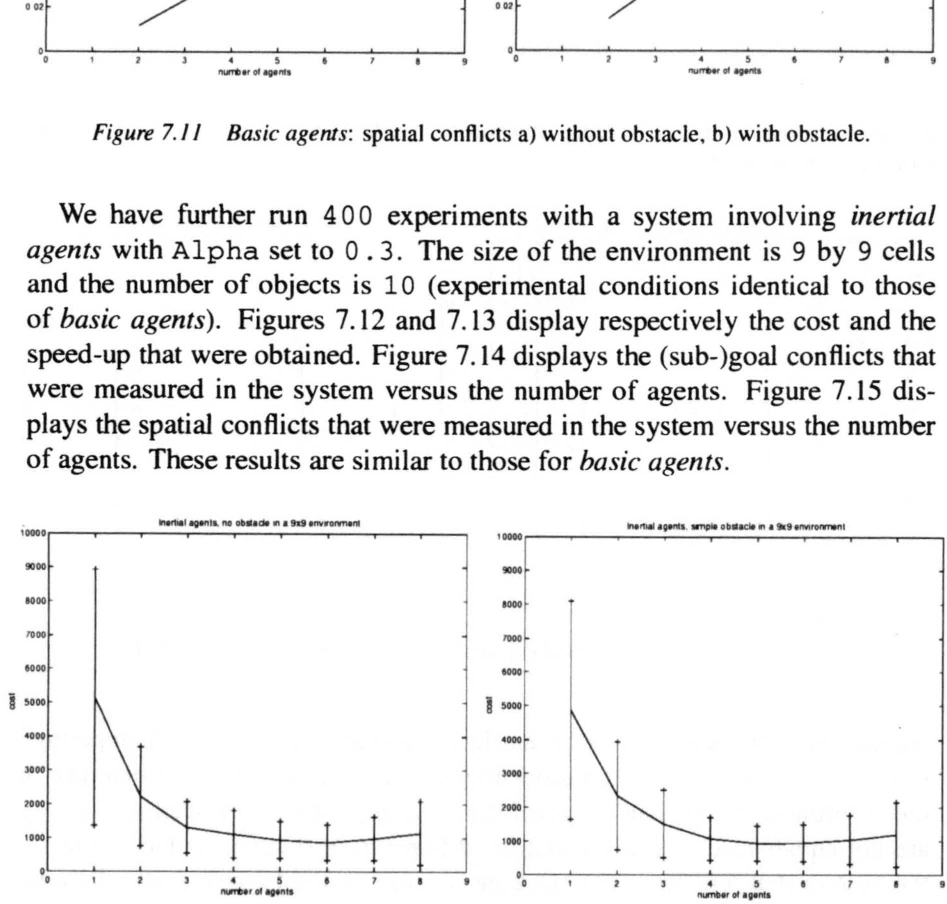

Figure 7.12 *Inertial agents*: cost to complete the task a) without obstacle, b) with obstacle.

We now concentrate on a particular result with the aim of illustrating our characterization of the concept of emergence. The result we focus on is the fact that the global task of object regrouping is always achieved in the system. There is a simple explanation, which is based on the modulation of the probability of picking an object up as a function of stack height (as already

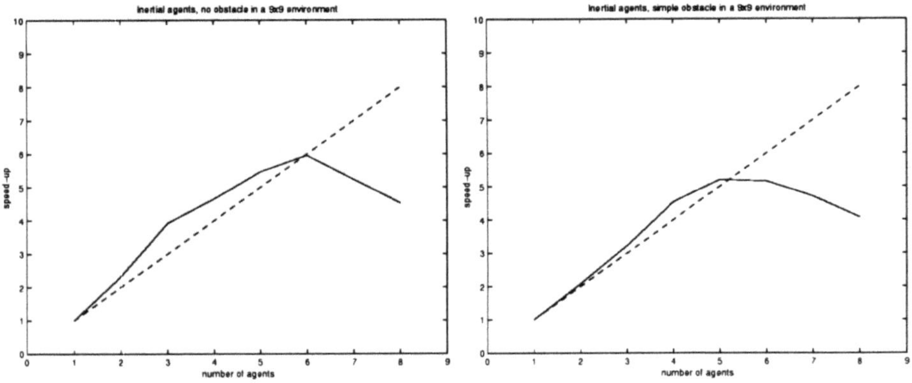

Figure 7.13 *Inertial agents*: speedup a) without obstacle, b) with obstacle. The dotted line indicates a linear speed-up.

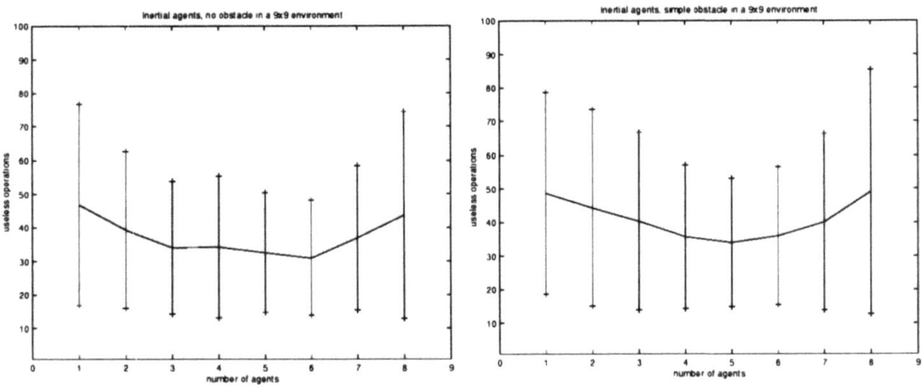

Figure 7.14 *Inertial agents*: (sub-)goal conflicts a) without obstacle, b) with obstacle.

mentioned); the process can be easily understood in terms of "competing" stacks as follows. Let us consider the situation of two stacks remaining in the environment (this can be generalized to any number of stacks). If they are not equal-sized, it is clear that the difference in size will induce a bias in the system that will favor the stacking process on the biggest stack. Finally, two equal-sized stacks constitute an unstable configuration; sooner or later a difference in size will appear.

In order to diagnose whether there is emergence or not in the system, let us first consider a probabilistic model describing the dynamics of this system essentially in terms of competing stacks. The explanation presented above could easily be completed and expressed in terms of such a model. The explanation cost would then certainly be low, and the benefit appears to be high enough (at least for most observers). Therefore, according to our characterization, there

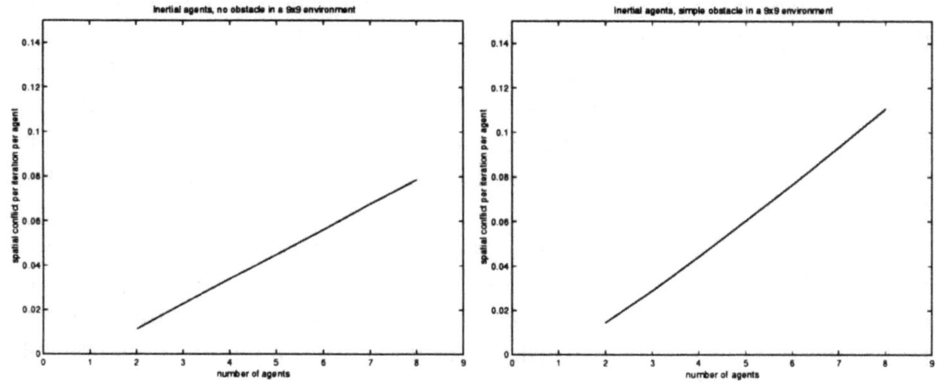

Figure 7.15 *Inertial agents*: spatial conflicts a) without obstacle, b) with obstacle.

is no emergence with respect to this model (this should be true for most observers). Let us now consider the (deterministic) model used to *implement* the simulation (or the simulation itself), which includes the pseudo random number generators as well as the seed values for these generators. For simplicity, let us just address the result "global task is achieved" for *a single run*. There is of course an explanation of the result in terms of this model (the run itself), so that there can not be strong emergence. Nevertheless, we clearly see that explanations in terms of this model tend to be extremely long (high cost) and the benefit is likely to be very low. The value of such explanations (as defined in section 3.) being very close to zero, we can speak of weak emergence.

6. CONCLUSION

In this chapter, simulations of a simple system of object-regrouping agents have been presented. The agents are operationally autonomous: they "decide" by themselves over time the action to take in relation to their internal state and their perception[8]. There is no supervisor in the system and the global task to be achieved, viz regrouping objects, is not encoded explicitly within the agents; the environment is not represented within the agents; there is no explicit cooperation protocol between agents, and there is no form of direct communication among agents. Therefore in the runs with a moderate number of agents, the global task is efficiently achieved by virtue of a form of implicit cooperation. This simple system is flexible and robust, since agents and obstacles can be added to or removed from the system to some extent without running severely into trouble. Incidentally, this study has lead to a preliminary implementa-

[8]Although the autonomy implemented in the agents is operational only, we can possibly speak of a certain behavioral autonomy at the level of the system.

tion with real robots, each endowed with a camera and infrared sensors (see (Chantemargue and Hirsbrunner, 1999)). A few modifications have been necessary so as to take into account specific constraints, among which the most important ones are the fact that the world is continuous and not discrete, and the fact that the robot will perceive, pick up and drop objects in front of it rather than underneath. A collective behavior of object regrouping has also been observed.

The chapter pointed out different kinds of conflict, and the system was observed under the effects of these forms of conflict, in the absence of explicit handling. Despite this absence, the results we obtained show that the system's performance on this particular task scales good up to a moderate number of agents; in some of the cases presented, it scales in a supra-linear way.

It was suggested that this good performance scaling could be due to the fact that there is in the system a highly influential type of conflict, which remains nearly constant or even decreases as the number of agents is moderately increased. Specifically, the number of agents in our system influences the amount of total useless operations: this amount is kept nearly constant or even decreased up to a moderate number of agents. One could possibly talk of implicit conflict "management". Further reflection and work on this point might lead to a systematic study of implicit ways of conflict handling.

Our partial characterization of the concept of emergence is preliminary but it should serve as a basis for an operational definition of emergence. Moreover, the briefly discussed relationship between conflict and emergence could contribute to open new directions in the study of conflict, as a source of novelty in autonomy-based multi-agent systems.

Acknowledgments

This work was financially supported by the Swiss National Foundation for Scientific Research, grants 20-05026.97 and 21-47262.96. Many thanks to P. Lerena for fruitful discussions and judicious suggestions, which allowed to improve this chapter.

III

APPLICATION CENTERED AGENTS' CONFLICTS

Chapter 8

STRATEGIC USE OF CONFLICTS IN TUTORING SYSTEMS

Esma Aïmeur
Université de Montréal, Québec, Canada
aimeur@IRO.UMontreal.CA

Abstract Tutoring strategies have evolved from direct learning to cooperative learning involving various agents, which are either computer simulated or real human beings. During these learning sessions conflicts then arise since the student must interact with several simulated participants such as the tutor, the companion, or the troublemaker (a companion able to mislead the learner). We call these conflicts **external conflicts**. Some of them are accidental but others are intentional in order to test the learner's self-confidence and to detect **internal conflicts** that oppose new knowledge to existing learner knowledge. In this chapter, we highlight the usefulness of conflicts in various **cooperative** learning strategies, showing that they contribute with social interaction to the development of cognition. In particular, we discuss the advantage of an intentional external conflict caused by a difference of opinion between the student and the troublemaker. This difference of opinion is introduced in order to get the student to evaluate his own opinion and cognitive schema. If the learner presents a cognitive dissonance (discord between ideas) a dialogue with the troublemaker will help him correct his internal conflicts. Then, the tutor and the troublemaker cooperate to manage a learning session. We present experimental results that show the gain brought by the troublemaker conflicts in learning improvement.

1. INTRODUCTION

Over the last few years, cooperative learning systems (Slavin, 1990a, Slavin, 1990b, Augustine et al., 1990, Schultz, 1990, Cumming, 1991) have been extensively studied in different domains both in terms of their design and in terms of their implementation. Since in such systems there is an interaction and a dialogue between several partners it is inevitable that conflicts would arise between them.

Researchers have asked many questions about these conflicts including: What to do in case of a conflict? Can one predict and avoid conflict? How does one resolve the conflict? Can conflict be quantified? It is however important to notice that conflicts can have negative but also positive impacts. In our opinion, although research has been done in the area of conflict resolution, not enough work has been done in taking benefit from the conflicts which arise (Aïmeur et al., 1997a).

In Intelligent Tutoring Systems (ITS) (Sleeman and Brown, 1982, Frasson and Gauthier, 1990, Anderson et al., 1995), one can find different learning strategies among which are cooperative strategies. It is interesting to note that these strategies can cause different types of conflict (tutor/learner, learner/co-learner (Gilmore and Self, 1988), learner/companion (Chan and Baskin, 1990), learner/troublemaker (Aïmeur and Frasson, 1996), etc.). This last one is strongly conflicting. We call these conflicts, external conflicts.

In this chapter we intend to consider, in the evolution of learning strategies, the role and importance of conflicts in the interaction between the learner and the other learners, or the tutor. In fact, various factors can play a role in the improvement of learning such as motivation, arousal, feedback, reinforcement, etc. We will focus on the learner/troublemaker conflict which is an intentional external conflict. It consists of a difference in opinion between the learner and the troublemaker (specialized tutor), and this difference is introduced to attain an obvious pedagogical goal: to make the learner evaluate his own opinion and cognitive schema. If learner is experiencing cognitive dissonance (discord between two ideas) (Festinger, 1989) then an argumentative dialogue with the troublemaker will help him correct conflicts with his own set of knowledge that we call internal conflicts. This discussion is organized according to a scenario set by the troublemaker (section 5).

In this chapter we first review the evolution of learning strategies towards cooperative environments that show the necessity of reciprocal interaction. These interactions can cause different types of conflicts that we present in section 3. In particular, we introduce the cognitive dissonance theory (Festinger, 1957) one of the best known and most researched frameworks pertaining to attitude change which is caused by conflicts among beliefs. We analyze in section 4 the different kinds of conflicts which exist in an ITS and especially for those that use cooperative learning strategies. We will show, in particular, how a new cooperative strategy that we have developed can correct the cognitive dissonance. We define in section 5 the notion of conflict management and the different forms of dialogues. In order to validate two hypotheses formulated on the utility of conflicts in cooperative learning improvement we present in section 6 experimental results concerning the comparison of two cooperative learning strategies.

This work was initiated in 1996 in the Safari project (Gecsei and Frasson, 1994, Frasson and Aïmeur, 1997) in which the various components of the strategies have been supported by a multi-agents architecture. Each strategy uses several pedagogical agents (Frasson et al., 1997).

2. EVOLUTION OF LEARNING STRATEGIES IN INTELLIGENT TUTORING SYSTEMS

Since the beginning of the eighties ITS evolved towards several directions. Initially ITS tried to incorporate into a single system reproductions of a super-teacher using multiple knowledge sources such as a student model, a pedagogical model, a subject matter model. However this architecture was gradually simplified to the benefit of specific modules able to achieve precise tasks such as advising the learner, providing learning in context, or strengthening self-learning or interaction between different learners. Why? Two reasons can be found in this orientation. First in real life, in industry for instance, people need to obtain specific and immediate help in problem solving situation or for short term objectives. They often need to involve teams working collaboratively. Another more important reason results from the studies in artificial intelligence (AI) which initially considered that reproducing human tutoring behavior was an intelligent criteria. This approach (also called one-on-one strategy (Sleeman and Brown, 1982)) consisted in having the computer simulate an intelligent tutor who can understand the learner and provide adaptive tutoring. In this case the learner receives knowledge directly from the tutor who communicates and acts according to a prescriptive behavior.

This approach became blurred when the AI community concluded that intelligence should finally result from a joint construction between the human and the computer. This orientation strengthened the opinion from a part of the education community convinced by the construction of knowledge.

The principle of cooperative tutoring systems (also called social learning systems) is based on the use of the computer not as a directive training means but instead as a way to exchange, control and build knowledge. Several experiments have shown that two persons working together will learn more than in individual training (Dillenbourg and Self, 1992, Weeb, 1989). Constructivist approaches assess that the learner builds his own knowledge using his [1] experience and interaction with the real working environment. Learning in context states that knowledge construction results from a common interaction with the real world (including not only specific aspects of the domain but also social, cultural, and historical aspects) using the context.

[1] Note that in this paper and for convenience he refers to he or she, and him refers to him or her.

In that sense, several models have been developed which generally are called social learning systems, cooperative systems, or collaborative systems.

Cooperative learning systems adopt a constructive approach using the computer more as a partner then as a tutor. Multiple agents that are either computer simulated (Vanlehn et al., 1994) or real human beings can work on the same computer or share a computer network.

Chan and Baskin proposed a three-agent learning situation (Chan and Baskin, 1990) which consists in a cooperation between a human learner and a simulated learning companion. They learn together under the guidance of the tutor. The companion and the learner perform the same task and exchange ideas on the problem. The learner and the co-learner (the companion) work together (collaboratively) and ask the tutor for help only if they cannot find a solution. A conflict may occur between the companion and the learner, fostering the discussion and the discover of the solution (Chan et al., 1992).

Several experiments have shown that students learn more when they explain examples to their teachers (Palthepu et al., 1991) or to themselves. A set of findings around this last principle has been called the self-explanation effect (Chi et al., 1989) and reproduced in models or simulation programs (Chi and Vanlehn, 1991, Vanlehn et al., 1992). The study by Chi et al was conducted on students involved in physics course (learning particle dynamics) and distinguished between two classes of students: Good solvers (students with the highest scores) from Poor solvers (the others).

Other variations of the reciprocal teaching were recently introduced (Aïmeur and Frasson, 1996, Retalis et al., 1996). In the learning by disturbing strategy (Aïmeur and Frasson, 1996) the computer simulates two agents: a tutor and a special companion called troublemaker. The level of competence of the troublemaker is superior that of the learner in order to provide reasonable competition. In addition it has some pedagogical knowledge which can help it to plan its interactions efficiently. The troublemaker proposes suggestions to the student emphasizing some of the finer points of the exercise at hand. A conflict may occur between the troublemaker and the learner as sometimes the suggestions are right but sometimes they are wrong.

- The tutor presents to the team of students both the lessons and the exercises to be solved. It is the tutor who controls both the content and the length of the session. At any time, the tutor may intervene to help one of the students in their task. Finally, it is the tutor who evaluates the performance of the learner.

- The learner is the human student who is using the ITS. The learner interacts with the other participants via either natural language or symbolic dialogue. The system maintains at all times a model of the learner which describes the state of the student's knowledge relative to the system's objectives. The later is particularly relevant to the troublemaker strategy since it is important to gage the student's confidence levels to plan the troublemaker's actions.

- The troublemaker appears to be a simulation of a student working with the learner. In fact the troublemaker possesses both pedagogical expertise and a level of knowledge of the domain comparable to that of the tutor (Aïmeur et al., 1997b). The troublemaker uses this pedagogical expertise to maximize the impact of its interventions. The role of the troublemaker is to unsettle the student by proposing solutions which are sometimes truthful but other times erroneous. This tests the student's self-confidence and obliges him to defend his point of view. We believe that this argumentation increases the student's motivation and increases learning.

The reader may ask why the tutor does not ensure both the teaching and the trouble-making functions. The answer is clear. In the framework of intelligent tutoring systems, one can not afford to have the student lose confidence in the tutor. In fact the troublemaker by making suggestions which are sometimes correct but also sometimes erroneous will inevitably lose credibility in the eyes of the student. We present the troublemaker as a student that will work with the learner without revealing its true intentions. The learner will never know that the troublemaker is in fact a tutor with a specialized role: that of testing and provoking the student.

The role of the troublemaker is to introduce an external conflict and in fact, as we will see in the next section, conflicts can strengthen learning when introduced efficiently.

3. NOTIONS OF CONFLICTS

3.1 PRINCIPLES

- **Definition 1 (Conflict)** *A conflict is a situation between humans having incompatible or exclusive goals or values. It can be considered as a mechanism to re-stabilize strengths that maintain and consolidate social systems. The conflict is also defined as the status of an entity subject to contradictory forces resulting from external conditions or from the entity itself. Conflicts are related to human psychological development and no evolution can exist without conflicts.*

The notion of conflicts was often used according to different forms. Festinger (Festinger, 1957) was the first to talk about dissonance, Berlyne (Berlyne, 1960) talked about competition within responses, Piaget (Piaget, 1975) talked about equilibrium perturbation. All these notions indicate a status of conflict between cognitive elements in a human and this conflict will be a source of evolution.

- **Types of conflicts** The conflict can bring individuals together (interpersonal conflict), groups (intergroup conflict), social organizations (social conflict) or nations (international conflict). All these conflicts will be called external conflicts. Conflicts which appear in the mind of an individual are called internal conflicts. Conflicts are of different kinds. For instance, the partners can aim at contradictory goals (for instance the employees of a company asking for a salary increase and the management who refuses), they can defend contradictory values (traditional education and present education), they can competitively aim at the same goal (two girls loving the same guy).

- **Conflicts resolution** Three modes of conflict resolution can be defined :

  - **negotiation** : negotiation is a discussion procedure established between two opposed parts for the purpose of reaching a common agreement.
  - **mediation** : mediation is a negotiation between two opposed parts in the presence of a third neutral part which will facilitate the research of a solution to the conflict.
  - **arbitration** : conflicting parts leave it to a third part decision.

Several works have been done on detection, prevention, or resolution of conflicts (Touzard, 1977, Zlotkin and Rosenschein, 1991, Fach et al., 1993, Baker, 1994, Kotenko, 1994, Stuller, 1995, Chu-Carrol and Carberry, 1996).

In this paper we will focus on conflicts between a real learner and a simulated learner. These conflicts will be deliberately provoked in order to make the learner realize his internal conflicts. We will refer to the arbitration of the tutor. To highlight these conflicts we will use the cognitive dissonance theory.

3.2 COGNITIVE DISSONANCE

Various learning theories exist in the literature, for instance : the ACT theory from Anderson (Anderson and Bower, 1973), the cognitive dissonance theory from Festinger (Festinger, 1957), the conditions of learning from Gagné (Gagné, 1984), the component display theory from Merrill (Merrill, 1980), the constructivist theory from Bruner (Bruner, 1966), the conversation theory from Pask (Pask, 1975), the operant conditioning from Skinner (Skinner, 1957), the situated learning from Lave (Lave, 1988, Lave and Wenger, 1991), the social development from Vygotsky (Vygotsky, 1978), the social learning theory from Bandura (Bandura, 1971), to cite only some of them among more than fifty theories. In the following section we will only consider the cognitive dissonance theory. Each of us memorize at a given moment a certain number of facts, both true and false, partly true or partly false, concerning ourselves or others. Social psychologists of the 50s called these facts cognition. These cognition refer to conscious representations of fact in our mind. They can be concepts, ideas, knowledge, opinions, beliefs, etc. They can refer to one-self ("I am interested in computer science"), to one's behavior ("I am waiting for Suzanne"), to one's social environment ("my neighbors are fighting again") or to one's environment ("the sky is blue"). Most of the cognition that constitute our cognitive environment are not independent of each other. On the contrary, they are related in ways that can be perfectly harmonious but might also be quite uncomfortable.

Between 1955 and 1960, several psychological theories appeared. Their main goal was to explain the relations between cognitions, and in particular how these relations were built and adjusted. The most important of these theories were the theory of cognitive-dissonance (Festinger, 1957), Heider's theory of equilibrium (Heider, 1958) and Osgood and Tannenbaum's theory of congruence (Osgood and Tannenbaum, 1955). These theories are traditionally grouped in one paradigm, that of cognitive consistency, since they all describe an organization of cognitions. More specifically these different theories suggest that when cognitions are not well linked, in other words, when they are not well organized, a cognitive readjustment has to be done to re-establish a more harmonious organization.

Cognitive-dissonance is a theory originally developed by Festinger which had a great impact on the social psychology community. According to this approach a cognition represents an element of knowledge. Cognitions can be, with respect to each other, in either a relevant relation or an irrelevant one. When they are in a relevant relation, they can interact, imply each other, contradict each other, or contribute to each other. The theory is only interested in cognitions which are in a relevant relation with each other and these can either be consonant (consistent) or dissonant (inconsistent). More formally, if x and y are cognitions, then they are in a consonant state if x implies y or if x contributes to y. They are in a dissonant state if x contradicts y. Like the motivational states of hunger or thirst, the state of dissonance is unpleasant and prompts the individual to attempt to reduce that dissonance.

Example

Consider someone who buys an expensive car but discovers that it is not comfortable on long drives. Dissonance exists between his beliefs that he has bought a good car and that a good car should be comfortable. Dissonance could be eliminated by deciding that it does not matter since the car is mainly used for short trips (reducing the importance of the dissonant belief) or focusing on the cars advantages such as safety, appearance, or handling (thereby adding more consonant beliefs). The dissonance could also be eliminated by getting rid of the car, but this behavior is much harder to achieve than changing beliefs.

Definition 2 *Festinger's definition of cognitive-dissonance is the perception, by a subject, of a difference, of variable intensity, between what has been previously perceived and learned and new information.*

This process is illustrated by Figure 8.1.

1. Perception of information
2. Storage in a cognitive schema
3. Perception of new information
4. Realization of dissonance
5. Psychological discomfort
6. Action taken to reduce dissonance
7. Modification of the cognitive schema

Figure 8.1 Steps in the cognitive-dissonance process adapted from (Aïmeur et al., 1997a).

Festinger strongly links cognitive-dissonance and internal motivation: "The existence of dissonance, being psychologically uncomfortable, will motivate the person to try to reduce the dissonance and achieve consonance. In short, I am proposing that dissonance, that is, the existence of non-fitting relations among cognitions, is a motivating factor in its own right." (Festinger, 1957).

A key feature of Festinger's theory is the expectations that the subject has. In fact, the subject seeks to corroborate his conception of the environment by what he perceives. "New information may become known to a person, creating at least a momentary dissonance with existing knowledge, opinion or cognition concerning behavior. Since a person does not have complete and perfect control over the information that reaches him and over events that can happen in his environment, such dissonance may easily arise." (Festinger, 1989).

The individual experiencing cognitive-dissonance triggered by another person can react in four ways (Festinger, 1989):

1. Dismissing the subject of dispute as being unimportant.

2. Dismissing the other person as being unimportant.

3. Attempting to eliminate the dissonance by changing his own opinion (by letting himself be convinced) or by attempting to change the opinion of the other person (in particular by initiating a debate with that person).

4. Seeking new information in his environment which would support his opinion. For example in a community (such as a system with several participants) the individual could seek social support.

Each of the theories previously cited (cognitive-dissonance, Heider's theory of equilibrium and Osgood and Tannenbaum's theory of congruence) has specific aspects that make it inapplicable to certain domains. We have paid particular attention to the theory of cognitive-dissonance because it is the one that allows us to best understand the internal conflicts that exist in the learner's mind and that best explains the importance of the troublemaker in the learning process. In fact, we believe that the troublemaker strategy is an ingenious way to detect internal conflicts and to make the learner aware of them. By provoking external conflicts between the learner and the troublemaker the latter must react to rectify an uncomfortable situation. Several conflicts can exist in an ITS. To be used positively (for improving learning) we need to distinguish the adequate steps to introduce them as we will see in the next section.

3.3 LEARNING-BY-DISTURBING AS A WAY TO CORRECT COGNITIVE-DISSONANCE

The following points describe the learning-by-disturbing strategy in the context of cognitive-dissonance theory (Aïmeur, 1998).

1. A cognitive-dissonance is triggered by the troublemaker's interventions;

2. At that time, the troublemaker is the only available source of information, even if there is an agreement between the troublemaker and the tutor for their respective interventions.

3. In order to reduce the dissonance the learner is motivated to search for new information in his environment;

4. The mechanisms used are dialogue and debate with the troublemaker, and this process has two outcomes : the student can let himself be convinced, or the student can change his environment by convincing the troublemaker.

Finally, two factors influence the outcome of this debate:

- the confidence that the student has in his cognitive schema, and
- the ability the troublemaker has to express its ideas in a convincing manner.

In the previous section, we have considered the conflict in general without any assumption about the domain of application. We will now focus on application of conflicts to intelligent tutoring systems.

4. COOPERATION AND CONFLICTS IN ITS

There exist several different definitions of cooperation in the literature and the distinction between cooperation and collaboration is not always clear (Brant, 1990, Davidson and O'leary, 1990, Dillenbourg and Self, 1992, Edouards and Stout, 1990, Ellis, 1990, Johnson and Pugach, 1996, Kagan, 1990, Slavin et al., 1990, Sharan and S., 1990). We adopt the definition of collaboration formulated by (Roschelle and S.D., 1989, Roschelle, 1992): "a coordinated, synchronous activity that is the result of a continued attempt to construct and maintain a shared conception of a problem. Cooperation is an activity in which each person is responsible for a portion of the problem solving." In addition, taking a decision requires the choice between several options. Since it is rare that making a decision is a cut and dried prospect conflict arises. Choice is more a weighing of good and bad points of equal force but of different distribution. The tale of Buridan's donkey illustrates this situation: as hungry as thirsty and placed at equal distance between hay and water the donkey does not know what to choose and hesitates until death. There exists several types of conflict in ITS:

- *internal conflicts* in the learner model [2] (Vanlehn, 1988): knowledge acquired by the learner is sometimes not firmly anchored in memory (poorly acquired), or even incorrectly understood and recorded (misconceptions). In addition, some knowledge may be missing either because the information has been insufficiently perceived, and therefore not recorded, or it is no more accessible due to a lack of indexing. All

[2] The learner model is a model which describes the state of the student' knowledge (cognitive), of his preferences (affective) and his way of thinking (inferential).

these conditions of learning will constitute a basis for potential conflicts with the tutor.

- *external conflicts* between the learner and different participants in a learning session. Here also, the learner model of each participant can be at different stages and consequently the learners do not have the same dialogue level. Therefore conflicts may arise. The degree of conflict may also vary according to the perception of the behavior of their peers, depending on the role of each participant (collaborator or competitor).

- *external conflicts* between tutors delivering the course or designers of a single course in a multidisciplinary setting. Instructional design can be undertaken according to various design theories (Bloom, 1969, Gagné, 1984, Klausmeier, 1990, Merrill, 1991). Even in using a single theory, designers can emphasize on learning objectives, on capabilities to acquire, or on available resources. This occurs because not enough is known about how to create a generic and re-usable curriculum. Designing a course is a considerable source of conflicts particularly in a cooperative environment (Murray, 1998).

- *external conflicts* between the protocols of learning strategies. This aspect is based on several factors such as:
  - the number of participants (for example one tutor, one companion and two real learners),
  - the type of strategy (one-on-one, learning companion, learning by teaching, learning by disturbing),
  - the role of each participant (collaborator, competitor, neutral),
  - the forms of intervention (hints, advice, critics, etc.),
  - the means of intervention or resources (demonstration, HTML documents, simulations).

Conflicts may arise in the protocol of each strategy. Figure 8.2 illustrates two types of cooperative learning strategies (learning companion, learning by disturbing), the different roles played by each participant (collaborator, competitor), and the conflicts.

A cooperation exists at the system level, between the tutor, the companion and the troublemaker, while these two last virtual components collaborate with the learner in a learning session. The conflicts between the companion and the learner happen when the suggestions of the companion throws doubt on the learner who has to inspect his knowledge base, but the conflicts are involuntary. The conflicts between the troublemaker and the learner happen when the

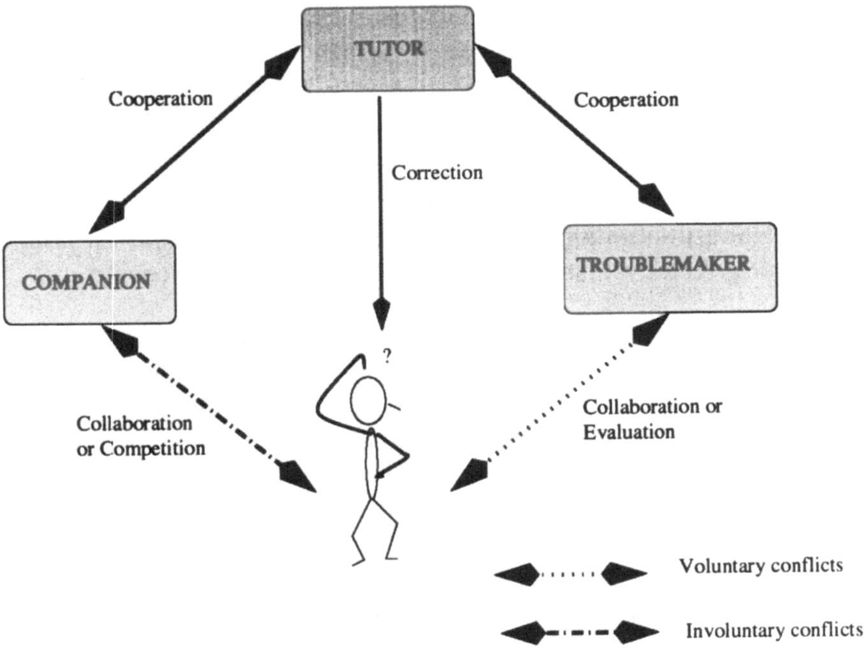

Figure 8.2 Different forms of collaboration, cooperation or conflicts

troublemaker tries to mislead him.

Dosing the conflicts To be efficient, conflicts in cooperative learning need to be adapted to the context of the learners and more precisely to their learning level. If the conflict is too high the learner will be discouraged and will look at the companion as a competitor, if it is too low he will not be sufficiently motivated to react to the stimuli and risks to stay on the same position (no progress). The pace and scale of the conflict must be related to the conditions of learning in which the learner is. Several mastery learning models support this gradation: the mastery learning initiated by John Caroll (Carroll, 1963), the conditions of learning from Gagné (Gagné, 1984), or the instructional transaction theory from Merrill (Merrill, 1991). The Gagné's conditions provide us with a precise scale for dosing conflicts. From level 1 to 4 motivation and recall can be made, levels 4 to 5 exercises can be realized, level 6 allows to present more complex exercises, level 6 to 7 allow generalization and abstraction and need self confidence. Thus, positive conflicts will be obtained if for level 1-4 the tutor and the companion are alternatively used, for level 5-6 the companion can intervene with more complex suggestions, and finally for level 6-7 the conflicts introduced by the troublemaker will contribute to strengthen the overall knowledge. Assessing (evaluation) the learner level with the type of conflicts will be used to select the best strategy at the right time. This tendency is reflected by several works in assessment (Herman et al., 1997, Schank and Jona, 1991, Smit and Van Der Molen, 1997, Wynne and James, 1997).

5. CONFLICTS MANAGEMENT

The introduction of a conflict by the troublemaker needs to be planned on precise points of the course. In fact, conflicts could arise in any points of the curriculum for a given learner but we have found, in a previous experience (Aïmeur and Frasson, 1996), that disturbing a learner could have a negative effect (discouragement) if his performance level was too low. On the other hand, disturbing can be positive for good learners. However, we need to know (1) where the conflict can be activated, (2) if the conflict has effectively introduced a dissonance into the learner knowledge, (3) how to repair this dissonance.

5.1 DEFINITIONS

Let us consider the following diagram in which a0, a2, . . . , a6, represent a sequence of actions that are necessary to achieve procedure A7 (Figure 8.3). For instance, procedure A7 is "Parking" and actions a1, . . . ,a6 are respectively: check traffic, indicate intention to park, relative disposition of the car, proximity of the car, wheel orientation, backup, steering wheel. A7 can be the result of another sequence of actions, for instance b1, b2, b3, that are actions to make "diagonal parking", A7 being a general procedure in which we consider the car as "parked".

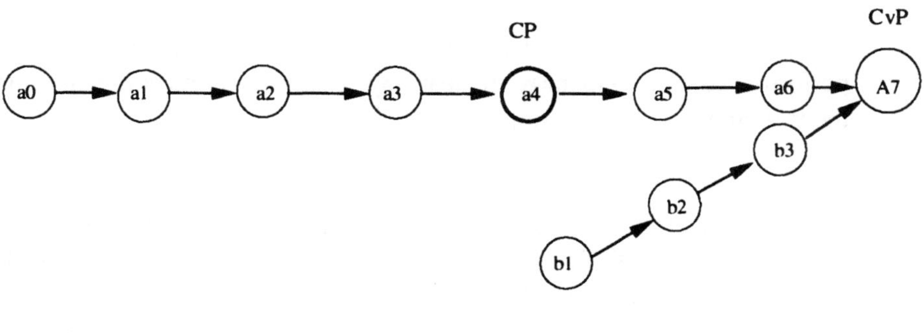

Figure 8.3 Conflict points in the curriculum

A Conflict Point (CP) is an action which is fundamental to reach correctly the end of the procedure. If this action is not well mastered the final procedure will be wrong. For instance, a4 consists in orienting the wheels to backup; a wrong orientation will lead to a failure. Learning through CP requires a methodology to apply in order to benefit from the introduction of CP. A Converging Point (CvP) is a procedure which can be realized according to different ways (for instance A7). A CvP is the result of a several sequences of actions involving one or several CP. A disturbance is a wrong suggestion given by the troublemaker on any action. Each question on an action may have several answers (multiple choice question). Among them we have a correct answer and three wrong answers. They correspond to three types of disturbance (D0, D1, D2) corresponding to three possible levels of the learner (weak, intermediate, high). The contradictions vary from obvious cases (for D0, the fallacy of the contradiction is obvious), to complex argumentation (for D2, the learner has normally some difficulty to immediately prove he is right). The CP and the disturbances are determined by the conceptual designer.

5.2 METHODOLOGY OF LEARNING THROUGH CONFLICTS

We consider the methodology to apply by different human or software agents for managing conflicts in learning : the conceptual designer (human), the tutor, the companion, and the troublemaker. We detail all these procedures (indicated in italic) in the next section.

- **The pedagogical designer**

  The role of the conceptual designer is to build the curriculum of a domain to be taught, to determine the conflict points (conflict planning), and to build the questions with their corresponding answers.

- **The tutor**

  The role of the tutor is to teach curriculum concepts, to evaluate learner performance, and to manage the learning session with the companion or the troublemaker (see section 2).

- **The companion**

  During the learning session a dialogue is introduced between the tutor and the learner, with the intervention of the companion (see section 2). The companion gives good recommendations to the learner. However, these recommendations can be wrong, introducing an involuntary conflict. In that case, the tutor acts as a referee and can correct both the learner and the companion.

- **The troublemaker**
  - **Step1** : learning session. A dialogue is introduced between the tutor and the learner with the intervention of the troublemaker. At a proximity of a CP the troublemaker may intervene before the answer of the learner, giving a wrong suggestion. The strength of disturbance depends on the learner's previous level of performance.
  - **Step 2** : conflict resolution. It consists in determining if the conflict resulted into a dissonance for the learner and how strong is this dissonance. In that case, we will help him to eliminate the conflict.

5.3 CONFLICT PLANNING

The determination of CP can be done by analyzing the curriculum, which contains all the knowledge elements to be taught. In the Safari project (Frasson and Aïmeur, 1997), we have determined a structure of the curriculum based on three networks of knowledge: capabilities or knowledge to acquire, objectives which represent the pedagogical goals to achieve, and the resources which support teaching material. Here, we will consider only the capabilities network to find the potential CP. A CP is initially determined by the pedagogical designer, who knows which knowledge element in the curriculum can be subject of discussion (due to past experience, the number of questions asked, ...). The procedure is as follows:

- For all CvP in a curriculum
- Consider a CvP as the root of a subtree and allot a weight (between 0 and 1) to each node of this subtree. The weight represents the importance of the node for the achievement of the CvP.
- Among the preceding nodes qualify as CP those that have the highest weights.

For each node in the subtree, the pedagogical designer builds a set of questions with multiple choices of answers, including true and false answers.

5.3.1 Learning session (for the troublemaker).

The tutor and the troublemaker control the performance of the learner through the different elements of the curriculum. In any action (which is not a CP) the troublemaker gives only right suggestions. However, the learner may not follow the suggestion and thus gives a wrong answer. It is an involuntary conflict provoked by the troublemaker. Again, the tutor will arbitrate the conflict by giving the right answer. The tutor is permanently evaluating the learner knowledge level through all the actions results. The knowledge level is the rate of correct answers. In case of CP, the troublemaker will use this knowledge about the learner to adjust the strength of the disturbance, choosing among the types D0, D1, D2 (Table 8.1). In case of CP two situations may arise: (1) the learner is influenced, which means that he followed the suggestions of the troublemaker. There is no conflict, but the tutor has to detect if there is a dissonance between the previous acquired knowledge. (2) the learner is not influenced. There is a conflict with the troublemaker since the learner did not follow his suggestion.

	Conflict Point		
Learner level	weak	intermediate	High
Troublemaker intervention before learner answer	D0	D1	D2
Troublemaker intervention after learner answer	NO	NO	D2

Table 8.1 Different dialogue situations

Perturbation D0 is an evident false suggestion. The objective is not to destabilize the learner but to catch his attention. D1 is a more ambiguous (false) suggestion. Finally, D2 is a wrong suggestion presented in a very subtle form, in which it is difficult to distinguish the truth. Examples of such suggestions are given in a next section.

5.3.2 Conflict resolution.

- **Case 1**: the learner is influenced, he agrees with the troublemaker. The learner seems to do not master the CP. The tutor will consider the preceding actions to know if they are also not understood and, for that purpose, ask a multiple choices question. If the action is correct the tutor continues the questioning process until the first action of the sequence. For actions not understood the tutor gives the right answer before continuing towards the first action. The goal is to find all the faulty actions. When the first node is reached the tutor resumes the repairing process by giving a complete correct sequence.

- **Case 2**: the learner is not influenced, he contradicts the troublemaker. The goals is now to detect on which previous actions there exists a contradiction in his reasoning or to maintain his confidence until the first action. For that, the troublemaker will ask the learner on previous actions, introducing again a new disturbance (at level D2, because we are in the presence of a good learner) starting from the last action of the sequence to the first one. Two situations may arise: (1) the learner steps backward, justifying each action correctly until the first one. The consequence is that the learner has proved the correctness of his reasoning and strengthened his knowledge by the self-explanation effect. (2) The learner fails on a certain action while he succeeded in achieving the final action. He discovers an unexpected contradiction with his reasoning and thus a dissonance (this may be a clue for the tutor for qualifying the action as a possible CP if several learners fail). The correction of the conflict will be achieved by the tutor, which will show him the contradiction between the two actions. There is no more conflict with the troublemaker.

Remark : in the learning session the tutor asks questions randomly. In a CP, he will ask questions sequentially, in a reverse order.

5.4 DIALOGUE MANAGEMENT

5.4.1 Architecture of the system. Figure 8.4 shows part of the architecture of the system, which handles the conflicts resolution.

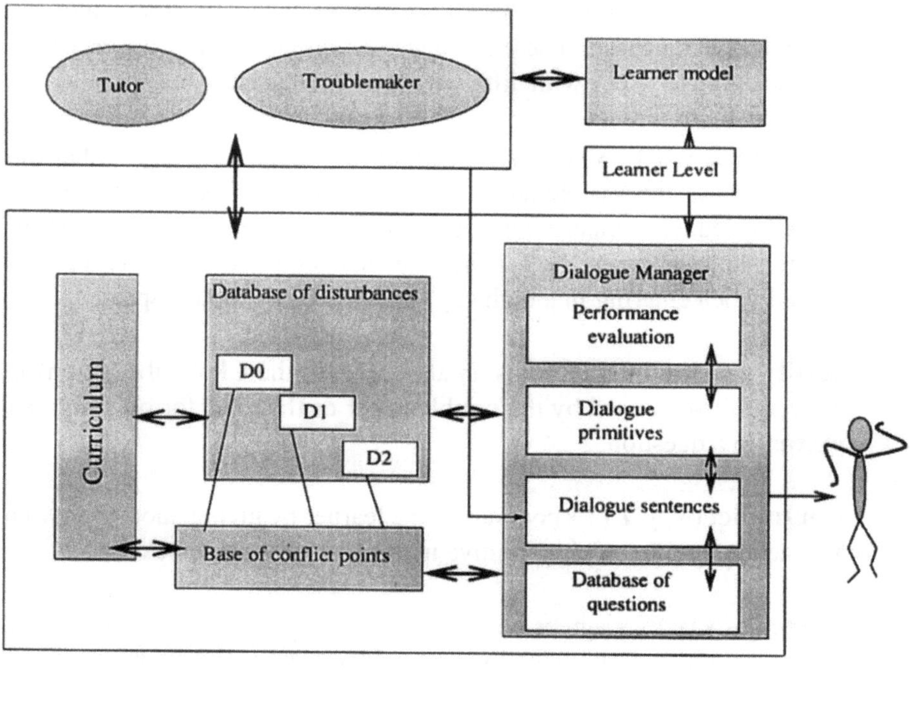

Figure 8.4 Dialogue management architecture

The base of conflict points results from an analysis of the curriculum. For each CP, three sets of disturbances are inserted in the database of disturbances, respectively D0, D1, and D2. The contradictions vary from obvious cases (for D0, the fallacy of the contradiction is obvious) to complex argumentation (for D2, the learner has normally some difficulty to immediately prove he his right). The CP and the disturbances are determined by the pedagogical designer. A database contains all the questions and answers related to each action of the curriculum. The knowledge level is evaluated by a performance evaluation module, which takes into consideration the level of Gagné (since the questions are categorized according to the different levels of Gagné) and the rate of learner good answers. Receiving the learner knowledge level, the dialogue manager informs the troublemaker about the type of disturbance to trigger (D0, D1, D2). Correspondingly, the troublemaker will dynamically chooses the type of disturbance. The sentences are built using predetermined elements of phrases (such as : I think that the answer about question . . . , or I propose that for the question relative to . . .), the content of the question, and the disturbance. The sentences are activated by the dialogue manager using a set of primitives detailed in the next section.

5.4.2 Dialogue primitives. The dialogue is handled by the following primitives. For each primitive a set of various sentences is stored into the dialogue sentences database. These sentences represent different forms of the same sentence type to apply with different types of suggestions.

- **Suggest (x, y, z) : x** suggests disturbance **y** at the CP **z**. x is either the companion or the troublemaker. For instance : I think that the answer about "speed when entering in a highway" is "reduce speed". A variation of the sentence would be : I propose that for the question relative to "speed when entering in a highway" the answer is "reduce speed"

- **Justify (x, y, z) : x** requests an answer y for the CP (or the action) **z**. This primitive is used by the troublemaker or the tutor for obtaining an answer to a question.

- **Contradict (x, y, z) : x** contradicts the learner by giving another answer y to action or CP **z**. This primitive is used by the troublemaker.

- **Agree (x, y, z) : x** agrees with the learner on answer **y** to CP or action **z**. This primitive is provided by the troublemaker or the tutor.

- **Ask-Learner (x, y, z) : x** asks the learner (with question **y**) on CP or action **z**. The question is issued from the troublemaker or the tutor.

- **Ask-Tutor (x, y)** : in case of conflict with the learner, the companion, or the troublemaker (**x**) can ask the tutor for additional precision on the CP or action **y**.

- **Answer (x, y)** : the tutor provides the correct answer **x** to action or CP **y**, with explanations.

5.4.3 Example of dialogue. We will use the elements of the curriculum indicated in Figure 8.3. The CP is on action a4 : car orientation and the goal is to do a parallel parking. The questions attached to each action are indicated below. Note that these questions are stored in the database of questions (Figure 8.4). Four answers are attached to each questions, 3 false answers, corresponding to D0, D1 and D2, and a correct answer. The correct answers are underlined for the reader.

- **a0 : Check traffic**

  1. <u>look behind</u>
  2. look ahead
  3. look at the parking spot
  4. look in the side-view mirrors

- **a1 : Indicate intention to park**

  1. push brakes
  2. indicate left light
  3. <u>indicate right light</u>
  4. put the hand outside the car

- **a2 : relative disposition of the car**

  1. place the head of the car even with the parked car
  2. stay with an angle of 30 degrees
  3. stay half to the parked car
  4. <u>stay parallel to the parked car ahead</u>

- **a3 : proximity of the cars**

  1. keep a distance of 1 meter
  2. <u>keep a distance of 60 cm</u>
  3. keep a distance of 30 cm

4. keep a distance of 45 cm

- **a4 : wheel orientation**

    1. the wheels form an angle of about 60 degrees with the sidewalk
    2. the wheels form an angle of about 30 degrees with the sidewalk
    3. the wheels are parallel to the sidewalk
    4. the wheels form an angle of about 45 degrees with the sidewalk

Comments of the dialogue are indicated between ** **. The dialogue begins by different questions related to the highway code. These questions are not linked. When we reach a question on a CP we consider all the actions preceding this CP. For instance, we will begin by a question on a given action, d12, related to "leave a vehicle".

d12 : leave an unoccupied vehicle

1. Yes, at all times
2. Yes, for a few minutes only
3. No, never
4. None of these answers

- **Ask-learner (Tutor,** Can you leave an unoccupied vehicle parked with doors unlocked ?, **d12)**

  Suggest (Troublemaker, 3, d12) : I think that the answer about question d12 is " No, never"

  Reply of the learner : (3) : No, never

  Answer ("correct answer", d12)

  ** The learner agrees with the troublemaker and is approved by the tutor. Then, the tutor asks a question on a CP**.

- **Ask-learner (Tutor,** How do you orient the car when you backup for a parking ?, **a4)**

Suggest (Troublemaker, 1, a4) : I propose that for the question relative to a4 the answer is "the wheels form an angle of about 60 degrees with the sidewalk"

Reply of the learner : (4) : the wheels form an angle of about 45 degrees with the sidewalk

Answer ("correct answer", a4)

**An external conflict appears with the troublemaker. The learner decided not to follow his recommendations. Detecting the right answer (case 2 (1) of section 5.3.2) the tutor steps backward asking on the previous actions. The tutor eliminates the conflict between the troublemaker and the learner by approving this one **.

- **Ask-learner (Tutor,** At which distance do you stay from the parked car ?, **a3)**

Suggest (Troublemaker, 4, a3) : I think that the answer about a3 is "keep a distance of 45 cm "

Reply of the learner : (2) : keep a distance of 60 cm

Answer ("correct answer", a3)

** The tutor continues to step backward. He eliminates the external conflict between the troublemaker and the learner by approving this one**.

- **Ask-learner (Tutor**, How do you place your car relatively to the parked car ?, **a2)**

Suggest (Troublemaker, 2, a2) : I propose that for the question relative to a2 the answer is "stay with an angle of 30 degrees"

Reply of the learner : (1) : I place the head of the car even with the parked car

Answer ("you are wrong, the correct answer is 4", a2)

** detecting the wrong answer (case 2 (2) of section 5.3.2)**.

An additional conflict (internal) happens here. This last case means that the learner was not aware about the dissonance which arises between a2 and a4. He discovers that he will never be able to orient the car correctly at 45 degrees if the car is not placed parallel to the ahead parked car. Consequently, A7 will not be achieved correctly. By providing the correct answer followed by a replay of the correct sequence of actions until A7, the tutor eliminates the dissonance and reinforces the knowledge of the learner.

6. EXPERIMENTATION

If the tutor cooperates with the companion and the troublemaker to improve learning we need to know, however, in which strategy the improvement is more significant. For this purpose, we have realized the following experiment. The conditions of experimentation are defined according to the participants, the material and the evaluation procedure.

Participants

The subject matter that we decided to choose for the experiment was the highway code. The participants for this evaluation were 30 learners of the computer science department (students or professors) at Université de Montréal. We wanted to compare the results of the learning by disturbing strategy with the learning companion (see section 2).

Materials

The data on which questions were asked dealt with highway code. A total of 42 questions were asked on the traffic signs. Questions were presented to the learner using texts or icons and were visualized on HTML documents. The advantage to use HTML documents is their accessibility on the WEB and their portability on various platforms.

Procedure

We have separated the set of learners into two groups using a random criteria: a reference group which was put through the learning companion strategy and a test group which experimented the learning by disturbing strategy. After a questionnaire in order to know the sex, age, self-confidence and experience of the learner (information that are not directly used in this experiment but that will be considered in further analysis), each group was successively submitted to a pretest, a training phase and a posttest. The pretest was used to (1) eliminate subjects having weak results (less than 60 %) or very high results (more than 90 %), (2) ensure that we have two groups with the same level of knowledge, (3) know the initial knowledge of each learner and be able to measure the progress in learning. Candidates to the pretest were evaluated using a set of 12 questions. For the training phase subjects of the two groups were submitted to a same set of 18 questions according to the two strategies, one group receiving suggestions (for the answers) from the companion and the other one from the troublemaker. The posttest allows to evaluate the knowledge of the learners in order to compare them with the results of the pretest and so appreciate the progress (or regress). Posttest contains 12 questions and 25 % of them have been proposed in the training phase. Learners were not aware that they could be exposed to wrong suggestions and they did not communicate in order not to introduce a bias during the test. During the training phase suggestions were given to the learner in each group by the companion or the troublemaker and they were inhibited during the evaluation phase in order to appreciate the effect of the two strategies.

Hypotheses

We make the following hypotheses:

- In general people learn better with the troublemaker.
- Improvements with the troublemaker are more significant.

7. RESULTS AND DISCUSSION

The two groups have been separated randomly and were submitted to the pretest in order to verify that they were of equivalent initial knowledge level. The pretest results are listed in Table 8.2. The relatively high P-value confirms that the learners in the two groups were not significantly different.

Table 8.3 allows us to conclude that learning was effective. The difference between the pretest and the posttest in each strategy is significant. As P-value are low there is a significant difference between the pretest and the posttest results for each strategy.

Results of pretest and posttest of each strategy are illustrated in Figure 8.5. The troublemaker strategy appears more efficient than the companion. In fact, for the questions which are repeated in the posttest the learners trained with the troublemaker performed better because the process of memorization is better activated due to a more striking interaction. For the new questions, the perfor-

Strategy	No. of learners	Mean	SD	SEM
Companion	13	75.00	6.80	1.89
Troublemaker	11	75.76	5.84	1.76
t-Value	0.60			
d.f.	22			
P-value	0.55			

Table 8.2 Pretest results

Strategy	Companion	Troublemaker
No. of learners	13	11
Pretest	75.00	75.76
Posttest	78.85	84.09
Paired differences		
Mean	3.85	8.33
SD	11.59	12.91
SEM	3.22	3.89
t-Value	2.04	1.88
d.f.	24	20
P-value	0.05	0.07

Table 8.3 Pretest vs posttest results

mance was also better because the learners used to justify their answers, and thus to link the knew knowledge to their previously acquired information.

We have evaluated the learning rate by measuring, for each learner the difference between the posttest and the pretest. In order to compare the increase in learning of the two strategies we have applied a t-test to demonstrate that people learn better with the learning by disturbing strategy. The very low P-Value indicated in Table 8.4 shows that there is a significant difference between the increase in learning for the two strategies. This confirms our first hypothesis "In general people learn better with the troublemaker".

We have established three categories of people who respectively improved their performance, were stable or regressed. Figure 8.6 shows such a distribution for each strategy. The proportion of people who increased their performance is higher with the learning by disturbing strategy.

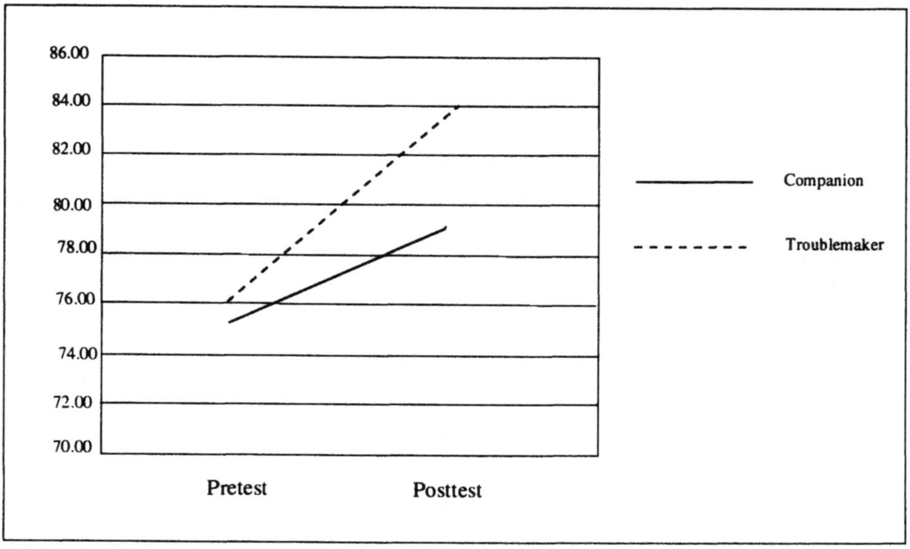

Figure 8.5 Performance of the two strategies

Strategy	No. of learners	Mean	SD	SEM
Companion	13	3.85	11.59	3.22
Troublemaker	11	8.33	12.91	3.89
t-Value	3.10			
d.f.	22			
P-value	0.01			

Table 8.4 Comparison of differences

Let us now consider the first category (people who increased their learning). Table 8.5 illustrates the difference of learning rate between the two strategies. This table is similar to table 8.4 but only for people who increased their learning. We observe the relatively low P-value which shows us that people who learn with the troublemaker performed better than people with the companion. This validates the second hypothesis "Improvements with the troublemaker are more significant".

Figure 8.7 illustrates, for category 1, the distribution of improvement within each strategy. We can see that the proportion of people who improved their performance by more than 25 % is clearly higher with the troublemaker.

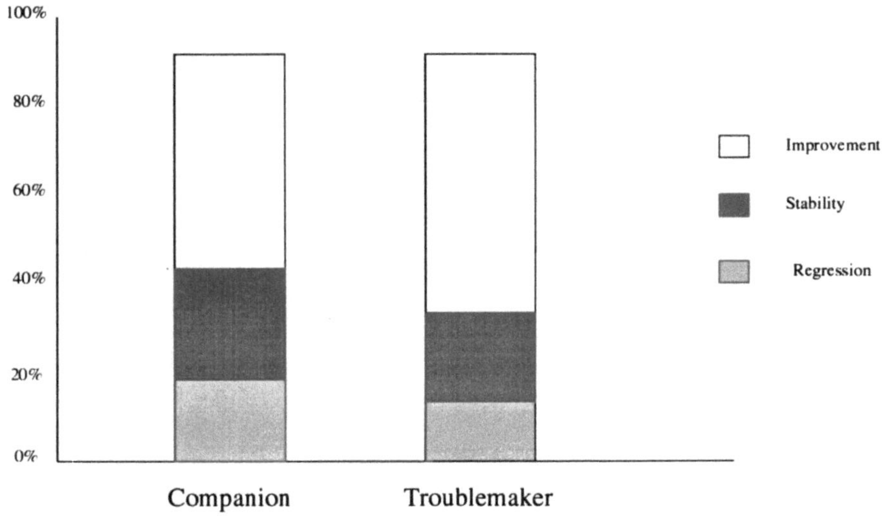

Figure 8.6 Distribution of categories within each strategy

Strategy	No. of learners	Mean	SD	SEM
Companion	6	13.89	6.80	2.78
Troublemaker	6	18.06	8.19	3.34
t-Value	1.58			
d.f.	10			
P-value	0.14			

Table 8.5 Comparison of differences for people who increased their learning

We have considered the difference of posttests within each category in order to compare it with the difference of pretests. We have made a bilateral test to check if the difference of posttests means were equivalent to difference observed for pretests. We have made the same hypothesis for high and poor levels learners: "if the difference between pretest means is equal to the difference of posttest means then progress in learning would be equivalent within each strategy for both categories of learners". Table 8.4 and 8.5 indicate results obtained for high level learners and poor learners. The low P-value shows that a significant difference effectively exists.

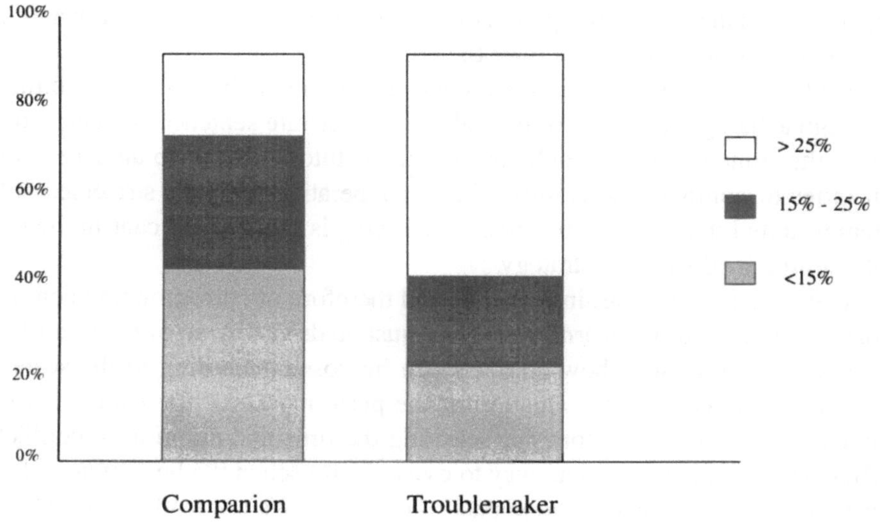

Figure 8.7 Distribution of improvement by category

8. CONCLUSION AND PERSPECTIVES

Cooperative learning strategies include both collaboration and conflicts aspects. If conflicts have negative impacts, they may have also positive contributions. Taking benefit from positive aspects of conflicts in learning is a way to optimize the selection of learning strategies. As we notice conflicts are necessary for the evolution of the learner. They provoke changes in his attitudes and performances.

Among the different types of conflicts we focused on internal and external conflicts for which the cognitive dissonance theory can bring an explanation. Cognitive dissonance can be reduced in several ways. We have found a double advantage in using learning by disturbing: this strategy at the same time reduces cognitive dissonance and clearly strengthens learning. The great advantage of this approach is to use an external conflict between the troublemaker and the learner to make him realize his internal conflicts which otherwise would remain hidden.

More precisely, we discussed an intentional external conflict caused by a difference of opinion between the learner and the troublemaker (specialized tutor). This difference of opinion is introduced in order to encourage the learner to evaluate his own opinion and cognitive schema. If a cognitive dissonance exists in the learner (discord between ideas) a dialogue with the troublemaker will help him correct his internal conflicts. The tutor and the troublemaker cooperate to manage a learning session, agreeing on the parts to intervene, the troublemaker being free to choose the remedy.

We have developed an architecture and a system which manage the conflicts through a dialog. A set of primitive allows to generate sentences that can come from the companion, the troublemaker, or the tutor. We set up an experiment in order to compare the results of two cooperative learning strategies. We demonstrated that the improvement of learning is more significant in the case of learning by disturbing strategy.

The selection of a learning strategy and therefore of corresponding conflicts that could be used in a learning session must be driven by an evaluation of the learner. We have seen how conflicts can be dosed according to the scale of Gagné and a permanent evaluation of the performance of the learner. Additional work needs to be done for selecting the time and duration of conflicts. They will provide a complete way to dynamically select the best strategy for a learner, and so to enhance the impact of conflicts. We are working on such an architecture involving distributed pedagogical agents that can react to stimuli (situations), plan their interactions, and also learn from the results obtained by the other agents.

Chapter 9

CONFLICT HANDLING IN COLLABORATIVE SEARCH

Jörg Denzinger
University of Calgary, Alberta, Canada
denzinge@cpsc.ucalgary.ca

Abstract We present an overview of the different kinds of conflicts arising in knowledge-based multi-agent search systems and the methods employed to deal with these conflicts. Based on an application-domain independent definition of sequential search processes, search agents and multi-agent search systems, we characterize three main ideas that are used to develop multi-agent search systems to solve given search problems, namely adding communication and cooperation to the competition approach, working on a common search state, and dividing the given problem into subproblems. For each of these ideas we describe several subtypes of multi-agent search systems based on the ideas and we collect the types of conflicts arising in these subtypes. For each type of conflicts we present the ideas used in literature to resolve these conflicts. Finally, we briefly sketch the requirements, advantages, and disadvantages of the three basic ideas for distributing search among agents and their subtypes.

1. INTRODUCTION

Knowledge-based search is one of the most prominent problem-solving techniques in AI systems and more and more other applications. Knowledge-based search, often also called heuristic or intelligent search, is characterized by the use of various kinds of knowledge to guide the search system through enormous, sometimes even infinite, search spaces whose systematic exploration would take too much time to be of any use.

This knowledge can be of use with respect to different levels of a search or search system, namely:

- the search problem or problem class,
  for example knowledge about how to divide a problem into subproblems,

- certain instances of the problem,
  for example knowledge about special solution methods for instances with certain properties,

- the used search model,
  for example knowledge about attributes of good and bad search states,

- the search process and its control,
  for example criteria to detect good successor states.

Usually, most of this knowledge is rather vague and may not be applicable to the instance of a search problem one is interested to solve. In addition, in most cases many different pieces of knowledge on each of the levels from above are potentially available for usage and it is even possible that some pieces contradict each other. Obviously, there is a large potential for conflicts between knowledge of different levels and also between pieces of knowledge on any of the levels. In single-agent search systems either the developers come up with a certain combination of the available knowledge to resolve the conflicts or, and this is the usual case, a user of the system has to decide which pieces of knowledge he or she wants to have employed in a particular search run.

The concurrent use of several search agents in a search system offers the possibility to model conflicts in the system, by, for example, having different agents using different pieces of knowledge, and to employ conflict solving techniques that can use information gathered in the actual search to either come up with better solutions to the given problem instance or to find a solution faster (or with less search runs)[1]. In addition, the agents can work on different processing units (processors or computers) in parallel. The price to pay for these advantages is twofold: Firstly, the use of several search agents results in an additional potential for conflicts, for example conflicts with respect to the task distribution among the agents. Secondly, conflict resolution often is a search problem itself and therefore can become rather expensive with respect to computing time. The later results in many multi-agent search concepts that either try to avoid or postpone conflicts and/or use rather simple methods for conflict resolution, like first-come-first-serve or survival-of-the-fittest. But there are also concepts that are centered around negotiation based conflict resolution.

There are three different basic ideas that are used in developing collaborative multi-agent search systems and that represent also different possibilities for conflicts, namely

- search based on improving on a competition between the search agents,

[1] Spoken in the terms of chapters 3 and 8, the internal conflicts of developers or users of the system (that are not easy to solve) are transfered into external conflicts between the different search agents (that, during search, may become easier to solve).

- search centered around a common search state for the search agents, and
- search based on dividing the given problem instance into subproblems for the search agents.

In the following, we will first describe more formally what collaborative search by a multi-agent search system is and then we will use these definitions to present the characteristics of systems following these three basic ideas. Naturally, we will mainly focus on the characteristics with respect to potential conflicts in such systems. For each of the three basic ideas, we will also present features of concrete multi-agent search systems based on such an idea and we will describe the different concepts for conflict resolution that have been employed in literature.

2. SEARCH AND MULTI-AGENT SEARCH

Usually, descriptions of search systems are centered around their application domains, i.e. the search problems they are intended to solve. In this chapter we are interested in general concepts for multi-agent search and the general potential conflicts in such systems. Therefore we have to abstract from concrete application domains. But this means that, before we characterize multi-agent search systems, we have to look at conventional (or sequential or single-agent) search and describe its elemental characteristics. All the following definitions are taken from (Denzinger, 1999).

On an abstract level, search is a process that generates out of a given state a new state (much like any program). Usually, to a state there are several successor states (in contrast to most other programs), so that the main task of the process is to select one of the possible successors. This task is done by the search control. In order to describe the possible search states, a *search process* is based on a *search model* that consists of a set of possible states and a transition relation between states. The *search control* bases its decision, in addition to the actual search state and the history of the search so far, on various pieces of knowledge and on other information not included in the search state, the so-called environment (this will be important in multi-agent search). More precisely, we have the following definition of a search process:

Definition 1 (Search model, search process)
Let S be a set of possible search states and $T \subseteq S \times S$ a set of transitions between states. Then $\mathcal{A} = (S,T)$ is a search model. *Let further be $\mathcal{E}nv$ a set of values of (data) structures. The triple $\mathcal{P} = (\mathcal{A}, \mathcal{E}nv, \mathcal{K})$ is a* search process, *if $\mathcal{K}$: $S \times \mathcal{E}nv \to S$ is a function for which $\mathcal{K}(s,e) \in \{s' \mid (s,s') \in T\}$ holds for all $s \in S$ and $e \in \mathcal{E}nv$. $\mathcal{K}$ is called the* search control *of the search process.*

Often used main data structures for states are sets of objects, trees, or graphs. Transitions for trees and graphs describe how to expand nodes in them. For example, in and-trees a leaf is expanded by dividing the problem described by this leaf node into several subproblems and for each of these subproblems a new leaf as successor of the original one is generated. In or-trees or -graphs, the successors of a node describe different possible solution alternatives. In addition to search problem specific knowledge, search controls often also employ some search model specific knowledge, for example to prefer transitions that generate only very few new nodes in and-trees and -graphs.

A search system usually is intended to solve many different instances of a search problem. What particular instance is to be solved is given by the input to such a system. On the level of search model and search process, the *search instance* determines from what search state the search starts and what criteria a state has to fulfill in order to represent a solution to the given instance. The search process then hopefully leads to a sequence of states that connects the start state to such an end state. This sequence is the *search derivation* produced by the search process to the given search instance.

Definition 2 (Search instance, search derivation)
Let $\mathcal{A} = (S,T)$ *be a search model and* $\mathcal{P} = (\mathcal{A}, \mathcal{E}nv, \mathcal{K})$ *a search process to* $\mathcal{A}$. *A* search instance *to* $\mathcal{A}$ *is a pair* $\mathcal{I}ns = (s_0, \mathcal{G})$, *where* $s_0 \in S$ *is the* start state *of the search and the predicate* $\mathcal{G}\colon S \rightarrow \{yes, no\}$ *is the* goal condition *that evaluates those states* $s \in S$ *to yes in which the search is successfully terminated. If* $e_0 \in \mathcal{E}nv$ *is the environment to* $\mathcal{P}$ *at the start of the search, then the sequence* $A = (s_i)_{i \in \mathbb{N}}$, $s_i \in S$, *is the* search derivation *to* $\mathcal{I}ns$ *produced by* $\mathcal{P}$, *if there are* $e_i \in \mathcal{E}nv$, *such that* $s_{i+1} = \mathcal{K}(s_i, e_i)$.

If the environment does not change then a search process always generates to the same search instance the same search derivation (if random factors are not included into the search control). As measure for the efficiency of a search process, in addition to the run-time of the system, often the number of necessary transitions in a search derivation in relation to the number of all performed transitions is used. A transition is unnecessary if it does not contribute to generating the parts of the found end state that represent the solution to the search instance. This depends on the particular search model of the search process. The set of all possible search derivations to a search instance is called the *search space*. Note that a particular search process might be very efficient for one search instance while it is very inefficient for another one.

To solve a given search problem, usually search processes with different search models can be used and even to a fixed search model many different search processes can be constructed (by using different search controls). Unfortunately, for nearly all interesting search problems there is no search process that is efficient for all search instances. Often, it is not even possible to identify a best search model to solve a certain search problem. Some concepts for multi-agent search try to overcome this problem of selecting a good search process to a given search instance.

As the name already suggests, a multi-agent search system consists of several *search agents*. The basis of a search agent is a search process. In addition, mechanisms to communicate information between the agents are needed. The environment of a search process already allows it to integrate data from outside into its search. Therefore we only need a means to put information into the appropriate environments. This is achieved by a *communication structure* and the communication function of a search agent.

Definition 3 (Communication structure, search agent)
A communication structure $\mathcal{K}om$ *is a structured set of data areas, i.e.* $\mathcal{K}om = (D_1, ..., D_l)$ *for sets* D_i *of objects. The actual* value val *of* $\mathcal{K}om$ *is defined as the tuple* $(d_1, ..., d_l)$ *with* $d_i \in D_i$. *The function* dat: $\mathcal{K}om \times \{1,...,l\} \rightarrow D_1 \cup ... \cup D_l$ *is defined as* $dat(val,i) = d_i$. *Let* $\mathcal{P} = (\mathcal{A}, \mathcal{E}nv, \mathcal{K})$ *be a search process and* mes: $S \times \mathcal{K}om \rightarrow \mathcal{K}om$ *a so-called communication function. Then the triple* $\mathcal{A}g = (\mathcal{P}, \mathcal{K}om, mes)$ *is a* search agent.

The data areas of a communication structure can be used both to structure data passed between agents and to provide access to data for selected agents. The later is achieved by allowing in a *multi-agent search system* the search agents to have several of these data areas in their environments. In addition, in such a system also components are needed to provide the search agents with their initial search states and to generate the found solution to a problem instance out of the results of the search agents. Finally, the search agents also need processing units to run their search processes (and communication functions) on. Since number and abilities of such processing units can be very important in some concepts for multi-agent search systems, they have to be part of the descriptions of such systems. More formally, we have:

Definition 4 (Multi-agent search system)
Let SP *be a search problem,* $\mathcal{K}om$ *a communication structure and let* $\mathcal{A}g_S$ (start agent) *and* $\mathcal{A}g_E$ (end agent) *be agents and* $\mathcal{A}g_1,...,\mathcal{A}g_n$ *a set of search agents,* $\mathcal{A}g_i = (\mathcal{P}_i, \mathcal{K}om, mes_i)$. *Further, let* $PU = \{pu_1,...,pu_z\}$, $z \leq n$, *be a set of processing units. Then the tuple* $\mathcal{MASS} = (\mathcal{A}g_S, \mathcal{A}g_E, \mathcal{A}g_1,...,\mathcal{A}g_n, \mathcal{K}om, PU)$ *is called a* multi-agent search system *to* SP, *if the following holds:*

- *For each* $\mathcal{P}_i = (\mathcal{A}_i, \mathcal{E}nv_i, \mathcal{K}_i)$ *there are* $D_{j_1},...,D_{j_{p_i}}$ *in* $\mathcal{K}om$, *such that* $\mathcal{E}nv_i = (D_{j_1},...,D_{j_{p_i}})$.

- *The agents can use the processing units to run their search processes and their* mes*-functions.*

- *The agent $\mathcal{A}g_S$ produces for each instance $Inst$ of SP n pairs $(s_{0_1}, \mathcal{G}_1)$, ..., $(s_{0_n}, \mathcal{G}_n)$, such that $(s_{0_i}, \mathcal{G}_i)$ is a search instance to $\mathcal{P}_i$.*

- *If A_1,...,A_n are the search derivations produced by $\mathcal{P}_1$,...,$\mathcal{P}_n$ to $(s_{0_1}, \mathcal{G}_1)$, ..., $(s_{0_n}, \mathcal{G}_n)$ then $\mathcal{A}g_E$ produces a solution to the instance $Inst$ of SP, if*

    - *$Inst$ is solvable and*
    - *all $\mathcal{A}g_i$ terminated their search in a regular fashion.*

Our description of a multi-agent search system from above only provides a mostly static view on multi-agent search. Most of the conflicts in such systems can be more clearly seen and analyzed using a dynamic component similar to search derivations for search processes. But in contrast to search derivations that are not depending on considerations about the points in time certain events take place, the points in time at which the search agents act, either to change their state or to change the value of the communication structure, are very important for the outcome of a multi-agent search. In fact, different sequences of actions often lead to a rather different behavior of the search system. Therefore any analysis of the dynamic behavior of a multi-agent search system has to take into account, what actions were performed at which points in time. This leads us to the need of having a *time frame* that provides us with the points in time that have been important in a particular search run of a multi-agent search system.

Definition 5 (Time frame)
Let SP be a search problem, $\mathcal{MASS}$ = $(\mathcal{A}g_S, \mathcal{A}g_E, \mathcal{A}g_1, ..., \mathcal{A}g_n, \mathcal{K}om, PU)$ a multi-agent search system to SP and let $Inst$ be an instance of SP. Further, let A_1,...,A_n be the search derivations produced by the search agents $\mathcal{A}g_1$,...,$\mathcal{A}g_n$ given the search instances generated by $\mathcal{A}g_E$ to $Inst$. A set $\mathcal{TF}$ = $\{t_1,...,t_m\}$ of points in time is called a time frame *to $\mathcal{MASS}$ and $Inst$, if the following holds.*

- *$t_i < t_j$, if $i < j$.*

- *For each state s_{ij} in an A_i there is a $t_k \in \mathcal{TF}$, such that s_{ij} holds in t_k but not in t_k-ϵ, for some $\epsilon \in \mathbb{R}^+$. t_k is called the* point in time *of s_{ij}: t_k = $time(s_{ij})$.*

- *Is s_{ij} a state in an A_i and val the value of $\mathcal{K}om$ at $time(s_{ij})$, then there are t_{r_1},...,t_{r_l}; $t_{r_k} \geq time(z_{ij})$ for all k, such that for all d_k in val holds: The value of data area k of $\mathcal{K}om$ at the point in time t_{r_k} is $dat(mes_i(s_{ij}, val), k)$.*

So, a time frame to a search run consists of all points in time at which either one of the search agents changed its search state or the value of a data area in the communication structure was changed (this is similar to the points in time and time frames that are used in chapter 6 to analyze the behavior of robot teams, see especially section 3.1). Especially if a multi-agent search system employs several processing units which are used by its search agents there are often many rather different time frames that result from search runs. But also some concepts for multi-agent search that are intended for one processing unit only may result in the possibility to produce rather different time frames, especially if the agents share the processing unit using time slicing techniques.

Having the time frame for a particular run of a multi-agent search system allows us to describe this run similar to a search derivation in the one-agent case, namely as a sequence of "states" that now are n+1-tuples that are some kind of snapshot of all the interesting states and data areas. This sequence is a *search course protocol.*

Definition 6 (Search course protocol)
Let SP be a search problem, $\mathcal{MASS} = (\mathcal{A}g_S, \mathcal{A}g_E, \mathcal{A}g_1, \ldots, \mathcal{A}g_n, \mathcal{K}om, PU)$ a multi-agent search system to SP and let $Inst$ be an instance of SP. Further, let $A_1, \ldots, A_n$ be the search derivations produced by the search agents $\mathcal{A}g_1, \ldots, \mathcal{A}g_n$ given the search instances generated by $\mathcal{A}g_S$ to $Inst$. Also, let $\mathcal{TF} = \{t_1, \ldots, t_m\}$ be a time frame to $\mathcal{MASS}$ and $Inst$ and let $runs$: $PU \times \mathcal{TF} \rightarrow \{\mathcal{A}g_S, \mathcal{A}g_E, \mathcal{A}g_1, \ldots, \mathcal{A}g_n, none\}$ be a function which assigns to each processing unit at each time at most one agent. Then the sequence

$$SCP = (s_{10}, \ldots, s_{n0}, val_0), \ldots, (s_{1m}, \ldots, s_{nm}, val_m)$$

is called the protocol of a collaborative search run *to $\mathcal{MASS}$, $Inst$ and $\mathcal{TF}$ (or* search course protocol*) if the following holds:*

- $s_{ik} \in S_i$.
- *For s_{ik} and $s_{i,k+1}$ holds: either $s_{ik} = s_{i,k+1}$ or $(s_{ik}, s_{i,k+1}) \in T_i$.*
- $val_k \in \mathcal{K}om$.

So, the search course protocol to a search run provides information about all data generated during the run and allows to determine what actions of agents followed what other actions. Especially, this means that the conflicts that occured and the processes that resolved those conflicts can be observed.

In the following, we will use the definitions of this section to briefly describe different types of concepts for multi-agent search systems with a special focus on the possible conflicts occuring in systems of these types. Then we will describe the solution methods for the possible conflicts that have been proposed in literature.

3. MULTI-AGENT SEARCH BASED ON IMPROVING ON THE COMPETITION APPROACH

An obvious solution to the problem of having different and even contradictory knowledge about a search problem and search processes is to let several different search processes try to solve a given instance of the search problem. If several processing units are available, then the search processes can work in parallel, else some time slicing techniques can be used or the processes can even be alloted certain time intervals and then be started one after the other has exeeded its interval. The search processes can use the same search model and differ only in their controls or they can even be based on different search models. In all cases, the search processes work independently from each other, no communication takes place, and after one process finds a solution to the given instance, the whole search is stopped. This rather simple idea has been employed in many different application domains and this concept is called the competition of search agents, or the *competition approach.*

From a multi-agent point of view the competition approach can just barely be seen as a multi-agent search system. Since only one agent really contributes to the found solution, this approach in general seems not to be very efficient. Also, since there are no conflicts between the search agents that are solved in any way (except that the best agents "wins"), this approach seems to be not very interesting for this chapter. But there are several concepts for multi-agent search systems that are based on the competition approach and improve on it by including communication between the search agents. In the following, we will present two general types of such systems, namely improvements of the competition approach

- without central control and
- with central control.

As we will see, the central control is closer to the general idea of a competition of agents and there is more potential for conflicts between the agents.

3.1 IMPROVEMENTS WITHOUT CENTRAL CONTROL

The central idea common to all multi-agent search systems improving on the competition approach without utilizing a central control is to periodically exchange selected pieces of information of various types. By integrating these pieces of information into its search a search agent shows a behavior different from the behavior when searching alone. The intended result is that one of the search agents in the system finds a solution to the given instance of the search problem faster using the information from the other agents (that itself might be the result of information from any of the agents, again).

More precisely, the start agent of the system provides each search agent with a search instance describing the full given instance of the search problem or those parts of this instance that the search agent can work with. During the search, the search agents exchange selected information of various types. Usually, there are different criteria for this selection process that is the task of the communication function of an agent, as for example the success the agent had with some particular piece of information (such criteria are used in most of the multi-agent search systems) or the demands of the agents to which a piece of information is transmitted to (such a criterion was used in the DARES system, see (Conry et al., 1990), and also in TECHS-based systems, see (Denzinger and Offermann, 1999)). In literature (namely in (Denzinger and Offermann, 1999) and (Denzinger and Fuchs, 1999)) four different types of information have been identified:

- positive information to be integrated into the search state (D_{pstat}),
- negative information to be integrated into the search state (D_{nstat}),
- positive information to influence the control of an agent or even its search model (D_{pcon}), and
- negative information to influence the control of an agent or even its search model (D_{ncon}).

Thus, the communication structure $\mathcal{K}om$ at most has to contain for each agent and each type of information a data area, i.e.

$$\mathcal{K}om = (D_{pstat,1}, D_{nstat,1}, D_{pcon,1}, D_{ncon,1}, \ldots, D_{pstat,n}, D_{nstat,n}, D_{pcon,n}, D_{ncon,n}).$$

Naturally, how the elements of these data areas look like is determined by the concrete search problem. Usually, these elements include some kind of partial solution to the given problem instance, either in the sense that these partial solutions should be worked upon in order to find the full solution (i.e. as positive information) or that solutions containing such partial solutions should be avoided (when used as negative information).

All the information a search agents gets can be filtered by it and parts that seem not useful can be thrown away. In a typical search course protocol, each search agent repeats a cycle consisting of a working period in which it concentrates on performing transitions, followed by selecting the information to be given to other agents, and then by integrating the information from the other agents. The timing of the cycles of all agents can be the same so that all agents are in a working period or all agents communicate – this results in a synchronous behavior – or each agent has its own cycle – which results in an asynchronous system behavior.

Possible conflicts and their solutions

Obviously, conflicts between search agents can only occur as a result of the exchange of information. In general, either received information conflicts with information of the agent receiving it or there is a conflict between information received from other agents. Beside conflicts due to the content of some information a conflict can also be caused just by the amount of information received that can be too much to be properly integrated into the search of an agent.

In concepts for a coarse-grained distribution of evolutionary algorithms only positive information to be integrated into the search state is exchanged (see (Cantu-Paz, 1995) for an overview). In (Cantu-Paz, 1999) was demonstrated, both theoretically and empirically, that selecting for the exchange the best solutions found so far and throwing away the worst solutions of an agent in order to make room for the received ones is the best realization of the exchange. In (Hogg and Williams, 1993) a randomly chosen (partial) solution replaces the solution of a so-called repair agent (that is in fact a local optimizer) after random time intervals, thus prefering received information.

In all known multi-agent search systems of the type discussed in this section, positive and negative information to be integrated into the search state must be valid with respect to the problem instance to solve, i.e. if negative information states that certain elements are not a solution then this is true and if a (partial) solution is exchanged as positive information, then this element is indeed a (partial) solution to the given problem. This way, conflicts with respect to the content of exchanged information of these types are avoided.

In contrast to this, control information cannot be valid, because if a good search path to a solution is known, search would not be necessary. Therefore, if some control information suggests to an agent to change its control then this might not result in the agent getting better at the given task. The known search systems that do exchange control information differ in handling such conflicts. In (Nangsue and Conry, 1998) the successes of the involved agents so far determine whether in case of a conflict the received information is just thrown away (if the receiving agent is not much worse than the sending one) or gets priority.

In the already mentioned TECHS concept, a search agent first filters all received information. Only information that is either very good (in the same sense as in (Nangsue and Conry, 1998)) or that fulfills the actual needs of the agent passes the filter (so that it is possible that all received information is filtered out). Control information that passed the filter is used with priority for a given number of transitions and then the original control of the agent takes over again. If the received control information has been good then a search state should have been reached for which also the original control should be able to prefer some transitions also favored by the received control. Else, only for a limited number of transitions bad decisions have been made and the agent should be able to get back on its original, better path. So, conflicts are solved by trying out the conflicting suggestions and making a judgement when enough (or at least more) information is available.

3.2 IMPROVEMENTS WITH CENTRAL CONTROL

A problem of the multi-agent search systems from the last subsection is that during a search run after some time search agents may not be able to really contribute to the search anymore –despite the pieces of information they get from other search agents. This results in not making good use of the resources of the system. As a solution to this problem several authors have proposed to use a central control in such multi-agent search systems that can exchange such "bad" search agents by hopefully better ones. So, the resulting multi-agent search system not only searches for a solution to the given problem instance but also for a good team of search agents for this search task.

More precisely, start and end agent are taken together into a control function that can be either realized as an individual agent (as in (Pedroso, 1996)) or that is a role of a search agent (as in (Denzinger, 1995)). The control agent determines which search agents are allowed to participate in the search, the search states these search agents continue the search from, and, if several processing units are available, which agent uses which unit how long. The communication structure can contain the data areas described in section 3.1 and in addition for each agent areas for assigning new search states (D_S) and assigning processing units (D_{PU}). Also, usually there is an area D_{con} in which all agents write information that the control function needs for its decisions.

In principle, the contributions of a single search agent to the search course protocol are the same as in section 3.1: a cycle consisting of working, selecting information for other agents (using their data areas and the D_{con}-area), and integrating information from other agents (also from the own D_S- and D_{PU}-areas). But all agents perform this cycle in a synchronous manner and the control has a large influence on the integration part. In all known approaches with central control, the control agent receives from all search agents that are assigned to a processing unit (the active agents) via D_{con} some kind of objective report about the performance of the agent (a *measure of success* for the agent). Based on these reports the search agents are selected that will also be active in the next cycle. Usually, the reports are also used to suggest new search agents for the remaining units. At least the new search agents must get search states to start their search from, but in some multi-agent search systems of this type also some (namely in (Pedroso, 1996)) or all (in (Denzinger, 1995)) other agents get new search states.

Possible conflicts and their solutions

Since the search systems presented in this subsection are an improvement of the ones of the last subsection, all the conflicts of the systems of the last subsection can also occur in the search systems of this subsection. And naturally, the same solutions to such conflicts can also be observed in systems with central control.

But there are now additional conflicts between the search agents, namely which of them are allowed to continue searching and what of the information represented in their search states "survives" the decisions of the control agent. The solutions to these conflicts in literature use some concepts we already presented in the general description, namely the use of measures of success for agents.

In systems based on the TEAMWORK-method (see (Denzinger, 1995)) this measure of success for an agent is computed by summing up computed measures for the quality of all performed transitions (these measures heavily rely on the ability to do an a posteriori analysis of the transitions) and also measures for the quality of all information contained in the actual search state of an agent. The control agent (the supervisor) is a role that is always assumed by the search agent with the best measure of success. Search agents whose measures of success have been much worse than that of the best agent for several cycles are exchanged. Their successors are chosen using information about the search agents and their interaction (collected by the developers of such systems), mainly information about which agents work well together and which agents should follow which other agents (see (Denzinger and Kronenburg, 1996)). But also agents that are not the best one and that are not exchanged loose in the conflict for "survival" of information. They have to use a new start state that is generated by the supervisor out of the state of the best agent and the selected positive information to be integrated into the search state sent by the other agents. This has the advantage that agents that got "lost" in the search space can be brought back on a good track.

Survival-of-the-fittest on the search agent level has also been proposed in (Pedroso, 1996) and (Corno et al., 1996) as solution to the conflict with respect to which agents continue the search. Niche-search, as described in (Pedroso, 1996), allows several search agents to continue their search with the state they reached so far (without having to integrate any information from other agents). These agents are the ones with the best measure of success (how many agents is a parameter chosen by the user). The other agents may also "survive" with a certain probability. If chance is against them, then not only a new agent is (randomly) selected, but also a new search state for this agent is generated by randomly choosing parts of the state of the exchanged agent and parts of the state of a randomly chosen agent of the set of best agents.

In the CGATTO system, described in (Corno et al., 1996), groups of search agents are formed that are based on the same control function scheme. The agents of a group share their work using the idea that will be discussed in section 4.2. The groups compete with each other and after certain periods of time the successes of the groups are evaluated. In contrast to the previous approaches, a bad group is not eliminated and all processing units its agents used are given to a new group. Instead, only a part of the processing units are taken away and given to more successful groups. While the successful groups then can employ more agents of their scheme, a bad group looses some of their agents. But if such a group gets better, it can get back units.

4. MULTI-AGENT SEARCH BASED ON USING A COMMON SEARCH STATE

If the main goal is to parallelize a certain process then a good idea is to look at actions within the process that can be done in parallel. Applying this idea to search results in doing some of the possible transitions in a search state in parallel, i.e. by several search agents. So, from the outside, such a multi-agent search system looks like a sequential search process in which in a given time interval more transitions are performed than by the usual sequential search process.

In order to achieve such a behavior, a *common search state* for all the search agents is needed. This common search state reflects the search state of the hypothetical sequential search process that we mentioned above. A search agent might use the whole common search state or parts of it as its own search state (or copies it in its own search state), performs one or several transitions (with respect to the hypothetical sequential process), and then has to integrate its local results back into the common search state. This can also be seen as a kind of *partitioning of the search space* (or at least parts of it) among the agents. Again, from the point of view of possible conflicts we have two general types of search systems based on a common search state, namely systems with

- a centrally stored common search state and
- a distributed common search state.

As we will see, distributing the common search state results in an additional potential for conflicts compared to a centrally stored common state. Note that these two types are only the two extremes of a large spectrum of possibilities that todays computers and networks offer. Multi-agent search systems that hierarchically combine aspects of both these types are described in (Diderich and Gengler, 1996) or (Correa, 1995).

4.1 CENTRAL COMMON SEARCH STATE

Multi-agent search systems that work on a central common search state represent this common state as the value of one data area of $\mathcal{K}om$ (or several such data areas that are stored in the same memory device, as in case of A-teams, see (Talukdar et al., 1993)). The search agents have only very limited own search states and they mainly manipulate the value of the data area(s). Examples for such systems can be found in (Huang and Davis, 1987), (Quinn and Deo, 1986), or (Kumar et al., 1988).

More precisely, the start agent of a search system based on a central common search state is a search agent itself that uses a search process similar to the one that can be seen as the behavior of the system from outside. It performs its search process until a state is reached that allows enough transitions so that to each search agent can be assigned at least one of them. The end state of the start agent is stored in the data area D_{com} whose value represents the common search state.

A search agent usually performs one or several transitions selected by its search control without looking at its environment. Then its communication function integrates its local search state back into D_{com}. There are different possibilities described in literature for getting a new start state for the agent. It can be assigned a new state by a central control agent, it can keep a part of its local search state, or it can select the new state itself from the actual value of D_{com}.

The working cycle described above, that can be observed in the typical search course protocols of systems of this type, can be performed both in an asynchronous manner and synchronous with the other search agents (as, for example, in (Quinn, 1990)). But if we want to look a little closer on this cycle then the known multi-agent search systems differ mainly in the integration of information in the common search state and the selection of a new start state, which is due to the potential conflicts that arise for these tasks (and the different methods to resolve them).

Possible conflicts and their solutions

In general, conflicts between the search agents can occur in two ways:

- several agents might want to perform the same transition
- an agent might want to integrate information into the common search state that contradicts information already in the common state or information another agent wants to integrate.

In fact, these two situations can also be combined, if information one agent integrates makes the intended (or worked-upon) transition(s) of another agent unnecessary.

All concepts for solving conflicts of the first type try to avoid such conflicts. This is possible either by extending the search model used for the common search state to allow markers at certain parts of the state, or by having a central instance (agent) that assigns the possible transitions (or transition sets) to agents, or by only using agents that are guaranteed to select different transitions. In search systems that are using tree- or graph-based search models marking nodes that are already processed by agents is an often used solution. In (Yokoo and Kitamura, 1996) and (Kitamura et al., 1996) markers are also used to help to direct other agents into promising regions of the search space (they use or-trees as search model).

Having a control agent (as in some concepts of (Kumar et al., 1988)) is an obvious solution to both types of conflicts and the management of the central common search state on a storage device is already a task of a processing unit that then is not totally available for the search agents. By completely assigning this processing unit to a control agent both types of conflicts can be resolved by this "higher instance" and it is also possible to use the control agent's global view of the problem to direct the search into promising directions. In systems with heterogeneous agents the control agent also can exchange agents to adapt the system on the actual state of the search (as suggested in (Rachlin et al., 1998)).

Using agents that prefer different transitions is usually used in search systems employing a set-based search model, as for example in systems based on the A-teams approach (see (Talukdar et al., 1993)). In such systems often the common search state consists of several sets of different types of objects so that several data areas are used (one for each type). In some realizations this is even coupled with having a central control agent.

Conflicts caused by contradicting information are also avoided in most search systems by using search models that do not allow conflicts between transitions. They might still allow for information that makes some transitions unnecessary (as for example a new bound in a branch-and-bound-based search that allows to close certain leafs) but usually performing a few unnecessary transitions is accepted (and if each agent performs only one transition in its working cycle, really only very few such redundant transitions occur).

However, search models that have a backtracking transition usually have to apply this transition because of contradicting information in the actual search state (as for example and-tree- or and-graph-based search). Then, if *intelligent* backtracking should be performed, an analysis is necessary in order to determine to which earlier state backtracking should be made. Although this analysis could be performed as joint effort of all search agents, so far only concepts employing a control agent are known, so that we have delegating the conflict to a "higher authority", again.

Another possibility to deal with conflicting information that requires backtracking is to change to another search model that makes backtracking unnecessary. More precisely, instead of having a search model whose states represent only one actual division of a problem (as it is the case in and-trees or and-graphs) for each node all possible divisions are incorporated into the search state. This then leads to using and-or-trees or and-or-graphs as basic data structure of the model (see (Sanders, 1995)). Still, information that a search agent integrates might have as a result that transitions performed by other agents become unnecessary (because the particular division is no solution to the given problem instance or a subproblem). But all agents that later on look for new nodes to process can decide for themselves at what alternatives to work. This again avoids this kind of conflict.

4.2 DISTRIBUTED COMMON SEARCH STATE

Requiring a central common search state rather limits the possibilities to implement a multi-agent search system, namely to architectures that provide a shared memory. Although it is possible to use processing units without a shared memory by letting the operating systems of the units form a virtual shared memory, this usually results in quite a loss in efficiency, so that it is better to develop concepts for multi-agent search systems that already take into account that it is not possible to have a central common search state (while still trying to have a common search state). On a high level the concepts for multi-agent search systems discussed in this subsection are very similar to the concepts discussed in the previous subsection, but we have some additional potential for conflicts and therefore need additional solutions.

More precisely, in a search system based on a distributed common search state we still have a start agent that is a search agent itself for the search model on which the common search state is based. But now it is not enough to produce a state allowing for assigning one transition to each search agent in the system. Instead, $\mathcal{A}g_S$ has to work until at least a certain number of transitions can be assigned to each agent so that agents do have enough transitions to not become idle very soon. Usually, this requires that the search agents do not use search models equivalent to the one used by $\mathcal{A}g_S$ but search models in which a state is a set of parts of the states that $\mathcal{A}g_S$ uses. For each part additionally there is its "history" that allows the end agent to put the parts of all agents together to form the end common state. In recursively defined search models a part can usually be described by the model itself, as for example subtrees of a tree or subgraphs of a graph. Then the history provides information about where to put a part back.

So, the common search state is not represented in the communication structure anymore, but distributed among the search states of the agents. The communication structure provides for each agent $\mathcal{A}g_i$ a data area $D_{req,i}$ in which it can receive requests (or wishes) from other agents and an area $D_{ans,i}$ for answers to its own requests. In addition, an area D_{con} as in section 3.2 may be used.

In order to perform a transition (and to be fair), a search agent usually first selects one part in its search state and then a transition that is applicable for the selected part. An agent continues to perform transitions until either there are no more possible or sensible transitions for its parts or another agent requests additional work (because it has no more transitions to its parts or thinks that its parts are not promissing) via the D_{req}-area. In the later case, the communication function of the agent has to decide whether the agent should transmit some of its work (i.e. parts of its parts) to the requesting agent or not. In the former case, the agent has to transmit requests itself, either to all other agents or only selected ones. The parts of a typical search course protocol for a search system of this type dealing with the communication with other agents depend on how the possible conflicts are handled, so that we will go into more detail later.

Possible conflicts and their solutions

As in case of a central common search state, a possible conflict between search agents can be due to contradicting information the agents want to integrate into the common search state. In contrast to the search systems in the last subsection, there is no possibility that several agents might want to perform the same transition, because all known search systems emploing a distributed common search state require that the intersection of the sets of possible transitions of two agents is empty.

Nevertheless, there is a rather similar possibility for conflicts for systems with distributed common state, namely the wish of an agent to get additional work from other agents. As already stated, the reason for such a wish does not have to be that the requesting agent is idle, but it can also be the case that the requesting agent "thinks" that its remaining transitions are not very promissing (and that it is therefore not sensible to perform them).

Conflicts due to contradicting information are mostly avoided, again. This is very important, because in a search system based on a distributed common search state, it should be avoided to inform all agents about all new information one agent has (although (Bonacina, 1997) does exactly this), because of the high communication cost. This would make it very difficult to detect contradicting or conflicting information, so that only search models (for the common state) are used, in which such conflicts are not possible (so: no backtracking).

Conflicts with respect to distributing transitions and work between the agents are also often solved by trying to avoid them. For example, in (Kumar et al., 1988) or (Quinn, 1990) search agents do not wait for wishes by other agents but send a certain percentage of their newly possible transitions to other agents after each transition they performed (these concepts were developed for tree-based search models, so that this can be accomplished by just sending away new nodes). But even in these search systems the situation can arise that an agent has no transitions to perform or that all transitions seem to be not sensible.

The concepts in literature that deal with the need of an agent to get new work, i.e. transitions to perform, from other agents differ in one, several, or all of three aspects, namely

- the detection of the need,
- the group of other agents that is brought into the process of filling the need (i.e. the agents that are taken into this conflict), and
- the selection criteria used by the other agents to fulfill the need.

Obviously, an agent needs new transitions if it cannot perform any transitions in its actual state anymore. But for some search models, as for example or-tree- or or-graph-based ones, it is necessary to rate transitions according to their likeliness to lead to a solution and all the transitions to a node might be much more unlikely to do so than transitions to other nodes. If an agent only has such "unlikely" nodes, the probability that it contributes to finding a solution is very low and it definitely needs new (and better) transitions. In (Vornberger, 1986), an agent can detect that it is in such a situation by looking at the value of the D_{con}-area, in which each agent writes the ratings of its last and actual transitions (according to the same rating scheme).

An agent might make requests to all other agents or only its "neighbors" (given by a neighborhood relation). Usually, the number of agents a request is sent to determines how many transitions (or nodes) an answering agent sends back (or at least the maximal possible number). The more agents might answer the fewer transitions should be sent by one agent. Otherwise, too much work might be sent to the agent (causing it to give it back to the other agents later).

There are various selection criteria that are used in literature. In (Finkel and Manber, 1987) an agent selects the transition it would do next. In (Quinn, 1990) the transition rated second-best by the answering agent is sent. In (Kumar et al., 1988) some search systems are presented in which an agent sends the transition (node) that became possible the latest. Many other criteria are possible.

5. MULTI-AGENT SEARCH BASED ON DIVIDING THE PROBLEM INTO SUBPROBLEMS

The general ideas to the types of multi-agent search systems presented in sections 3. and 4. stem from concepts that are somewhat process-oriented and therefore specific for the handling of (sequential) search in computer science. However, the typical problem solving behavior of groups of human beings suggests a distribution idea that is not oriented on looking at the solution process but instead on structuring and distributing the given problem. Basis for such a distribution are usually the different abilities of the individuals in the group.

For solving search problems this idea translates to dividing the given instance of a search problem into instances of this or other search problems that hopefully each are easier to solve than the given instance and whose solutions taken together constitute a solution to the given instance. The intention of employing this idea is to assign to each of the subproblem instances its own search agent that uses the best (or at least a good) search process for this task. If the subproblems are independent from each other, then the main problem is to achieve a good load-balance between the processing units that are used by the agents. Therefore this case is not very interesting for us and in the following we will assume that the resulting subproblem instances depend on each other (or at least a few of them do).

The division on the problem level requires a kind of language so that the agents can communicate. In section 4. the search model on which the common search state was based made such a language unnecessary (or better already provided such a language that is both problem- and process-dependent). For the systems based on the competition approach of section 3., the search problem (or better its general description) provides a problem-dependent language that usually is easily integrated into the different search processes. Since in general, systems based on dividing the problem into subproblems might employ agents with both different search processes and different search problems that are solved by them, finding such a language can become difficult (some remarks to this problem for the application domain constraint satisfaction problems can be found in chapter 3 section 2.3 with regard to problem specification).

Many known multi-agent search systems of this type therefore try to employ search agents using similar search models and the problem division sometimes is more artificial (i.e. oriented on features of these search models) than natural (i.e. oriented on the problem). Often used information that is exchanged between agents are values of problem- (solution-) specific variables. But note that there is a wide range for aggregating such information (as, for example, alternative values and combinations of values of different variables) which can lead to rather complex languages to express such information.

As in case of the other two types of multi-agent search systems we can distinguish also for the type of this section two subtypes, namely

- systems using a static division into subproblem instances and
- systems employing a dynamic division.

Again, the second subtype is some kind of improvement of the first subtype which also means that there is a larger potential for conflicts and additional concepts to deal with them. In addition, the second subtype is related to the subtype presented in section 4.2 that also dynamically shifted search tasks between the agents.

5.1 STATIC DIVISION OF THE GIVEN INSTANCE

As the term "static division" already suggests, the general idea of search systems of this type is to have an initial division of the given problem instance into instances of subproblems and an initial assignment of subproblem instances to search agents. And neither division nor assignment changes during the search. Then the task of the search agents is to find solutions to their subproblem instances that are compatible with the solutions to the other subproblems. Here, compatibility means that there are no inconsistencies when the solutions to the subproblems are put together to form a solution to the given problem instance.

More precisely, the start agent $\mathcal{A}g_S$ is responsible for the division of the given problem instance into subproblem instances and for finding appropriate search agents to solve them. Since the agents have to produce compatible solutions, the communication structure has to allow the exchange of some kind of requirements on solutions (usually in form of partial solutions) that certain agents have and also some kind of negotiation about such requirements whenever inconsistencies occur. If it is not possible to determine the other search agents that need to fulfill the requirements of an agent then one data area D_{req} that is part of the environment of each agent should be used. Else, each agent $\mathcal{A}g_i$ should have an individual data area $\mathrm{D}_{req,i}$ so that it can be directly addressed. The form of a requirement depends on the search problem the multi-agent search system is intended to solve, but in addition to such a problem specific part the agent having a requirement has to identify itself.

Obviously, the resolution of inconsistencies will be the topic of our later presentation of conflicts and their solution. All known resolution concepts need to be able to adress an agent, so that a minimal requirement for $\mathcal{K}om$ is that each agent has a data area $\mathrm{D}_{confl,i}$ (but splitting it in several areas and also additional areas that are in the environment of all agents may be necessary). The search process of an agent must be able to integrate requirements of other agents in its own search, resp. its search state. Even more, since requirements can change, the agent must be able to withdraw them as part of the conflict resolution. As already stated, we will go into more detail (especially with respect to the tasks of the communication functions) later.

The task of the end agent is to put together the solution of the given problem instance. In some search systems of this type it is also responsible for detecting the unsolvability of the given instance (a task that might be impossible for the search agents due to their limitation to a local problem view). Naturally, typical time frames and search course protocols can only be given with respect to the concepts used to resolve conflicts.

Possible conflicts and their solutions

In multi-agent search systems based on a static division of the given problem instance into subproblems conflicts between the search agents occur when the requirements of an agent (resp. its actual solution) are not compatible with the requirements of other agents. For example, if the solution of an agent to its subproblem instance requires that a certain problem variable has a value greater than 4 while another agent has to set this variable to a value of less than 2, then obviously the two solutions to subproblems cannot be combined to a solution to the given problem instance.

This type of conflict is very similar to conflicts that are the result of different goals of agents and therefore there is a wide variety of conflict resolution concepts available in literature. Still, the special requirements of search have to be taken into account, namely the need to resolve conflicts rather fast. Therefore the conflict resolution concepts used in search systems of this type in literature do not employ rather long negotiation dialogs but try to determine the agent that has to change its requirements by means of orderings and hierarchies. As a result, a wrong decision might be made so that later, when the wrongness becomes known or obvious, another solution to the conflict has to be tried out. Obviously, the conflict resolution then becomes a kind of search itself that is interleaved with the agents own search processes.

In (Yokoo et al., 1992) conflict resolution is based on a problem-induced ordering of the search agents. Whenever an agent finds a solution to its subproblem that also agrees with all known requirements of the other agents it sends its own solution as requirement to all other agents. If this causes a conflict (either due to not already announced requirements or due to later changes in requirements), the agent that is higher in the ordering has to withdraw its own requirements and must search for another solution to its subproblem. Since the ordering of the agents has to be determined a priori, false decisions of agents that are low in the ordering can cause much unnecessary work. Therefore, in (Yokoo, 1995) an improvement was presented in which the ordering of agents was dynamic. The more conflicts an agent is involved in, the lower in the ordering it gets and therefore the more important it is. Then also its actual solution gets more important and the other agents become responsible for solving conflicts with this agent. This approach was in (Hirayama and Yokoo, 1997) improved to deal with agents employing more complex search processes (namely processes using and-or-trees instead of simple or-trees).

Instead of using a total ordering among agents, in (Liu and Sycara, 1994) the agents are put in different priority groups. In what a group an agent is put depends on the flexibility its subproblem allows. The more flexibility, the less priority is given. Agents of the same priority group solve conflicts among them by exchanging information about their specific subproblems so that the normal local view of an agent gets more global. This way, an agent can select the solution to its problem that has the greatest chance to conform with the other agents (and their requirements). If still the agents of the priority group cannot solve the conflict (or if the conflict solution process takes too much time) then the agents of the next higher priority group are asked to change their requirements, by switching to a less optimal solution of their subproblem (see also (Liu and Sycara, 1995)).

Sending more information about the own problem, resp. the own solution possibilities, is also the conflict solution technique propossed in (Lander and Lesser, 1992). If an agent receives a requirement of another agent that conflicts with its own (optimal) solution then it reacts by sending a "critique" to the agent with the requirement, indicating the problem (i.e. the own solution requirements) and also possible relaxations the agent might allow in its own requirements. If an agent receiving a critique can fulfill the requirements of the critizing agent without having to relax its own requirements (i.e. there is a solution for its subproblem meeting the requirements and being of acceptable quality) it withdraws its own requirements and switches to the other solution. Else, nothing happens at first. Only if all the solutions to its subproblem of sufficient quality were critizied the agent has to relax its definition of sufficient quality which allows for new compromises.

Also the multi-phase agreement finding, presented in chapter 3, bases its conflict resolution on getting more and more relevant information about the problems of other agents into the own search state of an agent so that its search process can deal with it. Here the requirements are values for certain variables and they have to be withdrawn if agents handling constraints detect inconsistencies.

It should be noted that all these conflict resolution methods require certain properties of either the search processes of the agents or the descriptions of problems and subproblems. Most prominent among these requirements is that the problems are formulated as sets of variables and sets of constraints among the variables. There are many search problems that can be formulated this way, but there are also problems that cannot and for some of the problems that can there are other formulations (and therefore search models and search processes) that are or might be better suited.

5.2 DYNAMIC DIVISION OF PROBLEM INSTANCES

Multi-agent search systems based on a static division of the given problem instance can have difficulties with respect to two phenomena. Firstly, if we are interested in employing several processing units then the different grades of difficulty the subproblems may have can result in agents (and their processing units) being idle, because they have solved their respective subproblem instances and just have to look for inconsistencies between their solutions and new requirements of other agents. This load-balancing problem has also occured in search systems of the type presented in section 4.2.

The other problem that can be observed is that usually it is very difficult to generate subproblem instances that in all their aspects are well-suited for a certain search agent. Often a search agent performs several or even many transitions and then it becomes obvious that certain sub-subproblems have to be solved that would be better dealt with by other types of search agents.

Both types of problems of a static division can be solved by allowing a dynamic (and recursive) division of the given problem instance. If the main objective of the dynamic division is to achieve a good load-balancing between agents (and processing units) then allowing agents to request work from other agents, similar to the general concept presented in section 4.2, is sufficient. If the general idea of a problem-oriented employment of agents –that is the basis for the division approach– is the goal of the dynamic division, then agents that encounter subproblems that are (or might be) better solved by other agents should announce such problems to other agents. These agents then can compete for these subproblem instances in order to find the best suited agent. Since agents that think they have too many or too hard subproblems can also announce some of their sub-subproblems, some handling of load-balancing problems is also included in this announcement approach.

More precisely, in search systems of this type a start agent is not needed. Instead, one of the search agents gets the given problem instance and starts to solve it. If this agent (and later on also other agents) encounters subproblem instances that it does not want to solve for itself then it announces them to the other agents so that suitable agents can solve them. Therefore the communication structure of search systems of this type has to have at least a data area D_{ann} for announcing subproblem instances and an area $D_{negot,i}$ for each agent that can be used to react to such announcements. If announcements can (or should) be directed towards certain agents, then individual data areas $D_{ann,i}$ for each agent can also be used. Since there can still be dependencies between subproblem instances, also the data areas D_{req} (resp. $D_{req,i}$) and $D_{confl,i}$ of the last subsection (for requirements of agents and to handle conlicts due to such requirements) may be needed in the search systems of the type presented in this subsection.

The search agents –as in case of the search systems in the last subsection– have to be able to integrate and withdraw requirements of other agents. In some search systems using a dynamic division they also have to be able to work on several subproblem instances so that their search models again are sets of the usual search states of such agents (see section 4.2). Obviously, the search agents must also be able to detect subproblem instances in their actual search states that should be given away, i.e. placed into the D_{ann}-area(s).

In addition to this task, the communication function of an agent also has to deal with selecting the own requirements and with the agent's reaction to requirements of other agents and announcements from other agents. The last two tasks are the conflict management and resolution in search systems of this type and therefore we will look closer into them later. Detecting subproblem instances that should be given away is based on knowledge about the search model an agent uses and about the search problems the agent can tackle. Sometimes also knowledge about the other search agents (and their abilities) is used but then integrating new search agents into such a multi-agent search system gets difficult, because all other agents have to be changed in order to integrate knowledge about a new agent's expertise. Only subproblems should be selected for announcement to other agents that cannot be solved easily by the search agent itself. If solving them takes less time than the whole process of giving them to other agents, obviously no gains in efficiency are possible.

Possible conflicts and their solutions

Since the type of search systems of this subsection are a kind of improvement of the ones of the last subsection, they have all the types of conflicts we presented in the last subsection. But the dynamic division adds an additional type of conflicts so that we have

- conflicts among search agents due to conflicting requirements resulting from their actual solutions to their subproblems and
- conflicts among search agents due to an interest in solving the same announced subproblem (that another agent wants to give away for solving it).

For resolving conflicting requirements all the concepts from subsection 5.1 can be used. But the need to solve conflicts of the second type also led to another concept –employed in the MARS system– that we will present after we dealt with other concepts for the second type. There are also search systems using a dynamic division of problems in which conflicting requirements are avoided by generating independent subproblems only. In fact, such search systems –especially if they employ only one type of search agents– are very similar to search systems based on using a common search state to distribute the search space (see section 4.), because a division on the problem level has to be achieved by using properties of the used search model.

An example of such a multi-agent search system was presented in (Smith, 1979). There, the contract-net-protocol was employed to achieve the dynamic division of problems and the assignment of the resulting subproblems to agents. The main objective in (Smith, 1979) was to achieve a good load-balancing between the search agents that each had its own processing unit. In the MARS system (see (Fischer et al., 1995)) an improvement of the contract-net-protocol was used to distribute newly arriving tasks among the search agents (that represent trucks of a forwarding agency). The improvement allows to additionally split a task into subtasks during the distribution. But still, the conflict resolution is achieved by letting the agents compete for tasks using bids based on estimates of their suitability for the task and their actual work load. The agent with the best bid is assigned the task.

A consequence of such a bidding process is that over time usually all the search agents get assigned some subproblems that other agents would be better suited to solve. The agents end up with being assigned those problems because the better suited agents had too much work assigned at the time of the announcement of them. If we are interested in optimizing the solution time, such subproblems can be seen as requirements of the better suited agents that should be withdrawn, so that these subproblems constitute a conflict of the first type in our list.

In MARS, these conflicts are solved by employing a central authority (a kind of control agent) and again an auction-like bidding process to get rid of the "bad" requirements while taking on better requirements (this is called simulated trading). Subproblems requireing much solution time are announced to the control agent that offers them to the other agents. The agent announcing such a problem can withdraw its requirements from its work load and then has free capacity to bid for announced subproblems of other agents. The control agent keeps track of the exchanges and if a chain of exchanges is found that is satisfactory it gives the okay to all agents and the real exchange takes place. It is also possible that not involved agents create new subproblems and then the whole simulated trading is cancelled and all requirements (subproblems) are put back into place until agents for the new subproblems are found.

Autonomous dynamic reconfiguration, as presented in chapter 3 section 4, also tries to dynamically change the subproblem instances assigned to an agent. Agent melting and agent splitting are the techniques used to resolve the conflicts. Agent melting is again a case of solving conflicts by sending relevant information about the conflict to one agent that then includes solving the conflict into its own search (now the relevant information is the whole actual state of the other agent). Agent splitting obviously follows the main idea of multi-agent search systems of this type, namely dividing problems into subproblems.

In case of MARS, the conflict resolution methods for both types of conflicts are very similar (announcement and bidding) so that a rather efficient problem solution is achieved. Potentially, also quite different methods for the different conflict types can be used, but the resolution method for one type of conflict will usually have effects on the other type (as can be seen by the concep presented in chapter 3). In order to find the agents the requirements of one agent should be sent to, not only the chain of divisions leading to the resp. subproblem must be followed but also the chains resulting from this chain. This very quickly means that all agents are involved in each occuring conflict. And this can result in quite some inefficiency. This might be the reason that not so many multi-agent search systems are known that deal with both types of conflicts.

6. CONCLUSION

In most multi-agent knowledge-based search systems conflicts are not caused by different goals of the agents but by how to achieve the common goal of finding a solution to the given search problem instance. Since for nearly all search problems the success of a particular search system can be measured rather well by the time needed for finding a solution of a certain quality, the resolution of conflicts between agents during the cooperative search has to be fast. In the time needed to find the best solution to a conflict, another system using a more quickly found conflict solution that is a little bit worse than the best one might be able to search through a larger part of the search space and thus come nearer to a solution.

Nevertheless, many multi-agent search concepts can make use of conflicting knowledge about search problems, instances, and controls and as a result have more success than single-agent search concepts. By exploring the consequences of conflicting information and combining achievements from all search agents as a result of their cooperation, hard problem instances can be solved faster and the set of problem instances that can be solved in acceptable time is usually much larger than the sets to each of the search agents when working alone. The search systems and concepts presented in (Bonacina, 1997) or (Denzinger and Fuchs, 1999) show that multi-agent search achieves gains in efficiency not only because several processing units are used but also because synergetical effects occur due to the exchange of information. The examples for the use of A-teams presented in (Rachlin et al., 1998) also demonstrate the ability to find better solutions due to collaboration of search agents.

The three different basic ideas for multi-agent search we presented in this chapter lead to different advantages and have different weaknesses. Improvements of the competition approach employ search agents that have the most global view on the given problem instance so that the agents in the system are rather loosely coupled. Therefore they decide for themselves how to act in a conflict situation which can lead to very good performances. But on the other side, also worse performances are possible, if the wrong information is exchanged or the wrong decisions are made by the agents. In addition, systems of this type cannot avoid a certain percentage of redundant transitions, because the conflicts due to a distribution of transitions are avoided.

Search systems based on a common search state can establish a global view on the search problem only if the processing units have a shared memory. Without such a shared memory, the view on the problem has to be localized, so that the probablity of wrong decisions rises. Although some synergetic effects in systems of this type have been reported (mostly if different types of search agents are used) the main goal of the known concepts is to distribute a certain sequential search process among several processing units without many conflict situations. As a consequence, the achieved speed-ups are more reliable but clearly less than linear.

Dividing the given problem instance into subproblems allows in a natural way to use different types of search agents. As a result, the subproblems can be solved in the best known manner. If the dependencies between the subproblems are few, so that not many conflicts occur, very efficient problem solving is possible. If a dynamic division of the given problem is used, also changes in (or additions to) the given problem instance do not cause problems, so that continous search problems (that often occur in planning tasks) can also be solved.

If too many conflicts between the agents (due to dependencies of their subproblems) occur, the improvements versus sequential search systems diminish and the performance of the multi-agent search system might even become inferior. A local view on the search problem –as employed in systems of this type– requires then too much information exchange to get a global picture of the problem. As was pointed out in (Yokoo, 1998), there are search problems (or requirements on the (hardware-) architecture used) for which a global view cannot be given (for example, due to security reasons) and then this type of search systems offers a solution method (see also the discussion in chapter 3, section 3.1 and section 5.2). It should be noted that not for all search problems sensible divisions of all instances into subproblems exist.

There are no clear boundaries between these three classes of multi-agent search systems so that search systems combining aspects of all three classes are possible. But future research into this direction must carefully weight the additional (or combined) conflicts and their solution processes against the potential gains such a combined system might provide. Promising are conflict resolution techniques that allow to use additional knowledge about the search problem to solve and the used search agents.

Chapter 10

CONFLICT AS A HEURISTIC IN THE DEVELOPMENT OF AN INTERACTION MECHANICS

William F. Lawless
Paine College, Augusta, USA
lawlessw@mail.paine.edu

T. Castelão
Grand Valley State University, Allendale, USA
castelat@gvsu.edu

C.P. Abubucker
Paine College, Augusta, USA
abubuckerc@mail.paine.edu

Abstract The prevailing belief that the replacement of conflict with cooperation among artificial or human agents improves performance was supported in the field for the solution of well-defined problems (*wdp's*), but ironically, only when the underlying hypothesis that logic concepts and reality correspond is no longer true. In contrast, our theory, based on the bistable information derived from action-observation complementarity, predicts that resolving conflict between autonomous agents reduces the available information, *I*, into skills which solve *wdp's*, but that conflict or social tension increases the *I* available to discover optimal paths for the solution of ill-defined problems (*idp's*). Earlier we confirmed both predictions; first, in an experiment with USAF combat pilots in simulated air-combat, we found that observations in extreme environments produce *I* that converges to form knowledge independent of reality, *R*; second, convergence underdetermines *R*, promoting multiple, independent worldviews of *R* and a tension between them which we enhanced at a DOE military nuclear facility to significantly improve its environmental remediation decisions. We extend our theory to model the transition from social statics to dynamics by combining action-observation complementarity with a model of feedback resonance. It indicates that cooperation to solve *wdp's* in social systems enhances acculturation and stasis, but that competition to solve *idp's* at the level of macroeconomics powers the evolution of new social structures to manage human interaction.

1. INTRODUCTION: TRADITIONAL VIEWS OF REALITY, R AND CONVERGENCE

Einstein's assumption (Einstein et al., 1935) that formal concepts and *R* must correspond to produce meaning is matched by similar assumptions in game (Von Neumann and Morgenstern, 1953), economics (Arrow, 1999), and social learning theory (Bandura, 1989). In contrast, Bohr (Bohr, 1955) questioned whether the convergence of observational information produces knowledge that corresponds to *R*. But while correspondence prevails, decision theorists and economists have recognized that if correspondence is not true (Lipshitz, 1997), it will greatly alter the traditional constructs of *R*. Based on previous work (Lawless et al., 2000), we have concluded that correspondence occurs in mundane social practices, the solution of well-defined problems (*wdp's*), and the transmission of culture to new generations of adherents in a process we know as education or acculturation (e.g., see chapter 4), but correspondence breaks down when cultures are confronted by ill-defined problems (*idp's*).

When physicists fail to link theory with *R* in their relatively narrow fields, a crisis is created which does not end until the failure is resolved (Von Neumann, 1961). In contrast, while it is widely agreed that social science (Hendrick, 1988) and mathematics (Von Neumann, 1961) do not account for social or physical *R*, no crisis is ever created. Gödel (see (Von Neumann, 1961)) proved that the rational logic of mathematics or any language cannot converge into a complete proof; rational theory was brought into question by Arrow (Arrow, 1999); and one of the founders of social convergence theory, Campbell (Campbell, 1996), rejected his own theory after recognizing that the information derived from interactions spontaneously converges into multiple, incommensurable views of *R* instead of the single convergence predicted by logical positivists. Yet, from the mainstream, economists assert that choices are only rational when information among interactants converges into common knowledge (Sen, 1996); social scientists assert that measurement is reliable only when concepts and observations converge (Judd and McClelland, 1998); and artificial intelligence scientists assert that action is only deterministic when there exists a convergent agreement among autonomous agents on the motivation behind an action (Meyer et al., 1999).

Given that the persistence of interactions among organisms implies that interaction is key to solving problems of varying functionality to the social community, interaction must be observed to improve the skills used by agents to solve problems. Yet, the rapidity of shifts between organisms, in contrast to the interactions between inanimate objects modeled by classical mechanics, is believed to be too complex to rationalize (Jones, 1998). But not being able to rationalize the interaction may preclude the rational control of distributed autonomous artificial agents employed without human assistance to solve physical and social problems of increasing complexity (e.g., the Mars Pathfinder required central control).

Early attempts to model the social interaction considered it as a rational process that consists of either decision exchanges (Von Neumann and Morgenstern, 1953), message communications, or as a bounded combination of both (Simon, 1992). The prevailing model of rationality holds that perceptions of reality, R, correspond to physical R, and that despite the rapidity of turn-taking in an interaction between autonomous agents, R is sufficiently stable such that the information, I, derived from the interaction is independent of the shifts between actors (transmitters) and observers (receivers). However, the application of the conventional model to social dynamics, including organizational dynamics or economics, has not yet succeeded (Arrow, 1999). There are many reasons. Tracking I from interacting autonomous agents can create a fusion overload (Hayes, 1999) that becomes a separate problem when agents replan during mobile military missions independently of their mission (see chapter 5; information fusion alone is already a difficult problem during rapidly changing situations, as in providing weather forecasts during unstable conditions (Palmer, 1999)). But we believe that some of the obstacles to a rational theory of social dynamics may be overcome by replacing correspondence with a theory of static bistability to model the I derived from the interaction; by construing the interaction as the generator of self-similar social structures; and by studying the transition from social statics to social dynamics.

The essence of rational models of the interaction can be generalized from a review of game theory (Von Neumann and Morgenstern, 1953). It poses artificial configurations of discrete choices for an agent in the laboratory to re-create the tension that precedes its decision to cooperate or compete with another agent. Social dynamics is then an iterative sequence of static configurations derived from the observable "snapshots" of an actual dynamic interaction. The underlying concept is that language maps the interdependent choices to create the tension between agents in an interaction that produces the rational behavior, B, predicted by the configuration of choices.

Von Neumann and Morgenstern's game theory concept of the interaction was predicated on stable *R*, lending itself to the direct application of language. However, Bohr speculated to Von Neumann that if social interactions are bistable (see p. 148 in (Von Neumann and Morgenstern, 1953)), the variables of action and observation would be conjugate and not correspondent. Possibly the result of his background with quantum bistability, Von Neumann concluded that if Bohr was correct, game theory underdetermined *R*. Two reasons are possible: language, including mathematics, underdetermines *R*; and underdetermination in a social environment spontaneously generates multiple, incommensurable interpretations of *R*. While a consensus agrees with the first condition, it rejects the second (Bandura, 1989). But a theory of conjugacity is the only one that accounts for the evolution of incommensurable beliefs within a single *R*. An example of perceptual bistabity is the very simple vase-faces illusion (i.e., an observer can perceive either the vase or the profile of two faces). It illustrates that observational correspondence produces meaning by converging into one view of *R* that excludes others. The consequence is that convergence makes any real or artificial agent incapable of viewing bistable aspects simultaneously–viewing one stable aspect physiologically precludes others (Cacioppo et al., 1996).

Common examples of bistable beliefs make the news almost daily. From a 1999 Public Opinion Strategies Poll, "Republicans, by 45% to 17%, think the Clintonesque movie "Primary Colors" is more truth than fiction; Democrats, 40% to 23% think the opposite". Thus, in bistable *R*, the stable character of convergence can be reversed not only by shifting conceptual reference frames from Group A to Group B (i.e., prospect theory (Tversky and Kahneman, 1981)), but also by shifting references from the observed object to the object observed, the key insight in physical science by Copernicus and Newton, and in political science by Madison.

Bistable *R* means that decision makers are confronted by both the content of a decision and its causes. From Heisenberg (see p. 129 (Heisenberg, 1958)), "we meet [bistability] when we reflect about a decision and the motives for the decision". This suggests that most rational generalizations predicated on stable *R* have no or limited validity (Poincaré, 1952). Kelley, the most prominent theoretician in social exchange theory, which was adapted from game theory (Kelley, 1979), said it well that the choices made by interactants presented a matrix of choices, such as the Prisoner's Dilemma Game, seemed to shift from rational responses to ones based neither on their own observations or on their previously established preferences. That is why Allport (Allport, 1962) concluded that the master problem in social psychology remained the discontinuous shift from the rational decisions made by an individual to the very different decisions by the same individual made as the member of a group. Arrow won the Nobel prize for proving that a rational path from the ordering of individual to group preferences was not possible. Society often disregards the *obiter dicta* from individual judges even as it enshrines as precedents the decisions they make in the courtroom (Polanyi, 1974). In forensic psychology, the failure to predict individual behavior across social contexts is the rule (Faust and Ziskin, 1988). And in reviewing decision science, Tversky (Shafir et al., 1993) concluded that the rational justifications by an individual subsequent to a decision often bear no correspondence to the decision, giving impetus to the new field of naturalistic decision-making research (see (Lawless et al., 2000)).

If *R* is stable, then convergent rational perspectives should be stable. An excellent example of a rational assumption made in social psychology, which has never been verified, is the one about self-knowledge championed and studied exhaustively by Baumeister (Baumeister, 1995). Given that the individual human agent has full access to its own stable *I*, then according to Baumeister, the individual agent should be the best source of information or knowledge about itself. This straightforward assumption is widely accepted in traditional sociology and psychology; indirectly, it has begun to find its way into the research of multiple autonomous agents (e.g., "internal conflicts can be solved more efficiently than external conflicts because of a better understanding of the situation and the missing communication overhead" in chapter 3; also see chapters 4 and 5). From the stable perspective of *R*, this assumption is logical, strong, and makes good common sense. But to Baumeister's credit, he reports that he has found no evidence to support it. He concludes that individual human agents have poor access to their local stores of knowledge. We believe that the problem is not poor access, but the bistable *R* between the action-agent and observer-agent that precludes access. Simply put, it is physically impossible for an artificial or human autonomous agent to play the role of actor-agent and observer-agent simultaneously, including the special case when actor and observer are the same agent. This bistability will become more apparent with the increasing sophistication of autonomous agents and the more ill-defined the problems they attempt to solve. As we will show, and as first put forward by Bohr (Bohr, 1955), these two mutually exclusive roles produce mostly mutually exclusive information ("mostly" because the rapidity with which agents shift between these two roles produces memory overlaps that interact with agent self-reports).

Yet traditional social, economic, decision, and artificial agent science perspectives of the interaction between autonomous agents remain predicated on the correspondence between the observations of an agent and its context or *B*. On the one hand, cognitive theorists recognize that the *I* to control expert skills becomes transparent to the agent, but they also conclude that "The shift in perspective does not transform an individual from an agent to an [observable] object" (see p. 1181 (Bandura, 1989)). Primarily based on laboratory research with nominal rather than functional groups (Levine and Moreland, 1998), conclusions continue to be drawn from rational theory that favor cooperation instead of competition (Axelrod, 1984), individual decisions over group decisions (Stroebe and Diehl, 1994), and rational decisions by central decision makers instead of democracy or majority rule (Ridley, 1996). But rational correspondence has been unable to account for the evolutionary existence of groups, to validate the simple link between theory and *B*, and more central to our work, to provide a means to improve the solution of *idp's*. We now believe that since perception shifts, from either action or the presence of another person, are transparent to cognitive awareness, measurements of the interaction interfere with observations drawn by either actors or observers, breaking correspondence. Thus, for a theory of the interaction to improve the solution of *idp's*, it must determine the limits of cognitive correspondence, differentiate action from observational *I*, and discriminate between individual and group decisions. We believe this can only be accomplished with a theory of the interaction between conjugate variables.

2. BISTABILITY

Information complementarity between the conjugate variables of action and observation in an interaction leads to the prediction that knowledge and behavior are more likely to correspond when practicing mundane or intuitive day-to-day tasks, but that the correspondence between knowledge and behavior breaks down in extreme or novel situations.

The conventional means of deriving *I* from the interaction with self-reports or observations of *B* assumes that the measurement of *B* is equal to *B* (Judd and McClelland, 1998). This assumption derives from Campbell, the leading social measurement theorist, who concluded that the correspondence between concepts and *R* could be proven with the convergence among independent techniques now known as cross-validation. But the consistent failure to find reliable links between *B* and the self-reported observations of an individual human agent led Campbell to conclude that the problem extended to all observation, that indeed it was his theory of convergence that was at fault. Before he died, he had begun to seek an alternative construction of *R* based on the postmodern concept that two cultures form incommensurable views of *R* (Campbell, 1996). Convergence within a cultural worldview gives meaning to its adherents, but since the statistical average between extreme worldviews is mathematically meaningless (Nash, 1950), Campbell had been unable to go further.

Incommensurable views may arise spontaneously partly because self-reports of *B* from subjects may be interdependent with actual *B*. Testing for this possibility solved a long-standing research problem in cognitive dissonance research (for a review, see chapter 8). Cognitive dissonance is the tension within a person who tries to resolve the discrepancy between two strongly held but conflicting beliefs. An example is the phobia of a target object, associated with anxiety, coupled with relaxation. As measured by the physical closeness in the approach *B* of phobic subjects to the object of their phobia (e.g., snakes), physical effort has been used to reduce the phobia, but while the approach *B* measured by scientists consistently improved after effort, self-reports did not. Axsom and Lawless (Axsom and Lawless, 1992) collected self-reports before and after approach *B* and found an interaction which indicated that observations of *B* are interdependent with actual *B*.

Bohr was the first to speculate that action and observation are conjugate variables. This means that a single agent is in two states simultaneously until a measurement or interaction occurs. An agent is simultaneously an actor and an observer, an individual and a group member, and a member of one incommensurable group or another until the initiation of action or the presence of another agent. Action or interaction shifts the agent from the dual to a single state either where *I* flow corresponds to *R* (e.g., a player passes a basketball to a teammate who drives to a hoop and scores), or external measurement of a target *B* leads to static *I* that corresponds to *R* (an observer witnesses the basketball pass from teammate A to teammate B who scores). However, discrepant accounts between agent-players and agent-observers are noted immediately (i.e., the difference is between the *I* flow experienced during action and the sequential static *I* images of a mental movie experienced during observation; see (Gibson, 1986)). Flow correspondence occurs during action to allow agents to navigate reliably and it also occurs in daily life when observations of *R* are not extreme. But the more that action and observation diverge, as can occur between action and concepts, or between cultures, measurement replaces *R* - *I* correspondences with conceptual correspondences that converge to form a stable worldview divergent from *R*:

$$\Delta a \Delta I \approx c \tag{10.1}$$

where c is a constant, Δa is uncertainty in action information and ΔI is uncertainty in observation information. Equation 10.1 means that as observational uncertainty in *I* goes to zero, implying a cultural worldview or convergence to knowledge, *K*, the uncertainty in the actions to solve an *idp* increases (e.g., during the world-wide economic crises in 1998, the Federal Reserve reported to the *Wall Street Journal* that its economic forecasts were "worse" than guessing).

Support for equation 10.1 should come from extreme environments. A field experiment with 125 USAF combat fighter pilots who had flown eight 3-min encounters in F-15 simulators against a machine and human opponent was designed by USAF trainers to determine that training improved the *K* of combat pilots and their outcomes in air combat (see (Lawless et al., 2000)). The *K* of air combat was determined by a multiple-choice examination weighted to favor training. Experience, $\sum B$, was the sum of flight-time histories (e.g., total flight time, total combat time) and training expertise (advanced tactical field exercises like Red Flag). Based on multiple regressions, experience significantly predicted the winners, total aircraft energy availability relative to opponents, and a judgment of performance from the subject matter expert who was also the human combat opponent. Contradicting Simon (Simon, 1992) about expert *K* and *B* and Einstein about concept-*R* correspondence, but in agreement with equation 10.1, air-combat *K* did not predict win-loss outcomes, energy scores, or expert ratings. For the solution of ill-defined problems, and in agreement with equation 10.1, as the certainty in observation in bistable *R* converges to form a single worldview or *K* (i.e., $\Delta I \rightarrow 0$), observation or measurement is no longer correspondent, making action unpredictable.

As an analog of the USAF study, we subsequently explored the relationship between the concept of self-esteem and academic performance, which Baumeister has long believed to be integral to academic success (Baumeister, 1995). Subjects (n=20) who rated themselves on their general skills, mathematics skills, and self-esteem were administered a mathematics test. Strong correlations were found between the general self-concepts of performance and self-esteem ($r = .59, p < .05$), the general self-concepts of performance and mathematics skills ($r = .63, p < .01$), and between the self-concept of mathematics performance and self-esteem ($r = .34, p > .05$ or $n.s.$). But in agreement with the USAF study and equation 10.1, weak correlations were found between self-esteem and actual mathematics scores ($r = -.05, pn.s.$), and the self-concept of mathematics performance and actual mathematics scores ($r = .00, pn.s.$). Our findings agree with previous results in the literature on the association between academic perceptions and actual grades earned ($r = .16$; in (Michael et al., 1989). Apparently, world-view convergence occurs independently from physical *R*.

Divergence between worldviews and *R* is not a problem when solving well-defined problems (*wdp's*). All cultures maintain instructions to solve the *wdp's* indigenous to their cultures. These instructions on how to build a house, drive a car, or operate a computer are generally sufficient to initiate novices into practices. Also, complex problems like agent navigation (see chapter 6) or computationally intensive problems can be included in *wdp's* (e.g., (Clearwater et al., 1991)). For multiple autonomous agents, *wdp's* include algorithms to solve NP-complete problems to schedule events or to perform extensive data searches (see chapters 3 and 9). Once human agents become experts, however, their newly acquired skills may be independent of the original instructions (Polanyi, 1974), separating the knowledge of skills from their practice. For example, experts who become teachers need to be retrained to think from a novice's viewpoint (e.g., active duty military pilots from the fleet retrain to become flight instructors; see `www.cnet.navy.mil/nascweb/ats/fitc/fitc.htm`).

Despite the separation between skills and *K* observed in the solution of *wdp's*, by definition, there are no guides to solve *idp's*. Equation 10.1 indicates that worldviews will interact with the solution of *idp's*, sometimes violently, leading to an evolution in knowledge (e.g., see the functional violation of norms in chapter 2). An excellent example is Planck's discovery of the equation to model black body radiation. His trial-and-error solution required discrete energy levels to model radiant energy. But when he realized that quantum theory would replace classical mechanics at the atomic level, Planck became so disturbed that he spent years trying but ultimately failing to replicate his findings with continuum classical mechanics (Cline, 1987).

3. SOLVING ILL-DEFINED PROBLEMS

Equation 10.1 indicates that *idp's* can be solved only by decreasing the certainty in stable *K*. But this provides no understanding of the effort or time required to make a decision. We introduce behavioral inertia, *j*, as the sum of personal reactive experience to information change and information flow. It is analogous to physical inertia in Newtonian mechanics, and represents the inertial resistance to the new information that anchors an agent in an interaction. If $j * a = B$ and $a = \Delta I/\Delta t$, then from equation 10.1,

$$j * \Delta a * \Delta I = j * \Delta[\Delta I/\Delta t] * \Delta I * \Delta t/\Delta t = \Delta[j * (\Delta I/\Delta t)^2] * \Delta t = \Delta E \Delta t \approx c \qquad (10.2)$$

where ΔE is the uncertainty in energy and Δt the uncertainty in time. Equation 10.2 means that as Δt is reduced to zero, the uncertainty in energy becomes unbounded.

Based on equation 10.2, a modern society of human agents should have evolved techniques to resolve detailed time aspects of bistable R (i.e., $\Delta t \rightarrow 0$). An example from the courtroom where defense attorneys are pitted against prosecutors is that the opportunity for justice improves if both attorneys pursue their individual self-interests to create independent, detailed views of R before a neutral jury; an example from government is that the best protection against tyranny is the I derived from the use of checks and balances inherent in a republic; and an example from science is that its practices pit formidable opponents against each other before relatively neutral observers (e.g., Galileo versus Aristotle, Chomsky versus Skinner). In these examples (see (Lawless et al., 2000)), the energy expended to peer within the smallest increment of time becomes unpredictable.

In sum, bringing incommensurable views into contact produces a tension and a consumption of energy that forces society to evolve as it solves *idp's*. Paradoxically, the solution to ill-defined problems occurs from reducing rational certainty.

4. ENVIRONMENTAL REMEDIATION

In 1993, the antiquated practices which had caused significant environmental problems at the U.S. Department of Energy (DOE) Savannah River Site (SRS) and other sites across the DOE complex had ended. But progress on new environmental remediation (ER) initiatives had slowed as well as the more intractable *idp's* long confronted by DOE like the disposal of radioactive high-level wastes (HLW) (for a review, see (Lawless et al., 2000)).

Within the DOE complex, SRS in South Carolina and Hanford in Washington are the two sites with the largest budgets (over $1 billion each in 1996 for ER and waste management). Both sites have Citizens Advisory Boards to help restore confidence in DOE decisions by making recommendations on ER and waste management practices. While both of these boards have been successful, the SRS Board (SAB) has focused on facilitating the cleanup between SRS, its regulators, and the public. Because the quality of science applied in the field by DOE had been poor, the first decision by SAB recommended independent scientific peer review (ISPR) as one factor to improve technology practices at SRS (written by the first author; see (Lawless et al., 2000)). By introducing external scientific worldviews that could conflict with the insider views of the scientists at the DOE-SRS site, peer review created a tension among the scientific worldviews that could be regulated for the benefit of the site and society (for a nice review, see chapter 4). In contrast, the Hanford Board (HAB) has focused on providing independent perspectives based on "core principles and values" to address major policy issues at Hanford. This primary difference between the two Boards reflects action convergence to problem solutions at DOE-SRS versus convergence to a single worldview of "values" at DOE-Hanford (i.e., $\Delta a \to 0$ versus $\Delta I \to 0$).

In addition, SAB uses traditional democratic voting (simple majority rule) to decide whether to make recommendations, while HAB is governed by the DOE policy to "strive for consensus" (cooperation). Majority rule promotes a competition of ideas among the factions that arise on a committee, producing a gain in I (Friedman, 1982). Majority voting also means that not all ideas win. The ideas with wide support survive criticism from the minority, but the better ones are those reached after a struggle to a compromise between the majority and minority (Schlesinger, 1949). Guided by equations 10.1 and 10.2, compromise indicates that the struggle by each group to promote their own worldviews as they search for the optimal solutions to ill-defined problems is a necessary ingredient for technological innovation and social harmony.

Struggle also occurs on HAB, but to build a consensus worldview for the advice it provides to DOE at Hanford. DOE suggests that its advisory panels "strive" to reach consensus under a policy of cooperation. This conventional view, which HAB follows but SAB does not, holds that groups are more effective decision-makers by seeking cooperation (Axelrod, 1984) instead of individual self-interest. The National Academy of Sciences (National Academy of Sciences, 1994) agrees that seeking a consensus is key to restoring trust in DOE. But this striving inverts the usual power relations between majority and minority, enhancing conformity to a single worldview, producing less I, narrower decisions, and, by expending its available energy to reach consensus, less innovation (Janis, 1971). In their research on distributed agents, Hannebauer and Denzinger reach similar conclusions (see chapters 3 and 9). They found that the search for consensus among distributed agents produces suboptimal solutions and higher overhead from communication costs. To reduce these costs and to improve the solutions, Hannebauer and Denzinger question whether it is better to favor central decision-making, or, as we have posed (see also (Lam and Suen, 1997)), distributed decision-making along with majority rule. We will address this question in the next two sections.

From survey and interview data, both DOE boards compared to all others have made significant contributions to improving DOE site decisions. However, compared to HAB, the SAB reported more support for DOE decisions, progress, and trust. And with conflict on SAB minimized by the combination of ISPR and majority rule to reach decisions, it has been more willing to obtain expert advice but less willing to accept the views of government regulators.

From the field data, significantly more progress has been made at SRS than Hanford (see (Lawless et al., 2000)). While SRS has unresolved technical issues (e.g., HLW salt precipitation), it has been a leader in ER, vitrifying HLW, incinerating low-level radioactive waste (LLW), closing HLW tanks, and even in applying innovative techniques developed at Hanford like plug-in-regulatory decisions. In contrast, Congress has investigated Hanford for its lack of progress, and it may be a decade behind SRS in vitrifying HLW or in closing its HLW tanks.

The results support bistability and equation 10.1. The clash of incommensurable views over the centuries among citizens and scientists makes little evolutionary sense unless R is bistable. Bistability means that the best approach to the solution of *idp's* is with a social mechanism that reduces the certainty in any single cultural or scientific view of R by bringing incommensurable worldviews into contact, moderates this clash by motivating compromise instead of conflict, and then keeps factions unstable by encouraging them to pursue the mutually exclusive self-interests that maintain bistability. The tension from incommensurability between majority and minority factions is the engine that drives the creative solution of *idp's*. When an *idp* is solved, participants act as if in response to a virtual K in the sense that this K influences the decisions of participants who cannot be relied upon to provide valid self-reports. While creativity requires social interaction, the I that emerges is bistable, making observation unreliable. Outside scientific observers of both SAB and HAB failed to grasp the differences between majority rule and consensus rule decision making, which agrees with equation 10.1 (see (Lawless et al., 2000); also, this finding follows the logic of emergence described in chapter 7). Unexpectedly, however, we found that the situational awareness of decision-makers at SAB was better than predicted. In retrospect, this does agree with our finding for the subject matter expert who participated in the air combat and whose judgment of air-combat success agreed with the more objective measure of energy availability. It may be that the struggle to solve *idp's* acts to prime situational awareness; later as the problem becomes a *wdp*, awareness is replaced with transparency.

When struggle solves problems, as it did on SAB, it leads to positive feelings. ISPR enhanced practices in the field by questioning technical decisions, democracy enhanced decisions on the Board by forcing majority and minority members to compete for ideas and struggle with each other for compromise, and the tension from both mediated decisions by the regulators and DOE to broaden the public mandate. But on HAB, as its members strove to produce a convergence between their advice and worldview, struggle was less successful, encumbering the cleanup of Hanford. This agrees with Feynman's conclusion that values (worldviews) do not solve physical problems (Feynman, 1967), but it must surprise those who believe that conflict (competition), which serves to break apart worldviews, is wasteful (Axelrod, 1984) (for support for our view, see the section on functional violation of norms in chapter 2). Indeed, the narrowness of ideas from conforming to consensus worldviews has generated more public conflict on HAB than SAB (Lawless et al., 2000). This finding agrees with research which indicates that majority votes among computational systems is simpler to apply and more effective than the computationally intensive schemes that depend on consensus (Lam and Suen, 1997).

Self-reports by agents represent snapshots of action which not only shift dramatically over time, but which also may be fallacious. While self-reports have been found to be as reliable as any other form of observation (Howard, 1994), McGuire (McGuire, 1976) concluded that the inability of social scientists to establish a reliable relationship between B and self-reports was a scandal. If language as epiphenomenon (Chomsky, 1995) is static at any moment, and if humans use it to construct convergent I to gain meaning, agent observations will always support the illusion that R is stable, even though equation 10.1 and our results indicate that it is bistable. The breakdown in correspondence between agent observations and R in solving well-structured problems like building a house becomes more noticeable with *idp's* (e.g., sellers and buyers in unstable stock markets). As each observation is constructed, one view of R is selected from at least two possibilities, breaking correspondence. Similarly, measurement constructs a convergent picture of R that excludes incommensurable views, preventing the reconstitution of R as Kelley has found.

Bohr concluded that there is no alternative to language to describe R even though the observational correspondences afforded by language dissolve into arbitrary distinctions in bistable R. This seems illogical because we are taught the fundamental discoveries in a discipline as an organized set of logical trajectories even though logic is not central to discovery (Poincaré, 1952). It seems more logical that bistable beliefs are innate human limitations which should be overcome by education (Shearer and Gould, 1999), or that beliefs rather than R determine B (Frith and Frith, 1999). And it seems illogical that concepts predicated on convergence have a cross-validity with other concepts but not with physical evidence (Campbell, 1996). Despite these appearances, however, the rational approach does not explain the results from the laboratory that changing frames of reference affects decisions (Tversky and Kahneman, 1981); nor the USAF test of knowledge which failed to measure air-combat performance (i.e., $\Delta I \rightarrow 0$), while a simple sum of experience did (i.e., $\Delta a \rightarrow 0$); nor the better experience of SAB compared to HAB. Bistability also clarifies the disconnect between public surveys, which have found an enormous fear of the geologic repository for nuclear wastes being constructed near Las Vegas, NV (Slovik et al., 1991), with the knowledge that Las Vegas continues to be the fastest growing city in the U.S. In sum, the logic of rational theory, such as game theory, must be modified to account for measurement and action in bistable *R*.

5. THE TRANSITION TO INTERACTION MECHANICS

The mainstream social perspective derived from Lewin (Lewin, 1951) is that *B* is a function of the correspondence between an agent's perception and construction of *R*. While Lewin's logic must be true at some level, our findings limit it in three important respects: first, the transparency between *R* and well-practiced *B* to an agent's cognitive executive authority permits multiple *B*'s (e.g., simultaneously driving a car, tuning a radio, and carrying on a conversation); second, the employment of language is a tool that breaks correspondence with *R*; and third, the indeterministic nature of *R* promotes multiple, incommensurable worldviews, and tension between them. The tension powers social evolution as different social mechanisms arise spontaneously to counter these limitations in order to solve ill-defined problems. When the interaction is transparent to outside viewers, as in democracy, new *I* from incommensurabilities or symmetry breaking is produced. By this logic, the effects of different interaction structures on decisions should be measurable. The static information modeled by equations 1 and 2 indicate that we can choose to model these effects by reducing either observational or action uncertainty, or time or energy uncertainty (e.g., from equation 10.2, if we assume that the uncertainty in time becomes unbounded, the uncertainty in energy goes to zero, allowing us to focus on the changes in energy near an interaction equilibrium).

Broadly, in an interaction between autonomous agents, pure or mixed visual, sound, and physical exchanges convey *I*. Visual exchanges are observation-guidance behaviors; aural-oral behaviors occur with sound; and in the physical realm, sensation-mechanical behaviors prevail. We loosely group the former activities (observation, aural, sensation) under observation, and the latter under action. The most common example of a mixed exchange is the visual observations in modern society reduced to symbols or text and converted into externally or internally voiced reading behaviors. Traditionally, speaking-reading behaviors are transparent to the process of observation and meaning. Instead of breaking apart transparency, we discount the convergence of observational *I* because it produces meaning only within a consensual worldview.

Progress towards a theory of social dynamics centered on the mechanics of interaction will include irreversibility (information entropy) and *E* (economic costs). In this section, we follow Prigogine's (Prigogine, 1997) suggestion to convert the static theory of quantum conjugacity into a theory of interaction mechanics with the phenomenon of resonance. It has been successfully employed to model interaction persistence in chemical science, music, and speech. We know that uttered verbalizations occur at or near the vocal resonance characteristic of an individual voice box. We speculate that vocal resonance factors into an observer's interpretations of interactions recalled from memory (according to Chomsky (Chomsky, 1995), language is sound with a meaning). Then if the purpose of feedback is to reduce transaction errors in the solution of problems, interaction persistence emerges with language feedback. In that voice and vocal memories represent feedback, by extension from individual to group dynamics, we assume that an interaction between two organisms can be characteristic of the participants and the interaction. We define this state as interaction resonance.

Resonance produces an *E* channel between two non-local objects. It "tunes" a radio or television set to receive *E* transmissions from a specific station while simultaneously damping off-frequency signals. A similar phenomenon known as the "cocktail party" phenomenon occurs when one person selects a single conversation from among many. And it may be a factor in the entrainment of oscillations from actor to observer in the interaction (Kelso, 1995). Resonance also represents the maximum output at a discrete energy level. At resonance, the change or loss in energy (*E*) is approximately zero:

$$\Delta E \approx 0 \qquad (10.3)$$

The channel created during resonance acts as an energy pump that is nature's approximation of a "free-lunch". Physiologically, resonance permits the vocal chords to operate with the least expenditure of energy (Ladefoged, 1996). The low cost permits an organism to perform extensive vocal *B*'s to convey sound *I* between coupled partners with the least investment in structural equipment.

The observational *I* transmitted between two organisms is the average uncertainty, unexpectedness or variance for a discrete value *x*.

$$I = I(x) = -\sum_{x} p(x) log_2 p(x) \qquad (10.4)$$

where $p(x)$ is the probability of occurrence and $log_2 p(x)$ transforms probability into bits of information. *I(x)* is entropy and ranges between $[0 = log_2 1 =$

certainty to $log_2 n = uncertainty$] as the probable outcome of one choice ranges from certain knowledge, K, to $1/n$ when all choices are equally likely to be true. The joint uncertainty $I(x_1, x_2)$ between two participants is

$$I(x_1, x_2) = I(x_1) + I_{x1}(x_2) = I(x_2) + I_{x2}(x_1) \tag{10.5}$$

which is the uncertainty in one variable combined with that in the other after removing knowledge of the first. $I(x_1, x_2)$ ranges between $I(x_1)$ or $I(x_2)$ at the minimum when both are equal and one controls the other, to $I(x_1)$ plus $I(x_2)$ when both are independent.

The *I* transmitted, or $I_T(x_1 : x_2)$, between two agents is the constraint of one on the other:

$$I_T(x_1 : x_2) = I(x_1) + I(x_2) - I(x_1, x_2) = I(x_2) - I_{x1}(x_2) \tag{10.6}$$

which measures the amount that knowledge of one variable interdependently reduces uncertainty in the other. The constraint ranges between [0 to $min[I(x_1), I(x_2)]$ as x_1 and x_2 range between independence to interdependence (i.e., conjugate). We can convert equations 10.5 and 10.6 directly into information flow equations without the loss of generality. Equation 10.5 becomes:

$$\partial I(x_1, x_2)/\partial t = \partial I(x_1)/\partial t + \partial I_{x1}(x_2)/\partial t \tag{10.7}$$

Considering $I(x_1, x_2)$ and $I_T(x_1 : x_2)$ together with our prior findings leads to an interesting prediction. Between two agents, maximum interdependence occurs at minimum joint uncertainty or when one agent is slaved to the other. Alternatively, minimum interdependence occurs at maximum joint uncertainty. Maximum interdependence implies minimum *I* uncertainty (independent of the state of knowledge; see below), and minimum interdependence implies maximum *I* uncertainty.

This means that the state of interaction resonance, recognized as consonance, cooperation, or consensus between two or more or groups of agents, occurs at maximum interdependence. In contrast, the state of interaction dissonance, recognized as conflict, competition, or dissensus, occurs at minimum interdependence (see chapter 9). As dissonance increasingly shifts the interaction from interaction resonance, reducing *I* constraints to zero, ΔE increases proportionately. We predict that for a problem domain that has been solved, maximum cooperation approximates a state of *K*; conversely, competition represents new *I* or the regulated destruction of prior *K*.

These striking parallels between cognitive and social dissonance suggest self-similarity across individual and social interactions. At the individual level, trivial beliefs for an individual are easily changed, but strongly held worldviews change only following cognitive dissonance (Axsom and Lawless, 1992). As a human agent approaches cognitive dissonance, ΔE increases to a maximum with increasing cognitive conflict, then subsides to $\Delta E \to 0$ as the previous belief valence is reversed. An example reviewed earlier was the surrogate effort used by Axsom and Lawless to change the worldview of subjects. From the literature, we know that compared to novices, experts performing well-practiced B's consume much less cognitive E (Landers and Pirozzolo, 1990). By extension, processing a worldview strongly held by cultural experts consumes less E than novices who are becoming acculturated (unless the experts are seeking consensus, e.g., DOE's HAB group). At the social level, in bistable R across groups, K ranges from roughly univariate at consensus to multivariate as the problem sets range between well-defined to ill-defined. Then social dissonance between groups maximizes I, minimizes K, and, as competition, represents the struggle to survive; in contrast, resonance between clusters minimizes I, maximizes K, and, as cooperation, represents adaptation to a given environment. Across groups, dissonance indicates that a problem has not been solved, consonance that it has. However, dissonant feedback under generally consonant conditions leads to acculturation (e.g., see chapter 8); under generally dissonant conditions, consonant feedback leads to new interaction mechanisms (e.g., a new business).

This leads to the speculation that striving to reach a single worldview by mutual consent or by force suppresses new I, while unbridled competition produces more I than can be accommodated, breaking apart existing social structures. Suppression of I becomes a problem for survival in an ill-defined environment when social influence in a group is used to reject one aspect of a bistable observation over another (e.g., forcing a consensus; closing a sale; using the Prisoner's Dilemma Game as a method of interrogating prisoners), reducing adaptability by increasing interaction costs. For survival under consensus, the goal becomes to retain the *status quo ante* independently of E consumption, reducing adaptability and increasing vulnerability. In contrast, while competition creates and then diffuses across the society the I that permits free markets to find the best prices, it breaks apart the social structures which cannot contain interaction stresses, a problem when competition can no longer be regulated or when compromises are no longer sought. Thus, the management of bistability generates the incommensurable worldviews between two groups that power the evolution of social structure.

Support for these speculations comes from the relation between ΔE and ΔI, free energy, ΔA, and temperature, T,

$$-W = \Delta A = \Delta E - T\Delta I(x_1, x_2) \tag{10.8}$$

As $\Delta A \to 0$, the available *E* for innovation is dissipated. In low availability situations, $\Delta E \approx \Delta I$, indicating, all things being equal, those social groups which consume the least *E* are those which cooperate to solve problems, while competition always consumes more *E*. Thus, resonance (cooperation) should be characteristic of low *E* consumption while dissonance should not be. Limited support comes from an analysis of speech wave forms by Kang (Kang and Everett, 1984) who was able to distinguish between mellifluous, normal, and tense voices. This finding at the individual level may indicate that vocal energy consumption correlates with interaction state.

For useful work to be derived from dissipative systems, whether dyads, groups, systems of groups, or nation states, the available energy must be greater than its uncertainty of use. If *T* is set to 1, $\Delta E/\Delta I > 1$ becomes a tool to spontaneously convert the available *E* into channels self-organized to solve *idp's*, measured by increasing material wealth as a byproduct. Conversely, if $\Delta A \approx 0$, ΔE is being converted into ΔI. In examples from what we reported, the worst pilots in the USAF experiment were those who were unable to manage their aircraft's position and velocity *E* relative to opponents; and the energy consumed to construct a single worldview for consensuses reduced the *E* available to solve *idp's* in the DOE field study. From more common experiences, mergers arise from the collapse of the available *E* represented by prices falling across a market, as with the planned Exxon and Mobile Oil merger in 1999; and wars are interrupted when the costs to keep logistical channels open become greater than the benefits supplied, as in the Sudan where warfare during the 1990's was interrupted each monsoon season. These examples suggest the importance of channeling the available *E* for the solution of *idp's*.

From equation 10.7 and Fick we find:

$$k\partial^2 E/\partial x^2 \approx c\Delta E \tag{10.9}$$

where k and c are constants. Equation 10.9 implies that as a system moves away from resonance, a structure must exist to channel *E* into interactions to allow them to persist. These channels are like filters which permit passage when the content resonates with the channel but increases its *E* cost by antiresonance (damping) when not in agreement with the desired worldviews (here, damping and resonance are both characteristic of an interaction). Consensus is the formation of an *E* channel that arises from increasing the interdependence of multiple agents; competition is the creative destruction of existing channels (Schumpeter, 1989); and an efficient firm is a business structure that channels in more profit than it costs to produce products.

6. MACRO ECONOMICS

We predicted at the beginning of the last section that differences in how autonomous agent interactions are structured should have measurable effects: competition will consume more of the available energy than cooperation; it will bring about more change; and it will produce more material wealth. Analyses and theory have also led us to predict that the structure of interaction at one level may be self-similar across other levels. And we predicted that these interaction structures will be associated with the information and *E* flowing through them. Since scale may not be an obstacle, and since information is readily available at the level of macroeconomics, we tested our predictions at that level.

Testing our predictions at the level of macroeconomics based on dissonance and information theory derived at the individual and group level does not follow from the Standard Social Science Model (SSSM) of Tooby and Cosmides reviewed by Kohler (see (Kohler, 2000)). In part, SSSM asserts: "In discussing culture, psychological factors other than a capacity for learning can be neglected, since learning by itself is sufficient to explain behavioral structure, within-group similarities, and between-group differences." On the contrary, we have theorized that one of the reasons conventional models such as SSSM do not predict well in the field is that cognitive dissonance and information factors generate patterns at the social and cultural level not predicted by learning factors. Kohler provides an opening for our argument when he concedes that even the practitioners of social simulation based on conventional models of behavior view their own simulations with suspicion, which casts doubt on the SSSM model.

Conventional studies of *E* consumption look at a factor known as *E* intensity or efficiency. At the macroeconomic level, efficiency is often measured as Gross Domestic Product per unit of energy consumed (e.g., GDP in dollars per kilogram of oil equivalent). We contrasted *E* efficiency with Commercial energy use per capita (kg of oil equivalent) to measure *E* availability; relative citation impact to measure the scientific wealth of nations (i.e., RCI, the scientific citations divided by scientific publications (May, 1997)); and economic freedom to measure the ability of agents to make individual decisions to compete versus central decisions made by government for the benefit of citizens (by Friedman; see www.cato.org/research). Because the RCI index was only published for 15 nations, we compared those nations across all measures (i.e., Australia, Canada, Denmark, Finland, France, Germany, India, Italy, Japan, Netherlands, P.R. China, Sweden, Switzerland, U.K., and U.S.). For GDP/kg oil equivalent and for *E* availability, we used the World Development Report 1999 (see `www.worldbank.org/wdr/2000/`).

We considered *E* efficiency to be important because as part of the Kyoto Protocol, a consensus exists at the U.N. to help nations become more energy efficient; to improve the efficient use of power and fuel by industry; and to encourage international cooperation in promoting energy conservation, research and development (see www.unido.org/doc/online.html). Further, a glance at the comparisons for these 15 nations finds that some of the more developed countries like Australia and the U.S. are not energy efficient when compared to others like Japan and Switzerland (i.e., in 1996, GDP/kg OE for Australia was 3.7; U.S. 3.4; Japan 10.5; and Switzerland 12.0). As such, the U.S. has long been described as a profligate or wasteful energy consumer (Landsberg, 1979).

Based on the reported data, *E* efficiency was marginally associated with economic freedom ($r = .07, pn.s.$), weakly associated with scientific wealth ($r = .24, pn.s.$), and moderately associated with *E* availability ($r = .40, pn.s.$). In contrast, *E* availability was significantly associated with scientific wealth ($r = .69, p < .01$) and economic freedom ($r = .67, p < .01$). And economic freedom was significantly associated with scientific wealth ($r = .81, p < .01$). Finally, partial correlations that removed the contributions of scientific wealth weakly improved the association between *E* efficiency and economic freedom ($r = .21, pn.s.$); removing economic freedom moderately improved the association between *E* efficiency and scientific wealth ($r = .31, pn.s.$); but removing scientific wealth slightly reduced the association between *E* efficiency and *E* availability ($r = .34, pn.s.$). However, all of the partial correlations were non-significant.

These results, especially the partial correlations, indicate that at the level of macroeconomics, *E* efficiency is a poor indicator of how autonomous human agents solve *idp's*. *E* efficiency is a well-established measure for stable, closed systems that have solved *wdp's* (e.g., power generation, heating systems, industrial operations). But as a measure of the performance of autonomous agents in open systems attempting to solve *idp's*, *E* efficiency confounds how these more intractable problems are attacked by humans through competition, dissensus, or conflict. Yet, its pervasive influence has led to the widely-held consensus that democratic decision-making is inefficient (even by the strongest defenders of democracy; see Associate U.S. Supreme Court Justice Scalia's comments (Scalia, 1999)). In contrast, we found that economic freedom, scientific wealth, and energy availability are significantly interrelated. Our finding is supported by May (May, 1997) who found that the most competitive countries were among the top five nations across the twenty separate disciplines of science.

We predicted and found that the solution of *idp's* depends on a set of interaction structures which combine regulated conflict (competition) and conflict-free (cooperation) zones into channels to power the evolution of social systems; that excess E must be available to solve difficult problems; and that based on the availability of E, these structures must be allowed to spontaneously organize into channels to transport the knowledge derived from decisions to locations where they can best be applied. Differences in wealth become the byproducts of interaction structures employed by individuals, systems, and nations to solve *idp's*. The Nobel physicist Steven Weinberg claimed that "inequality in wealth is itself a social evil, which poisons life for millions" (Weinberg, 2000). However, these inequalities are a byproduct of suboptimal interaction structures. An alternative is to use consensus decision-making as an interaction structure, but as has been found with humans and artificial agents, consensus decision-making also produces suboptimal solutions. The alternative studied in this section was central decision-making. But we found that as a system of agents becomes more centrally controlled, the less I and E it has to solve *idp's*, the more vulnerable it becomes to conflict (Chagnon, 1988), and, as a consequence, the more inequalities it experiences in scientific and material wealth. Our results indicate that the most attractive interaction structure entails distributed agents using majority-rule to make decisions.

7. PATH FORWARD

A series of empirical questions await further study. A non-inclusive list:

- In the USAF experiment, the human combat opponent's judgment (he was also the subject matter expert) was the best indicator of air-combat success. Since he participated as the opponent in half of the combat flights, did his expenditure of "effort" in the cockpit lead to better agreement with action R outcomes? Further, in general, and as suggested by Kuhn (Kuhn, 1977), does moderated conflict in the form of competition (like DOE's SAB) or consensus (like DOE's HAB) lead to greater situational awareness of the decisions associated with R?

- Are the solution of *idp's* associated with dE/dt (energy consumption), new technology, and bistable perspectives? Can $\Delta E/\Delta I$ be applied to organizational or business management decisions to demonstrate similarities with what we found for macroeconomics? Is R&D associated with E efficiency or E availability? Can Kang's (Kang and Everett, 1984) ability to distinguish between normal and tense voices be duplicated for interacting dyads, groups, and systems of agents (e.g., negotiations during the DOE Advisory Board meetings are taped and available for speech wave-form regularity and energy analyses)? In these questions, the fundamental assumption in need of confirmation is whether the total E expended by a group of competitive agents is greater than a equal sized group of cooperative agents, and, in turn, whether E consumed by the cooperative group will range from a minimum that reflects K to a maximum that reflects no K.

- We assumed a temperature of one in this study (i.e., $\Delta A = \Delta E - T\Delta I \approx \Delta E - \Delta I$), but a more fruitful path from Landers suggests that temperature in social systems may be analogous to social activation. If $T = \partial E / \partial I$, the greater the social activation (conflict), the higher the temperature and the more E consumed. This suggests that activation may correlate with competition or conflict. Conversely, if tension from acculturation is like the surface tension of a group, the stronger the tension, the more quickly the group will respond to activation. Since Chagnon (Chagnon, 1988) has found that the rapidity to react implies evolutionary fitness (e.g., military responses to national interests; and by, extension, civil responses to fire and crime), does a lack of structure to moderate and channel activation imply a lack of fitness? Finally, as T is reduced, does measurement improve?

- Game theory should be revised with the concepts of action-observation uncertainty and information inertia in order to account for measurement and choices in bistable R.

- For social dynamics, feedback cycles between agents as oscillators offer a promising path forward. We plan to study whether the interaction can be modeled as a linear and non-linear series of entrainment between two or more agents oscillating from visual, sound, and physical exchanges (Kelso, 1995).

8. CONCLUSION

The focus of recent research in economics and artificial intelligence is to discover the replicator equations that establish a model of basic decision and learning processes in static and dynamic environments for single and multiple autonomous agents. Our approach to the discovery of these equations has been to develop an interaction mechanics. The transition from social statics (equations 1 and 2) to dynamics appears to be possible by encompassing the traditional perspective of information derived from the observation and the individual with a revised perspective of action and the group based on the speculation from Bohr that the factors of observation and action or individual and group behavior in the interaction are conjugate. The literature and our experimental evidence not only support Bohr, but have also made significant contributions to the environmental decisions at the DOE Savannah River Site.

The transition to a social dynamics developed from a proposal by Prigogine to make the static conjugate variables in the quantum interaction dynamic with the model of resonance, a phenomena which is common to both physical and social science. The assumption that resonance, and the departure from it, occurs between conjugate factors in an interaction revises the conventional view of cooperation, competition, and social creativity for the solution of *idp's*; introduced into interaction mechanics the concept of E availability, diffusion, and interaction channels; and led to a testable hypothesis that interaction structures (e.g., to manage decision-making processes) should produce measurable outcomes. Based on a theory of interaction developed at the cognitive and social levels, support at the level of macroeconomics was found.

The new perspective of a social statics and dynamics between conjugate factors in the interaction opens to research a domain of diversity, breadth, and scalability. The interaction between agents encompasses static and dynamic effects; the possibility of a mathematical model of the coupling between harmonic oscillators; vocal measures; models of correspondence, convergence, and divergence; and a fruitful parallel to interactions at the quantum level.

We draw two broad conclusions about conflict. The first is attributed to a perspective from Von Neumann (Von Neumann, 1961). Gödel's incompleteness theorem implies that the limits of rational convergence are signaled by conflict, that avoiding conflict is never productive, and that the management or resolution of conflict leads to the largest advances in rational thinking.

Finally, social structures are the physical and social mechanisms developed by trial-and-error methods to manage the interaction. Interaction mechanics can be a new approach with artificial intelligence and mathematics to control the interactions between multiple human and autonomous artificial agents. Our integration of cognitive and social dissonance with information theory and interaction uncertainty suggests that a new rational approach to the control of interactions between humans and autonomous artificial agents may one day be fully realized.

Acknowledgments

1. The first author is deeply grateful to Dr. J.A. Ballas, Ph.D., and the Information Technology Division, Naval Research Laboratory, Washington, DC, where most of this research was conducted with funds from the Office of Naval Research through American Society Engineering Education grants.

2. The first author is also very thankful to Chris R. Fuller, Professor, Director, Vibration and Acoustics Laboratory, Department of Mechanical Engineering, Virginia Tech, Blacksburg, VA, for computer time and for his guidance.

References

Aïmeur, E. (1998). Application and assessment of cognitive dissonance theory in the learning process. *Journal of Universal Computer Science*, 4(3):216–247.

Aïmeur, E., Dufort, H., and Frasson, C. (1997a). Profiting from conflict in intelligent tutoring systems. In *Workshop on Collaboration, Cooperation and Conflict in Dialogue Systems, IJCAI-97*, pages 1–7.

Aïmeur, E., Dufort, H., Leibu, D., and Frasson, C. (1997b). Some justifications for the learning by disturbing strategy. In *AI-ED 97, World Conference on Artificial Intelligence and Education, Japan*, pages 119–126.

Aïmeur, E. and Frasson, C. (1996). Analyzing a new learning strategy according to different knowledge levels. *Computers in education*, 27(2):115–127.

Alami, R., Fleury, S., Herrb, M., Ingrand, F., and Robert, F. (1998). Multi-Robot Cooperation in the Martha Project. *IEEE Robotics and Automation Magazine*, 5(1).

Alexander, J. C., Giesen, B., Münch, R., and Smelser, N. J., editors (1987). *The Micro-Macro Link*. University of California Press.

Allport, F. H. (1962). A structuronomic conception of behavior: individual and collective. *Journal of Abnormal and Social Psychology*, 64:3–30.

Anderson, J. and Bower, G. (1973). *Human Associative Memory*. Washington, DC: Winston.

Anderson, J., Corbett, A., Koedinger, K., and Pelletier, R. (1995). Cognitive tutors : Lessons learned. *The Journal of the Learning Sciences*, 4(2):167–207.

Arrow, K. J. (1999). Information and theory of industry. In Chichilnisky, G., editor, *Markets, information, and uncertainty: Essays in honor of Kenneth Arrow*, pages 19–25. Cambridge University Press.

Augustine, D., Gruber, K., and Hanson, L. (1990). Cooperation works! Cooperative learning can benefits all students, even those who are low-achieving, gifted, or mainstreamed. *Educational Leadership*, 47(4):4–7.

Axelrod, R. (1984). *The evolution of cooperation*. Basic.

Axsom, D. and Lawless, W. F. (1992). Subsequent behavior can erase evidence of dissonance-induced attitude change. *Journal of Experimental Social Psychology*, 28:387–400.

Baas, N. (1994). Emergence, hierarchies, and hyperstructures. In Wesley, A., editor, *Proceedings of Artificial Intelligence II*, pages 515–537, Santa-Fe, New Mexico, USA.

Baeijs, C., Demazeau, Y., and Alvares, L. (1996). Sigma: Application of multi-agent systems to cartographic generalization. In *Proceedings of the 7th Workshop On Modelling Autonomous Agents in a Multi-Agent World (Maamaw'96)*, Eindhoven, The Netherlands.

Baker, M. (1994). A model for negotiation in teaching-learning dialogues. *Journal of artificial intelligence in education*, 5(2):199–254.

Bandura, A. (1971). *Social Learning Theory*. New York: General Learning Press.

Bandura, A. (1989). Human agency in social cognitive theory. *American Psychologist*, 44:1175–1184.

Barnard, S. T. and Simon, H. D. (1994). A fast multilevel implementation of recursive spectral bisection for partitioning unstructured problems. *Concurrency: Practice and Experience*, 6:101–107.

Barnes, E. R. (1982). An algorithm for partitioning the nodes of a graph. *SIAM Journal on Algebraic and Discrete Methods*, 3(4):541–550.

Barták, R. (1999). Constraint programming: What is behind? In *Proceedings of the Workshop on Constraint Programming for Decision and Control (CPDC-99)*, Gliwice, Poland.

Baumeister, R. F. (1995). Self and identity: an introduction. In Tesser, A., editor, *Advanced Social Psychology*, pages 51–97. McGraw-Hill.

Bay, J. (1995). Design of the army ant cooperative lifting robot. *IEEE Robotics & Automation Magazine*.

Beckers, R., Holland, O., and Deneubourg, J. (1994). From local actions to global tasks: stigmergy and collective robotics. In Brooks, R. and Maes, P., editors, *Fourth Workshop on Artificial Life*, Boston, MA, USA. MIT Press.

Berlandier, P. and Neveu, B. (1995). Problem partition and solvers coordination in distributed constraint satisfaction. In *Proceedings of the Workshop on Parallel Processing in Artificial Intelligence (PPAI-95)*, Montréal, Canada.

Berlyne, D. (1960). *Conflict arousal, and curiosity*. New York: McGraw-Hill.

Beslon, G., Biennier, F., and Favrel, J. (1995). A Flexible Conveying System Based on Autonomous Vehicles. In *Proceedings of CARs and FoF'95*, volume 1, pages 115–120, Pereira, Colombia.

Béziau, J.-Y. (1994). Théorie législative de la négation pure. *Logique et Analyse*, (147-148):209–225.

Bloom, B. S. (1969). *Taxonomie des objectifs pédagogiques: domaine cognitif*. Montréal, Éducation nouvelle.

Blumer, H. (1966). Commentary and debate. Sociological implications of the thought of George Herbert Mead. *American Journal of Sociology*, 71:535–544.

Bohinc, T. (1999). Umgang mit Konflikten. *Deutsche Telekom Unterrichtsblätter*, (52 (9)):504–514.

Bohr, N. (1955). Science and the unity of knowledge. In Leary, L., editor, *The unity of knowledge*, pages 44–62. Doubleday.

Bonabeau, E., Dessalles, J., and Grumbach, A. (1995). Characterizing emergent phenomena (1) and (2): a critical review. *Revue internationale de systémique*, 9(3):327–346 and 347–371.

Bonabeau, E. and Theraulaz, G. (1994). *Intelligence collective*. Hermes, Paris.

Bonacina, M. (1997). The Clause-Diffusion Theorem Prover Peers-mcd. In *Proceedings CADE-14, Townsville*, pages 53–56.

Bond, A. H. (1989). Commitments, some DAI insigths from symbolic interactionist sociology. In *Proceedings of the 9th International AAAI Workshop on Distributed Artificial Intelligence*, pages 239–261.

Bond, A. H. and Gasser, L. (1988). An analysis of problems and research in DAI. In Bond, A. H. and Gasser, L., editors, *Readings in Distributed Artificial Intelligence*, pages 3–35. Morgan Kaufmann Publishers.

Boppana, R. B. (1987). Eigenvalues and graph bisection: An average-case analysis. In *Proceedings of the 28th Annual Symposium on Foundations of Computer Science*, pages 280–285, Los Angeles, USA.

Brant, R. (1990). On cooperative learning : a conversation with Spencer Kagan. *Educational Leadership*, 47(4):8–11.

Brooks, R. (1986). A robust layered control system for a mobile robot. *IEEE Robotics and Automation*, RA(2):14–23.

Brooks, R. (1991). Intelligence without Reason. In *Proceedings of IJCAI-91*, Sydney, Australia.

Bruner, J. (1966). *Toward a Theory of Instruction.* Cambridge, MA: Harvard University Press.

Bui, T. N. (1986). *Graph Bisection Algorithms.* PhD thesis, Department of Electrical Engineering and Computer Science, Massachusetts Institute of Technology.

Cacioppo, J. T., Berntson, G. G., and Crites, S. L. J. (1996). Social neuroscience: principles of psychophysiological arousal and response. In Higgins, E. and Kruglanski, A., editors, *Social Psychology Handbook of Basic Principles.* Guilford.

Calder, R. B., Smith, J. E., Courtemanche, A. J., Mar, J. M. F., and Ceranowicz, A. Z. (1993). ModSAF behavior simulation and control. In *Proceedings of the Conference on Computer Generated Forces and Behavioral Representation.*

Cammarata, S., McArthur, D., and Steeb, R. (1983). Strategies of cooperation in distributed problem solving. In *IJCAI'83*, pages 767–770.

Campbell, D. T. (1996). Can we overcome worldview incommensurability / relativity in trying to understand the other? In Jessor, R. and Shweder, R., editors, *Ethnography and human development*, pages 153–171. University of Chicago Press.

Campbell, J. (1981). George Herbert Mead on intelligent social reconstruction. *Symbolic Interaction*, 4:191–205.

Cantu-Paz, E. (1995). A summary of research on parallel genetic algorithms. Technical Report 95007, University of Illinois at Urbana-Champain.

Cantu-Paz, E. (1999). Migration Policies, Selection Pressure, and Parallel Evolutionary Algorithms. Technical Report 99015, University of Illinois at Urbana-Champain.

Cariani, P. (1990). Emergence and Artificial Life. In Wesley, A., editor, *Proceedings of Artificial Intelligence II*, pages 775–797, Santa-Fe, New Mexico, USA.

Carroll, J. B. (1963). A model of school learning. Technical Report Record, 64, 723-733, Teachers College.

Castelfranchi, C. (1991). Social power: a missed point in DAI, MA and HCI. In Demazeau, Y. and Müller, J. P., editors, *Decentralized AI*, pages 49–62. Elsevier, Amsterdam.

Castelfranchi, C. (1996). Commitment: from intentions to groups and organizations. In *Proceedings of the International Conference of Multi-Agent Systems (ICMAS'96)*.

Castelfranchi, C. (2000). Conflicts ontology. In Müller, H. J. and Dieng, R., editors, *Computational conflicts - Conflict Modeling for Distributed Intelligent Systems*, pages 21–40. Springer.

Castelfranchi, C. and Falcone, R. (1997). From task delegation to role delegation. In Lenzerini, M., editor, *AI*IA97: Advances in Artificial Intelligence*, pages 278–289. Springer-Verlag.

Castelfranchi, C. and Falcone, R. (1998a). Principles of trust for MAS: cognitive anatomy, social importance, and quantification. In *Proceedings of the International Conference of Multi-Agent Systems (ICMAS'98)*, pages 72–79.

Castelfranchi, C. and Falcone, R. (1998b). Towards a theory of delegation for agent-based systems. *Robotics and Autonomous Systems*, 24:141–157.

Cesta, A., Miceli, M., and Rizzo, P. (1996). Effects of different interaction attitudes on a multi-agent system performance, agents breaking away. In *Proc. MAAWAW 1996, Van de Velde, Perram (eds.)*. Springer Verlag.

Chagnon, N. A. (1988). Life histories, blood revenge, and warfare in a tribal population. *Science*, 243:985–992.

Chaib-draa, B. (1996). Interaction between Agents in routine, familiar and unfamiliar situations. *International Journal of Intelligent and Cooperative Information Systems*, 5.

Chan, T. and Baskin, A. (1990). Learning companion systems. In Frasson, C. and Gauthier, G., editors, *Intelligent Tutoring Systems : at the crossroads of Artificial Intelligence and Education*. New Jersey: Ablex.

Chan, T., Chung, Y., Ho, R., Hou, W., and Lin, G. (1992). Distributed learning companion systems WEST revisited. In *The 2nd International Conference of Intelligent Tutoring Systems, Lecture Notes in Computer Science, 608*, pages 643–650. Springer-Verlag.

Chantemargue, F., Courant, M., Dagaeff, T., and Robert, A. (1998). A pragmatic approach to conflict. In Tessier, C. and Chaudron, L., editors, *Conflicts among agents: avoid or use them?*, pages 87–93. Working Notes of the ECAI-98 Workshop.

Chantemargue, F. and Hirsbrunner, B. (1999). A collective robotics application based on emergence and self-organization. In *Proceedings of Fifth International Conference for Young Computer Scientists (ICYCS'99)*, Nanjing, China.

Chattergy, R. (1985). Some heuristics for the navigation of a robot. *Int. J. of Robotics Research*, 4(5966).

Chaudron, L., Fiorino, H., Maille, N., and Tessier, C. (2000). Difference: a key to enrich knowledge. Concepts and models. In Müller, H. J. and Dieng, R., editors, *Computational conflicts - Conflict Modeling for Distributed Intelligent Systems*, pages 82–102. Springer.

Chi, M., Bassok, M., Lewis, M., Reimann, P., and Glaser, R. (1989). Self-explanation: how students study and use examples in learning to solve problems. *Cognitive Science*, 13:145–182.

Chi, M. and Vanlehn, K. (1991). The content of physics self-explanation. *Journal of the Learning Science*, 1(1):69–106.

Cholvy, L. (1993). Proving theorems in a multi-source environment. In *IJCAI'93*, pages 66–71.

Chomsky, N. (1995). *The minimalist program.* MIT Press.

Chu-Carrol, J. and Carberry, S. (1996). Conflict detection and resolution in collaborative planning. In Wooldridge, M. J., Müller, J. P., and Tambe, M., editors, *Intelligent Agents II - Agent Theory, Architecture, and Languages*, pages 111–125. Springer Verlag.

Chu-Carroll, J. and Carberry, S. (1995). Generating information sharing subdialogues in expert-user consulation. In *Proceedings of International Joint Conference on Artificial Intelligence.*

Clearwater, S. H., Huberman, B. A., and Hogg, T. (1991). Cooperative solution of constraint satisfaction problems. *Science*, 254:1181–1183.

Cline, B. (1987). *Men who made a new physics.* University of Chicago Press.

Cohen, P. R. and Levesque, H. (1990). Rational interaction as the basis for communication. In Cohen, P. R., Morgan, J., and Pollack, M., editors, *Intentions in Communications*, pages 221–255. The MIT Press.

Cohen, P. R. and Levesque, H. J. (1991). Teamwork. *Nous*, 35.

Conry, S., MacIntosh, D., and Meyer, R. (1990). DARES: A Distributed Automated REasoning System. In *Proceedings AAAI-90*, pages 78–85.

Corno, F., Prinetto, P., Rebaudengo, M., and Reorda, M. S. (1996). A Parallel Genetic Algorithm for Automatic Generation of Test Sequences for Digital Circuits. In *Proceedings High Performance Computing and Networking, Brüssels*, pages 454–459.

Correa, R. (1995). A Parallel Formulation for General Branch-and-Bound Algorithms. In *Proceedings IRREGULAR'95*, pages 395–409.

Coser, L. (1956). *The Functions of Social Conflict*. New York.

Cumming, G., J. (1991). *Teaching knowledge an intelligent tutoring*, chapter Learning modeling in collaborative intelligent educatinal systems. Norwood, NJ: Ablex.

Dalla Chiara, M.-L. (1986). Quantum logic. In Gabbay, D. and Guenthner, F., editors, *Handbook of Philosophical Logic*, volume III, pages 427–469. D. Reidel.

Davidson, N. and O'leary, P. (1990). How cooperative learning can enhance mastery teaching. *Educational Leadership*, 47(5):30–34.

Decker, K. and Lesser, V. (1993). A one-shot dynamic coordination algorithm for distributed sensor networks. In *Proceedings of the Eleventh National Conference on Artificial Intelligence (AAAI-93)*, pages 210–216.

Decker, K., Sycara, K. P., and Williamson, M. (1997). Cloning for intelligent adaptive information agents. In Zhang, C. and Lukose, D., editors, *Multi-Agent Systems: Methodologies and Applications*, volume 1286 of *LNAI*, pages 63–75. Springer.

Decker, K. S. and Lesser, V. R. (1992). Generalizing the Partial Global Planning algorithm. *International Journal of Intelligent Cooperative Information Systems*, (1):319–346.

Dehais, F. and Pasquier, P. (2000). Approche générique du conflit. In *Ergo-IHM 2000*, Biarritz, France.

Demazeau, Y. (1995). From cognitive interactions to collective behavior in agent-based systems. In *Proceedings of the First European Conference on Cognitive Science*, Saint Malo, France.

Deneubourg, J.-L., Goss, S., Franks, N., Sendova-Franks, A., Detrain, C., and Chretien, L. (1991). The dynamics of collective sorting: robot-like ant and ant-like robots. In Meyer, J. and Wilson, S., editors, *Simulation of Adaptive Behavior: from Animals to Animats*, pages 356–365. MIT Press.

Denzin, N. (1996). Post-Pragmatism. Review Essay. *Symbolic Interaction*, 19(1):61–75.

Denzinger, J. (1995). Knowledge-Based Distributed Search Using Teamwork. In *Proceedings ICMAS-95, San Francisco*, pages 81–88.

Denzinger, J. (1999). Distributed Knowledge-based Search. Habilitationsschrift, University of Kaiserslautern.

Denzinger, J. and Fuchs, D. (1999). Cooperation of Heterogeneous Provers. In *Proceedings IJCAI-99, Stockholm*, pages 10–15.

Denzinger, J. and Kronenburg, M. (1996). Planning for Distributed Theorem Proving: The Teamwork Approach. In *Proceedings 20th Annual German Conference on Artificial Intelligence (KI-96)*, pages 43–56.

Denzinger, J. and Offermann, T. (1999). On Cooperation between Evolutionary Algorithms and other Search Paradigms. In *Proceedings CEC-99, Washington*, pages 2317–2324.

Dewey, J. (1991). Logic. The theory of inquiry. In Dewey, J., editor, *The Later Works (Vol. 12)*. Carbondale/Edwardsville.

Diderich, C. and Gengler, M. (1996). Solving Traveling Salesman Problems Using a Parallel Synchronized Branch and Bound Algorithm. In *Proceedings High-Performance Computing and Networking, Brüssel*, pages 633–638.

Dillenbourg, P. and Self, J. (1992). People power : A human-computer collaborative learning system. In *The 2nd International Conference of Intelligent Tutoring Systems, Lecture Notes in Computer Science, 608*, pages 651–660.

Dolev, D., Dwork, C., and Stockmeyer, L. (January 1987). On the minimal synchronism needed for distributed consensus. *J. of the Ass. for Computing Machinery*, 34(1):77–97.

Drogoul, A. and Ferber, J. (1992). Multi-agent simulation as a tool for modeling societies: Application to social differentiation in ant colonies. In *4th European Workshop on Modelling Autonomous Agents in a Multi-Agent World (Maamaw'92)*. S. Martino al Cimino, Italy.

Dubois, D. and Prade, H. (1988). *Possibility Theory : An Approach to Computerized Processing of Uncertainty*. Plenum Pub. Corp.

Durfee, E. H. (1999). Distributed problem solving and planning. In Weiss, G., editor, *Multiagent Systems — A Modern Approach to Distributed Artificial Intelligence*, pages 121–163. MIT Press.

Durfee, E. H., Lesser, V. R., and Corkill, D. D. (1987). Coherent cooperation among communicating problem solvers. *IEEE Transactions on System, Man and Cybernetics*, C-36(11):1275–1291.

Easterbrook, S. (1991). Handling conflict between domain descriptions with computer-supported negotiation. *Knowledge Acquisition*, 3(3):255–289.

Easterbrook, S. M., Beck, E. E., Goodlet, J. S., Plowman, L., Sharples, M., and Wood, C. C. (1993). A survey on empirical studies of conflict. In Easterbrook, S. M., editor, *CSCW: cooperation or conflict?* Springer.

Edouards, C. and Stout, J. (1990). Cooperative learning : The first year. *Educational Leadership*, 47(4):38–42.

Einstein, A., Podolsky, B., and Rosen, N. (1935). Can a quantum mechanical description of reality be considered complete? *Physical Review Letters*, 47:777–780.

Ellis, S. (1990). Introducing cooperative learning. *Educational Leadership*, 47(4):34–37.

Fach, P., Bannert, M., and Kunkel, K. (1993). From conflict to dialogue : On attack and defense in on-line assistance. In *Proceedings of Vienna Conference, VCHCI'93*, pages 103–113.

Faust, D. and Ziskin, J. (1988). Expert witnesses in psychology. *Science*, 241:31–35.

Ferber, J. (1995). *Les systèmes multi-agents, vers une intelligence collective*. InterEditions, Paris.

Ferber, J. (1999). *Multi-Agent Systems. An Introduction to Distributed Artificial Intelligence*. Addison-Wesley Pub Co.

Festinger, L. (1957). *A Theory of Cognitive Dissonance*. Stanford, CA: Stanford University Press.

Festinger, L. (1989). The arousal and reduction of dissonance in social contexts. selected works of Leon Festinger. In S.Schachter and M.Gazzaniga, editors, *Extending Psychological Frontiers*, pages 238–257. Russell Sage Foundation.

Feynman, R. (1967). *The character of physical law*. MIT Press.

Fikes, R. E. (1982). A commitment-based framework for describing informal cooperative work. *Cognitive Science*, 6:331–347.

Finkel, R. and Manber, U. (1987). DIB – A Distributed Implementation of Backtracking. *ACM Transactions on Programming Languages and Systems*, 9(2):235–256.

Fiorino, H. (1998). *Élaboration de conjectures par des agents coopérants*. PhD thesis, Supaéro, Toulouse, France.

Fischer, K., Müller, J., Pischel, M., and Schier, D. (1995). A Model for Cooperative Transportation Scheduling. In *Proceedings ICMAS-95*, pages 109–116.

Forrest, S. (1990). Emergent Computation: Self-organizing, Collective and Cooperative Phenomena in Natural and Artificial Computing Networks. *Physica D*, 42.

Franklin, S. and Graesser, A. (1996). Is it an agent, or just a program? A taxonomy for autonomous agents. In Müller, J. P., Wooldridge, M., and Jennings, N. R., editors, *Intelligent Agents III*, pages 21–35. Springer LNAI 1193.

Frasson, C. and Aïmeur, E. (1997). Lessons learned from a university-industry cooperative project in tutoring systems. *Int. Journal of Failures and Lessons Learned in Information Technology Management*, 1(2).

Frasson, C. and Gauthier, G. (1990). *Intelligent Tutoring Systems: at the crossroads of Artificial Intelligence and Education*. New Jersey: Ablex.

Frasson, C., Mengelle, T., and Aïmeur, E. (1997). Using pedagogical agents in a multistrategic intelligent tutoring system. In *Workshop on Pedagogical agents in AI-ED 97, World Conference on Artificial Intelligence and Education*, pages 40–47.

Freeman, K. and Farley, A. (1993). Towards formalizing dialectical argumentation. In *Proceedings of the Conference on Cognitive Science Society*.

Freuder, E. C. (1978). Synthesizing constraint expressions. *Communications of the ACM*, 21(11):958–966.

Friedman, M. (1982). *Capitalism and freedom*. University of Chicago Press.

Frith, C. and Frith, U. (1999). Interacting minds - a biological basis. *Science*, 285:1692–1695.

Frühwirth, T. and Abdennadher, S. (1997). *Constraint-Programmierung*. Springer.

Fujimara, K. (1991). Motion planning in dynamic environments. In *Lecture Notes in Artificial Intelligence*. Springer Verlag.

Gagné, R. (1984). *The Conditions of Learning*. New York: Holt, Rinehart & Winston, 4 edition.

Galliers, J. (1990). The positive role of conflict in cooperative multiagent systems. In Demazeau, Y., editor, *Decentralized AI*, pages 33–49. Elsevier.

Garagnani, M., Fox, M., and Long, D. (1998). Belief systems for conflict resolution. In Tessier, C. and Chaudron, L., editors, *Conflicts among agents: avoid or use them?*, pages 55–60. Working Notes of the ECAI-98 Workshop.

Garey, M. R., Johnson, D. S., and Stockmeyer, L. (1976). Some simplified NP-complete graph problems. *Theoretical Computer Science*, 1(3):237–267.

Garrido-Luna, L. and Sycara, K. (1996). Towards a totally distributed meeting scheduling system. In Görz, G. and Hölldobler, S., editors, *Advances in AI. 20th Annual German Conference on AI*. Springer, Berlin u.a.

Gaschnig, J. (1979). Performance measurement and analysis of certain search algorithms. Technical Report CMU-CS-79-124, Department of Computer Science, Carnegie Mellon University.

Gasser, L. (1991). Social conceptions of knowledge and action: DAI foundations and open systems semantics. *Artificial Intelligence*, 47:107–138.

Gasser, L., Rouquette, N., Hill, R., and Lieb, J. (1989). Representing and using organizational knowledge in distributed AI systems. In Gasser, L. and Huhns, N., editors, *Distributed Artificial Intelligence II*, pages 55–87. Pitman.

Gaussier, P. and Zrehen, S. (1994). A constructivist approach for autonomous agents. In Thalmann, I. D. and N., editors, *Artificial Life in Virtual Reality*, pages 97–113, London. John Wiley and Sons.

Gecsei, J. and Frasson, C. (1994). Safari: an environment for creating tutoring systems in industrial training. In *EdMedia, World Conference on Educational Multimedia and Hypermedia*, pages 25–30.

Gent, I. P., MacIntyre, E., Prosser, P., and Walsh, T. (1996). The constrainedness of search. In *Proceedings of the Thirteenth National Conference on Artificial Intelligence (AAAI-96)*, pages 246–252. AAAI Press.

Georgeff, M. and Ingrand, F. (1989). Decision-making in an embedded reasoning system. In *Proceeding IJCAI*, pages 972–978.

Gibson, J. (1986). *An ecological approach to visual perception*. Erlbaum.

Giegel, H.-J. (1998). *Konflikte in modernen Gesellschaften.* Frankfurt.

Gilmore, D. and Self, J. (1988). *Artificial Intelligence and Human Learning, Intelligent Computer-Assisted Instruction*, chapter The application of machine learning to intelligent tutoring systems, pages 179–196. New York: Chapman and Hall.

Ginsberg, M. L. (1986). Multi-valued logics. In *5th National Conference on Artificial Intelligence*, pages 243–247, Philadelphie, PA.

Goodwin, R. (1993). Formalizing properties of agents. In *Technical Report.*

Grasso, F. (1998). Better learning through conflicts. In Tessier, C. and Chaudron, L., editors, *Conflicts among agents: avoid or use them?*, pages 69–75. Working Notes of the ECAI-98 Workshop.

Grosz, B. (1996). Collaborating systems. *AI magazine*, 17(2).

Grosz, B. and Kraus, S. (1996). Collaborative plans for complex group action. *Artificial Intelligence*, 86:269–357.

Haddadi, A. (1996). *Communication and Cooperation in Agent Systems.* Springer-Verlag.

Haferkamp, H. (1985). Mead und das Problem des gemeinsamen Wissens. *Zeitschrift für Soziologie*, 14(3):175–187.

Hannebauer, M. (2000a). A formalization of autonomous dynamic reconfiguration in distributed constraint satisfaction. *Fundamenta Informaticae*, 43.

Hannebauer, M. (2000b). How to model and verify concurrent algorithms for distributed CSPs. In *Proceedings of the Sixth International Conference on Principles and Practice of Constraint Programming (CP-2000)*, LNCS. Springer.

Haralick, R. M. and Elliot, G. L. (1980). Increasing tree search efficiency for constraint satisfaction problems. *Artificial Intelligence*, 14:263–314.

Hayes, B. (1997). Can't get no satisfaction. *American Scientist*, 85(2):108–112.

Hayes, C. (1999). Agents in a nutshell-a very brief introduction. *IEEE Transactions on Knowledge and Data Engineering*, 11:127–132.

Heider, F. (1958). *The Psychology of Interpersonal Relations.* New York : Wiley.

Heisenberg, V. (1958). *Physics and philosophy.* Harper.

Hendrick, C. (1988). An opinion. In Leary, M., editor, *The state of social psychology*, pages 125–132. Sage.

Hendrickson, B. and Devine, K. (1999). Dynamic load balancing in computational mechanics. *Comp. Meth. Applied Mechanics & Engineering (to appear)*.

Hendrickson, B. and Leland, R. (1994). An empirical study of static load balancing algorithms. In *Proceedings of the Scalable High Performance Computing Conference*, pages 682–685. IEEE Press.

Hendrickson, B. and Leland, R. (1995). The chaco user's guide version 2.0. Technical Report SAND95-2344, Sandia National Laboratories, Albuquerque, USA.

Herman, J., Klein, C., and Wakai, S. (1997). American student's perspectives on alternative assessment: do they know it's different? *Assessment in Education*, 4(3):339–352.

Hestenes, D. (1986). *New Foundations for Classical Mechanics*. Reidel Publishing Company, Dordrecht.

Hewitt, C. (1977). Viewing control structures as patterns of passing messages. *Artificial Intelligence*, 8:323–364.

Hewitt, C. (1986). Offices are open systems. *ACM Transactions on Office Information Systems*, 4(3):271–287.

Hewitt, C. (1991). Open information systems semantics for distributed artificial intelligence. *Artificial Intelligence*, 47:79–106.

Hewitt, C. and Inman, J. (1991). DAI betwixt and between: From "intelligent agents" to open system sciences. *IEEE Transactions on Systems, Men, and Cybernetics*, 21(6):1409–1419.

Hirayama, K. and Yokoo, M. (1997). Distributed Partial Constraint Satisfaction Problem. In *Proceedings CP 97, Linz*, pages 222–236.

Hogg, T., Huberman, B. A., and Williams, C. P. (1996). Phase transitions and the search problem. *Artificial Intelligence*, 81:1–15.

Hogg, T. and Williams, C. (1993). Solving the Really Hard Problems with Cooperative Search. In *Proceedings AAAI-93, Washington*, pages 231–236.

Hollmann, O., Müller, H. J., Ranze, K. C., and Herzog, O. (2000). Conflict resolution in distributed assessment situations. In Müller, H. J. and Dieng, R., editors, *Computational Conflicts - Conflict Modeling for Distributed Intelligent Systems*, pages 182–201. Springer.

Horaud, R. and Monga, O. (1993). *Vision par ordinateur: outils fondamentaux*. Hermes.

Houdé, O., Kayser, D., Koenig, O., Proust, J., and Rastier, F. (1998). *Vocabulaire de sciences cognitives*. Presses Universitaires de France. ISBN 2-13-049400-5.

Howard, G. (1994). Why do people say nasty things about self-reports? *Journal of Organizational Behavior*, 15:399–404.

Huang, S. and Davis, L. (1987). A Tight Upper Bound for the Speedup of Parallel Best-First Branch-and-Bound Algorithms. Technical report, Center for Automation Research, University of Maryland.

Ishida, T., Gasser, L., and Yokoo, M. (1992). Organization self-design of distributed production systems. *IEEE Transactions on Knowledge and Data Engineering*, 4(2):123–134.

Janis, I. (1971). *Groupthink*. Houghton.

Jennings, N. R. (1993). Commitments and conventions. The foundation of coordination in multi-agent systems. *Knowledge Engineering Review*, 8(3):223–250.

Jennings, N. R. (1994). *Cooperation in industrial multi-agent systems*. Number 43 in Computer Science. World Scientific.

Jennings, N. R. (1995). Controlling cooperative problem solving in industrial multi-agent systems using joint intentions. *Artificial Intelligence*, 75.

Joas, H. (1992). *Die Kreativität des Handelns*. Frankfurt.

Johnson, L. and Pugach, M. (1996). Role of collaborative dialogue in teachers' conceptions of appropriate practice for students at risk. *Journal of Educational and Psychological Consultation*, 7(1):9–24.

Jokiinen, K., Sadek, D., and Traum, D., editors (1997). *Collaboration, cooperation and conflict in dialogue systems*. Working Notes of the IJCAI-97 Workshop.

Jones, E. (1998). Major developments in five decades of social psychology. In Gilbert, D., Fiske, S., and Lindzey, G., editors, *The Handbook of Social Psychology*, volume I, pages 3–57. McGraw-Hill.

Judd, C. and McClelland, G. (1998). Measurement. In Gilbert, D., Fiske, S., and Lindzey, G., editors, *The Handbook of Social Psychology*, volume I, pages 180–232. McGraw-Hill.

Kagan, S. (1990). The structural approach to cooperative learning. *Educational Leadership*, 47(4):12–16.

Kang, G. and Everett, S. (1984). Improvement of the narrowband linear predictive coder, part 2. Report 8799, Naval Research Laboratory, Washington, DC.

Kanzali, R. (1996). Behavioural and neural basis of instinctive behavior in insects - odor-source searching strategies without memory and learning. *Robotics and Autonomous Systems*, 18.

Karypis, G. and Kumar, V. (1995). A fast and high quality multilevel scheme for partitioning irregular graphs. Technical Report 95-035, Department of Computer Science, University of Minnesota, Minneapolis, USA.

Kelley, H. (1979). *Personal relationships*. Earlbaum.

Kelso, J. (1995). *Dynamic patterns: The self-organization of brain and behavior*. MIT Press.

Kernighan, B. W. and Lin, S. (1970). An efficient heuristic procedure for partitioning graphs. *The Bell System Technical Journal*, 49(2):291–307.

Khatib, O. (1986). Real-time obstacle avoidance for manipulators and mobile robots. *Int. J. of Robotics Research*, 5.

Kinny, D., Ljungberg, M., Rao, A., Sonenberg, E., Tidhar, G., and Werner, E. (1994). Planned team activity. In Castelfranchi, C. and Werner, E., editors, *Artificial Social Systems*. Springer-Verlag.

Kitamura, Y., Teranishi, K., and Tatsumi, S. (1996). Organizational Strategies for Multiagent Real-time Search. In *Proceedings ICMAS-96, Kyoto*, pages 150–156.

Kitano, H., Asada, M., Kuniyoshi, Y., Noda, I., and Osawa, E. (1997). Robocup: The robot world cup initiative. In *Proceedings of the first international conference on autonomous agents*.

Klausmeier, H. (1990). *Dimensions of Thinking and Cognitive Instruction*, chapter Conceptualizing, pages 93–138. Lawrence Erlbaum Associates, NJ.

Klein, M. (1990). Conflict resolution in cooperative design. *International Journal for Artificial Intelligence in Engineering*, 4(4):168–180.

Klein, M. (1991). Supporting conflict resolution in cooperative design systems. *IEEE Transactions on Systems, Man, and Cybernetics*, 21(6):1379–1390.

Klein, M. and Lander, S., editors (1994). *Models of conflict management in cooperative problem solving.* Technical Report WS-94-08. AAAI Press.

Kohler, T. (2000). Putting social sciences together again. In Kohler, T. and Gumerman, G., editors, *Dynamics of human and primate societies.* Sante Fe Institute.

Kotenko, I. (1994). Conflict resolution in computer-supported cooperative design. In Brad Blumenthal, J. G. and Unger, C., editors, *Proceedings of 4th International Conference, EWHCI'94*, pages 152–163.

Kraus, S., Sycara, K., and Evenchik, A. (1998). Reaching agreements through argumentation: a logical model and implementation. *Artificial Intelligence*, 104:1–70.

Kube, C. and Zhang, H. (1994). Collective robotics, from social insects to robots. *Adaptive Behavior*, 2(2). The MIT Press, Cambridge.

Kube, C. R. and Bonabeau, E. (2000). Cooperative transport by ants and robots. *Robotics and Autonomous systems*, 30:85–101.

Kuhn, T. (1977). *The essential tension.* University of Chicago Press.

Kumar, V. (1992). Algorithms for constraint satisfaction problems: A survey. *AI Magazine*, 13(1):32–44.

Kumar, V., Ramesh, K., and Rao, V. N. (1988). Parallel Best-First Search of State-Space Graphs: A Summary of Results. In *Proceedings AAAI-88, Saint Paul*, pages 122–127.

Ladefoged, P. (1996). *Elements of acoustic phonetics.* University of Chicago Press.

Lakatos, I. (1984). *Proofs and refutations.* Cambridge University Press.

Lam, L. and Suen, C. (1997). Application of majority voting to pattern recognition. *IEEE Systems, Man, and Cybernetics*, 27(5):553–568.

Lambrinos, D., Moller, R., Labhart, T., Pfeifer, R., and Wehner, R. (2000). A mobile robot employing insect strategies for navigation. *Robotics and Autonomous systems*, 30:39–64.

Lander, S. (1994). *Distributed Search and Conflict Management Among Reusable Heterogeneous Agents.* PhD thesis, Computer Science Department, University of Massachusetts Amherst.

Lander, S. and Lesser, V. (1992). Customizing Distributed Search Among Agents with Heterogeneous Knowledge. In *Proceedings 1st Intern. Conf. on Information and Knowledge Management, Baltimore.*

Landers, D. and Pirozzolo, F. (1990). Panel discussion: Techniques for enhancing human performance. Annual meeting of the american psychological association, National Academy of Sciences, Boston, MA.

Landsberg, H. (1979). The future demand of energy. In Landsberg, H., editor, *The Energy report: The next twenty years*, page 84. Harper & Row.

Latombe, J. (1991). *Robot Motion Planning*. Kluwer. Boston.

Lave, J. (1988). *Cognition in Practice: Mind, mathematics, and culture in everyday life*. Cambridge, UK: Cambridge University Press.

Lave, P. J. and Wenger, E. (1991). *Situated Learning: Legitimate Periperal Participation*. Cambridge, UK: Cambridge University Press.

Lawless, W., Castelão, T., and Ballas, J. (2000). Virtual knowledge: bistable reality and the solution of ill-defined problems. *IEEE Transactions on Systems, Man and Cybernetics*, 30(1):3–30.

Lemaître, M., Verfaillie, G., and Bataille, N. (1999). Exploiting a common property resource under a fairness constraint: a case study. In *IJCAI'99*, pages 206–211.

Lerena, P. and Courant, M. (1996). Bio-machines. In *Poster booklet of Artificial Life V*, Nara, Japan.

Levesque, H. J., Cohen, P. R., and Nunes, J. H. T. (1990). On acting together. In *Proceedings of the 8th National Conference on Artificial Intelligence (AAAI'90)*, pages 94–100.

Levine, J. and Moreland, R. (1998). Small groups. In Gilbert, D., Fiske, S., and Lindzey, G., editors, *Handbook of Social Psychology*, volume II, pages 415–469. McGraw-Hill.

Lewin, K. (1951). *Field theory and social science- Selected theoretical papers*. Harper. Edited by D. Cartwright.

Lipshitz, R. (1997). Naturalistic decision making perspectives on decision errors. In Zsambok, C. and Klein, G., editors, *Naturalistic decision making*, pages 49–59. Erlbaum.

Liu, J. and Sycara, K. (1994). Collective Problem Solving through Coordinated Reaction. In *Proceedings IEEE Intern. Conf. on Evolutionary Computation, Orlando*.

Liu, J. and Sycara, K. (1995). Exploiting Problem Structure for Distributed Constraint Optimization. In *Proceedings ICMAS-95, San Francisco*, pages 246–253.

Luck, M. and d'Inverno, M. (1995). A formal framework for agency and autonomy. In *proceedings of the First International Conference on Multi-Agent Systems (ICMAS-95)*, pages 254–260.

Luhmann, N. (1982). *Liebe als Passion*. Suhrkamp, Frankfurt.

Luhmann, N. (1984). *Soziale Systeme*. Suhrkamp, Frankfurt.

Luhmann, N. (1986). *Ökologische Kommunikation*. Opladen.

Luhmann, N. (1987). The evolutionary differentiation between society and interaction. In Alexander, J. and others, editors, *The Micro-Macro Link*, pages 112–131. Berkeley, London.

Luhmann, N. (1992). *Die Wissenschaft der Gesellschaft*. Suhrkamp, Frankfurt.

Luhmann, N. (1997). *Die Gesellschaft der Gesellschaft*. Suhrkamp, Frankfurt.

Luo, Q. Y., Hendry, P. G., and Buchanan, J. T. (1992a). Heuristic search for distributed constraint satisfaction problems. Research Report KEG-6-92, Department of Computer Science, University of Strathclyde, Glasgow G1 1XH, UK.

Luo, Q. Y., Hendry, P. G., and Buchanan, J. T. (1992b). A hybrid algorithm for distributed constraint satisfaction problems. Research Report RR-92-62, Department of Computer Science, University of Strathclyde, Glasgow G1 1XH, UK.

Luo, Q. Y., Hendry, P. G., and Buchanan, J. T. (1992c). A new algorithm for dynamic constraint satisfaction problems. Research Report RR-92-63, Department of Computer Science, University of Strathclyde, Glasgow G1 1XH, UK.

Luo, Q. Y., Hendry, P. G., and Buchanan, J. T. (1993). Comparison of different approaches for solving distributed constraint satisfaction problems. Research Report RR-93-74, Department of Computer Science, University of Strathclyde, Glasgow G1 1XH, UK.

Mackworth, A. K. (1977). Consistency in networks of relations. *Artificial Intelligence*, 8(1):99–118.

Mackworth, A. K. (1992). Constraint satisfaction. In Shapiro, S. C., editor, *Encyclopedia of Artificial Intelligence*, pages 285–293. Wiley-Interscience Publication, second edition.

Maes, P. (1990a). *Designing Autonomous Agents*, chapter Situated agents can have goals, pages 49–70. The MIT Press.

Maes, P., editor (1990b). *Designing Autonomous Agents. Theory and Practice from Biology to Engineering and Back.* The MIT Press.

Maines, D. (1982). In search of mesostructure. Studies in negotiated order. *Urban Life*, 11(3):267–279.

Malsch, T. (2000). Naming the unnamable: Socionics or the sociological turn of/to distributed artificial intelligence. Technical report, Technical University Hamburg-Harburg, Department of Technology Assessment.

Mammen, D. L. and Lesser, V. R. (1998). Problem structure and subproblem sharing in multi-agent systems. In *Proceedings of the Third International Conference on Multi-Agent Systems (ICMAS-98)*, Paris, France.

Manciulli, M., Potesta, L., and Ruggeri, F. (1986). *Il dilemma organizzativo. L'inosservanza funzionale delle norme (The Organizational Dilemma: The Functional Disregard of Norms).* Franco Angeli, Milano.

Marriot, K. and Stuckey, P. J. (1998). *Programming with Constraints — An Introduction*. MIT Press.

Martinoli, A. and Mondada, F. (1995). Collective and Cooperative Group Behaviours: Biologically Inspired Experiments in Robotics. In *Proceedings of the Fourth Symposium on Experimental Robotics ISER-95*, Stanford, USA.

Martinoli, A. and Mondada, F. (1998). Probabilistic Modelling of a Bio-Inspired Collective Experiment with Real Robots. In *Proceeding of the Third International Symposium on Distributed Autonomous Robotic Systems DARS-98*, Karlsruhe, Germany.

Mataric, M. (1992). Minimizing complexity in controlling a mobile robot population. In *Proceedings of the International Conference on Robotics and Automation*, Los Alamitos. IEEE Computer Society Press.

Mataric, M. (1995). Issues and approaches in the design of collective autonomous agents. *Robotics and Autonomous Systems*, 16.

Maturana, F., Shen, W., and Norrie, D. H. (1998). Metamorph: An adaptive agent-based architecture for intelligent manufacturing. *International Journal of Production Research.*

Maturna, F. P. and Norrie, D. H. (1996). Multi-agent mediator architecture for distributed manufacturing. *Journal of Intelligent Manufacturing*, 7:257–270.

Maudet, N. and Evrard, F. (1998). Using implicature to avoid conflicts in dialogue. In Tessier, C. and Chaudron, L., editors, *Conflicts among agents: avoid or use them?*, pages 61–66. Working Notes of the ECAI-98 Workshop.

May, R. (1997). The scientific wealth of nations. *Science*, 275:793–796.

McGuire, W. (1976). Some internal psychological factors influencing consumer choice. *Journal of Consumer Research*, 2:301–319.

Mead, G. (1934). *Mind, Self and Society from the Standpoint of a Social Behaviorist*. Chicago.

Merrill, M. (1980). Learner control in computer based learning. *Computers and Education*, 4:77–95.

Merrill, M. D. (1991). An introduction to instructional transaction theory. *Educational Technology*, 31(6):7–12.

Meyer, J.-J., van der Hoek, W., and van Linder, B. (1999). A logical approach to the dynamics of commitments. *Artificial Intelligence*, 113:1–40.

Michael, W., Smith, R., and Michael, J. (1989). *Dimensions of self-concept*. Edits Publishing.

Minar, N., Burkhart, R., Langton, C., and Askenazi, M. (1996). The SWARM simulation system. a toolkit for building multi-agent simulations. Technical report, The Santa Fe Institute. n. 96-06-042.

Montanary, U. (1974). Networks of constraints: Fundamental properties and applications to picture processing. *Information Sciences*, 7:95–132.

Mottez, B. (1971). *La sociologie industrielle*. CNRS, Paris.

M.R. Jean et al. (1997). Emergence et SMA. In *Proceedings of JFIADSMA'97*. Hermes.

Müller, H. J. (1996a). Negotiation principles. In O'Hare, G. and Jennings, N. R., editors, *Foundations of Distributed AI*, pages 211–230. Wiley Interscience.

Müller, H. J. (1997). Towards agent system engineering. *Data & Knowledge Engineering*, (23):217–245.

Müller, H. J. and Dieng, R., editors (2000). *Computational Conflicts. Conflict Modeling for Distributed Intelligent Systems*. Springer.

Müller, H. J. and Dieng, R. (2000). On conflicts in general and their use in AI in particular. In Müller, H. J. and Dieng, R., editors, *Computational conflicts - Conflict Modeling for Distributed Intelligent Systems*, pages 1–20. Springer.

Müller, H. J. and Siekmann, J. (1991). Structured social agents. In *Proceedings of the 4th GI Congress on Knowledge Based Systems, München*, pages 42–52. Springer IFB 291.

Müller, J. P. (1996b). *The Design of Intelligent Agents*. Springer LNAI 1177.

Murray, T. (1998). Authoring knowledge-based tutors: tools for content, instructional strategy, student model, and interface design. *The Journal of the Learning Sciences*, 7(1):5–64.

Nangsue, P. and Conry, S. (1998). Fine-Grained Multiagent Systems for the Internet. In *Proceedings ICMAS-98, Paris*, pages 198–206.

Nash, J. F. (1950). The bargaining problem. *Econometrica*, 18:155–162.

National Academy of Sciences, N. A. S. (1994). *Building consensus*. National Academy Press.

Newell, A. (1990). *Unified Theories of Cognition*. Harvard Univ. Press, Cambridge, Mass.

Nguyen, T. and Deville, Y. (1998). A distributed arc-consistency algorithm. *Science of Computer Programming*, 30(1-2):227–250.

Nollmann, G. (1997). *Konflikte in Interaktion, Gruppe und Organisation. Zur Konfliktsoziologie der modernen Gesellschaft*. Opladen.

Noreils, F. (1992). Multi-robot coordination for battlefield strategies. In *Proc. IEEE/RSJ Int. Conf. on Intelligent Robots and Systems*, pages 1777–1784.

O'Leary, D. E. (1999). Identifying conflicting probabilistic knowledge in multiple knowledge base systems. In Tessier, C. and Chaudron, L., editors, *Agents' conflicts - Papers from the AAAI workshop - Technical report WS-99-08*, pages 7–13. AAAI Press.

Osgood, C. and Tannenbaum, P. (1955). The principle of congruity in the prediction of attitude change. *Psychological Review*, 62:42–55.

Palmer, T. N. (1999). Predicting uncertainty in forecasts of weather and climate. *Reports of Progress in Physics*, 63:71–116.

Palthepu, S., Greer, J., and Mccalla, G. (1991). Learning by teaching. In *The Proceedings of the International Conference on the Learning Sciences*.

Parsons, S. and Jennings, N. R. (1996). Negotiation through argumentation — a preliminary report. In *Proceedings of the International Conference on Multi-agent Systems*.

Parsons, S., Sierra, C., and Jennings, N. (1998). Agents that reason and negotiate by arguing. *Journal of Logic and Computation*, 8(3).

Pask, G. (1975). *Conversation, Cognition, and Learning*. New York: Elsevier.

Pawlak, Z. (1984). On conflicts. *International Journal on Man-Machine Studies*, 21:127–134.

Pedroso, J. (1996). Niche Search: An Evolutionary Algorithm for Global Optimisation. In *Proceedings Parallel Problem Solving from Nature IV, Berlin*, pages 430–440.

Peirce, C. (1991a). Die Lehre vom Zufall. In Peirce, C., editor, *Schriften*, pages 215–228. Suhrkamp, Frankfurt. (First published in *Popular Science Monthly*, 12 (1878), pp. 604-615, "The doctrine of chances".).

Peirce, C. (1991b). Wie unsere Ideen zu klären sind. In Peirce, C., editor, *Schriften*, pages 182–214. Suhrkamp, Frankfurt. (First published in *Popular Science Monthly*, 12 (1878), pp. 286-302, "How to make our ideas clear".).

Penders, J. (1991). Autonomous vehicles avoiding one another: A case study of obstacle avoidance procedures. In *Proc. Computing Science in the Netherlands*, pages 439–452. Stichting Mathematisch Centrum Amsterdam.

Penders, J. (1994). Conflicts in the spatial interaction of autonomous agents. pre-publication NT-PU-93-1728, PTT Research. (abstract appeared in Proceedings KI-94, Springer Verlag, 1994).

Penders, J. (1999). *The Practical Art of Moving Physical Objects*. PhD thesis, University of Maastricht.

Penders, J. and Braspenning, P. (1997). Situated actions and cognition. In *Proceeding IJCAI-97*, pages 1372–1377.

Perrussel, L. (1998). Contextual reasoning. In *ECAI'98*, pages 366–367.

Pfeifer, R. (1995). Cognition - Perspective from autonomous agents. *Robotics and Autonomous Systems*, 15:47–70.

Piaget, J. (1975). *L'équilibration des structures cognitives*. Paris, Presses Universitaires de France.

Poincaré, H. (1952). *Science and hypothesis*. Dover.

Polanyi, M. (1974). *Personal knowledge*. University of Chicago Press.

Pollack, M., Israel, D., and Bratman, M. (1987). Towards an architecture for resource-bounded agents. *CSLI Report*, CSLI-87-104. Stanford.

Prasad, M. V. N., Decker, K., Garvey, A., and Lesser, V. (1996). Exploring organizational designs with TAEMS: A case study of distributed data processing. In *Proceedings of the Second International Conference on Multi-Agent Systems (ICMAS-96)*, pages 283–290.

Prigogine, I. (1997). *The end of certainty*. Simon and Schuster.

Quinn, M. (1990). Analysis and Implementation of Branch-and-Bound Algorithms on Hypercube Multicomputers. *IEEE Trans. Computation*, 39(3):384–387.

Quinn, M. and Deo, N. (1986). An upper bound for the speedup of parallel branch-and-bound algorithms. *BIT*, 26:35–43.

Rachlin, J., Goodwin, R., Murthy, S., Akkiraju, R., Wu, F., Kumaran, S., and Das, R. (1998). A-Teams: An Agent Architecture for Optimization and Decision-Support. In *Proceedings ATAL-98, Paris*.

Reisig, W. (1998). *Elements of Distributed Algorithms — Modeling and Analysis with Petri Nets*. Springer.

Retalis, S., Pain, H., and M., H. (1996). Arguing with the devil: Teaching in controversial domains. In *ITS'96 Conference, Third International Conference on Intelligent Tutoring Systems*, pages 659–667.

Reynolds, C. (1987). Flocks, herds and schools: a distributed behavioral model. *Computer Graphics*, 21(4):25–34.

Ridley, M. (1996). *The origins of virtue*. Penguin.

Ronald, E., Sipper, M., and Capcarrère, M. (1999). Design, Observation, Surprise! A Test of Emergence. *Artificial Life*, 5(3):225–239.

Roschelle, J. (1992). Learning by collaborating: convergent conceptual change. *The Journal of the Learning Sciences*, 2(3):235–276.

Roschelle, J. and S.D., B. (1989). The construction of shared knowledge in collaborative problem solving. In O'Mally, C., editor, *Computer Supported Collaborative Learning*.

Rosenschein, J. S. and Zlotkin, G. (1994). *Rules of encounter: Designing convention for automated negotiation among computers*. Artificial Intelligence. The MIT Press.

Rossi, F., Petrie, C., and Dhar, V. (1990). On the equivalence of constraint satisfaction problems. In *Proceedings of the Ninth European Conference on Artificial Intelligence (ECAI-90)*, pages 550–556.

Sanders, P. (1995). Towards Better Algorithms for Parallel Backtracking. Technical Report IB 6/95, University of Karlsruhe.

Sandholm, T. (1999). Distributed rational decision making. In Weiss, G., editor, *Multi-Agent Systems*, pages 201–258. The MIT Press.

Sandholm, T., Larson, K., Andersson, M., Shehory, O., and Thomé, F. (1999). Coalition structure generation with worst case guarantees. *Artificial Intelligence*, 111(1–2):209–238.

Scaglione, M. (1998). Les Modèles de la Vie Artificielle et les Concepts d'Emergence: de la métaphore à la réalisation. In *Quelles relations entretenons-nous avec nos modèles?*, Rochebrune, France. Rencontres interdisciplinaires sur les systèmes complexes naturels et artificiels.

Scalia, A. (1999). Essay: How democracy swept the world. *Wall Street Journal*, page A24.

Schank, R. and Jona, M. (1991). Empowering the student: new perspectives on the design of teaching systems. *The journal of learning sciences*, 1(1):7–35.

Schlesinger, A. (1949). *The vital center. The politics of freedom.* Riverside Press.

Schneider, W.-L. (1994). *Die Beobachtung von Kommunikation. Zur kommunikativen Konstruktion sozialen Handelns.* Westdeutscher Verlag, Opladen.

Schultz, J. (1990). Cooperative learning : Refining the process. *Educational Leadership*, 47(4):43–45.

Schumpeter, J. A. (1989). *A theoretical, historical, and statistical analysis of the capitalist process.* Porcupine Press.

Sen, A. (1996). Comment. In Arrow, K., Colombatto, E., Perlman, M., and Schmidt, S., editors, *The rational foundations of economic behavior*, pages 101–105. St. Martin.

Sen, S., editor (1999). *Negotiation: settling conflicts and identifying opportunities.* Working Notes of the AAAI-99 Workshop.

Shafir, E., Simonson, I., and Tversky, A. (1993). Reason-based choices. *Cognition*, 49:11–36.

Sharan, Y. and S., S. (1990). Group investigation expands cooperative learning. *Educational Leadership*, 47(4):17–21.

Shaw, M. and Gaines, B. (1994). Knowledge support systems for constructively channelling conflict in group dynamics. In Klein, M. and Landers, S., editors, *AAAI-94 Workshop on models of conflict management and cooperative problem solving*, pages 107–116.

Shearer, R. R. and Gould, S. J. (1999). Essay on science and society: of two minds and one nature. *Science*, 286:109–110.

Shehory, O., Sycara, K. P., Chalasani, P., and Jha, S. (1998). Increasing resource utilization and task performance by agent cloning. In *Proceedings of the Fifth International Workshop on Agent Theories, Architectures and Languages (ATAL-98)*, pages 305–318, Paris, France.

Shen, W. and Norrie, D. H. (1998). A hybrid agent-oriented infrastructure for modeling manufacturing enterprises. In *Proceedings of the Knowledge Acquisition Workshop (KAW-98)*, Banff, Canada.

Shoham, Y. and Tennenholtz, M. (1992). On the synthesis of useful social laws for artificial societies. In *Proceedings of the AAAI-92*, pages 276–281.

Shoham, Y. and Tennenholtz, M. (1995). On social laws for artificial agent societies: off-line design. *Artificial Intelligence*, (75):231–252.

Sichman, J., Conte, R., Castelfranchi, C., and Demazeau, Y. (1994). A social reasoning mechanism based on dependence networks. In Cohn, A. G., editor, *Proceedings of the 11th European Conference on Artificial Intelligence*, pages 188–192.

Simmel, G. (1892). *Einleitung in die Moralwissenschaft (Band 2)*. Stuttgart and Berlin.

Simmel, G. (1908). *Soziologie*. Leipzig.

Simon, H. A. (1992). What is an explanation of behavior. *Psychological Science*, 3:150–161.

Singh, M. P. (1995). *Multiagent Systems: a Theoretical Framework for Intentions, Know-how, and Communications*. Springer Verlag.

Skinner, B. (1957). *Verbal Learning*. New York: Appleton-Century-Crofts.

Slavin, R. (1990a). *Cooperative Learning: Theory, Research, and Practice*. Englewood Cliffs, NJ: Prentice Hall.

Slavin, R. (1990b). Research on cooperative learning : Consensus and controversy. *Educational Leadership*, 47(4):52–54.

Slavin, R., Madden, N., and Stevens, R. (1990). Cooperative learning models for the 3R's. *Educational Leadership*, 47(4):22–28.

Sleeman, D. and Brown, J. (1982). *Intelligent Tutoring Systems*. London : Academic Press.

Slovik, P., Flynn, J. H., and Layman, M. (1991). Perceived risk, trust, and the politics of nuclear waste. *Science*, 254:1603–1608.

Smit, G. and Van Der Molen, H. (1997). The construction and evaluation of simulations to assess professional interviewing skills. *Assessment in Education*, 4(3):353–364.

Smith, R. (1979). *A Framework for Distributed Problem Solving*. UMI Research Press.

Smith, R. G. (1988). The contract net protocol: High-level communication and control in a distributed problem solver. In Bond, A. H. and Gasser, L., editors, *Readings in Distributed Artificial Intelligence*, pages 357–366. Morgan Kaufmann Publishers.

Solotorevsky, G., Gudes, E., and Meisels, A. (1996). Modeling and solving distributed constraint satisfaction problems (DCSPs). In *Proceedings of the Conference on Constraint-Processing (CP-96)*.

Steels, L. and Brooks, R. (1994). *The artificial life route to artificial intelligence. Building Embodied, Situated Agents*. Lawrence Erlbaum, Hillsdale, NJ, USA.

Strauss, A. (1978). *Negotiations. Varieties, Processes, Contexts, and Social Order*. San Francisco.

Stroebe, W. and Diehl, M. (1994). Why groups are less effective than members. *European reviews of social psychology*, 5:271–303.

Stuller, J. (1995). Inconsistency conflict resolution. In *Proceedings of SOFSEM'95 : Theory and Practice of Informatics, Lecture Notes in Computer Science, 1012*, pages 469–474.

Svesta, P. and Overmars, M. (1998). Coordinated path planning for multiple robots. *Robotics and Autonomous Systems*, 23:125–152.

Sycara, K. (1985). Arguments of persuasion in labour mediation. In *Proceedings of the 9th International Joint Conference on Artificial Intelligence*, pages 294–296.

Sycara, K. (1990). Persuasive argumentation in negotiation. *Theory and Decision*, 28(3).

Sycara, K. P., Roth, S. F., Sadeh, N., and Fox, M. S. (1991). Distributed constrained heuristic search. *IEEE Transactions on Systems, Man, and Cybernetics*, 21(6):1446–1461.

Talukdar, S., de Souza, P., and Murthy, S. (1993). Organizations for Computer-based Agents. *Journal of Engineering Intelligent Systems.*

Tambe, M. (1997). Towards flexible teamwork. *Journal of Artificial Intelligence Research (JAIR)*, 7:83–124.

Tambe, M. and Jung, H. (1999a). The benefits of arguing in a team. *AI Magazine*, 20(4).

Tambe, M. and Jung, H. (1999b). Towards conflict resolution in agent teams via argumentation. In Tessier, C. and Chaudron, L., editors, *Agents' Conflicts*, pages 1–13. Working Notes of the AAAI Workshop.

Tessier, C. and Chaudron, L., editors (1998). *Conflicts among agents: avoid or use them?* Working Notes of the ECAI-98 Workshop.

Tessier, C. and Chaudron, L., editors (1999). *Agents' Conflicts.* Working Notes of the AAAI-99 Workshop.

Teubner, G. and Willke, H. (1984). Kontext und Autonomie. Gesellschaftliche Steuerung durch reflexives Recht. *Zeitschrift für Rechtssoziologie*, pages 4–35.

Toulmin, S. (1958). *The uses of argument.* Cambridge Univ Press, London.

Touzard, H. (1977). *La médiation et la résolution des conflits*, chapter Considération sur le conflit social, pages 19–115. Presses universitaires de France.

Trullier, O. and Meyer, J.-A. (1997). Biomimetic navigation models and strategies in animats. *AI Communications*, 10:79–92.

Tsang, E. P. K. (1993). *Foundations of Constraint Satisfaction.* Academic Press.

Tversky, A. and Kahneman, D. (1981). The framing of decisions and the psychology of choice. *Science*, 211:453–458.

Vanlehn, K. (1988). Student modeling. In Polson, M. and Richardson, J., editors, *Foundations of Intelligent Tutoring Systems*, pages 55–78, Hillsdale, NJ : Erlbaum.

Vanlehn, K., Jones, R., and Chi, T. (1992). A model of the self-explanation effect. *The Journal of the Learning Sciences*, 2(1):1–59.

Vanlehn, K., Ohlsson, S., and Nason, R. (1994). Application of simulated students: an exploration. *Journal of artificial intelligence in education*, 5(2):135–175.

Varela, F. (1994). The Re-Enchantment of the Concrete: Some Biological Ingredients for a Nouvelle Cognitive Science. In L. Steels and R. Brooks, editor, *The artificial life route to artificial intelligence. Building Embodied, Situated Agents*, pages 11–22. Lawrence Erlbaum, Hillsdale, NJ, USA.

Verfaillie, G. and Schiex, T. (1994). Dynamic backtracking for dynamic constraint satisfaction problems. In *Proceedings of the ECAI-94 Workshop on Constraint Satisfaction Issues Raised by Practical Applications*, pages 1–8, Amsterdam, The Netherlands.

Von Neumann, J. (1961). The mathematician. In *Collected works*, volume I. Pergamon.

Von Neumann, J. and Morgenstern, O. (1953). *Theory of games and economic behavior*. Princeton University Press.

Vornberger, O. (1986). Implementing Branch-and-Bound in a Ring of Processors. In *Proceedings CONPAR 86*, pages 157–164.

Vygotsky, L. (1978). *Mind in Society*. Cambridge, MA: Harvard University Press.

Wagner, T., Shapiro, J., Xuan, P., and Lesser, V. (1999). Multi-level conflict in multi-agent systems. Technical Report 1999-17, Department of Computer Science, University of Massachusetts.

Walshaw, C., Cross, M., and Everett, M. (1998). Mesh partitioning and load-balancing for distributed memory parallel systems. In *Proceedings of Parallel and Distributed Computing for Computational Mechanics*, Lochinver, Scotland, UK.

Wang, P. (1989). Interaction dynamics of multiple mobile robots with simple navigation strategies. *J. of Robotic Syst.*, 6(1):77–101.

Wansing, H. (1996). *Negation: a notion in focus*. Walter de Gruyter.

Watzlawick, P., Helmick Beavin, J., and Jackson, D. D. (1967). *Pragmatics of human communication. A study of interactional patterns, pathologies, and paradoxes*. New York, Norton.

Webb, B. (1995). Using robots to model animals: A cricket test. *Robotics and Autonomous Systems*, 16(2-4).

Weeb, N. (1989). Peer interaction and learning in small groups. *International Journal of Educational Research*, 13:21–40.

Weinberg, S. (2000). Five and a half utopias. *The Atlantic Monthly*, pages 107–114.

Werner, E. (1990). Cooperating agents: a unified theory of communication and social structure. In Cohen, P., Morgan, J., and Pollack, M., editors, *Distributed Artificial Intelligence: II*. Morgan Kaufmann Publishers.

Wooldridge, M. (1994). Coherent social action. In *ECAI'94*, pages 279–283.

Wooldridge, M. and Jennings, N. (1995a). Intelligent agents. theory and practice. *Knowledge Engineering Review*, 10(2).

Wooldridge, M. and Jennings, N. R., editors (1995b). *Agent Theories, Architectures, and Languages: a Survey*, volume ECAI-94 workshop on Agent Theories, Architectures, and Languages, chapter Intelligent Agents, pages 1–39. Springer Verlag, Berlin.

Wynne, H. and James, M. (1997). Assessment and learning: differences and relationships between formative and summative assessment. *Assessment in Education*, 4(3):365–379.

Yokoo, M. (1995). Asynchronous weak-commitment search for solving distributed constraint satisfaction problems. In *Proceedings 1st Conf. on Principles and Practice of Constraint Programming*, pages 88–102.

Yokoo, M. (1998). Distributed Constraint Satisfaction: Foundations and Applications. In *Proceedings ICMAS-98, Paris*, pages 14–15.

Yokoo, M., Durfee, E., Ishida, T., and Kuwabara, K. (1992). Distributed constraint satisfaction for formalizing distributed problem solving. In *Proceedings 12th IEEE Conf. on Distributed Computing Systems*, pages 614–621.

Yokoo, M., Durfee, E. H., Ishida, T., and Kuwabara, K. (1998). The distributed constraint satisfaction problem: Formalization and algorithms. *IEEE Transactions on Knowledge and DATA Engineering*, 10(5).

Yokoo, M. and Hirayama, K. (1998). Distributed constraint satisfaction algorithm for complex local problems. In *Proceedings of the Third International Conference on Multi-Agent Systems (ICMAS-98)*, pages 372–379, Paris, France.

Yokoo, M. and Ishida, T. (1999). Search algorithms for agents. In Weiss, G., editor, *Multiagent Systems — A Modern Approach to Distributed Artificial Intelligence*, pages 165–199. MIT Press.

Yokoo, M. and Kitamura, Y. (1996). Multiagent Real-Time-A* with Selection: Introducing Competition in Cooperative Search. In *Proceedings ICMAS-96, Kyoto*, pages 409–416.

Zeghal, K. and Ferber, J. (1993). Craash: a coordinated avoidance system; modelling and simulation. In Pave, A., editor, *Proc. of the 1993 European Simulation Multiconference*, Lyon.

Zhang, Y. and Mackworth, A. K. (1991). Parallel and distributed algorithms for finite constraint satisfaction problems. In *Proceedings of the IEEE-Symposium on Parallel and Distributed Processing*, pages 394–397.

Zhao, J., Wang, F., and lin Wu, Z. (1992). The development of ship collision avoidance automation. *The Journal of Navigation*, 45(1).

Ziemke, T. (1997). Adaptive Behavior in Autonomous Agents. *Autonomous Agents, Adaptive Behaviors and Distributed Simulations' journal*.

Zlotkin, G. and Rosenschein, J. S. (1991). Cooperation and conflict resolution via negotiation among autonomous agents in non-cooperative domains. *IEEE Transactions on Systems, Man and Cybernetics*, 21(1):1317–1324.

Index

MIX
Papier aus verantwortungsvollen Quellen
Paper from responsible sources
FSC® C105338

If you have any concerns about our products,
you can contact us on
ProductSafety@springernature.com

In case Publisher is established outside the EU,
the EU authorized representative is:
Springer Nature Customer Service Center GmbH
Europaplatz 3, 69115 Heidelberg, Germany

Printed by Libri Plureos GmbH
in Hamburg, Germany